PRESENTED BY

THE UNIVERSITY OF WINNIPEG
ALUMNI ASSOCIATION

IN MEMORY
OF
EDWARD W. HAWKINS, QC
CLASS OF 1934

Lawyers and Citizens

Lawyers and Citizens

*The Making of a Political Elite
in Old Regime France*

David A. Bell

New York   Oxford
OXFORD UNIVERSITY PRESS
1994

Oxford University Press

Oxford   New York   Toronto
Delhi   Bombay   Calcutta   Madras   Karachi
Kuala Lumpur   Singapore   Hong Kong   Tokyo
Nairobi   Dar es Salaam   Cape Town
Melbourne   Auckland   Madrid

and associated companies in
Berlin   Ibadan

Library of Congress Cataloguing-in-Publication Data
Bell, David Avrom.
Lawyers and citizens : the making of a political elite in
Old Regime France / David A. Bell.
p. cm.   Includes bibliographical references and index.
ISBN 0-19-507670-2
1. Lawyers—France—Paris—History.   2. Practice of law—France—
Paris—History. 3. France—Politics and government—1589–1789.
I. Title.   KJV173.B44   1994
320'.08'8344—dc 20   93-23089

The following journals have kindly granted permission to include in this book portions of
articles that were first published in their pages in somewhat different form:

French Historical Studies—"The 'Public Sphere,' the State, and the World of the Law in
Eighteenth-Century France," 17:4 (Fall 1992): 912–934.

Past and Present: A Journal of Historical Studies—"Lawyers and Demagogues: Chancellor
Maupeou and the Transformation of Legal Practice in France, 1771–1789," no. 130
(February 1991): 107–141. (World copyright: The Past and Present Society, 175
Banbury Road, Oxford England).

The Publisher gratefully acknowledges the financial support of the Frederic W. Hilles
Publications Fund of Yale University.

1 3 5 7 9 8 6 4 2

Printed in the United States of America
on acid-free paper

For Donna

Preface

Long before the period with which this book is principally concerned, lawyers already formed a highly visible stratum of French society. It was as early as 1573 that François Hotman put the following complaint into his treatise *Francogallia:* "Everywhere in France today a class of men predominates whom some call lawyers . . . in every town where [a court] is located, nearly a third of the citizens and residents, attracted by the great rewards, have applied themselves to the practice and study of the art of verbal brawling."[1] To present-day readers, it may be surprising to come across such a passage in a book more than four hundred years old, because today lawyers seem such quintessential creatures of modern industrial and commercial society. The numerous college students to whom history courses form but a prelude to law school most often end up as counsel to large modern businesses, to agencies of the modern welfare state, or to those citizens who have fallen into the vast pit of litigation dug by these two frequent antagonists. Many social scientists have reinforced lawyers' "contemporary" image by arguing that the professions themselves are essentially creatures of modern capitalism.

Yet in fact, as a long line of historians has shown, lawyers were present at the very creation of modern European society, and the modern European state. They designed and staffed the chanceries and exchequers of late medieval and early modern kingdoms. They served as agents of the new state institutions, devising and administering laws, collecting taxes, even performing as diplomats.[2] They acted as counsel for nobles and prelates who now had to accept the rule of law, and settle disputes with each other in court. According to William Bouwsma, they "possessed skills essential to the development of a more complex social order" and were in fact "essential in devising the institutions and conventions of early modern Europe."[3] Nowhere were lawyers thicker on the ground or more successful, moreover, than France, a nation where the state itself has always been the principal growth industry. Throughout the last centuries of the Old Regime, lawyers continuously made up the most prominent, if not the most wealthy sector of what we now call the middle classes. They were the elite of the Third Estate.

This book is concerned with the way in which this elite profession, already old and established by the reign of Louis XIV, refashioned itself between 1660 and 1790 into a training ground for the political leadership of a nation where the voice of the "public" was counting for more and more. It is concerned with the way in which lawyers, who could never be a true political elite in the hierarchical world of the Old Regime, became such an elite once that regime began to unravel. As historians know well, during the French Revolution, it was overwhelmingly lawyers and government office-holders, rather than merchants or industrialists, who took the political leadership of the Third Estate, and thus of the nation. For more than a century afterwards, lawyers remained a political elite, providing France with a long succession of deputies, prime ministers, and political troublemakers. But this transformation did not happen all of a sudden in 1788–89, with the calling of the Estates General. Long before any lawyers had dreamed of France becoming a democracy, the changes in the profession formed part and parcel of the process by which, as Keith Michael Baker puts it, "French politics broke out of the absolutist mold."[4] These changes therefore not only help explain why politically ambitious lawyers found themselves so well situated to take advantage of events in 1789; they also help explain why the larger transformations in French political culture under the Old Regime took the form they did.

I first became interested in this subject when, in the mid-1980's, I began reading "revisionist" historians of the French Revolution. Although the place of lawyers in the development of early modern French politics had not been exactly ignored before, the revisionists, starting in the 1950's and 1960's, had put new emphasis on it. After all, for anyone arguing that the Revolution did not arise out of a conflict between a declining aristocracy and rising bourgeoisie, it helped to point out that the revolutionary middle classes were predominantly legal and administrative, not commercial or industrial.[5] The revisionists' work also seemed to invite new research on lawyers. By calling into question the very notion of a distinct, self-conscious "bourgeois" class, whose interests dictated its members' political conduct, they left one wondering if there was anything distinct about the Old Regime legal profession itself that influenced its members' extraordinary political ideas and actions. What political atmosphere prevailed in the bar during the Old Regime? What connections could be drawn between the ideas that circulated there, the structure of the profession itself, and the position of lawyers in French society and culture?

To my surprise, I found that with a few honorable but brief exceptions (notably that of Colin Lucas), historians had not done much to answer these questions.[6] The profession's general concentration on social history aside (and interesting work was being done on lawyers from this perspective), two reasons seemed to explain why the political angle had remained largely untouched since a useful but quirky 1927 study on lawyers and the Enlightenment by Francis Delbeke.[7] First, new research was being done on lawyers *after* 1789, and it struck a cautionary note. It emphasized that the profession as a whole generally lost its enthusiasm for the Revolution with remarkable speed, and if anything, was quite counter-revolutionary even before the onset of the Terror. The bar might have supplied much of the Revolutionary leadership, but as a whole it no longer appeared the revolutionary profession *par excellence*.[8] Secondly, did the sources exist? The obvious site for such a study had to be Paris, whose bar was by far the largest, most prestigious, and most important to Old Regime political life. Yet the Parisian Order of Barristers had left relatively few documents from the Old Regime, and certainly none of the endless shelves of bound records that has made research on the political history of the French *parlements* so rewarding.

By the mid-1980's, however, the subject had come to seem both more exciting and more accessible. Several important works had reinvigorated the study of the Old Regime's political history, and in the process they had further highlighted lawyers' contributions to prerevolutionary political culture.[9] Names such as Le Paige, Maultrot and Saige had become familiar outside a tiny côterie of specialists, as men whose works may have lacked the profundity of the *philosophes*, but whose political influence was in some respects comparable. It had also become clear that whatever the eventual revulsion felt by many lawyers towards the Revolution, before 1789 the leadership of the profession, particularly in Paris, had been massively involved in the ideological struggles that helped bring the Revolution about. The rank-and-file tended to follow eagerly, and in the prerevolutionary crisis of 1787–89, lawyers of all stripes rallied massively to the *patriote* party. At the same time, the new political history pointed the way to several rich veins of largely untapped sources, in the pamphlet collections of the Bibliothèque Nationale, in the wilderness of the B.N.'s Joly de Fleury papers, in the astonishing Le Paige Collection of the Bibliothèque de Port-Royal. The suggestions of generous colleagues, plus further investigation on my part, later opened up further profitable research avenues, including the rich caches of printed trial briefs called *mémoires judiciaires,* the archives of the French Foreign ministry, and especially the library of the *Ordre des avocats* itself, where I found there was more to be gleaned than I had originally suspected.

Thus fortified with the promise of sufficient source material I began work on a subject that has now occupied quite a few years of my life, as the project evolved from ideas and hopes to stacks of note cards, to a dissertation, and finally to a book. In the process, I have accumulated many debts, and it is a pleasure to acknowledge the individuals and institutions who helped me along the way, and who thus helped shape the final product. The faults that remain are, of course, wholly my responsibility.

From the project's first phase as a dissertation at Princeton, my chief debt is to Robert Darnton, whose writings first inspired me to become a historian and whose encouragement and criticism made this project possible. I would also like warmly to thank my teachers Lawrence Stone, Natalie Zemon Davis, and Theodore Rabb. At Princeton I had financial support from the History Department and the Ogden Porter Jacobus Fellowship, and also from the Mellon Fellowships in the Humanities.

During my research in France, the staffs at the Archives Départementales de la Côte d'Or, the Archives Nationales, the Bibliothèque Nationale, the Archives des Affaires Étrangères and the Bibliothèque de la Cour de Cassation all provided unusually hospitable working conditions. M. Yves Ozanam of the Bibliothèque des Avocats à la Cour d'Appel de Paris, and Mlle. Odette Barenne of the Bibliothèque de la Société de Port-Royal were especially helpful and generous. Thanks also to M. Alain de Mézeray and M. Michel Vinot Préfontaine for allowing me access to papers in their possession, and to the Marquis de Rosanbo for permitting me to consult the Malesherbes papers at the Archives Nationales. In France, I have further debts to Prof. Michel Antoine, who discussed the project at length and led me to the manuscript of Jean-Louis Julien de Prunay, to M. Lucien Karpik, who helped me define the sociological issues, and to M. Albert Poirot of the Bibliothèque Municipal de Dijon, whose own work on the barristers was an invaluable guide. In France, I also benefitted from discussions with Roger Chartier, Christian Jouhaud, Robert Descimon, Arlette Farge, Catherine Maire and the late Annik Pardailhé-Galabrun. My trips to France were supported by the Bourses Chateaubriand of the French government, the Social Science Research Council, and the National Endowment for the Humanities.

The process of turning the dissertation into a book took place largely at Yale. Many thanks here go to my colleagues John Merriman, Peter Gay, Linda Colley, Thomas Head, Mark Shulman, David Stebenne, and my students in History 413a from the fall of 1990. The Yale History Department kindly funded trips to two conferences.

In the broader milieu of English-speaking historians of France, I want above all to thank Dale Van Kley, who has blazed the trail for everyone working in eighteenth-century French political history, and who went far beyond the call of duty in his readings of the manuscript. Sarah Maza kindly shared the fruits of her work on *causes célèbres*, and offered extensive, valuable advice. I also received very useful suggestions and criticism from Keith Michael Baker, David Bien, Michael Fitzsimmons, Vivian Gruder, Patrice Higonnet, Carroll Joynes, Donald Kelley, Jeffrey

Ravel, Isser Woloch, the anonymous readers from Oxford University Press, and the participants in the Center for the History of Freedom seminar at Washington University in 1991–92. Peter Campbell and Carroll Joynes kindly allowed me to consult their excellent dissertations.

Along the way, I presented papers deriving from this project to the Society for French Historical Studies, the Western Society for French History, the New York City French Historians Group and the Princeton Graduate Student Colloquium. Pierre Chaunu, Edna Lemay, and the late Denis Richet generously invited me to speak to their research seminars at the Sorbonne and the École des Hautes Études en Sciences Sociales. I am grateful to the participants in these forums for their advice and criticism. Portions of this book appeared in quite different form in the journals *Past and Present, French Historical Studies,* and the forthcoming volume *The French Idea of Freedom,* published by Stanford University Press. I am grateful to the various editors for allowing me to use the material here, and also to Nancy Lane, my editor at Oxford, who does her valiant best in a difficult period to maintain high standards of academic publishing.

Finally, a few personal acknowledgements. Joël Félix has been a guide to the archives and an intellectual companion during my research and since. Dror Wahrman has been an acute critic and inexhaustible source both of ideas and ruinous phone bills. Doron Ben-Atar has helped make starting out as a junior faculty member remarkably enjoyable. My "famille française," the Lemerles, taught me as much about France as I learned in the archives and gave me a true home away from home in Paris. To my parents, Daniel and Pearl Bell, and to my wife, Donna Farber, I can only say: for everything, thank you. *L'dor va-dor.*

New Haven   D. A. B.
May 1993

Contents

Examinons donc, en quoi consiste cette liberté tant exaltée et tant critiquée des avocats, et nous verrons que ce n'est qu'une portion de la liberté naturelle à tous les hommes, dont les autres hommes ont été frustrés, et que les avocats seuls ont conservée.

Malesherbes, *Mémoire sur les avocats* (1774)

Let us examine, then, the nature of this freedom which belongs to the barristers, and which has been so glorified and so criticized. We will see that it is but a portion of the liberty that is natural to all men, which other men have been deprived of, and which only barristers have conserved.

Lawyers and Citizens

MEMOIRE

POUR les Sieurs Samson Curé d'Olivet, Coüet Curé de Darvoi, Gaucher Chanoine de Jargeau, Diocèse d'Orleans, & autres Ecclesiastiques de différens Diocèses, Appellans comme d'abus;

CONTRE Monsieur l'Evêque d'Orleans & autres Archevêques & Evêques de différens Diocèses, Intimés.

Sur l'effet des Arrests des Parlemens, tant Provisoires Que Définitifs en matiere d'Appel comme d'Abus des Censures Ecclesiastiques.

Es moyens de ce Mémoire sont pris d'une Consultation fort étendue faite en 1718, qui fut dès lors rendue publique avec les noms de 14 Avocats qui l'avoient déliberée, dont quelques-uns sont décedés; les moyens qui subsistent, ont paru si décisifs pour la cause dont il s'agit, qu'on s'est seulement proposé de les mettre dans un plus grand jour, en suivant à peu près le même ordre dans lequel cette Consultation a été faite.

Le Conseil soussigné qui a vû le Memoire du sieur le Cointre Prêtre du Diocèse de Reims, & l'Arrêt du Parlement de Paris du 25 Oct. 1717, qui l'a reçu Appellant comme d'abus de l'Ordonnance du sieur d'Autherive Vicaire Général de M. l'Archevêque de Reims, rendue dans un cours de visite, par laquelle, sur ce que le sieur le Cointre n'avoit pas paru devant lui, il est ordonné que pour apprendre son devoir, il se retirera pendant six semaines dans le Seminaire; pendant lequel tems *Il demeurera suspens de ses saints Ordres*: lequel Arrêt fait des défenses indéfinies d'exécuter cette Ordonnance, Est d'avis que cet Arrêt empêche l'exécution provisoire de l'Ordonnance en question dans toutes ses parties, même par rapport à la suspense.

Cela s'établit par des principes généraux & incontestables, & par l'autorité de la chose jugée *in terminis*.

Les principes généraux sont, que, suivant les Constitutions du Royaume, les Par-

* A

François de Maraimberg's 1730 legal brief, which provoked a political crisis with its assertion that "all laws are contracts between those who govern and those who are governed." Photo courtesy of the Bibliothèque Nationale, Paris.

Introduction

Jurisconsultus hoc est Homo politicus. *

François Baudouin, *Commentarius de jurisprudentia Muciana* (1559).

Between the months of October 1730 and December 1731, a political duel took place in France between two seemingly mismatched combatants. On one side stood the French crown, represented by the unofficial prime minister, Cardinal André-Hercule de Fleury, and the venerable chancellor (head of the judiciary), Henri-François d'Aguesseau. On the other side was ranged the Parisian Order of Barristers, five hundred men of predominantly moderate means, predominantly bourgeois origins, and little obvious political influence. The duel began when the royal council condemned a printed legal brief, signed by forty barristers, that contained several allegedly "seditious" statements, notably, "all laws are contracts between those who govern and those who are governed."[1] The council ordered the signatories to retract or disavow the brief within forty days, but the Order of Barristers resisted, and a dramatic standoff began. The dispute soon became intertwined with long-running debates over the political role of France's *parlements* (sovereign courts) and the temporal powers of the Catholic church in France. It produced a plethora of pamphlets, decrees, secret negotiations, and conspiracies, and culminated in a three-month strike by the barristers that shut down every court of law in Paris. At one point a frustrated member of the royal council suggested that twenty barristers be exiled, twenty thrown in the Bastille, and twenty

---

*"The jurist is a political man." I owe this citation to Donald Kelley, *The Beginnings of Ideology: Consciousness and Society in the French Reformation* (Cambridge: Cambridge University Press, 1981), p. 203.

more summarily hanged.[2] Instead, the crown itself retreated, and the barristers celebrated a "triumph."

While this unusual "affair" has interested several historians of early modern France, one of its most intriguing facets has managed to escape their investigation.[3] Throughout the complicated course of events, the barristers' unsettling defiance elicited from the leading figures in the French government a series of strikingly candid, confidential observations about the nature of political power under a supposedly absolute monarchy. D'Aguesseau, a diligent and insightful jurist who dominated the French judicial scene for more than fifty years, wrote in a set of private reflections in 1730:

> To accustom subjects of a monarchy to believe that laws are nothing but contracts, and that consequently they are only subject to laws to the extent that they have given their consent, is to invite revolt and rebellion against all legitimate forms of power.... If laws are indeed contracts between those who govern and those who are governed, then would the nation not have the right to say that it has not entered into any contract, that therefore it wishes to make the laws, and that it has given no power to the *parlements* to enter into contracts on its behalf...?[4]

D'Aguesseau expanded on the theme in another note to himself in 1731: "The King does not rule over the opinions of men: he judges individuals, and the public judges him." The chancellor then continued, in a passage that underlined the monarchy's fear of public debate itself:

> It is wise to spur men to examine the source and true nature of all forms of human power? This is the way to expose its weakness. There is no power whose principal instrument is not some sort of persuasion. Monsieur Law ruined everything by teaching the world the intrinsic value of money: is it less dangerous to reveal the mystery of the intrinsic value of power?[5]

Another leading minister, Germain-Louis de Chauvelin, himself a former magistrate, touched on the same theme in a letter to the French ambassador in Rome. "The barristers' opinions," he commented, "[are] stronger in the Public than those principles whose observation is prescribed by legitimate authority."[6] Meanwhile, the young Marquis d'Argenson, an ambitious and widely read courtier who would later produce several notable works of political theory, was writing starkly in a confidential report to Fleury:

> Opinion governs men. It is by opinion that Kings rule, and with more or less power. Opinion is thrown into disorder more easily than it is set in place, and this occurs when the slightest degree of disobedience is permitted. ... If ever [the barristers'] ideas penetrate into the minds of the multitude, there will remain only the course of prudent temporization, sustained by solid and constant maxims, to destroy little by little the monster that we neglected to strangle in its cradle.[7]

The elderly, perennially anxious archbishop of Paris, Charles-Gaspard-Guillaume de Vintimille du Luc, was most pessimistic. "Would one accustom us to make the people believe that you can cut off our Kings' heads as they do in England in formal trials?" he asked Fleury.[8]

These passages stand in striking contrast to the prevailing theories of monarchy (articulated most forcefully by Bossuet), according to which the king's semi-divine nature itself commanded complete obedience to his rule. The practical, experienced men who served the young Louis XV recognized that whatever the king's divine *right* to rule, his actual *ability* to do so depended on the "opinions" of his subjects, of "the public." Opinion, however, was by definition unstable and irrational, the opposite of knowledge, and this fact made the monarchy fragile indeed.[9] The king himself could not command such a shifting, elusive phenomenon, yet— and this was the monarchy's terrible "weakness" for d'Aguesseau—he could not rule without it. If "opinion governed men," then even the divinely ordained principles of French government could have no status other than "opinion" in the minds of the king's subjects. It was opinion that let kings rule "with more or less power," and it was opinion that mere barristers could seduce away from principles sanctioned by "legitimate authority."

From the perspective of the later eighteenth century, these writings, and particularly d'Aguesseau's, seem not only dangerously candid, but eerily prophetic. In 1789, "the nation"—in the form of a National Assembly dominated by barristers—indeed decided that it wanted to make the laws, and that it had given the *parlements* no power to enter into contracts on its behalf. Nonetheless, in the context of the "affair" of 1730–31, these frank avowals of royal impotence present something of a puzzle. Why should the writings of a group of largely unknown barristers prompt the most powerful men in the kingdom to such somber reflections? If the barristers in fact posed such a serious threat, why did the crown not take stronger steps to bring them under control?

It would be tempting to answer these questions by saying that the events of 1730–31 represented an aberration, a lone incident in which the crown lost control of "opinion," but, in fact, this was not the case. The complaint that "the barristers' opinions [are] stronger in the Public than those principles whose observation is prescribed by legitimate authority" would have held true at many different moments between 1710 and 1790. In the 1750's, when an older and embittered Marquis d'Argenson confided to his journal that winds of revolution were blowing into France from England, Parisian barristers were writing nearly all the important polemical works in the conflicts opposing the *parlements* and the crown, and experimenting with notions of the sovereignty of the nation.[10] In the 1770's, they directed the massive pamphlet campaign against the judicial "coup d'état" of Chancellor Maupeou and led the broad-based "patriotic opposition" to the monarchy. In the decade immediately preceding the Revolution, many of them became political celebrities, attracting hordes of spectators to the Palais de Justice in great *causes célèbres* which became a focus for political discontent.[11] When the crown finally took d'Argenson's observations to heart and began to issue its own appeals to "public opinion," it did so on the advice of yet another Parisian barrister, and recruited its own publicists in large part from this small stable of legal writers.[12]

Some of the most farseeing contemporary observers did not fail to notice the seemingly anomalous freedom and influence enjoyed by low-ranking men of the law at this time. The barrister Pierre-Louis de Lacretelle later recalled the eighteenth-century Paris bar as a "sort of democracy working in favor of the debris of public liberty." Malesherbes, the renowned magistrate and administrator who did much to facilitate the publications of the *philosophes*, wrote in 1774, in the epigraph to this book, that only barristers still preserved a full portion of "the natural liberty possessed by all men." The astronomer Jean-Sylvain Bailly, who presided over the National Assembly in the early days of the French Revolution, came to a similar conclusion in his memoirs: "Men of letters and barristers were the freest men under the *ancien régime*. The powers that be could never close the mouth of a courageous barrister. . . ." An adviser to Cardinal Fleury (probably d'Argenson) perhaps went furthest, calling the Paris bar "a sort of absolutely independent little republic at the center of the state."[13]

It is a commonplace that lawyers take to politics with unquenchable enthusiasm, but they do so mostly under democratic systems of government. They formed a numerous bloc in the Long Parliament of seventeenth-century England and in the American Continental Congress. They continue to do so in the American Congress and executive branch today. Modern France has not deviated from this pattern, and a recent book on its nineteenth-century regimes even bears the title *Les républiques des avocats*. When the deputies of the Third Estate convened in Versailles in May 1789, forty-six percent of them—by far the largest single professional group—belonged to the bar. Among the lawyers who stood out in this or subsequent revolutionary assemblies were men named Brissot, Danton, and Robespierre.[14]

The reasons for the prominence of lawyers in democratic politics are generally straightforward. Consider the case of France in 1789. Lawyers, by common agreement, then represented the social pinnacle of the bourgeoisie. Thanks to the exceptional social mobility it offered, the law also acted as a particularly strong magnet for ambitious young men.[15] Because of the grotesquely swollen nature of the legal system (a problem common to many modern and early modern societies), lawyers had sheer numbers on their side as well. In France, in fact, they almost certainly represented a greater proportion of the population than they do today, and in some cities their absolute numbers were higher than in the late twentieth century, despite increasing population and industrialization.[16] As Tocqueville commented, "one might almost say that the whole middle class was concerned in one way or another with the administration of justice."[17] Standing as they did on the porous border between public and private spheres, lawyers also had skills and experiences of obvious use to future legislators. As one of their number argued in 1789:

> Is it a mediocre advantage to have among one's Representatives men accustomed to speaking in public . . . ? Is it not important to have men accustomed to rules, to order and forms, and whose knowledge is most analogous to the grand purposes of constitution-making and legislation which principally claim our attention at this time?[18]

In short, the political prominence of lawyers in 1789 was overdetermined.

Yet if the position of lawyers in the Revolution needs little explaining, the same cannot be said for their achievements in 1730 and throughout the eighteenth century. After all, their social qualifications meant little in a society governed by aristocrats and based largely on privilege— on the *principle* of inequality. Their oratorical skills had no political outlets in a society that lacked permanent representative institutions, and where no licit political debate was supposed to take place outside the king's inner circle. Indeed, early modern French barristers frequently lamented the lack of "great objects" worthy of their rhetorical prowess.[19] Therefore, the question of why this group inspired such pessimistic reflections on the part of the kingdom's leading ministers demands a different sort of explanation.

This book will attempt to explain the peculiar influence achieved by Parisian barristers under the *ancien régime*. It will examine the motivations that drove them to intervene in political debate, the strategies they employed to ensure that their interventions had an impact, and the effects of these activities on the profession itself. It will also explore the consequences of this story for French politics as a whole, both under the Old Regime and during the early years of the Revolution. It will seek to demonstrate that the barristers' increasing confidence that they could shape what was called "public opinion"—and government policy as well—ultimately helped change their attitudes towards fundamental questions of political power. In the early eighteenth century, the law was still a profession broadly suspicious of political power in all forms. It was highly receptive to lugubrious Jansenist teachings about the political consequences of original sin, and it tended to define itself as part of France's immemorial constitutional restraints on the sovereign power of the king. By the late eighteenth century, however, its members had gained a great degree of optimism about the potential uses of power, and had come to think of themselves as organs for the expression of a sovereign political will. They used their highly visible platform in the law courts not to restrain the power of the crown, but to push it to make reforms. This change occurred in part because the late eighteenth century legal profession attracted a very different sort of membership from its early eighteenth-century counterpart, but it was no less striking for all that. And it was a change that would have wide repercussions, both because of barristers' very real influence on the political debate of their time, and because of their massive presence in the revolutionary assemblies.

Most immediately, this book focuses on institutional factors—on the development of the legal profession itself—and this approach itself needs a word of justification. In the hierarchical, corporate society of the *ancien régime*, where "rights" were largely a synonym for "privileges," access to public forums and the printing press depended in the first instance on a degree of institutional protection. Even men of letters, who had no official institutional status, still depended intimately upon the good will of powerful institutional patrons, whether to receive the *permissions tacites* that allowed their books to circulate, to obtain pensions and sinecures, or simply to avoid arrest.[20]

While these institutional factors had only incidental importance for some groups, for barristers they were absolutely central. Barristers owed their livelihood to their expertise in the legal codes that bound French institutions together. In a very real sense, they were the institutional technicians of the *ancien régime*, the men who knew the historical precedents and understood the arcane regulations undergirding the creaky remains of a medieval judiciary and administration. If their political ideas had an impact, the reason did not lie simply with the ideas themselves, but in the fact that barristers exploited their expert technical knowledge to create conditions under which they could speak and publish with virtual impunity. It was for this reason that Malesherbes and Bailly believed they possessed a degree of freedom denied to most of their compatriots, and for this reason that d'Argenson called the bar a "little republic."

This "republic," an autonomous space within the institutions of French government, is thus this book's principal subject. D'Argenson may have exaggerated the extent of its independence. Nonetheless, it was what allowed barristers to become privileged midwives for the new, critical "public politics" that arose in France over the course of the eighteenth century. From their protected position, barristers could wage a permanent publicity campaign against "despotism" in the crown and church, and unlike men of letters they could do so openly, signing their names and often publishing legally, without censorship.

These institutional developments, however, need to be placed within a broader social, political, and cultural canvas. Until recently, efforts to link the history of the bar to such a canvas usually took one of two relatively predictable paths. Either the historians in question concentrated heavily on questions of economic development and class conflict, most often treating barristers as an example of the "rising bourgeoisie," or they rejected "materialist" interpretations altogether and portrayed barristers solely as vehicles for "Enlightenment thought."[21] In the first case, the research took place largely on the terrain of social history, in the second, intellectual history. In recent years, however, it has become clear that while the *ancien régime* hardly existed in a condition of social and economic stasis, the transformations underway in its last century did not fit neatly into any Marxian scheme of class conflict. At the same time, developments in intellectual history have called into question the very idea of a monolithic "Enlightenment" that won converts by the sheer force of its ideas. Was it really a unified movement? Was it the great *philosophes* whose ideas proved most damaging? What factors predisposed French readers to accept what they read?[22]

For these reasons alone, the "bourgeois" and "Enlightenment" interpretations of barristers' political stances no longer provide satisfying intellectual fare. They also fail in another regard, however, because they assume that a previously apolitical and inward-looking bar only turned its attention to broader political issues in the mid-eighteenth century. In fact, whether as counselors to great nobles, advisers to royal legislators, assistants to magistrates, or commentators on the laws, barristers had believed for centuries that they held an honorable and indispensable position within the constellation of estates and institutions that made up the French polity. Politics was the central axis along which they conceived of their relationship to the world outside the Palais de Justice. Hence the barrister François Baudouin's 1559 statement: "Jurisconsultus hoc est Homo politicus." Any study of the barristers, however predicated on broad interpretations of the eighteenth century, must take this preexisting relationship to French political life into account. At the same time, any argument that seeks to cast barristers as outsiders (bourgeois, *philosophique,* or otherwise) bent on drastically changing the regime must take into account the *perception* that most Parisian barristers—including those elected to the Estates General in 1789—held of themselves as consummate insiders, without whom the polity could not function.

Thus the barristers' story must be understood first of all in relationship to what scholars have taken to calling the "political culture of the old regime."[23] As recently as 1987, one prominent historian could still remark: "We still understand little of the dynamics of French political culture under the *ancien régime,* and the processes by which revolutionary political practices were invented within the context of an absolute monarchy."[24] Fortunately, in the years since then, the profession's attention has begun to swing back over this fascinating and treacherous territory. New works have appeared on the *parlements,* the *corps,* journalism, municipalities, villages, and many other subjects, much of it strongly influenced by the work of François Furet on the political culture of the French Revolution, and by Jürgen Habermas's early writings on the notion of the "public sphere."[25] These works have revealed a far more vibrant and complex political scene than earlier scholars (who themselves paid attention largely to class relations and the *philosophes*) had led us to expect. These works thus provide a new starting point for evaluating the story of the men of the law who would, more than any other single professional group, rule France during the years of revolutionary turmoil.

* * *

The "new political history" of eighteenth-century France has concentrated above all on the weakening of royal authority, on the processes by which large numbers of the French first lost their habit of obedience to the idea that open political debate had no place in a (theoretically) absolute monarchy, and second their obedience to the monarch himself. Research has dwelled on the mental changes by which the assumption of sovereignty by a National Assembly became possible in a nation long accustomed to treating its kings as semi-divine.[26] Collectively, the new work has argued persuasively that long before the monarchy lost its physical power, a new, critical attitude had grown up (at least among the French elite) towards all forms of political authority, an attitude that involved holding justifications for power and privilege up to abstract standards of reason and utility. Furthermore, the application of this rational criticism led men and women to identify political legitimacy less with the sovereign himself than with "public opinion," which had lost its earlier reputation for instability and irrationality, and had come to be considered the embodiment of reason. Thus the crown surrendered its symbolic centrality in French political life. When the king's ministers themselves decided to campaign openly for the support of the public, they implicitly confirmed this surrender.[27]

This weakening of royal authority itself entailed a fundamental shift in the structure of French politics. As long as the king had remained theoretically absolute, any attempt by the French to press claims upon each other (which is what politics is ultimately about) could proceed licitly only in the form of appeals to the king himself, or to bodies that acted in his name.[28] Furthermore, most such claims were inevitably articulated in the language of privilege—that is to say, they were justified by reference to "rights" and "liberties" that the monarchy had explicitly granted or sanctioned in the past. All sides in disputes ranging from the proper manner of collecting feudal dues to the right of the *parlement* of Paris to participate in the legislative process invoked dusty, ambiguous precedents and ancient, half-forgotten instances of royal favor. Linked to what might be called this "politics of privilege" was the assumption that the king and his magistrates would judge all conflicting claims according to the strict rule of impartiality, even when their own interests came into play. If the king constantly modified or revoked his grants of favor, of course, royal privileges would be *ipso facto* worthless. Royal justice might have lived up only rarely to this ideal of equity, but the ideal itself survived.[29]

After the middle of the eighteenth century, however, as royal authority declined, political claims increasingly took the form of appeals to the judgment of the "public" in printed pamphlets and periodicals, and were increasingly articulated in the language of natural rights. As the magistrate Pierre Gilbert de Voisins recognized in 1753, this shift had serious consequences for the existing order: ". . . in France, people always reasoned frivolously and without consequence concerning the conduct of the government, but today, it is the very foundations of the constitution and the order of the state that they are calling into question."[30] Just as importantly, however, the participants in disputes of all sorts, not just overtly political ones, now increasingly came to believe that they could best serve their cause by mobilizing "public opinion" on their behalf. As for the king, instead of serving as the guarantor of an ideal of impartial justice, he now became simply another litigant before this new "tribunal." Obviously, pamphlet debates, invocations of the "public," and even appeals to the "law of nature" were nothing new in France. Nor was the existence of an active, interested audience for polemical works a novelty. But in the last decades of the *ancien régime* the argument goes that the *idea* of the "public" gained a centrality and legitimacy it had not before possessed, while the use of publicity for political ends became so common—and not only in moments of political crisis—that even a nobleman imprisoned by royal order sought release not by asking for the help of a powerful patron, but by launching an appeal in print.[31] In other words, broadly speaking, the "politics of privilege" was now losing ground to a "politics of public opinion" (although appeals based on privilege did not disappear).

Why did this shift occur? For the most part, the new political history has tended to invoke long-term social and cultural factors such as the increasing market for printed matter, the rise of a "commercial culture," the decline in religious belief, and even changes in modes of reading. Jürgen Habermas's argument associating rational criticism of authority with a new "civic public sphere" that took shape primarily in "bourgeois" literary institutions has had particular influence, steering research in the direction of such institutions as salons and newspapers. Thus the continuities between the two forms of politics have been minimized. It has been assumed that a "public" first took shape outside what Habermas calls the "representative public sphere" of kings, courtiers, and administrators, then became aware of itself, and finally began to assert its rights.[32]

While providing a useful starting point for analysis, the notion of a public "sphere" is itself somewhat vague (Habermas himself actually used the German word *Öffentlichkeit*, meaning, roughly, "publicity"). How did such a "sphere" take shape? What were its limits? Who participated in it? On these questions, the historians have been divided. Some, following Habermas himself, have chosen to emphasize the social context of the phenomenon. They thus examine the workings of salons or the periodical press, linking them closely to the fortunes of the commercial bourgeoisie. "Public opinion," to them, is the name contemporaries gave to a new, visible category of society. The historian Keith Baker, on the other hand, has preferred to see "public opinion" principally as a "discursive invention" for which the social changes formed a necessary, but insufficient precondition.[33]

Habermas's 1962 model itself now appears to have some important shortcomings. First of all, any attempt to link the "public sphere" to the social changes he discusses runs up against the notorious weakness of capitalism under the Old Regime. In France, as a generation of revisionist scholarship has demonstrated, the expanding reading "public" of the eighteenth century was not a public of merchants and industrialists, of outsiders to the sphere of government. It was a public of officeholders, financiers, idle *rentiers*, nobles, and, of course, lawyers—precisely the same groups that participated in the "politics of privilege."[34] Furthermore, Habermas took his model of the "public sphere" from England, which in the eighteenth century possessed a largely free press, as well as swarms of coffeehouses, literary circles, and other such forums for critical debate. France, by contrast, lacked an indigenous free press (although foreign French-language journals had large circulations), while it possessed a powerful police force that watched closely over nongovernmental institutions such as coffeehouses for the slightest murmur of dissent.[35] In France, the forms of criticism Habermas describes, and the notion of "public opinion" itself, paradoxically had greater freedom to develop within the ambit of French government, in forums quite familiar to practitioners of the politics of privilege. It is significant, as Keith Baker has stressed, that the idea of a sovereign public first took hold in the 1750's in the context of a long-running, *political* crisis dominated by the crown and the *parlements*. Baker himself, however, does not explore why a largely conventional constitutional debate should suddenly unleash such a massive upheaval in French political life. He directs his own analysis to the evolution of new conceptual tools, which he believes occurred at a remove from any broader social and institutional context.[36]

Strikingly, few historians have tried to connect the origins of the "public sphere" with a subject that normally dominates discussion of early modern French politics: state centralization. They have also largely passed over the author who has explored this topic most profoundly: Alexis de Tocqueville. Consider, briefly, Tocqueville's well-known description of the effects of royal centralization upon French social relations. Thanks to the monarchy's effective consolidation of all authority within itself, he argued, other, previous ties of obligation, whether of vassals to lords, clients to patrons, or members of *corps* to each other, all withered away. There remained only artificial, dessicated barriers of privilege between atomized individuals, who were essentially equal because they stood in the same relation to the central power. An organic, unified nation thus gave way to one effectively divided between state and society, the latter composed wholly of private individuals—private, because they could neither discuss nor participate in affairs of state.[37]

Although aspects of Tocqueville's analysis have not fared particularly well in recent years, this insight into changing social relations remains suggestive. A possible "revised Tocquevillian" argument might proceed as follows. Over the course of the seventeenth and eighteenth centuries, the crown did much to build up national lines of communication. Its new administrative officers, even if they often served principally as conduits of information rather than as governors, nonetheless brought vast numbers of Frenchmen into direct contact with the central government for the first time. The monarchy itself—rather than the capitalist interests described by Habermas—first sponsored a national press in France, with the institution of the *Gazette de France*, followed by the *Mercure* and the *Journal des Savants*. Under Louis XIV, the monarchy bound members of ruling elites around France into large, and increasingly bureaucratized, patronage networks.[38] Yet even as the kings helped create a national community for the first time, they also became increasingly distinguished *from* this community. The great public ceremonies in which their predecessors had made manifest the bonds between them and the nation disappeared or saw their meanings twisted; royal ceremonial now focused on the grandiose but remote court rituals of Versailles. The Bourbons also rejected any notion of the monarchy as merely the greatest link in an interlocking chain of corporate bodies possessing an independent, divinely-sanctioned existence. They defended the idea that the king could modify the institutions of his realm as he pleased. As we will see, the royal administration encroached on the rights of the judiciary, which had long considered itself an autonomous restraint upon the actions of the monarch.[39]

These changes occurred mostly on the level of political symbolism, but they arguably had the effect of making large numbers of French men and women aware of a dichotomy between state and society. They also raised fears that the king would violate the delicate, tacit foundations upon which the politics of privilege had been built, and proceed to rule in an arbitrary manner, violating rules of equity and property. They demonstrated the transient, malleable nature of all associations below the level of the royal administration, and therefore encouraged the formation of new, less formal, noncorporate ties. Thus, while an expansion of the literary market and the growth of an educated, largely bourgeois audience for books and pamphlets certainly provided one precondition for the politics of public opinion, it was not the only one. In France—the country that gave birth to the word *étatisme*, and where to this very day political philosophers mourn the weakness of "civil society" vis-à-vis the state—the sort of changes Tocqueville describes also proved of vital importance, both in undermining the "politics of privilege," and in making "the politics of public opinion" possible.

In order to understand how and why this "politics of public opinion" took hold, therefore, we must look not simply at men of letters and bourgeois entrepeneurs, but at members of the governmental elites (taken in a broad sense) who had heretofore pursued their goals in a very different manner. And it is in this way that the story of Parisian barristers offers a particularly useful case study. Not only did barristers explicitly define their calling in terms of politics, they also proved adept at redefining it to suit the successive forms of French politics. The dictum *jurisconsultus hoc est Homo politicus* was equally valid, whether one defined the *homo politicus* as an adviser to great nobles maneuvering at court, as an author of deliberately inflammatory pamphlets and legal briefs, or, for that matter, as a member of a National Assembly. If barristers tended to use phrases such as "oracles of justice" about themselves in the waning years of Louis

XIV, by the days of Louis XVI they had become "the voices of the nation," and had recast the profession around the idea of publicity.

Under the "politics of privilege," the barrister was a political man
because appeals to royal authority frequently tended to take the form of
lawsuits waged by barristers in the royal courts. A number of studies have
recently underscored this point. William Beik, for instance, has written in
his important study of absolutism in seventeenth-century Languedoc: "It
cannot be emphasized enough that law suits were the society's principal
form of regulation and enforcement."[40] Michael Sonenscher has shown
that thanks to the organization of the Parisian trades into corporate bodies with sufficient funds to hire lawyers, artisans as well as nobles and
bourgeois depended on the court system for vindication: "The 'typical
form of protest' in the eighteenth-century trades was neither the food
riot nor the strike, but . . . the lawsuit."[41] Hilton Root, Maurice Gresset,
and Yves Castan have all argued that even peasants, through their collective village assemblies, had frequent recourse to the courts against their
seigneurs.[42] In some of these areas, the court system retained its importance until the end of the Old Regime, although in general, the ability of
the judicial system to act autonomously came increasingly into question,
and the specter arose of its functions being usurped by the royal administration.[43] Thus while barristers might not have occupied a particularly
high station in the polity, they were vital to its functioning.

Barristers also profited from the fact that even claims pressed outside
the venue of law courts—for instance, in the "remonstrances" of the
parlements and the clergy—tended to involve the sort of interpretation of
formal written texts at which they excelled. From the sixteenth century
onward, as the crown established a firm monopoly over the use of coer-
cive force in France, political conflicts came to center ever more explicitly
on disagreements over the interpretation of key words and phrases such
as *puissance spirituelle, loi fondamentale,* or indeed *constitution française.*[44]
Historians eager to excavate the "public language" of the *ancien régime,*
and to define unambiguous meanings for each term, have all too often
occluded this fundamental feature of early modern French politics. If
anything, its public language was a creature of poststructuralist delirium,
a web of *mis*understandings and *mis*interpretations in which meaning forever seemed to recede below the horizon.[45] As early as the sixteenth century, jurists such as Budé and Pasquier tellingly blamed the most serious
social conflicts, and even heresies, on the vagaries and imperfections of
language.[46] It was the barristers, professionally schooled in the painstaking
analysis of legal texts, who naturally emerged as acknowledged experts in all
sorts of textual interpretation, gaining preeminence in early modern historical and philological scholarship.[47] Thus their assistance became increasingly desirable not only in lawsuits, but in all conflicts that involved
attempts to "fix" the meaning of ambiguous terms. It was their style of
analyzing problems, moreover, which became increasingly authoritative
to an expanding world of readers.

As the "politics of public opinion" began to take shape in the eighteenth century, barristers did not fade in importance. Instead, they again found themselves at the center. Above all, because of their privilege of publishing legal briefs without preliminary censorship, these documents —in theory, internal court memoranda—became an important means of appealing to, and speaking for, the new and nebulous creature called the "public." The ministry's panicked reaction to the 1730 brief illustrates the importance the genre had already achieved by this date. Moreover, thanks to the barristers' long experience in this sort of polemical writing, by 1750 they had established themselves as the leading political publicists in the kingdom. The protégés of the barristers who signed the 1730 brief dominated the debate over the "Maupeou crisis" in 1771, and *their* protégés contributed as heavily as any other group to the debate over the Estates General in 1788–89.[48]

But was it simply a publishing privilege that gave barristers their continuing central role? Hardly, and the reason lies in the continuities between the two forms of politics that the Habermasian approaches to the subject have minimized. The concerted pamphlet campaigns that greeted every major political crisis of the eighteenth century, and particularly those between the *parlements* and the crown, continued to dwell on the same "rights" and "liberties" that had been fought over for generations. The fact that the abstract figure of "public opinion" had now gained some sort of symbolic legitimacy did not immediately change matters. Arguably, given that the intended readers of these pamphlets themselves mostly possessed privileges of various sorts, were accustomed to justifying them by recourse to precedent, and depended on the familiar standard of impartial royal justice for their preservation, it would have been initially difficult to press political claims in any other sort of language. Even in the last fifteen years of the *ancien régime*, as French readers learned the language of natural rights, and as the grip of royal censorship loosened, sensational trials remained an ideal means of drawing attention to claims of all sorts. In fact, for reasons explored in Chapters 5 and 6, trials now served these purposes better than ever. Barristers remained very much in the limelight.

Even as this book attempts to situate barristers in relation to different forms of politics, it will not treat them as a monolithic corporate group, or as motivated principally by collective interests whether oriented towards material gain, status, or power. In this respect, it will differ from most previous investigations of the subject. Tocqueville himself assumed, in *Democracy in America*, that French lawyers' thwarted professional ambitions dictated their political conduct, and in fact played an important part in bringing about the Revolution.[49] More recently, Maurice Gresset, in his path-breaking social history of *"gens de justice"* in Besançon, similarly links the barristers' enthusiasm for the Revolution to their inability to gain promotion to the magistracy under the Old Regime.[50] Michael

Fitzsimmons has interpreted their subsequent hostility to revolution as a reaction to the National Assembly's attempt to destroy their cherished corporate ethos.[51] The sociologist Lucien Karpik has written that French lawyers in the eighteenth and nineteenth centuries naturally fell into an oppositional political stance because the pose of representing the "public" served a collective "strategy" for increasing their social status.[52]

The assumption that collective interests dictated political behavior has itself been bolstered by a common perception of early modern French barristers as members of a *corps* rather than of a modern profession. Historians and sociologists who specialize in the field generally argue that if modern professions define themselves in part around standards of ethics and performance, and a dedication to the common weal, *corps* are concerned far more with protecting specific privileges.[53] Thus while a profession might allow its members a degree of latitude in choosing political positions, a *corps* keeps more vigilant watch, ensuring that individuals remain oriented towards the pursuit of the collective good (as defined, of course, by the corporate leadership). The corporate groups of the Old Regime have a particularly strong, if somewhat exaggerated reputation as close-knit, suffocating institutions which forced their members to put the interests of the *corps* above all else.[54]

Yet did barristers really fit this model? Was it their collective interests that most often dictated their political conduct? I will contend that this was not always the case. To begin with, as British historians have already shown conclusively, the somewhat rigid contrast between modern professions and pre-modern *corps* has been greatly overstated as far as the law is concerned. Furthermore, even though the term "profession" in the modern sense did not exist in eighteenth-century France (the French word *profession* meant simply "occupation"), the Paris bar, like that of London during the same period, in fact bore a great resemblance to modern professional bodies.[55] Matthew Ramsey has usefully suggested that what the French now call *professions libérales* can be most readily defined in terms of a loose set of simple criteria, particularly a distinct identity as a professional group, an established body of theory taught in institutions of higher learning, uniform standards for training and performance, an independent governing body, and a monopoly on certification and practice. One might add to this list the standards and service ethic discussed above.[56] By these criteria (as the next chapter will make clear), Parisian barristers certainly resembled modern "professions" by 1700.[57] Moreover, they themselves strove vehemently to distinguish the bar from privileged corporate bodies. They did not always do so persuasively, and the tension between corporatism and an early version of "professionalism" stood as a defining feature of the history of the French legal profession between 1660 and 1790. Yet the bar most emphatically cannot be considered a corporate body single-mindedly concerned with its rights and privileges.

In fact, the barristers' motivations cannot be easily reduced to any single factor, for if some men used politics as a vehicle to advance the interests of the bar, others used the bar as a vehicle to advance their own political agendas. Resentment at the lack of opportunities for advancement certainly existed. However, most often it expressed itself not in experimentation with new forms of political engagement, but rather (as Chapter 2 will make clear) in quarrels with magistrates over precedence and protocol, quarrels which allowed the barristers to affirm their status within a milieu where etiquette was worshiped just as fervently as at Versailles. In many other cases, barristers willingly put their own professional futures, and those of their colleagues, in jeopardy because of a commitment to political goals (for instance, the advancement of religious toleration) that they had defined well before embarking on legal careers. Quite a number of barristers, though they gladly exploited the privileges accorded in the bar, had little concern for the future of the profession itself. Indeed, many of the same barristers who identified themselves most vociferously as the "voices of the nation" in the 1780's would soon call for the abolition of the legal profession entirely.[58] In general, barristers could afford to act against their narrow professional interests more easily than their modern counterparts because, as will be shown in the next chapter, most of them possessed independent forms of wealth, and did not rely wholly on their practice for their revenues.

The most important single group of barristers studied here—the so-called Jansenists, who provoked the 1730 incident—tended to think not in terms of the interests of their own Order, but rather in terms of the ideal of impartial justice, which held such an important place in the "politics of privilege." They envisaged this standard of justice as the pillar that supported French society. Without it, as one jurist wrote in 1711, "cities, provinces and kingdoms would be mere brigandages, rather than civil societies and legitimate and well-ordered States."[59] In essence, they conceived of French government as what might be called a "judicial monarchy." Furthermore, they saw any challenge to their cherished standard of justice from sovereign authority, whether the king's or the pope's, as "arbitrary despotism," a dark specter threatening literal ruin and damnation for the kingdom. (In a society where so many people depended on this ideal of justice, of course, the message had wide resonance.) This concern for justice did reflect a distant material interest on the barristers' part, for they themselves, as the principal repositories of legal expertise, had an obvious and indispensable role to play in a society organized on the basis of royal justice mediating between competing individuals and institutions. But this concern also reflected a broad, deeply Augustinian view of the world, and a desire to organize the city of man in a manner most conducive to salvation.

Thus in this book, the transformation of the legal profession and its role in the birth of the politics of public opinion will not be ascribed to

any single set of "interests." Indeed, it will be argued that while the
Jansenists had more importance than any other group of barristers in the
emergence of the politics of public opinion, for the most part they looked
on it with distaste. They regarded the tools of publicity, which they used
with previously unknown virtuosity, as unsavory weapons that they had
only picked up *in extremis*, to impede the progress of despotism. It would
take another generation of barristers, less influenced by Jansenism, to ap-
plaud the politics of public opinion for its own sake, and to treat the prospect of democracy in a nation of twenty-six million with something other
than dread.

While this book tells the story of the French legal profession in the eighteenth century, it will not go over familiar ground. For a social history of
lawyers, in the tradition of the *Annales*, the reader is advised to turn to
the works of Maurice Gresset, Lenard Berlanstein, and Albert Poirot.[60]
For a narrative account of lawyers' past glories, the careful, but uncritical
studies by Jean-François Fournel, Joachim Gaudry, Charles Bataillard,
and André Damien—all themselves members of the French legal profession—are recommended.[61] Nor will the reader find here a sociologically-
oriented "history of the professions" such as Matthew Ramsey has written on French medicine, or Wilfrid Prest and David Lemmings on English
law.[62] While the book closely examines the political ideas advanced by
eighteenth-century lawyers, and particularly what Dale Van Kley has
dubbed "Jansenist-*parlementaire* constitutionalism," it will situate them
less in the story of French political thought as a whole than in their cultural and institutional milieux.[63]

Unfortunately, the word *institutional* itself tends to suggest a dry
and dusty survey of law codes, finances, and organizational structures.
This, I hope, will not be the case here. Barristers have much in common
with actors. They must perform before a public, and often, forgetting
they have left the stage at the end of the day, continue to perform as they
go through the other aspects of their daily lives. The legal profession in
eighteenth-century Paris seemed especially hospitable to eccentric, colorful men of this sort. The *dramatis personae* of this work include the hulk-
ing, unkempt figure of Claude-Joseph Prévost, nicknamed "the bear"
both for his plebeian origins and his wild, uncontrollable rages. They
include Louis-Adrien Le Paige, one of the great *éminences grises* of French
history who directed the *parlementaire* opposition from his rooms in the
gloomy fortress called the Temple, writing thousands of pages of pamphlets and coordinating the activities of scores of correspondents, all the
while presiding over the strange sect of the Convulsionaries. They include
the pale, skeletal Simon Linguet, whose shrill voice and childish antics
somehow mesmerized the Parisian public more than any actor of his generation, and Linguet's great adversary, the haughty, corrupt, grandiose
orator Pierre Gerbier.

The book is also not concerned with "typical" barristers, even assuming this species could be located in a country so large, unsettled, and diverse as early modern France.[64] First, it concentrates on the bar of Paris, the largest and wealthiest in the kingdom (although comparisons are offered, where possible, with the provinces). Furthermore, while it pays considerable attention to the organization called the Order of Barristers, which included all practicing barristers in Paris, the leading members of the bar, sometimes no more than fifty or sixty men at a time, have been singled out for special scrutiny. These leading members could hardly compete socially with magistrates and *maîtres des requêtes*, let alone with barons and dukes, but (as the next chapters will show) they were frequently nobles, and possessed sizeable fortunes, which to some extent freed them from financial considerations when deciding, for instance, to go on strike. These were the men who, if not "typical" of French barristers as a whole, participated in political debate at a high level, provoked incidents such as the 1730 "affair," and directed the activities of their Parisian colleagues. These were men whose actions had the greatest impact on French political culture, and whose story best illuminates the changes in that culture over time.

Nonetheless, the book does have implications for the study of the French legal profession beyond this Parisian elite (and thus for the role barristers played in 1789 and thereafter). The very fact of the Parisian barristers' eminence meant that they served as models for their colleagues in all ranks of the profession. When lawyers elsewhere had questions about the organization of the bar, they appealed to their Parisian colleagues.[65] Parisian barristers largely wrote the gigantic dictionaries of jurisprudence that served as the indispensable reference books for lawyers elsewhere.[66] They also wrote the largest share of important polemical works, and figured most often in periodicals such as the widely-read *Mémoires secrets* and the *Gazette des tribunaux*.[67] If the tens of thousands of lesser-known French barristers, hundreds of whom ended up in the revolutionary assemblies, came to see themselves as "voices of the nation" in the eighteenth century, it was due in no small part to the Parisian example.

The Barristers' Seminar, by Gabriel de Saint-Aubin, illustrating the Barristers' Library on the Ile de la Cité. Photo courtesy of the Bibliothèque Nationale, Paris.

1

The World of the Law

The practices of the law courts had entered in many ways into the pattern of French life. Thus the courts were largely responsible for the notion that every matter of public or private interest was subject to debate and every decision could be appealed from; as also for the opinion that such affairs should be conducted in public and certain formalities observed. Obviously incompatible with the concept of a servile state, such ideas were the only part of a free people's education furnished by the old regime.*

Tocqueville, The Old Regime and the Revolution

Lawyers are easily stereotyped, and the stereotypes are rarely favorable. In this respect, early modern France differed not at all from contemporary Europe or America.[1] A particularly nasty 1782 critic went so far as to call lawyers "gnawing vultures who do not let their prey escape until they have fully gorged themselves."[2] Of course, a few images, generally produced by the legal profession itself, have always gone to the other extreme. In them, lawyers are depicted as a secular priesthood, the conscience of a nation, and generally the thin wedge protecting civilization from barbarian hordes. Early modern France produced its share of such writings as well (Chapter 2 will examine how they in fact contributed to the formation of an organized legal profession in Paris). Between the Scylla of overwrought hostility and the Charybdis of unrestrained praise, is it possible to sail through to a point where the social, cultural, and institutional contours of the early modern French legal profession become more clearly visible? Fortunately, the wealth of the archives, and the efforts of several dedicated French specialists, make such a trip possible. It is best to begin with the legal institutions, for without a sense of how they

*Translation by Stuart Gilbert (New York: Doubleday, 1955), p. 117.

functioned, it is difficult to see why barristers came to occupy such an important niche in the French polity.

General Outlines

Although twentieth-century government rarely approaches the Weberian ideal of bureaucratic rationality, we like to pretend that it does nonetheless. We like to believe that it can be accurately represented in a complex flowchart, with the different branches clearly separated, the different functions and jurisdictions clearly delineated, and the chain of authority clearly spelled out. When looking at the "government" of the Old Regime, however, these preconceptions must be ruthlessly suppressed. Any modern bureaucrat asked to prepare a flowchart of the early modern French administration and judiciary would soon likely abandon the task in despair, leaving behind drafts bearing more resemblance to expressionist art than to any known structure of government. Nor is the problem simply one of complexity, for many of the concepts dear to modern political systems— the "separation of powers," "bureaucratic responsibility," even a clear distinction between "state" and "society"—had at best a protean existence in the seventeenth and eighteenth centuries.

For the Old Regime, it is hardly an exaggeration to say that the operative concepts of government were duplication, ambiguity, and competition. Ever since the Middle Ages, French kings had hesitated to anger powerful vested interests by abolishing existing institutions, but preferred to create parallel ones to slowly take over their functions. Every century thus brought an accretion of new agencies devoted to old and familiar purposes (*intendants* supplanting royal governors, *Grand conseil* paralleling *parlements*, *présidiaux* demoting *sénéchaussées*). For this reason, several different bodies often shared the authority to take a particular action, or to judge a particular case, and the actual ability to act could depend less on the formal institutional structure than on influence or favor. The different bodies, moreover, often fought over turf with far more energy than they devoted to their nominal functions. The stakes were high, since the dimensions of a jurisdiction determined, in fairly direct measure, the amount of an official's revenue, the value of his office, and even the extent of his honor, measured quite tangibly by his rank in public processions. It is not surprising that jurisdictional quarrels—fought with the lawyers' weapons of tortuous reasoning and mind-numbing recourse to precedent—featured in nearly every important political battle of early modern France.[3]

The nature of French law itself did very little to alleviate the confusion that arose from this state of affairs. Nothing could be further from the concise, coherent precepts of the *Code Napoléon* than what Mercier memorably called "the mire and abominable chaos" of pre-revolutionary jurisprudence.[4] The country did not even have a single law code, as England did. Roughly speaking, the south of France followed Roman law, a distant inheritance from the Roman Empire. The north followed customary law—but not a united Common Law, because each region, and sometimes each village, had its own "custom" (*coutume*). Royal ordinances formed an uneven layer on top of these codes, while the church followed canon law, and the courts' own rulings (*arrêts*) had great force as judicial precedents.[5] The flamboyant and rebellious barrister Simon Linguet asked acerbically: "Has any man managed to learn one percent of the laws which our ancestors' fertile imaginations have bequeathed to us, and which we follow with a most stupid respect?"[6] Manuals for aspiring barristers routinely warned that a basic mastery of French jurisprudence took *decades* of applied study.[7]

The court system did its part to maintain the general level of complexity. Seigneurial courts, church courts, commercial courts, courts for admiralty law and excise taxes, courts for royal forests and waterways, courts for salt depots and the constabulary—all teetered beside or atop each other. The barrister Pierre-Nicolas Berryer noted in his memoirs in the early nineteenth century that his birthplace, Ste. Menehould, with a population of only three thousand, had possessed nine different courts under the Old Regime, all of which the Revolution later replaced with a single panel of four judges.[8] As for appeals, hapless litigants found themselves climbing a tall and rickety ladder from *prévôtés* and seigneurial courts to *bailliages* and *sénéchaussées*, thence to *présidiaux* and finally to the *parlements* and other sovereign courts, while the king's privy council stood as the absolute final court of appeal for all of them. Linguet justly complained about these "cascading jurisdictions, which drag litigants further and further down into a pit from which few are fortunate enough to escape."[9]

The city of Paris exemplified all the most baroque features of this system. The city contained thirty-five separate courts, whose jurisdictions ranged from a third of the kingdom to a quarter of the Ile de la Cité. Nearly all were crammed into the center of the city, and sixteen squeezed into the Palais de Justice itself, a collection of architecturally-diverse structures located on the site of a former royal palace.[10] Across the Seine from the Palais sat the vast medieval hulk of the Châtelet, or municipal courts, making the Pont au Change into a thoroughfare for black-robed clerks and lawyers streaming between the two. The courts practically constituted cities of their own: if one counted clerks and the boutique-owners whose stands crowded the halls and corridors, as many as forty thousand people spent their days within the Palais de Justice alone.[11] The courts thus dominated the center of the city, and, after the creation of Versailles in the late seventeenth century, they did so without competition from government ministries or the royal household.

What strikes the modern eye as intolerable confusion could, however, have very different meanings for contemporaries. Indeed, the occupants of the Parisian courts had long swathed the ramshackle and disorganized physical structures in a rich blanket of symbolism and ceremony that conveyed a message of order, dignity, and organic unity. The very location of the Palais de Justice on the Ile de la Cité had important symbolic meaning. In 1607, the magistrate Louis d'Orléans had written in *Les ouvertures de Parlemens* that Paris had three parts: the "sacred" Left Bank, seat of the Sorbonne's faculty of theology; the "profane" Right Bank devoted to commerce; and mediating between them, the Cité, home of royal Justice.[12] Every November 12, the day on which the *parlement* began a new year of business, its magistrates would march in procession dressed in brilliant red robes, attending mass in a chapel lit by thousands of flickering candles, and reverberating to the voices of choristers. The lawyers followed, silent, subservient, and attentive.[13] For this moment, at least, all quarrels over jurisdiction were stilled, and all the members of the legal world took their ordained place in a complex, but coherent living tapestry. To borrow the useful schema devised by Jürgen Habermas, the courts belonged wholly to the "representative public sphere," a place where public authority took the form of a giant pageant put on "not for but 'before' the people."[14]

At the pinnacle of the judicial system sat the sovereign courts called the *parlements*, with the *Parlement* of Paris predominant among them. Numbering eight separate chambers and over one hundred magistrates in 1700, this court heard appeals from a bloated jurisdiction that covered a full third of the kingdom, corresponding roughly to the old royal domain (in 1789, sixteen smaller *parlements* and equivalent *conseils supérieurs* divided up the other two-thirds). It also judged certain cases in the first instance, notably those involving peers of the realm. With the *ducs et pairs* in attendance, it could sit as the Court of Peers. Its magistrates, who owned their offices as a valuable form of property, mostly stood in the highest ranks of the "nobility of the robe," the elite stratum of royal officers which had grown up since the Renaissance.[15]

While the *parlement* primarily functioned as a law court, it also performed many of the functions modern observers would associate with the administrative or legislative branches. It regulated certain aspects of Parisian life, particularly in regard to the grain trade, and its judgments (*arrêts*) had such force as judicial precedents that they effectively constituted a sort of legislation—as Sarah Hanley has brilliantly demonstrated in the case of family law.[16] This sweeping authority derived from the fact that in late medieval and Renaissance France, the crown, lacking other well-developed administrative structures, had used the courts as organs of royal government. Even after they began to develop alternate systems of administration, the kings still recruited their leading corps of administrators in large part from the *parlements*. France still, in a real sense, had the form of a "judicial monarchy."[17]

Most important, the *parlements* maintained that they had a role of sorts in the national legislative process. The king might promulgate laws, but each *parlement* needed to "register" physically these statutes on its books before they took effect in its jurisdiction. This seemingly technical point took on vast, almost metaphysical significance for the *parlements*, for it made them into the "repository of the laws," the channels through which the king's decisions had to flow. The "right of registration" did not constitute a veto power on laws (except as construed in the most extreme *parlementaire* propaganda), but the *parlements* also insisted on another right: to "remonstrate"—interminably—with the king before registration when they disagreed with him.[18] French political theorists, notably Claude de Seyssel, characterized this right as a fundamental element of the unwritten French constitution, one of a number of "bridles" that guided the monarch and prevented him from abusing his authority. As the influence of the great noble magnates waned in the seventeenth century, the right of remonstrance made the *parlements* the most important remaining form of opposition to the monarchy, and the only quasi-independent institution to survive under its shadow.[19]

To a large extent, the political history of early modern France revolved around the crown's desire to secure its own direct authority at the expense of this powerful and independent judicial system. True, as we have seen, historians no longer accept Tocqueville's powerful vision of the crown's agents as single-minded, bureaucratic royal agents greedily crushing intermediate powers to build a centralized state (Napoleonic prefects *avant la lettre*). These agents now appear as fairly pragmatic sorts, who had their greatest success when they coopted or cooperated with established elites instead of trying to run roughshod over them. Far from abolishing corporate privilege, constant fiscal pressure generally forced them to strengthen it (the better to milk it for revenue).[20] Yet if "absolutism" poorly describes the crown's actual attempts to govern a variegated nation of over twenty million, it captures quite well the crown's ultimate goal, and the vision of the French polity it pursued, at least in the eighteenth century. In this vision, royal authority flowed *directly* from the monarch to each of his subjects. The institutions of government—including the *parlements*—amounted to no more than emanations of his own person, and could be modified at will. Under Louis XV in particular, royal publicists constructed this absolutist dogma with a vigor that put the crown's actual institutional reforms to shame.[21] The magistrates in turn reacted by seeking to anchor themselves ever more deeply in the elusive bedrock of the unwritten constitution dear to Seyssel, arguing by various means that the *parlements* were as immutable as the monarchy itself, and that the king had no right to change or bypass them. The more insistently the crown advanced its claims, the more the magistrates pushed their own, so that the two tended to radicalize each other.[22]

In practice, the conflicts between the crown and the *parlements* mostly took place on the level of day-to-day governance. Magistrates and royal officials constantly engaged in petty jurisdictional squabbling. Moreover, since the *parlements* claimed a role in the national legislative process, every royal law had the potential to bog down in remonstrance after remonstrance, "humble representation" after "humble representation," and finally judicial strikes. Following traditional patterns, the Bourbon kings sought to weaken the *parlements* by extending the powers of other, competing courts. On a few occasions they also succumbed to the temptation to call out musketeers and break the impasse by force, but these attempts rarely lasted long. More often, relations between the two sides took the form of unrelenting, but tolerable friction enlivened by occasional sparks of angry rhetoric.

It can be argued that these quarrels amounted to a de facto system of checks and balances, and posed little threat to the regime. William Doyle has gone so far as call them an element of "a stable political system working by well-understood, if sometimes tacit, rules."[23] Yet while the system's durability should certainly not be underestimated, nonetheless, over time, the constant friction clearly did reshape the French polity in important ways. The attempt to strip royal power of all fixed, institutional restraints, to set the king himself firmly apart from his subjects and transform him into a virtual demigod, contributed to the emergence of separate spheres for "state" and "society," and to the growth of an independent public sphere in the latter. The *parlements'* radicalization in the eighteenth century led to a revival (largely by barristers) of notions of popular sovereignty and social contracts long banished into the outer circles of heresy along with the Huguenots who had first professed them in France.[24]

The legal profession featured prominently in these changes, and indeed, had a greater stake in them than other groups. Magistrates at least received some compensation for reduced independence in the form of entrée into the high nobility and influential government positions. For barristers, the threatened advent of an "administrative monarchy" promised little but declining caseloads and diminished prestige. It is hardly surprising, then, that they would emerge as the most tenacious defenders of the "judicial monarchy."

The Barristers

Lawyers are mediators in many different senses. Most obviously, they mediate between their clients and the legal system, between private individuals and public authority. But they are also *social* mediators. The profession confers a certain degree of status and, at least potentially, a substantial income, yet admission into its ranks generally stresses learning, not capital. For these reasons, it functions in modern societies as a classic avenue of social mobility, particularly where a stigma attaches to trade and industry.[25] Yet the very nature of the profession as an avenue or a channel can make it far less homogeneous than others, and thus far more treacherous to generalize about as a social group. Early modern France conforms well to this general pattern, particularly since, unlike nearly all other legal occupations, the bar did not impose a *numerus clausus* or demand that its members purchase venal offices. Jacques Godard, just starting out as a barrister, wrote to a cousin in 1783: "It is only really a social station (*état*) when some consideration is joined to it. The title of barrister by itself is the smallest of all titles, because it is the easiest to obtain."[26]

As illustration of these points, consider two very different Parisian legal careers. Georges Le Roy was born in the mid-1650's, the son of a wealthy barrister in the king's council. He entered the bar himself in 1675, and soon compiled a glittering list of clients, including the King of Sardinia and Liselotte, the Princess Palatine, wife of the Duc d'Orléans. This work took him into the realm of high international politics, where he helped develop the Princess's claim on the Palatine succession, which served as a pretext for France's aggression in the War of the League of Augsburg. Le Roy remained throughout his life a loyal client of the house of Orléans, and as a reward, when Liselotte's son Philippe became regent in 1715, he granted Le Roy transmissible nobility by letters patent. At his death in 1747, the barrister possessed a sizeable mansion in Paris, a fourteen-room country house in Orly, and a fortune that rivaled that of some magistrates.[27]

Louis Babille, on the other hand, began his legal career in the 1730's as a humble clerk, copying writs and briefs. Although he grandly styled himself "Babille de Marsaneix" after entering the Order of Barristers in 1739, he lived in a squalid, fifth-floor, one-room apartment with his common-law wife, and found few clients. To support himself, he charged a small fraction of the prices established barristers generally demanded for various services, a practice which, though common enough among struggling barristers, earned him the enmity of his colleagues. In 1749, these colleagues suspended him from practice, and while he reapplied for admission to the bar six years later, offering plaintive descriptions of his family's misery, he was definitively disbarred.[28]

While these cases admittedly illustrate the extremes, modern social historians have confirmed the overall social heterogeneity of the French legal profession.[29] What, then, united its members? Any answer to this question must focus not only on quantitative measures of socioeconomic status, but also on training, professional discipline, and what might generally be called the "culture of the law courts." These things changed greatly over the course of the seventeenth and eighteenth centuries, but a few generalizations are still in order.

Merely identifying barristers is a subject that confused many contemporaries, and has baffled modern historians as well. Thousands of men held the title of "barrister" (*avocat*), but only a small percentage of them belonged to the Order of Barristers, whose members had the sole right to practice before the *parlement* and the other courts of the city.[30] The confusion arises from the fact that the *parlement* conferred the title on any university graduate in law who, sponsored by a barrister of twenty years' standing, took the "barrister's oath" (*serment d'avocat*). The magistrates rarely posed any objections, and senior barristers generally sponsored candidates without hesitation.[31] Many members of the legal world—including notaries, police commissioners, even bailiffs—thus took advantage of the simple procedure to acquire a prestigious honorific. In addition, all magistrates acquired the title in order to comply with royal laws stipulating that they belong to the bar.[32] Albert Poirot and Martine Acerra, who both studied the register of certificates (*matricules*) granted after the oath, estimate that for every practicing barrister, as many as twenty other men held the title for purely decorative reasons. The distinction is easy to miss, and unfortunately, some social historians of early modern Paris—notably François Furet and Adeline Daumard in their study of Parisian social structure—seem to have treated every self-styled *avocat* as a real one.[33]

Luckily, barristers made the distinction clear to themselves. Before 1660 the system proceeded informally: practicing barristers made themselves known to the magistrates and their colleagues, and their names were noted on a handwritten list (*rôle*). Then, between 1660 and 1700 a more formal set of distinctions came into being (the reasons will be explored in Chapter 2). In order to practice, aspiring barristers now needed to complete a two-year internship (*stage*) and then gain formal acceptance by the so-called Order of Barristers—which only came into existence as a functioning bar association during this period. The Order identified its members by an annual printed list, or *Tableau*.[34] According to these lists, which began appearing regularly only in the eighteenth century, numbers varied from a low of 346 (1710) to a high of 712 (in 1738), with an average of 540 between 1700 and 1789, making the Paris bar by far the largest in France. In theory, the men listed on the *Tableau* went by the title *avocats au parlement* whereas titular barristers presented themselves as *avocats en parlement*.[35] However, this overly subtle nomenclature, while spelled out in dictionaries of jurisprudence, never really caught on. Barristers themselves used the terms interchangeably, and to make things worse, Maupeou's reforms of 1771–74 temporarily created a new species of lawyer called *avocats du parlement*.[36]

If barristers had any socioeconomic group identity, it came less in the area of wealth and income than in family background, for a majority came from families already established within the world of the law. Maurice Gresset has shown, in his study of Besançon, that in general *gens de justice* tended to reproduce themselves, although social mobility—albeit at a slow, generational pace—was possible within the confines of the judiciary. Two-thirds of all Parisian barristers from the period 1661–1715, and fifty-four percent from 1760 to 1790, were sons of barristers, notaries, or other servants of the courts (the rest came principally from trade, finance, and medicine).[37]

Still, common origins within the world of the law did little to overcome the vast social gulf between nobles like Georges Le Roy and the sons of provincial notaries. In fact, one of the most important divisions in the bar lay between a relatively small number of established families (perhaps ten percent of all barristers), and outsiders like Louis Babille. Like the *parlement*, the bar had its great dynasties. Georges Le Roy was the son of a barrister in the king's council, and had two brothers and two sons in the bar. Louis-Adrien Le Paige, the great Jansenist *éminence grise*, was a third-generation barrister, and nephew and brother of men in other branches of the legal profession.[38] Legal dynasties naturally tended to perpetuate themselves, for success in the bar, especially in the early years, depended almost entirely on contacts. Le Paige began his career pleading in the *Grand conseil* thanks to his uncle, who worked there as a *procureur* (roughly, a solicitor).[39] Not surprisingly, barristers from outside the close-knit family networks had far more difficulty. Several men disbarred in 1729 complained, in an unsuccessful attempt at reinstatement, that certain families, whom they labeled "ant-hills of barristers," jealously maintained a virtual monopoly on legal practice.[40]

The great social divisions in the bar emerge clearly in studies of their wealth and income. Albert Poirot examined the fortunes of fifty Parisian barristers who died between 1760 and 1790, and his results show a vast range in fortunes: from 3,630 to 882,500 *livres* (with an average of 50,000). Thirty-six percent left more than 100,000 at their deaths, but a full quarter seem to have lived in very modest conditions, and left less than 15,000. More exhaustive studies of the provincial *parlements* reveal similar patterns.[41] Professional revenues also varied considerably. Pierre-Jean-Baptiste Gerbier, the most renowned orator of his day, received as much as 1,200 *livres* per court appearance, and as much as 300,000 *livres* from a single drawn-out case. Louis Babille and many like him hardly earned anything at all.[42]

For what it is worth, the median member of the bar (in terms of wealth and income) lay squarely in the upper middling ranks of society, better off than artisans and most tradesmen, but far below the glittering heights of the magistrature and *haute finance*. According to Poirot, he rented a four-to-six room apartment, and received an average of 3,000 *livres* a year in annuities (*rentes*), which allowed him to live in modest comfort regardless of professional revenues.[43] He also had a considerable library: 900 books on average, at a time when 250–300 books designated a significant collection. Libraries represented fully 16.9 percent of the average barrister's fortune, far above the level for any other group in Paris, including magistrates. In these libraries, as one would expect, works of jurisprudence predominated.[44]

Disparities in social contacts mirrored the disparities in wealth. Those barristers whose wealthy practices brought them into everyday professional contact with the aristocracy also tended to have frequent social contacts with the second estate. The barrister Edmond Barbier, a witty, acerbic man who kept an invaluable journal for more than forty years, often mentioned dining in the company of aristocrats and ministers. Gerbier had the honor of welcoming the Prince de Conti to his country home, and was known as a close friend of high-ranking magistrates.[45] Louis-Adrien Le Paige maintained close friendships with many magistrates, and while he did not deal with them wholly as social equals, the relationships went beyond mere deference, as revealed in a letter he received in 1775 from the magistrate Durey de Meinières:

> It is a pleasure, on this idle Sunday, to chat with you, my old and good friend, but I must start by scolding you for the formal language you use with me. You put a *Monsieur le Président* at the start of your letters, and a *Your very humble servant*, and then *Respect &c.* at the end. This is hardly the way to treat your friends. . . . From now on, do away with these frills, and tell me simply that you still love me, as I love you, and you will make me happy, very happy.[46]

In sum, the more eminent portion of the bar, by its social contacts as well as its wealth, clearly formed part of an emerging broad class of *notables*. Most of the Order, however, fell outside this class. The extent to which one can speak of its *overall* economic interests is, therefore, limited.

When asking what the great dynasties and the strugglers had in common, one must start with the nature of the legal profession itself. The activities of early modern French lawyers had much in common with those of their modern French and American counterparts, but there were also important differences. First of all, the barristers had strikingly narrow practices, for the French legal profession was then split into several branches. Contracts, wills, conveyancing and the like were the province of notaries (*notaires*). Clients in search of other forms of legal representation first approached not a barrister, but a *procureur* (essentially the equivalent of a modern English solicitor). He was the man who handled the procedural aspects of cases, collecting evidence and filing motions. Only if more than procedural expertise were required would the *procureur*—not the client— then proceed to engage a barrister (this arrangement obviously made family ties with *procureurs* extremely important).

   The barrister himself mostly provided two services: offering legal advice, and, if necessary, making oral or written arguments to a court. These services were themselves fairly limited. Oral and written arguments touched only on questions of law, for it was the *procureur* who established the facts of a case and presented them to the court. Nor did barristers frequently take part in much courtroom drama. Indeed, few of them spent much time in court at all, for the *parlements* judged most cases essentially on the basis of written material.[47] Even when barristers did appear, they generally did no more than make concluding speeches, since in France's civil law system, the magistrates themselves examined witnesses (and, before the Revolution introduced the jury system, determined the final verdict too). Finally, barristers appeared only in civil cases, since criminal defendants had no right to counsel.[48] The regulations governing the profession loosely divided practicing barristers into three classes, corresponding in theory to the three stages of a career: young *avocats écoutants*, still completing their training, who did nothing but study and attend trials; mature *avocats plaidants*, who made oral arguments; and venerable *avocats consultants*, who did not plead but merely offered consultations. In practice, the paucity of trials involving oral arguments, and sometimes personal preference as well, led many barristers to skip the second stage.[49]

Like modern lawyers, barristers also had several auxiliary forms of legal employment which complemented these otherwise-limited activities. Trainees and senior barristers made a practice of offering *pro bono* consultations for the poor. Large institutions such as the archbishopric and the tax collection company called the Ferme Générale generally kept one or more barristers on permanent retainer, as did the great princely houses of the realm. Finally, in cases where both parties agreed to submit to his judgment, a barrister would take on the role of "arbiter" and rule on the matter out of court to spare clients the time and expense of a trial.[50]

One of the most striking differences with modern legal practice concerned the written arguments, or legal briefs (called either *mémoires judiciaires* or *factums* in French). After producing these documents, generally in collaboration with the *procureur*, the barrister did not simply submit them to the judges, but often had them printed and distributed to the public, sometimes along with auxiliary briefs called *consultations*, cosigned by a number of colleagues. Briefs could run from as little as three printed pages to as many as five hundred, and complicated cases produced scores of them, drafted by teams of barristers. Even the most inconsequential trial might easily generate three or four. In the course of the eighteenth century, barristers produced at least a hundred thousand, making legal briefs one of the most common forms of printed matter in early modern France. Jurists justified the practice by arguing that publicizing the facts of cases protected their clients from courtroom intrigue. In fact, however, the briefs had other uses as well. Because of their technical status as internal court documents, and the need to print them rapidly, royal legislation exempted them from preliminary censorship as long as they bore a barrister's signature. They were practically the only documents published under the Old Regime that did not require preliminary censorship to circulate legally. They thus often served political as well as strictly legal purposes.[51]

Beyond the substance of legal practice, yet another difference between French barristers of the Old Regime and their modern descendants stands out in high relief: few, even among those listed on the *Tableau*, practiced full time, and many never practiced at all.[52] Edmond-Jean-François Barbier, who himself practiced little, confided to his journal in 1743 that "all sorts of people become *avocats au parlement* while young, and then devote themselves to an entirely different occupation." Eugène Hua dubbed these men "*avocats pour rire.*" Nicolas Berryer estimated that fully half the men listed in the *Tableau* did not practice.[53] Quite simply, the caseload in the Parisian courts did not require more barristers. In 1735, the *premier président* estimated that only 75 barristers, out of 513 then listed on the *Tableau*, were needed for the courts to function normally. Similar situations prevailed in the provincial *parlements*.[54]

Yet it would be anachronistic to conclude that only those men who practiced full time deserve treatment as full-fledged members of the profession. While some *avocats pour rire* did little but live off their *rentes*, or tried their hand as men of letters, most spent their spare time in positions that required some degree of legal expertise, and made sure to maintain their good standing among their colleagues. In the archives and the pages of the *Almanach royal*, barristers frequently turn up as judges in seigneurial and inferior royal jurisdictions, administrators in the hospitals of Paris, censors, and even functionaries of sorts in the royal administration, posts that conferred a small salary and other perks.[55] Claude-Joseph Prévost, the unofficial secretary of the Order in the first half of the century, provides a typical example: in addition to his legal practice he served at various times as *bailli royal* in Meudon, *avocat de l'université*, *avocat du roi de la capitainerie des chasses de Vincennes* (a post that came with an apartment near the Château de Vincennes), and archivist of the ancient registers of the *parlement*.[56] Barristers generally obtained these positions through the usual Old Regime system of clientage, but their perceived competence in legal matters also counted heavily. In 1723, when the abbé Dubois asked *procureur général* Joly de Fleury to recommend candidates for the diplomatic service, seven of the eight men proposed were barristers.[57] In one sense, the Order thus served as a sort of precursor to the modern *grandes écoles*, supplying various branches of the government with well-trained legal experts.

Barristers filled such positions not only in government, but in the great princely houses as well. In the eighteenth century, all the French princes—most prominently Orléans, Conti, Condé, and, after 1774, the two brothers of Louis XVI—possessed "councils" that managed their vast real estate holdings and provided legal and political advice to the current prince. In general, barristers figured prominently in these institutions. The barrister Pierre-Louis-Claude Gin even claimed that barristers serving on princely councils determined the princes' often-rebellious political positions.[58] More likely, opposition-minded princes sought out opposition-minded barristers. It can hardly be a coincidence that the two princely houses most consistently opposed to the crown during the century—Conti and Orléans—staffed their councils in very large part with Jansenist barristers.[59] Conversely, the diarist Edmond Barbier was attached through his father to the d'Argensons, a leading family of royalists and *dévots*, which perhaps explains his caustic view of the *parlement*.[60] Service in these households could demand considerable time and effort. In 1773, the barrister Élie de Beaumont, then *intendant* to the Comte d'Artois (brother of Louis XVI) spent two and a half months in the duchy of Angoulême investigating a dispute over lands belonging to the prince.[61]

Even barristers who did not practice continued to regard the bar as their ultimate calling. Charles Arrault, a mid-eighteenth-century barrister who never appeared in court and spent most of his time embroiled in the complicated affairs of the *Hôpital général,* nonetheless insisted, in a letter to the *procureur général,* that his reputation in the bar was "the only thing which matters to me and that has mattered to me."[62] Far from treating full-time practice as the primary criterion for membership of the Order of Barristers, its leaders often looked with suspicion on those who concentrated on earning money from their practice at the expense of self-cultivation. In 1718, the spokesman of the Order (Charles Arrault's father, as a matter of fact) condemned these strivers in harsh terms:

> How many young barristers, scarcely arrived in the Palais de Justice and impatient for material gain rather than for glory, unable to wait for the light of study to pierce the cloud of their darkness and pluck them from obscurity, rush after work from the very beginning . . . ?[63]

The young barrister was expected to study, live modestly from his *rentes* (hardly an option for men like Louis Babille), and only gradually acquire a clientele.

One experience that all barristers had in common, at least in theory, despite their wide range of activities, was their education. One could not become an *avocat au parlement* without earning a three-year *license* in the law faculty, and then completing the *stage.* This experience forced future barristers to spend a number of years in each others' company, and to acquire a common body of knowledge. The program did not, however, introduce them to social or political ideas different from those offered to Parisians in primary schools and *collèges.* At no point did it expose them to the more advanced theoretical currents of continental jurisprudence, such as the natural law theory that left such a mark on generations of German jurists. The emphasis was relentlessly practical.[64]

The university program, as in modern France, was determined by government legislation, and frequently modified. The latter years of the seventeenth century saw a complete overhaul of French legal education, thanks above all to Colbert, who wanted to make it more modern and conducive to commerce. As part of this effort, the University of Paris, which had previously taught only canon law, finally introduced Roman and French law into its curriculum in 1679. Legal education failed, however, to pick up many historical or theoretical dimensions. Students, who entered at a minimum age of sixteen years, spent the first year on Justinian's *Institutes,* and the remaining two on a narrowly focused three-part program consisting of Roman law, canon law, and French law (the first two taught in Latin). They also wrote short, largely perfunctory theses.[65] "One would never guess," writes the barrister and historian Francis Delbeke, "that the programs and professors' notebooks . . . had been written by contemporaries of Montesquieu, Beccaria, Voltaire and Rousseau."[66]

While this was the theory of university training, the practice was quite different, rather sordid, and even less conducive to any sort of intellectual molding, for in the eighteenth century, the sale of law degrees was an open scandal. The future revolutionary Brissot denounced the practice bitterly in 1781: "Law schools . . . are a public market, where, without any shame, avaricious professors sell ignorant men a title that only learning should be able to earn."[67] The outburst was more than slightly hypocritical, since just two years before, Brissot himself had bought a law degree. In his memoirs, he later described the farcical scene in Reims, the law faculty with the loosest reputation, where he and many others acquired their *licenses* in a few days for the sum of 500–600 *livres*. The sole "examination" consisted of absurd questions (for instance, can eunuchs legally marry?) posed with the greatest gravity, while the candidates gritted their teeth to keep from laughing. Danton, Roland, and many other contemporaries made the same "pilgrimage" to Reims.[68]

The leading Parisian barristers were all too aware of the imperfections of university training. To correct them, in 1693 they formally instituted their own training program, the *stage*. For two years (four after 1751), aspiring barristers now had to attend court hearings assiduously, and immerse themselves further in the study of law.[69] To complete the *stage* successfully, candidates needed certificates from six senior members of the Order, attesting to their assiduity.[70]

In 1710, the senior barristers also instituted a series of seminars, or *conférences*, on selected legal topics. Like the university courses, these meetings had a wholly vocational nature, dealing mostly with questions that frequently came before the courts. The lecturers—both senior barristers and magistrates—took pains to cite relevant precedents and references that the students might later draw on. While these *conférences* proceeded on a formal basis for only ten years, they continued in one form or another until the end of the Old Regime.[71] If university education only provided a common experience for those barristers who had the energy, interest, and leisure time to pursue them, all members of the bar went through this second, less formal stage of legal education.

In addition to the university and the Order's own training program, a great many barristers (though not the Georges Le Roys) also shared another sort of experience, serving as clerks to *procureurs* either before or during the *stage*. Clerkship, as Louis Babille knew, meant chilly, uncomfortable accommodations in a *procureur's* house, and long dreary days spent copying documents, but it also offered some advantages to future barristers. It provided a means of support for young men without independent incomes who had not yet finished their studies, and it gave contacts to outsiders who lacked family ties within the Parisian legal world (two chroniclers of the bar, Nicolas Berryer and Eustache-Antoine Hua, both received their first cases from the *procureurs* under whom they had clerked).[72] It also offered an all-too-thorough grounding in the minutiae of legal procedure, a subject that no barrister, however exalted his calling, could afford to ignore. As clerks, these men also took part in the legendarily raucous activities of the confraternity called the "Kingdom of the Basoche." They carried swords in imitation of the nobility (and in strict defiance of the magistrates' regulations), held mock courtroom sessions in the august Chambre Saint-Louis, and indulged in a proclivity for dueling.[73] It is difficult to say exactly what percentage of barristers went through the Basoche, because only one, fragmentary list of clerks (from 1735) has survived. Comparing this list to the *Tableaux* of barristers, however, it appears that at least a third of all barristers spent time as clerks.[74] The barristers Hua and Berryer both did stints as clerks, and so did Brissot (who never actually became a practicing barrister). Several commentators described clerkship as a normal stage of a barrister's career.[75] Needless to say, this immersion in the almost wholly formulaic detail of legal procedure only heightened the practical, mundane aspects of a barrister's training.

Does this relentless emphasis on practical skills reflect, as Delbeke and William Church have both argued, a decline in the prestige of the legal profession?[76] In fact, something of the reverse may have been true. The sociologist Mark Osiel has recently examined the comparative status of contemporary lawyers in common law and civil law systems.[77] He argues cogently that the higher prestige of lawyers in modern England and America, compared to continental Europe, derives not from their superior powers of abstraction, but, to the contrary, from common law systems' greater need for "hands-on" practical legal skills. In civil law systems, a lawyer needs only to apply the general principles contained in unambiguous legal codes to particular cases. In common law systems, a lawyer must have countless precedents at his or her fingertips, and also an instinctive feel for the myriad ambiguities and conflicts inherent to the common law tradition.[78] Lawyers in common-law countries therefore become prized for a high level of practical skill, judgment, and experience that no amount of theoretical training can replace. Thus their social prestige rises. While modern France, of course, possesses a civil law system, under the *ancien régime* common law still prevailed throughout most of the jurisdiction of the *Parlement* de Paris.[79] Thus the great emphasis on such "hands-on" skills during the eighteenth century can be seen not as "decadence," but as a means of training expert, highly sought-after professionals.

Education and the nature of legal practice played their part in bonding a socially-diverse group of men, but the most important source of unity lay elsewhere, in what might best be called a common culture. Throughout the seventeenth and eighteenth centuries, the Parisian Order of Barristers consciously attempted to set itself apart from both the miseries and refinements of the city that surrounded it. It set down standards of conduct and appearance for its members, enforced them with draconian discipline, and did in fact manage to create and maintain a distinct cultural sphere. This sphere overlapped with that of the magistrates and other legal professionals at many points, but even so, in the late seventeenth and early eighteenth centuries (as will be seen in later chapters), it took on a separate—and intense—character of its own.[80] By 1715, if a man took the trouble to complete the *stage* and seek admittance to the Order, then he was publicly embracing the culture of the Order, and subjecting himself to humiliating expulsion if he broke its rules. In a word, he was taking on not only a title, but an identity.

The common culture began with the Latin barrister's oath, whose terms had changed little since the fourteenth century. It enjoined men to obey the regulations and decisions of the court, to carry out their functions honestly and expeditiously, and to represent their clients faithfully. It committed them to accept only cases they believed to be just, and to abandon a case immediately should they come to think it unjust. It stipulated that barristers could not receive a percentage of their clients' winnings, or indeed any large fee (originally, one larger than 30 *livres*). However, it permitted theoretically free gifts (*honoraires*), which indeed constituted the barrister's principal source of revenue. Dating from a period in which priests probably constituted a majority of the bar, the oath's religious aspects should not be ignored. It defined legal practice as a vocation, a public service that demanded a degree of self-sacrifice.[81]

Beyond the oath, a profusion of treatises, manuals, and orations sponsored by the Order emphasized that the barrister's every gesture should reflect the sobriety, seriousness, and self-sacrifice of his calling. *Stagiaires* were expected to wear black gowns in public, long hair rather than wigs, and to carry their ceremonial hats (*bonnets carrés*) with them at all times. Eustache-Antoine Hua remembered that "it was no small business to go to the Palais every day, in all weather, down the rue St. Louis and through the Marais wearing my gown . . . and carrying the *bonnet carré* under my arm." Once past the *stage*, barristers retained much the same costume, though they now had the privilege of wearing wigs.[82] The Order also imposed what amounted to an unwritten code of conduct on both professional and personal behavior. Under its terms, barristers had to treat magistrates and opposing counsel with deference and respect. They could never sue to recover honoraria from a client, no matter how solemnly the gift had been promised. A certain standard of general moral probity was also expected, to the extent that the Order admonished barristers for keeping mistresses. Outside employment was limited to those positions judged "compatible" with the bar. Infringement of these rules, the *parlement*'s statutes or the barrister's oath, brought about swift expulsion (*radiation*) from the *Tableau*, a fate that victims called "civil death."[83]

If these aspects of the life at the bar seem dour and austere, the Order tempered them by trying to infuse its members with a sense of pride—even arrogant pride—in their calling. In this sense, of course, the bar was hardly untypical of a nation where "even the most common artisans cannot resist quarreling over the excellence of their respective occupations," as Montesquieu put it in *The Persian Letters*.[84] Nonetheless, the leaders of the Order approached the task with their characteristic zeal, missing no occasion to praise their profession not merely as worthy, but, quite literally, as "noble."

What exactly did they mean by this claim? In the late eighteenth century, roughly twenty percent of the Order legally belonged to the nobility, but for the rest, the authors of legal reference books asserted that the term "noble" amounted to no more than a "simple epithet" which did not confer legal status.[85] At most, they explained, barristers "living nobly" earned an exemption from a few unpleasant "commoner's" tasks such as serving as involuntary tax collector, or joining the militia. Barristers also took pride in the fact that nobles of any rank could enter the bar without derogating.[86]

Yet the situation was not quite so simple. Barristers liked to claim (inaccurately) that in the late Middle Ages, all members of the Order could, like soldiers, earn personal nobility by performing their functions in a distinguished manner. They even asserted that Charles V had created certain barristers "knights of the law" (*chevaliers ès lois*). They also pointed out that in certain parts of France, the profession did indeed confer personal nobility on some members.[87] And in Paris itself, one prominent barrister—none other than Georges Le Roy—had earned his nobility precisely through the distinguished exercise of his calling (i.e., his services to the house of Orléans). To quote the letters patent issued by the Regent:

> Since laws contribute no less than arms to the glory and tranquility of a state, the Kings our predecessors have bestowed no less dignity on the men they have charged with the administration of justice than on those whom they have armed for their defense. . . . We believe it would not be unjust for those who have been retained in this profession [of barrister] by continuous and assiduous study, protecting the weak and using their work and experience to facilitate the application of the rules for our judges, to have their share of the honors with which we reward virtue.[88]

The Order proudly kept a copy of these letters in its archives, so their terms were probably quite well known.[89]

Given these examples, it is not surprising that barristers frequently called on the crown to grant them full noble status. In 1733, the Dijonnais barrister Cocquart asked in an unsigned pamphlet: "Who other than the Barrister better deserves the quality of Noble, since he makes himself known every day by his mind and his virtue, while the Nobility we call hereditary often remains buried in obscurity . . . ?" Six years later, a Jansenist tract, dedicated to the Parisian Order (and to Le Paige in particular), called for the "restoration" of nobility to the barristers with the words "this profession, once judged worthy of the Empire, is as fallen into common estate." In 1778, the Parisian barrister François Chavray de Boissy defined nobility essentially as a reward for merit.[90] In this way, even barristers such as Louis Babille could hold up their membership in The Order as a badge of status.

This short profile of the barristers touches on a venerable historical question. Is such a group better understood by invoking the notion of "orders" such as Roland Mousnier has defined them, or rather by using the concept of social class? In fact, neither of these analytical tools apply terribly well to French barristers of the Old Regime. The group certainly does not fit into a single "order," for, as Mousnier uses the term, membership in an "order" depended above all on "esteem" as defined by people's social interactions, and the evidence shows that different members of the bar traveled in very different social worlds.[91] Similarly, all the barristers hardly belong in the same social class, given the wide divergence of wealth and income, and the fact that one-fifth formally belonged to the nobility. Thus, according to either model, barristers should have had no fundamental social interests in common, and hence no reason to act in unison. Yet throughout much of the period 1660–1790, as we shall see, the Order of Barristers in fact formed a strikingly cohesive group.

Why was this the case? Any explanation clearly has to go beyond notions of either "orders" or "classes" to take into account the common culture of the bar. More broadly, it also has to examine the role of the legal profession within the French polity as a whole. Throughout the seventeenth and eighteenth centuries, there were men who found the position of barrister a peculiarly useful one for achieving their personal, political, and even their literary ambitions. The reasons for this usefulness changed over time, and the self-styled "priest of justice" of 1660 would have had difficulty recognizing the 1780 "voice of the public" as a colleague. Nonetheless, as the following chapters will show, the desire to preserve the usefulness of the bar itself drew barristers—and particularly the elite of the profession—together throughout the early modern period. It led some members of the profession to attempt to forge their humble order into a veritable *organisation de combat*.

A Point of Comparison: The Procureurs

To illustrate the importance of the culture and institutional structures of the bar, as opposed to income and birth, it is useful to compare barristers briefly to their close neighbors in the world of the law, the *procureurs*. The *parlement* had long divided up legal work between these two groups according to the principle that everything requiring legal knowledge and reasoning belonged to the "noble" barristers, while the lowly *procureurs* took charge of the mechanical side of legal business: filing motions, drawing up writs, collecting evidence, in short, the minutiae of legal procedure. We have seen that beyond their collaboration on cases, barristers and *procureurs* had many links: principally family relations, and the fact

that perhaps a third of barristers first gained experience in the world of the law as *procureurs'* clerks. Furthermore, although they generally came lower than barristers on scales of income and wealth, their overall social profile was broadly similar. Yet despite these connections, the experiences of the two groups between 1660 and 1790 differed enormously. Unfortunately, compared to barristers, the *procureurs* have received hardly any attention from historians. Still, the broad outlines of their history can be discerned.[92]

Procureurs obviously needed a high degree of literacy, but unlike barristers, they did not necessarily train at a university (in Paris, as many as two-thirds did in fact possess diplomas, but recall Brissot's experience: the piece of paper was easily acquired). Instead, they served a long apprenticeship, working as clerks from roughly the ages of sixteen to twenty-six years. After completing this requirement, they then—like most denizens of the world of the law—needed to purchase a venal office, of which four hundred existed in the *Parlement* of Paris (three hundred after 1776). The possession of an office made them royal "officers": official representatives of the French state and hence subject to direct royal discipline.[93] In the middle of the eighteenth century, the offices sold for an average of 18,940 *livres*, but towards the end of the century prices seem to have risen exorbitantly.[94]

Historians have often portrayed venal offices as a straightforward sale of public authority, but as David Bien has noted, they also functioned as a system of state finance. The officeholder advanced a sum of money to the crown, in return for which he received regular payments (either in the form of wages or, in the case of *procureurs*, a share of the state revenue generated by his practice)—just as if he had purchased a bond. The difference lay in the fact that this "bond" never matured: as long as the office existed, the state would neither return the original sum, nor stop the payments. Royal officials also proved fiendishly clever at devising new ways to squeeze additional sums out of the officeholders (usually as payments for minor privileges, or to keep new offices, whose sale might hurt the price of the old ones, off the market). To borrow Max Weber's vivid metaphor for medieval Jewish usurers, officeholders were a "sponge" the crown used to squeeze revenues and credit from the general population.[95]

This unfortunate position had two important consequences for the *procureurs*, one involving their corporate organization, the other their personal finances. In the first case, as David Bien has observed, the system forced members of a given occupation to form tightly-knit corporate organizations. Such a body was needed both to negotiate with the crown over finances, and to raise the loans needed when the crown demanded that its officers purchase further privileges.[96] In the second case, the effect can be summed up in a single word: debt. In one sample of twenty-five contracts of sale from the eighteenth century, not a single purchaser paid the entire price up front. Instead, they took out loans using the office itself as collateral. Anecdotal evidence suggests that most *procureurs* were constantly in debt and in danger of losing their offices.[97]

The combination of debt, modest income, and the constant threat of further extractions by the crown meant that *procureurs* needed to squeeze every possible *denier* out of their unfortunate clients, and in the process they earned a public reputation that Shylock might have pitied. Louis-Sébastien Mercier left this vivid, biting portrait of the men he called "public, privileged vampires":

> Enter into a *procureur*'s bureau, which is improperly called a "study." Eight to ten young men sitting uncomfortably on hard stools are employed from morning to night scratching away on stamped paper. Fine work it is! They copy citations, writs, notices and appeals. They "engross." What does "engross" mean? It is the art of stretching out words and lines to use as much paper as possible, and thus to sell it all scribbled-over to unhappy litigants in the form of thick *dossiers*. . . . The *procureur* in his bureau surrounds himself with these dossiers, piled up like trophies all the way up to the ceiling, rather like the American savage in his hut surrounds himself, and hangs up the hairpieces of the people he has scalped.[98]

Duvigneau, a Bordeaux *procureur*, lamented that his profession was surrounded by "an insurmountable barrier of humiliation and shame," and manuals for aspiring members routinely began by denouncing the "unjust prejudices" against them.[99]

Given these difficulties, it is hardly surprising that the *procureurs*, beyond demonstrating an instinctive loyalty to the *parlement*, generally kept an extremely low political profile under the Old Regime, and during the Revolution as well (there were, of course, a few notable individual exceptions).[100] Officially limited to "mechanical" tasks, tightly bound up in the silver chains of debt, and generally reviled as human birds of prey, the best a *procureur* could hope for was to amass a fortune out of the public view. Then, he might be able to place a son in the bar, over the all-too-tangible barrier that separated a "noble" and "independent" profession from a "vile" and "subservient" one. Only in this way might he yet hope for his family to take part in the larger dramas of the world of the law. The comparison with the barristers, with whom the *procureurs* were bound by such close ties of family and work, illustrates the tremendous importance not only of the barristers' status as legal experts, but also, crucially, of the bar's institutional autonomy. It is to this subject that we now turn.

2

Building an
Independent Profession

In this general subjection which has affected all conditions of men, an order as old as the magistracy, as noble as virtue itself, and as necessary as justice, has distinguished itself by its own special character; alone among all the estates, it still maintains itself in the happy and peaceful possession of its independence.

Henri-François d'Aguesseau, "L'indépendance de l'avocat"*

The law is an old profession in Paris. Its origins go back to the high Middle Ages, and by the Renaissance, barristers possessed most of the criteria generally associated with modern professions, such as a distinct vocational identity, an established body of theory taught in universities, and uniform standards for training and performance.[1] An independent bar association, however, dates only from the time of Louis XIV. Over the long span of the king's "personal rule" and the Regency that followed (1661–1723), Parisian barristers gradually constructed a powerful, cohesive organization for themselves. It had a governing committee, a mandatory training program, and a library that also served as a meeting place. Most importantly, it controlled who could become, and remain, a barrister.

Theories of "professionalization" would normally attribute the creation of such an organization either to the growing importance of market forces, or, alternately, to the increasing regulatory activity of the French state. The latter hypothesis gains particular credence because of Colbert's massive creation of corporate bodies during this period.[2] The origins of the Parisian Order of Barristers, however, were different. Far from being

*In *Discours de Monsieur le Chancelier d'Aguesseau* (Paris, 1773), pp. 124–25.

sponsored by the state, its founding amounted to a gesture of opposition to two broad aspects of seventeenth-century state-building. First, there was the royal administration's encroachment on the political role of the judiciary, which also curtailed the activities of the legal profession. Second, there was the elevation of sovereign court judges into a new, noble stratum of French society, which increasingly turned barristers into second-class citizens in the world of the law. These twin developments made the seventeenth century seem like a long twilight to Parisian barristers, an age in which the legal profession lost its previous luster, and the religious and political ideas it stood for fell into eclipse. The perception of decline ultimately imposed a new sense of solidarity on the bar, and led its members to seek institutional remedies for their social and political ills.

The Barristers on the Defensive

The early history of the organization known as the Parisian Order of Barristers has never quite escaped from the linguistic confusion that lies, like a fog, over so much of the history of the Old Regime. Seventeenth and eighteenth-century barristers themselves, fearing interference from the *parlement* or the crown, took care to present all institutional innovations as mere formalizations of practices that dated from time immemorial. Since barristers were recognized experts in the manipulation of legal language, they succeeded, and thus gave what was essentially a new organization the same musty legitimacy coveted by all manner of early modern institution. Any reconstruction of their actions is further hampered by their antipathy towards record-keeping. As Ambroise Falconnet remarked in frustration in the late eighteenth century: "Where are the Barristers' Statutes? There is nothing written, nothing permanent with them. An oral tradition, even more versatile than it is imperfect, serves as the basis for their resolutions, which are not written down in order that they may be better forgotten."[3]

Previous historians of the seventeenth-century French bar, mostly barristers themselves, have had little incentive to peer too closely at what is in effect an "invented tradition."[4] Antoine-Gaspard Boucher d'Argis published his pioneering *Histoire abrégée des avocats* in 1778, just seven years after Chancellor Maupeou's reforms caused the Order's temporary disappearance, and just three after the turmoil accompanying the disbarment of Simon Linguet nearly put an end to its independence. Jean-François Fournel published his more elaborate, if rambling history in 1813, just two years after Napoleon placed the Order under draconian political restraints. Joachim Gaudry contributed the first systematic study in 1864, when these restraints were still partly in place. In short, these authors—whose works were echoed in scores of training manuals and ceremonial orations—had every reason to present a strong and independent Order as an unassailable inheritance from the distant past.[5]

Even in the eighteenth century, however, this version of events did not pass entirely uncontested. Voltaire, in his history of the *Parlement* of Paris, located the origins of the Order of Barristers not in the Middle Ages, but in 1730.[6] His less-than-rigorous scholarship did not carry much weight, but the same could not be said of the work of Ambroise Falconnet, an aspiring barrister excluded by the Order in the 1770's. In a 1786 legal brief that caused a sensation (and which he later revised and lengthened into a blistering pamphlet), Falconnet charged that the Order of Barristers had not come into being until the late seventeenth century.[7] The claims made by Boucher d'Argis and others, he argued, amounted to nothing more than a fiction, designed to justify an organization that functioned as a corporation without submitting to the controls and restrictions usually imposed on such bodies.

Falconnet's critique was soon forgotten in the revolutionary maelstrom, but in 1886, the archivist Roland Delachenal made a careful study of the legal profession between 1300 and 1600 and found no trace whatsoever of an "Order of Barristers." Indeed, Delachenal discovered that during these years the barristers had possessed no formal organization at all. The *parlement* itself had enforced a short *stage* (internship) and kept lists of those men who actually practiced in the Parisian courts. The barristers themselves had no fixed numbers, no meeting place, no registers, and no officers, even after the great expansion of the sixteenth century, when their numbers passed four hundred. They left matters of discipline, and the defense of their collective interests, entirely to the magistrates.[8] This arrangement was congenial, rather than subservient, Delachenal added, because the relationship between bar and bench was practically symbiotic. Many barristers won royal judicial appointments (although some sort of payment was often involved after the fifteenth century), and afterwards made a habit of consulting their former colleagues. Magistrates protected barristers from the wrath of powerful legal opponents, thereby ensuring that they enjoyed considerable freedom of speech (although they had no immunity from judicial reprimands or the king's displeasure).[9]

The barristers did possess a separate religious confraternity, dedicated to Saint Nicholas, which they shared with the *procureurs*, but this organization, while eventually taking the name of *communauté des avocats et procureurs*, never evolved into a true corporate body. It limited its functions to the celebration of masses, occasional discussion of ordinances and professional regulations in the great hall of the Palais, and an annual festive assembly on St. Nicholas's day (May 9). By 1600, most barristers only frequented it once a year, and during the seventeenth century it began functioning almost exclusively as the corporate body of the *procureurs* alone.[10] In only one way did it contribute to the life of the bar: every year its members elected a barrister to the ceremonial leadership post of *bâtonnier* (so named because he held the community's sacred *bâton*).[11]

The barristers also claimed, however, to constitute an "order," a particularly ambiguous word in the social lexicon of the Old Regime. Old

Regime dictionaries listed dozens of different definitions: as in modern English, it could designate both a physical organization—generally monastic or chivalric—or a general category of society, as in the phrase "the order of the nobility."[12] For the members of the legal profession, the phrase "the order of barristers" originally had a meaning which fell somewhere between these poles. It was best expressed by the early seventeenth-century barrister Charles Loyseau, who, in his *Traité des ordres*, presented "orders" as the most important constituent elements of French society. The kingdom divided on roughly functional grounds into the classic three orders of the clergy, the nobility, and the Third Order, and then subdivided into many others, including the "order of barristers." Yet "properly formed orders" amounted not only to social categories, but to semisacred vocations which in fact excluded most of the population (notably women and peasants). Only those occupations enjoying particular consideration or honor (*dignité*) deserved the title, and birth by itself was not sufficient to confer full membership. Candidates only became full members after special training and purification, their admission marked with special "solemnities."[13]

Loyseau made a clear distinction between orders, to which men belonged for life, and offices (such as judgeships) that they could give up or be dismissed from. The phrase "the order of barristers" thus described less a single occupation than a group of men qualified for a wide variety of positions under the crown—an apt description given the variety of positions barristers actually held in addition to their legal practice. Other contemporary authors expressed the same point by defining the Order of Barristers as the "nursery" or "seminary" for the highest officers of the state (*la pépinière ou séminaire des dignités*).[14] Looking at things this way, the magistrates of the *parlement* themselves belonged to the "order of barristers," and in 1579, the crown put this idea into law by stipulating that all magistrates serve time in the bar before entering office.[15]

Loyseau remained very ambiguous on the actual organization of "orders." These bodies clearly differed from a corporation endowed with officers, meeting places, and a disciplinary apparatus. Yet the word also clearly designated more than a simple social category. Otherwise, who would manage the process of purification and preparation by which men entered an order, not to mention the requisite "solemnities"? And who would expel malefactors, as Loyseau indicated might be necessary? Loyseau indicated in passing, however, that members of orders could belong to parallel corporate bodies that took care of organizational questions. In the case of the legal profession, the *parlement* itself—staffed by members of the "order of barristers"—presumably served this function. This concept worked well as long as a cozy relationship continued to prevail between barristers and magistrates.[16]

This cozy relationship did not, however, survive the Renaissance intact. Indeed, by 1600 barristers who wrote on the subject of their profession routinely lamented the fact that the traditional cordiality and mutual respect between bar and bench had given way to an atmosphere of tension and mutual resentment. "It now seems to some of them," the barrister Antoine Loisel wrote of the magistrates, "that we are cut from different wood or different cloth than they are, that we are almost nonexistent [*quasi des gens de néant*]." Loisel, Guy du Faur de Pibrac, and Loyseau himself all warned that because of these changing attitudes, the bar was prey to "waste and deterioration" and stood to lose its prestigious function as the *pépinière des dignités*.[17] In 1602, the barristers' growing resentment against the magistrates erupted into a successful two-week boycott of the courts after the *parlement*, backed by Henri IV, had tried to force barristers to declare their honoraria—a demand they rejected as a blow to their honor.[18]

The most important cause for the deteriorating relationship was the practice called "venality of offices." As early as the reign of François I, French kings, driven by an ever-deepening thirst for revenue, had openly sold judgeships to the highest bidder (covert office-selling was older still). By the early seventeenth century, high judicial offices conferred nobility upon their owners and had become inheritable, severely limiting openings in the court. Barristers, therefore, no longer had special access to judgeships. They needed to buy their way in like anyone else, and as prices increased, this possibility became a hopeless dream for all but a tiny minority (between 1653 and 1673 exactly one barrister became a magistrate).[19] Inevitably, venality soon lowered the standards of legal learning in the magistracy, and left barristers as the acknowledged repositories of legal expertise. Loyseau himself complained in the early seventeenth century about "mostly ignorant young magistrates." A hundred years later, one of Montesquieu's fictional Persian travelers could ask a magistrate, without mention of venality: "How can one apply the laws if one doesn't know them?" The magistrate replied: "If you knew the *Palais de Justice*, you would not ask that question: we have living books, the barristers. They work for us and take charge of our education"[20]

Beyond these changes, venality also brought subtler shifts in *mentalité*. When judgeships became valuable forms of property, the delicate distinction Loyseau had made between "orders" and "offices" lost all relevance to reality. Families made offices into centerpieces of their strategies for entering and advancing within the nobility, and had little patience left over for the niceties of lengthy training periods and arduous selection criteria. Generally, they tried to put their offspring into an office as soon as possible, and so the average age for entering the *parlement* plummeted, reaching twenty-three years by the early eighteenth century.[21] Under such conditions, it became impossible to maintain the fiction that magistrates belonged first and foremost to the "order of barristers." Only among the barristers themselves did the notion of an "order" retain the vigor it had had for Loyseau.

Unluckily for the barristers, the consolidation of the system of venality coincided with what Marc Fumaroli has termed a flight of oratorical talent from the Palais de Justice to the royal court. In the sixteenth century, the Palais had been a center of literary activity, attracting aspiring poets who found an outlet for their talents in the art of judicial rhetoric. Under Henri III, Henri IV, and Louis XIII, however, the royal court, deploying formidable weapons of patronage, came to challenge the *Palais* in this respect. Cardinal Richelieu in particular sponsored a new revival of classical eloquence—on the condition that it take as its object the praise of royal majesty and the absolute monarchy. Fumaroli interprets the political and religious struggles of the time as a competition between two cultures, one puritanical, Gallican (i.e., committed to the autonomy of the French Catholic church), and *parlementaire*; the other more sensual, Jesuitical, and "absolutist." The sight of the most promising young orators abandoning the Palais for the blandishments of the Louvre only accentuated the general malaise of the legal profession.[22]

Initially, Parisian barristers did not respond to these challenges by attempting to form a separate organization. Instead, a number of the most influential legal scholars—notably, Loisel, du Faur, and Etienne Pasquier—took a different course. These men were Gallicans, humanists, and *politiques* (advocates of the royalist, middle-of-the-road party during the Wars of Religion). They all eventually became magistrates themselves, serving as the king's representatives (*gens du roi*) in the *parlement*, but their primary allegiance remained to the "order of barristers." In a series of published letters and treatises, they sought to repair relations between bar and bench and to define an honored place for the legal profession in the increasingly centralized, royal state that they were helping to construct. Their works remained highly influential among barristers for the next two centuries, and therefore deserve some attention here.[23]

Loisel, du Faur, and Pasquier did not hesitate to criticize venality of offices for magistrates, and to evoke a supposed golden age in which barristers had advanced freely to the bench. Loyseau in particular lamented the fact that cases were now judged by "mostly ignorant" magistrates, while Loisel wrote bitterly in his *Dialogue of the Barristers*: "The day is past when men were sought for their merit and value."[24] Nonetheless, none of these men openly called for the abolition of venality. Instead, they sought to underline the purity, impartiality, and indispensability of the bar. Pasquier went so far as to compare barristers to preachers, asserting that these two callings, more than any others, allowed men to make what he called "public demonstration of the graces with which God has infused them." Loisel, meanwhile, asserted that "a state cannot exist without justice, and justice cannot be done without the help and advice of its ministers, above all barristers."[25] All the authors put stress on the need for an equitable court system in which barristers could defend their clients without fear or favor, even against great noblemen. Thus Pasquier urged his son, just starting out in the bar: "virtuously support the poor and oppressed, and make your conscience your armor against the efforts of the powerful, who wish to abuse their authority and their grandeur to ruin those who are weaker than they."[26] Loisel and du Faur also compared barristers to soldiers, and brought out the familiar argument that like soldiers they deserved nobility for particularly valiant service.[27]

To a certain extent, these paeans to the glory of the profession can be read as standard bar association boilerplate, the sort of ritual praise that resounds at any gathering of lawyers. Yet these royalist, *politique* authors were articulating their vision of the legal profession within a specific model of royal power. In this model, justice flowed from God to the world through the divinely-ordained king, making indisputable royal authority a necessary precondition for barristers to do their jobs. The king and his secular court system thus had jurisdiction over all important disputes that occurred within France, especially those that involved the church, despite the claims of popes and bishops to a degree of independent temporal power. At the time, French bishops were struggling to retain this power, and the dispute came to center in large part on the scope of the church court system. All the authors took the side of the king, and in his *Dialogue*, Antoine Loisel issued a strong Gallican warning against clerical "enterprises and usurpations" on royal justice—a phrase that, in 1602, could not help but stir memories of the Catholic League's recent rebellion.[28]

While generally supporting the king, the authors stressed that he should not interfere directly in the judicial process. Society, as Loyseau wrote in his *Traité des ordres*, had its own divinely-ordained form, which imperfectly mirrored the celestial hierarchy. The king should not try to rearrange the social order, and when disagreements arose within it, he should let his judges, advised by lawyers, decide independently where justice lay. In other words, like the early sixteenth-century jurist Claude de Seyssel, the authors believed French kings should submit themselves to certain "restraints" (*freins*) on their power, notably the obligation to take counsel from their judges. To use Michel Antoine's terminology, they wanted a judicial, but not an administrative monarchy.[29]

Concern for a limited monarchy, however, did not entail any encouragement of political participation by individual subjects. Indeed, while these authors generally sought out every possible means of glorifying the legal profession, they deliberately rejected the most obvious favorable models: Cicero and Demosthenes. Du Faur and Pasquier in particular argued that what Shakespeare called the "glib and oily art" of political persuasion, practiced by these orators in ancient times, had no place in a Christian monarchy. To quote Pasquier, as paraphrased by Loisel:

> In short, I desire in barristers the opposite of what Cicero required of orators, which is to say eloquence first, and then some legal science; quite to the contrary, I believe barristers must be above all learned in law and legal procedure, and only passably eloquent [*médiocrement éloquent*], more dialecticians than rhetors, more men of business and judgment than men of great or long speeches.[30]

Barristers should address themselves not to any *agora* or forum, but to the magistrates alone, helping them to interpret the divine *logos*. In sum, they should gain prestige from their expert ability to advise the Great, not from appealing to public outside the courtroom.[31]

Marc Fumaroli has suggested that both this "anti-Ciceronianism," and the barristers' general vision of the French polity, was undergirded by a highly pessimistic, Augustinian understanding of human nature. Unlike the followers of Luis Molina's Counter-Reformation theology, these authors did not believe that human beings could save themselves simply through good works and the help of the clergy. They placed great stress on human fallibility, even in the physical person of the king himself. For lawyers in particular, they advocated an austere, self-sacrificing life. Not surprisingly, these *politiques* numbered among the greatest enemies of the Jesuits (the primary advocates of Molinist theology) and worked closely with the barristers Simon Marion and Antoine Arnaud, whom one might call the literal begetters of French Jansenism.[32]

While the idealized image of the legal profession that these men projected had deep intellectual roots, it was also arguably well suited to the challenges that faced the legal profession in the aftermath of the Wars of Religion. Most obviously, depicting barristers as uniquely indispensable, impartial, and pure served the immediate task of improving their poor public image. More subtly, these works can be interpreted as a plea for defending the role of the judicial system—and thus of barristers themselves, along with judges—as the principal means of regulating the increasingly complex and increasingly centralized society of the early seventeenth century. On the one hand, the authors wanted the royal government—and, more specifically, the royal courts—to have jurisdiction over all important social disputes. Not only should the church, with its vast landed holdings, submit to secular arbitration; noble magnates should also presumably settle quarrels in lawsuits, rather than in duels or pitched battles. The urban trades, organized into corporate bodies, should let the courts rule on their disagreements. Yet, on the other hand, the authors also warned against the king himself taking too direct a role in this project of regulation. He should not attempt to settle social disputes by administrative fiat, all too easily influenced by the hubris and fallibility of individual officials, but rather leave them to a theoretically neutral, independent judiciary.

Did these authors speak for the entire legal profession of the late sixteenth and early seventeenth centuries? Not quite. In fact, one group of barristers represented the antithesis of everything they stood for. Between 1589 and 1594, the Catholic League controlled the city of Paris, defying first Henri III and then Henri IV in the name of an unforgiving, ultramontane Catholicism. Commandeering all the available presses, it waged an unprecedented, extraordinarily prolific campaign of pamphlets that called on the French nation (in a Catholic version of the doctrines of the Monarchomachs) to rise up and overthrow the king. Along with priests, barristers dominated the leading council of the League (called the *Seize*), and wrote a majority of the pamphlets.[33] Robert Descimon has argued that these barristers came largely from the lower ranks of the profession, and joined the League in reaction against a royal government that excluded them—unlike luminaries such as Pasquier and Du Faur—from its patronage. Whatever the reason for their actions, these men offered something of a countermodel of the legal profession: one characterized by hostility to the central government, a rejection of Gallicanism, and, in their direct appeals to the French nation through pamphlets, a distinct tendency to play Cicero.[34]

In the short run, Henri IV's triumph in 1594 ensured the victory of the Gallican *politiques*, not the ultramontane *ligueurs*. It was men such as Pasquier and Loisel whose texts became the theoretical bibles of the French legal profession over the next two centuries. Yet despite this success, these men's paeans had little impact outside the sheltered corridors of the Palais de Justice. Barristers never rose to the high position in the Bourbon state that Pasquier and Loisel had envisaged for them. Instead, over the next century, at least in the minds of the leading members of the bar, the decline of the profession continued unabated.

Why was this the case? The reasons are complex, but one fact stands out: the crown's growing encroachment on the judicial system in the seventeenth century. Even though this encroachment did not take place in the way Tocqueville imagined, namely with the advance of a centralized, authoritarian, proto-Napoleonic bureaucracy that replaced the rulings of the law courts with administrative fiat, nonetheless, it did occur. According to Sarah Hanley and Ralph Giesey, it occurred on a symbolic level, as the Bourbon kings abandoned the intricate, painstakingly orchestrated royal ceremonies of the Renaissance which had made manifest the restraints on the monarch and the bonds between him and his people. Now royal ceremonial focused on the court itself, with its dazzlingly complex codes of etiquette, and while the king was still on view, now the public had to come see him, not vice versa. The growing prominence of the royal court, where Jesuit theology and baroque art flourished, both exalting the king as a sort of demigod, represented an implicit repudiation of the austere, Augustinian mores of the Palais de Justice.[35]

The encroachment occurred in other ways as well. On a theoretical level, the Bourbon monarchs promulgated their new political maxims stating that absolute power inhered in the person of the king alone, not in the institutions of the monarchy. The political theory of Bossuet emphasized, on the irrefutable evidence of scripture, that "the entire state lies in the person of the prince," and that the prince therefore had the right to order the state as he pleased.[36] On the administrative level, the growth of the Versailles bureaucracy and the institution of the *intendants* at least raised the specter of the royal administration replacing the courts as the principal regulator of social conflict. Finally, on the political level,

Louis XIV curtailed the *parlements'* right to remonstrance, which had previously acted as a check on royal legislation.[37]

All of these developments affected the world of the law as a whole, from the highest magistrates to the lowest law clerks. They played a part in provoking the notoriously complicated civil war known as the Fronde, which began with a revolt of the *parlement* of Paris in 1648. But they arguably affected barristers more than most other groups. Under Richelieu and Louis XIV, the magistrates of the *parlements* did lose much of their independence. However, as a sort of compensation, they gained firm acceptance into the nobility. As François Bluche has shown, their families provided the basis for the new administrative elite, particularly at the rank of the *maîtres des requêtes*. In many provinces, they eased their way into royal patronage networks, got their fingers into a greater percentage of tax revenues, and, in William Beik's telling phrase, had the chance to "bask in the sun"—that is to say, in the rays of the triumphant Sun King.[38] But what did barristers gain? Not only did they suffer from the general encroachment upon the judiciary, but they received no form of social compensation whatsoever—quite the reverse. Those who could not afford the price of venal offices (which reached its height under Louis XIV), now found themselves deprived of any chance of promotion into the magistracy. Whereas they had previously seen themselves as the near social equals of magistrates, now they had been firmly demoted to the rank of second-class citizens in the courts.

In other words, the attempts by Loisel, Pasquier, and du Faur to define a high position for barristers in the Bourbon state, commensurate with their talents and their importance to the legal system, eventually failed. This failure did not immediately provoke tensions with the magistrates beyond the 1602 work stoppage. Myriam Yardeni has suggested that this affair in fact gained the barristers a "breathing space" in their relation with the *parlement*.[39] A common *parlementaire* culture also persisted for some time, and leading magistrates continued to serve substantive *stages* in the bar, fostering close personal and professional contacts between the two groups. Although barristers do not appear to have played a substantial role in the Fronde, the stormy events of 1648 could hardly have failed to reinforce solidarities within the *Palais de Justice*.[40] By the second half of the century, however, the barristers no longer could pretend that the *parlement* represented their own interests. Worse, the *parlement* was failing to block the encroachments on the legal system which threatened to push them to the margins of French society. It was time to form an association of their own.

The Birth of a Bar Association

Sometime in the year 1660, a number of barristers began to assemble regularly at the home of *bâtonnier* François de Montholon, a nobleman. Each claimed to represent one of the thirteen "benches" of the great hall of the Palais de Justice, around which barristers congregated while waiting for clients. They called the meetings *conférences de discipline*, and used them to discuss subjects of interest to all practicing barristers, including who had a right to practice law, and how best to respond to the insulting behavior of some magistrates.[41] Although the participants carefully avoided a confrontational stance, the meetings nonetheless represented a tentative declaration of independence from the *parlement*. The minutes for December 14, 1661 read in part:

> Resolved . . . that those affairs which depend on the barristers alone and which can settled by amicable agreement [*une bonne intelligence*] will be dealt with by them. . . . As for those affairs which call for the intervention of higher authority, *monsieur le Bâtonnier* will visit the *premier président* to inform him that the bar has worked by itself to maintain its discipline.[42]

In short, the barristers, while still acknowledging the ultimate authority of the *parlement*, were now asserting their ability to manage their own affairs.

To a contemporary observer, it would have seemed that the barristers were doing what hundreds of other groups of Frenchmen—often under pressure from Colbert—were doing at the time: organizing themselves into a cohesive corporate body. In the meeting for August 22, 1661, for instance, the barristers established elaborate rules for the *conférences*, covering meeting times (three a year), the election of "deputies" from each bench, the order of discussion, and the keeping of minutes. At a *conférence* in late 1661, they resolved to take all necessary steps to ensure "conformity of sentiments" in the bar.[43] Yet they refrained from referring to themselves as a *corps*, and made no attempt to obtain a royal charter for their new organization. Instead—and here the linguistic confusion so typical of the Old Regime began to come into play—they continued to use the familiar title of "order," even though their organization bore less and less resemblance to Loyseau's conception of an "order." They thereby managed to make it look as if the new arrangements amounted, at most, to a formalization of earlier practices.

The distinction between an "order" and a "corps" may seem slight to modern observers, but it clearly mattered to early modern French jurists. Chancellor Henri-François d'Aguesseau, a renowned legal authority and a firm supporter of the barristers, wrote to a Breton correspondent in 1750:

> Can one say that those who practice the profession of barrister in a *parlement* form a *corps* or society which really deserves the name? . . . Barristers are only linked to each other by the fact that they have the same calling [*ministère*]; they are Subjects who devote themselves equally to the defense of litigants, but they are not members of a *corps*.[44]

Alexis-Jean-Baptiste Durot, a Parisian barrister, put it even more strongly in an unpublished 1770 treatise. The very idea of a *corps* was, in his words, "repugnant to the essence" of the legal profession. "The barristers of the *parlement* do not form a *corps,*" he continued, "and can have neither officers, nor leaders nor registers nor even a place of assembly." The great legal dictionaries of the period, largely composed by Parisian barristers, faithfully echoed these ideas, as did Boucher d'Argis's 1778 history of the bar.[45] When pressed to give an alternate definition for the Order, the barristers tended to opt for the term "a society of men of letters."[46] Provincial barristers imitated the Parisians' noncorporate stance, taking care to call their own associations, generally created in imitation of the Parisian model, "orders" or "colleges," and resisting formal incorporation.[47]

In addition to outlining this theoretical stance, barristers took great care to eschew some of the most common outward manifestations of a *corps.* They appointed no officers beyond the *bâtonnier* of the confraternity (the "deputies" remained resolutely unofficial), held no formal assemblies, and kept no formal registers. In 1735, they even decided to stop keeping minutes of the *conférences de discipline,* because, as the young barrister Louis-Adrien Le Paige put it, "this smells too much of the corporation."[48] From some perspectives, however, the effort to liken the Order to a mere literary society amounted to no more than a polite fiction. "The *Barristers* are subject to none of the rules that politics, justice and common sense have forced all *Corps* to adopt," Simon Linguet wrote on the eve of his disbarment in 1775, "yet they have all the privileges of a *Corps.*"[49]

Why did the barristers so strenuously resist forming a *corps* during this period that saw the creation of so many? Montholon and his colleagues remained silent on the subject, but a 1782 pamphlet issued by the Order forthrightly mentioned one reason: fear of undue interference by the crown or the *parlement,* which might insist on writing specific oversight powers into a charter for a *corps des avocats.* "All corps are subject to a superior authority which makes them act as it pleases," the anonymous author declared.[50] This reasoning runs counter to the assumptions made by some modern historians who (following Montesquieu) have assumed that corporate bodies, by providing a trade or profession with a unified voice, give its members greater autonomy than otherwise. Barristers, however, clearly regarded themselves as an exception to this rule, and with some reason. Given the sensitivity of many of the cases that came before the *parlement,* it is reasonable to suppose that powerful magistrates or ministers would have used every instrument at their disposal—including the mechanisms of corporate discipline—to keep members of the bar under tight rein.[51]

Other factors arguably contributed to the barristers' "noncorporate" stance as well. Under French law, a *corps* was a "fictional person" which theoretically served as a conduit between its members and the rest of French society, subsuming their identity into its own. Thus a *corps des avocats* might have constrained a barrister's ability to represent fully the interests of his clients.[52] In addition, it would hardly have suited a profession which Pasquier had compared to the priesthood, a profession desperate to assert its own uniqueness and to arrest the rapid erosion of its prestige, to adopt a form of organization shared by the most common trades, from butchers to lemonade-sellers. By retaining the title of "order," the barristers instead underscored their similarity to clerics and knights, and thus their uniqueness and indispensability.

Incidentally, the perception of a unique status for barristers may help explain why they, unlike the *procureurs*, record-keepers, bailiffs, and nearly all other denizens of the *Palais de Justice*, not only never formed a *corps*, but never became venal officers. In the early seventeenth century, the crown had forced venality upon many of these "lower" occupations, sometimes against their strenuous objections and those of the *parlement* (these offices, unlike those in the *parlement* itself, did not confer nobility).[53] The precise reasons for its forbearance in the case of the barristers remain a mystery. It is probable, however, that the barristers' most powerful clients—particularly the leading princely houses and ecclesiastical institutions—feared that in the case of the bar, venality might directly threaten their own interests. Would advocates readily oppose royal demands if the crown could dismiss them from office and thereby deprive them of valuable property? The barristers themselves certainly believed so. In 1696, the participants at a *conférence de discipline* asserted that all true barristers opposed venality for the profession, and said that the king himself had "made it a principle . . . never to damage an order of men of letters which has always been considered the nursery of dignities." The Order's anonymous 1782 pamphlet declared: "Discharging the functions of offices is harmful to the perfection of [our] liberty, because it is done by force, and subject to an authority that demands obedience."[54] When combined with the barristers' own evident ability to paralyze the judicial system by a work stoppage, as demonstrated in 1602, these concerns may well have dissuaded the ministry from adding barristers to the ranks of the so-called *officiers ministériels*.[55]

The early activities of the newly constituted "Order of Barristers" mostly fell into four categories. First, it lobbied the crown to obtain titles of nobility for each successive *bâtonnier*, but met with no success.[56] Second, François de Montholon and his colleagues struggled to compile an accurate list (*rôle*) of those *avocats en parlement* who actually practiced law, even if only part-time. The list would distinguish between the thousands of men who had gained a *license* in law and taken the barrister's oath, and those men who actually identified themselves principally with the bar, and behaved accordingly.[57] Third, the Order began actively to police itself, and to take control over recruitment and disbarment. According to the "deputies," many *avocats en parlement* routinely demeaned their high calling. They took on forms of work "incompatible" with the bar. They hired themselves out to unscrupulous *procureurs*, accepting far less than the going rate for drawing up certain documents in order to remain employed (Louis Babille was expelled for precisely this infraction eighty years later). Worst of all, they openly "solicited" cases from clients, as if they were common tradesmen, instead of letting the clients come to them. To eliminate such practices, the participants at the *conférences* had no doubt about the proper course of action: the offenders "must be excluded from the Order and measures taken to strike them from the *rôle* and from the registers of the *parlement.*"[58] With these measures, the Order clearly sought to remove itself from the *parlement*'s disciplinary aegis.

The fourth, and in some ways most important set of activities concerned a word that has no exact English translation: *préséance.* It literally means "precedence," but in the early modern context it referred to precedence in ceremonial processions, and more generally to codes of etiquette and deference. Few observers have overlooked the crucial importance of *préséance* at the court of Louis XIV, but the same concerns permeated the *parlement* as well. Just as a duke expected certain marks of respect from a baron, so a magistrate expected them from a barrister—and vice versa. The system of etiquette allowed participants to symbolize graphically status and power relations, but as Norbert Elias shrewdly observed about the royal court, deference was an end as well as a means, pursued with the same rational intensity that stockbrokers devote to the pursuit of profit. Many courtiers of Louis XIV would happily have sacrificed large fortunes, or the real power that came from command of an army, in return for a more honored place at the king's bedside during the ritual of the *lever du roi.* Similarly, many barristers would have traded several rich and powerful clients for an appropriate mark of respect from the bench, particularly at periods, such as the mid-seventeenth century, when they believed the prestige of their profession to be at a dangerous low.[59]

The degree of pomp and circumstance that has accompanied legal proceedings in nearly every Western society by itself gave barristers nearly endless scope for anxiety over *préséance.* Where should barristers stand in the court? Need they keep their heads covered at all times? What color robes could they wear? What constituted contempt of court? They measured their status in every such matter and also compared themselves with the magistrates, on the one hand, and the despised *procureurs* on the other. Thus, early in the month of September 1661, the sovereign court dealing with fiscal matters, the *Cour des aides,* peremptorily summoned a barrister named Roizé to appear before it. Instead of obeying, he went to the *conférence de discipline* to ask the opinion of his colleagues. They told him that the terms of the summons were "against the order and honor of the bar," and advised him to ignore it, which he did.[60]

In November 1662, a more serious dispute erupted between the barristers and the *substituts du procureur général,* the lowest-ranking magistrates in the *parlement* (they functioned as aides to the king's attorney general). Traditionally, the *substituts* came from the ranks of the barristers, and considered themselves members of the bar even after taking office.[61] In 1662, however, they claimed the right to enter the Sainte-Chapelle in procession ahead of the rest of the Order. The other barristers perceived this action as an affront, and immediately resolved to cease dealing with the *substituts* on all court business—a move that greatly disrupted judicial proceedings—until the *substituts* renounced all formal distinctions between themselves and members of the bar.[62] The quarrel continued for nearly six months before the barristers (for unspecified reasons) finally gave in. Soon afterwards, however, the Order had a chance to assert its prerogatives more successfully, this time in a dispute over the circumstances in which *procureurs* could orally address the *parlement*.[63]

By taking these steps, as well as by attempting to "purify" their own ranks, the newly reorganized Order of Barristers was clearly trying to arrest the declining prestige of the legal profession. On the one hand, they insisted on their prerogatives vis-à-vis the magistrates, and on the other, they sought to distinguish themselves clearly from the lowly *procureurs*. To accomplish these goals, they also needed to ensure a high degree of cooperation, and, more important, obedience to the dictates of the *conférences de discipline*. Without it, an action such as a strike would have had no chance at all of success.

Despite this period of vigorous activity, after 1665 the *conférences de discipline* fell into abeyance for more than thirty years.[64] Why they did so is uncertain. Part of the answer probably lies in the participants' refusal to form an actual *corps*, for in the absence of statutes spelling out the duties of established officers, the functioning of the Order depended on vigorous leadership by volunteers. In the early 1660's, François de Montholon had provided leadership, along with the unofficial secretary of the Order, a man named Abraham. But no one picked up the torch from them until 1696. In fact, widely varying levels of activity for the Order persisted throughout the late seventeenth and eighteenth centuries, following the character of its leaders and the willingness of the membership to follow them. The sleepy, almost moribund association of the 1680's bore little resemblance to the frenetic *organisation de combat* dominated by Claude-Joseph Prévost in the 1720's and 1730's, which in turn had little in common with the deeply divided Order of the 1780's.

After 1665, beyond the lack of leadership, the members of the Order probably felt less of a need to defend the prestige of the profession, for on that score the barristers were staging something of a comeback. In the second half of the 1660's, Louis XIV issued his great ordinances on civil procedure and criminal law, and this overhaul of large parts of the French legal code put a premium both on legal expertise, and on the sort of backbreaking intellectual labor that barristers prided themselves on. Chancellor Lamoignon himself convened a special committee of barristers to work on the projects. Barthélemy Auzanet later wrote a long description of the meetings held at the chancellor's mansion, concentrating particularly on the clothing and seating arrangements—elements of *préséance*—and noting with pride that mere barristers sat at the same table with the chief magistrates of the *parlement*. After the projects had been completed, the king himself thanked the Order for its services.[65] In a 1667 speech, the *bâtonnier* dwelt at length on the barristers' contribution to the reform process, and, striking a note of optimism that contrasted with Loisel's earlier anxieties, asserted that despite venality, "our occupation is no less illustrious today than it was in the past."[66]

The royal ordinance on civil procedure issued in these years incidentally had another important consequence for the Order. In order to keep better track of who wrote official legal documents, it ordered Parisian barristers not merely to keep a written list of practicing barristers, but to publish it annually under the title of the *Tableau des avocats.*[67] Early historians of the bar portrayed this measure as a mere formalization of existing practices, but in fact it transformed the way the Order managed its recruitment. Inclusion on the handwritten, easily revised *rôle* had been a *sign* that a man practiced law. Inclusion on a *Tableau* that was printed and distributed to the public, however, soon became a *condition* for practicing. By the eighteenth century, aspiring barristers were not considered full members of the Order until the physical publication of the *Tableau* each year. Its contents carried such high stakes for barristers that its composition routinely degenerated into ferocious squabblings and stalemate.[68]

Despite the ordinance, for several years the *Tableau* only appeared irregularly.[69] In 1693, however, the *parlement*, which still retained its titular authority over the Order, issued a ruling intended to clarify the division of labor between barristers and *procureurs,* which in passing reiterated the need for a printed list. The barristers later took to reprinting this ruling in each successive *Tableau,* and put the following passage in italics:

> Procedural documents allocated to barristers will not be accepted unless they are prepared and signed by a Barrister listed in a Tableau which will be presented to the Court by the Bâtonnier of the Barristers; only those who are presently practicing the profession of Barrister can be listed in the Tableau, and they cannot prepare procedural documents unless they have practiced for at least two years.[70]

This dry, legal language had important implications. Beyond mandating the yearly publication of the *Tableau,* it formalized the difference between practicing and titular barristers and effectively mandated a *stage,* lasting two years. It officially recognized the *bâtonnier* as the leader of the barristers and delegated the composition of the *Tableau* to him. From this point on, the *Tableau* began to appear every year.

While their participation in Louis XIV's great legal reforms temporarily relieved the barristers' perpetual anxieties about their status, by the 1670's this ambitious effort at codification had begun to sputter and slow down. At the same time, the king took unprecedented measures to limit the *parlement*'s independence. In 1673 he obliged them to register all laws and edicts before issuing remonstrances, thereby effectively gutting this traditional means of protest. Throughout the reign, the attempt to glorify the king as a sort of demigod continued apace, while the royal administration stealthily increased the scope of its activities. Once again, therefore, the bar began to seem a marginal, declining part of a marginal, declining institution.[71]

In the last years of the seventeenth century, the brief note of optimism sounded in the 1660's had disappeared entirely. François Levesque, *bâtonnier* in 1696–97, gave an oration that again portrayed a profession in deep crisis. Like Loisel and Loyseau before him, he blamed the decline on venality of offices, which he attacked as an "ingenious deception" that would leave a legacy of shame. He spoke of the paltry "vestige of honor [*reste d'honneur*]" left to the bar and told his colleagues they could hope only to persevere in the face of adversity:

> If that happy age when personal merit alone decided appointments [to the magistracy] is no more, let us not cease to live as if such a just and wisely-established state of affairs, one so useful to individuals and the public alike, did not still prevail. Let us continue to cultivate our field as if it could still produce the venerable and glorious harvest it once did.[72]

Similarly, when the venerable barrister Etienne Gabriau de Riparfonds wrote his will (which he later made public) in 1702, he spoke bitterly of the poor opinion some magistrates had developed for the bar. He noted that certain magistrates openly snubbed barristers, and added: "I am obliged to acknowledge that their manners have been one of the leading causes that have contributed to the diminution of the *éclat* of the bar." A scalding 1698 speech by the future Chancellor d'Aguesseau on the "decadence of the bar" added to the chorus. He told barristers that despite their grand traditions they no longer took sufficient care to monitor who joined the Order, and that therefore, "the bar has become the profession of those who have no profession."[73]

Faced with these challenges, François Levesque and another barrister named Claude Berroyer decided to revive the *conférences de discipline* begun in 1660. Like François de Montholon, they began to police the Order, once again ferreting out instances of solicitation and illicit arrangements with *procureurs*. They also acted to defend barristers on issues of *préséance*. In a move that would have lasting effects, they also began to lay down a code of conduct for barristers in both oral and written arguments. According to the minutes of the *conférences*, barristers had regularly been insulting each other in the most vituperative terms, and thereby harming the Order's reputation. The deputies of the benches threatened to haul repeat offenders before general assemblies of the Order, and, in extreme cases, to report them to the *parlement* for further action.[74]

After Levesque stepped down as *bâtonnier* in May 1697, the *conférences* again began to take place only erratically. It took another energetic leader, Louis Nivelle, to revive them in 1707, now on a monthly basis.

During Nivelle's term, however, steps were taken to ensure that the Order of Barristers functioned continuously and with complete autonomy from the *parlement*.[75]

To function on a regular basis, the Order needed something quite mundane: a meeting place (the *conférences* had so far taken place mostly at the homes of *bâtonniers*). In 1705, the opportunity to obtain one arose when Riparfonds died and bequeathed to the Order both his considerable legal library, and sufficient funds to hire a librarian. In his will, Riparfonds had criticized the bar's low standards of learning and eloquence, and urged that the new library become the site of seminars on the law. After his death, the Order rented space in the building of the archdiocese, on the Ile de la Cité, and the library opened on May 5, 1708. From this time on, it provided not only an informal meeting place, but also a site for the Order's numerous seminars, assemblies, and oratorical exhibitions.[76]

The Order's automomy depended on one basic question: Who had ultimate authority over the *Tableau*, and thus over the membership: the *parlement* or the barristers themselves? The judicial ruling of 1693 had left the point ambiguous. In 1699, the *parlement*'s *gens du roi* took it upon themselves to review the list, and to make several changes.[77] In 1708, however, they refused to intervene when the bulk of the Order forced Louis Nivelle to redraft the *Tableau* he had composed for the next year. This affair carried great weight as a precedent, and barristers subsequently took pride in the fact that the Order had determined the *Tableau* itself, without interference from above.[78] In 1707, the Order also asserted its authority over the membership in another way—by striking one of its members from the *Tableau;* in other words, disbarring him.[79] With these events, control over the Order definitively shifted from the magistrates to the barristers. Although the *gens du roi* continued to claim some authority over the bar until the end of the Old Regime, and were occasionally consulted on questions of disbarment (even issuing *arrêts* confirming the Order's decisions), they only tried to intervene in the composition of the *Tableau* on two occasions, and both times ultimately acquiesced to the Order's wishes.[80] In 1739, the *procureur général* even acquiesced in the disbarment of a barrister to whom he had extended his personal "protection."[81]

In 1710, the final plank in the framework of a fully autonomous bar association fell into place. In this year, in accordance with Riparfonds's wishes, the barristers began to hold legal seminars (called *conférences de doctrine*) in the new library. These seminars, while instructional in nature, were open to all interested barristers, and magistrates as well. They focused on all manner of legal problem, and various barristers even published records of the deliberations. They proved vital for *stagiaires* trying to make up for the defects of their university education, and by later in the eighteenth century they had become a required part of the training program.[82] Incidentally, the seminars, as well as many other aspects of the barristers' organization, soon found parallels in the provinces.[83]

Even as the barristers were setting up their new library, a man came on the scene whose powerful, bizarre personality made him a leading force in the Order for nearly twenty years: Claude-Joseph Prévost (1673–1753). The son of a Parisian merchant of modest means, Prévost was known for a ferocious temper (which had led him to break off contact with his own family) and for relentlessly Jansenist religious opinions.[84] His nickname in the Order was "the bear." The best description of him comes from a 1735 journal kept by his protégé Louis-Adrien Le Paige:

> This man, who has an excellent heart and excellent, rare qualities, always makes everything a personal affair, however inappropriate the occasion. . . . He is a true colossus, and makes himself even taller by standing on his toes. He raises and lowers his head, shakes his long wig, opens his great big eyes, and exposes a great big mouth which emits the most absorbing things in an indescribable tone. . . . Best of all, his hands, like his entire body, never stop moving. He will seize a man by the lapel and shake him marvelously; or else he will gesticulate with such gestures as one rarely sees outside of the marketplace.[85]

Another barrister, Jean-Louis Julien de Prunay, had a similar, if slightly more critical appraisal: "I have never doubted his rectitude, but he is so strange, so irascible, so bizarre, so enigmatic that it is impossible to come to agreement with him."[86]

For all his raging emotion, Prévost also had enormous reserves of energy, which he applied not only to the arcana of criminal and canon law, but to the Order itself. Once the Barristers' Library opened, he took it upon himself to collect as many books and manuscripts as possible bearing upon the history of the French legal profession. Soon afterwards, the registers of the *conférences de discipline* started identifying him as the "secretary" of the Order, and for the next twenty years he kept the minutes in a rushed, barely legible hand. A correspondence between him and *bâtonnier* Charles Arrault from 1717 to 1718 reveals that Prévost did the actual work of drafting the *Tableau* each year. On one occasion, Arrault wrote him: "after all, you are the master."[87]

Prévost, like François Levesque and François Montholon before him, believed that the Order of Barristers could recover much of its earlier luster by a rigorous purification of its own ranks. In August of 1717, in a meeting with other senior barristers to discuss the *Tableau*, he made the following observations:

> It has become intolerable to those who believe in the rigorous purity of the profession to take part in the *conférences de doctrine* with those who do not believe themselves subject to such great rigidities. This disregard for the public, this lack of duty to the intentions of a benefactor [i.e., Riparfonds]

who so deserves our gratitude . . . must engage us to put an end to the cause of our troubles.[88]

Despite his idiosyncratic personality, Prévost did manage to convince many senior colleagues of the necessity for a purge. *Bâtonnier* Arrault, in his valedictory speech to the Order in May 1717, echoed his complaints closely, blaming the problems particularly on "*procureurs*' clerks turned barristers" who continued to serve their former employers and kick back a share of their earnings.

The purge desired by Prévost and Arrault did not come for several years, quite possibly because of the confusion resulting from the *parlement*'s 1720 exile to Pontoise. When it did come, as will be seen in the next chapter, the notion of "purification" had become enlarged to cover not merely professional standards of behavior, but also what can only be called political conformity. In the meantime, however, Claude-Joseph Prévost found another way of defending the prerogatives of the legal profession: the now-venerable practice of *querelles de préséance*.

Thanks to the increased autonomy now enjoyed by the Order, and Prévost's own violent brand of leadership, the *querelles* took on a new intensity and bitterness in the early eighteenth century. In the single decade between 1717 and 1727 they culminated in work stoppages no less than six times. In 1717, for instance, the barrister Geoffroy-Jacques Sicauld showed up late for a hearing, leading the presiding magistrate to threaten to ban him from future appearances in that chamber of the *parlement*. *Bâtonnier* Arrault warned that all barristers would henceforth boycott the chamber unless the *parlement* acknowledged its "esteem" for Sicauld in particular and the Order in general. According to a 1733 pamphlet, the *parlement* gave in on the issue. In 1720, another quarrel arose, this time over whether the *avocats généraux* should enjoy any special prerogatives (such as the right to always plead last) when arguing a case against a barrister. Again, the magistrates bowed to the threat of a strike.[89]

The most important and revealing *querelle* took place in 1720, over a point of order which, while derided as hairsplitting even at the time, mattered dearly to an Order obsessed with etiquette.[90] Traditionally, barristers had the right, as university graduates, to plead in court without removing their hats (*bonnets*). However, when they interrupted their arguments to engage in the "mechanical" task of reading from the evidence—a task usually performed by *procureurs*—the custom was for them to "uncover themselves."[91] But what should they do when reading from a passage of law, as opposed to a piece of evidence? On this point, the lore of the Palais de Justice was ambiguous. On July 5, when the barrister Louis Gin read aloud from a statute, the *président* of the chamber insisted he remove his *bonnet*. Gin indignantly refused, and when he persisted in his refusal the next Monday, the *président* suspended the hearing. Immediately, the barristers held a meeting to discuss the affair, in which Prévost chided his colleagues for not expressing greater shock at the magistrate's conduct. "It is surprising," he exclaimed melodramatically, "that . . . we have not been overcome with vertigo that someone has challenged the right of barristers to plead with covered head when citing [legal] authorities. . . ." The barristers decided to boycott the chambers in question, and the quarrel continued for more than a week. Finally, after ten days and lengthy negotiations between the *premier président* and a delegation of barristers, the *parlement* gave in.[92]

Three other, similar affairs occurred in the 1720's, involving both the *parlement* and the Châtelet, but in every case, the barristers forced the judges to back down.[93] For this reason, the *querelles* mark the final steps on the barristers' path to professional independence. The slow divorce between the *parlement* and the bar, begun in 1660 with the establishment of the *conférences de discipline*, and helped along in 1708–10 by the assertion of control over the *Tableau*, and the founding of the library, now culminated in the symbolic reassertion of the barristers' position vis-à-vis the noble magistrates. If the new Order of Barristers was hardly "parallel" to the magistracy (as Levesque still claimed in 1697), at least it could claim a position of honorable, stable subservience. Of course, this divorce did not amount to a full-fledged revolt. On larger political issues, barristers and magistrates were still in broad agreement, and when the magistrates themselves went on strike to protest actions by the crown, the barristers supported them. However, they made clear that from now on, their support had a price.[94]

It seems clear that the principal motivation for the Order's activities in the late seventeenth and early eighteenth centuries was status, particularly vis-à-vis the magistrates. It is true that on a few occasions the *bâtonniers* did stoop to acknowledge a pecuniary motivation for the Order's actions (Charles Arrault blamed dishonorable barristers for depriving fifty "honorable" colleagues of work). According to some critics of Claude-Joseph Prévost's policies, simple avarice underlay his desire for greater "purity" in the bar as well: after he had finally purged the ranks in the 1720's, they claimed, honoraria quadrupled.[95] The barristers' hard-won freedom not to declare their honoraria, however, makes such (clearly biased) accusations impossible to substantiate. In any case, in the *querelles de préséance*, barristers clearly demonstrated their readiness to foresake income and go on strike when a question of status had been raised.

The story of the *procureurs* once again offers a useful point of comparison with this account of the barristers' growing professional independence. A 1639 edict, protested by the *parlement*, fixed the terms of venality for them, and soon afterwards the *communauté des avocats et procureurs* became their official corporate body.[96] In theory, the *communauté*, as a full-fledged guild, should have had far more freedom of action than any organization possessed by the barristers. In practice, it spent most of its time negotiating complex financial transactions related to the venal offices, which tied its members ever more inexorably to the royal treasury by a sticky web of financial obligation.

David Bien has well described how venal offices and *corps* were transformed into a system of state credit which bore more than a passing resemblance to a protection racket.[97] The process worked in two stages. First, the crown issued an edict threatening the livelihood of a particular corporate group. In the case of the *procureurs*, the edict often established a superfluous office in the courts whose owner would either compete with the *procureurs* or otherwise cut into their fees.[98] Each time, however, the crown invited the *procureurs* to forestall the edict by buying the new offices themselves (for a total price that could vary from as little as 10,000 *livres* to as much as 300,000). In the bargain, the *procureurs* would also collect the small royal salaries that came with these new offices.[99] All these transactions amounted to forced loans in which the price of the offices represented the capital and the salaries represented the interest. According to a 1790 claim, the *procureurs* paid the crown a total of 3,384,400 *livres* between 1687 and 1790, amounting to 8,461 *livres* per *procureur*, or more than two-thirds of the original price of the office.[100]

Once instituted, this system of state credit incidentally proved a very effective muzzle on the *procureurs*. Not only could the crown force them to come up with large sums almost whenever it chose; the increased value of the offices also forced the *procureurs* to go even deeper into debt, making the possibility of the office's suppression potentially ruinous to them. Throughout the eighteenth century the crown itself recognized the *procureurs'* relative weakness by consistently making them its first targets when it tried to break judicial strikes. According to the royalist barrister Pierre-Louis-Claude Gin, the *procureurs* never took the political initiative themselves, but only followed the lead of the barristers.[101] In general, therefore, the *procureurs'* experience lends credence to the barristers' fear of venality and incorporation.

A New Raison d'Etre

The construction of an independent bar association did not occur without efforts to rethink the place of barristers in the French polity. The idea of the "judicial monarchy," in which judges and barristers regulated all important social conflicts, remained attractive. But barristers could no longer expect many tangible rewards for their services to this monarchy. The idea of the bar as a *pépinière des dignités*, leading to high office, had lost all relevance by the end of the seventeenth century. Nor did barristers still serve as the most visible advisers to the great noble households. Even as they created the Order to defend their interests, they needed new justifications for pursuing the "laborious" career of law.

A number of men attempted to satisfy this need by writing manuals of legal practice, of which at least five appeared between 1664 and 1713.[102] The most successful of them, a 1711 work by Pierre-François Biaroy de

Merville, devoted much of its space to practical advice on all aspects of a barrister's work, and particularly the physical aspects of courtroom arguments: it urged readers to speak from the lungs, not the head; to keep their heads straight, not shrug; and always to appear in court on an empty stomach. In general, Biaroy provided a safe, conventional model of legal practice which aspiring advocates could copy.[103] Yet the manual also offered new glorifications for the barrister's laborious calling.

These glorifications did not differ entirely from those advanced a century earlier by Loisel and Pasquier. Biaroy too noted the indispensable place of the profession in a properly organized polity:

> It cannot be doubted that the Corps of Barristers is the soul of Justice, as Justice is the soul of States, and without which Cities, Provinces and Kingdoms would be mere brigandages, rather than civil societies and legitimate and well-ordered States. Barristers are the Priests, the Ministers and the Oracles of Justice.[104]

Biaroy too compared the profession to the military.[105] But unlike the earlier authors, he preferred to dwell less on the glory that the profession had achieved in contemporary France, than on its standing in classical Rome. He also did not hesitate to evoke the example of Cicero and Demosthenes, which Pasquier had dismissed as unsuitable for a Christian monarchy.[106]

The work that best satisfied the needs of the profession, however, was not a manual, but an oration delivered to the barristers by the magistrate and future Chancellor Henri-François d'Aguesseau, the very same man who would challenge the barristers in the "affair" of 1730–31. D'Aguesseau, though largely forgotten today, was one of the great, indefatigable public servants of the Old Regime, in the tradition of Michel de l'Hôpital and Malesherbes. Raised in the most demanding traditions of the *noblesse de robe* to devote himself to the state and the Gallican church, he steadily climbed the ladder of dignities of the legal system, ending as chancellor for more than thirty years. Had he lived in a less placid age than that of the Regent and Cardinal Fleury, he might have made a great statesman, despite what Fleury (who was hardly one to talk) called his "natural indecision." Had he lived in an age of more vigorous jurisprudence, his keen legal mind might have produced a noted body of reforms. As it is, he presided over the legal system with dignity, and left behind a solid body of writings.[107]

In 1698, the same year that he warned the Order of the need for greater exclusivity, d'Aguesseau chose as the subject of another oration "the independence of the barrister." Thanks to the eloquent praise that he lavished on the profession on this occasion, his words remain common currency in the Paris bar to this day.[108] Eighteenth-century barristers cited them in almost everything they wrote about their calling, and "independence" became the central motif in the annual orations delivered by *bâtonniers* to their colleagues. By 1735, when Louis Adrien Le Paige recorded his bored reactions to one such speech, it had become as familiar and ritualized as prayer. In 1763, when *bâtonnier* Jacques Merlet sat down to compose his oration, he cribbed liberally from d'Aguesseau, noting to himself that "everything in the oration presents admirable material for imitation."[109]

D'Aguesseau began, in stoic fashion, by assuring the barristers that the "dignities" to which they aspired were hardly worth the moral price demanded. The more honor and wealth men acquired, the more enslaved they became to their terrestrial desires. This form of "voluntary servitude" (the term owes something to La Boétie) had become so general in the France of Louis XIV that "it seems that liberty, banished from the commerce of men, has fled a world which despises it." And yet, d'Aguesseau added, one exception remained to the trend: the barristers, who alone amidst the "general subjection" had remained independent and free.[110]

In effect, d'Aguesseau was applying a balm to the barristers' tender antennae by declaring that whatever had happened to their formal social position vis-à-vis the magistrates, their relative moral position had improved. Barristers were quite simply less dominated by their passions than other men, he said. Furthermore, in the Order of Barristers, honor amounted to more than empty flattery, for it came only as the reward of merit:

> Those distinctions which are based only on the hazard of birth, those great names with which most men flatter themselves, and which dazzle even the wise, are no help in a profession where virtue is the source of all nobility, and where men are reputed not for what their fathers did, but for what they do themselves. In entering this famous body, they abandon the rank which prejudice attributed to them in the world, to resume the rank that reason has given them in the order of nature and truth.[111]

The bar was France's last bastion of natural equality.

Had d'Aguesseau offered the barristers only the inner comfort derived from a sense of moral superiority, his oration would doubtless not have achieved canonical status. The oration also seemed to justify both the "noncorporate" stance of the bar, and its antipathy to venality, but these were common sentiments to barristers.[112] D'Aguesseau, however, offered one further form of gratification: "glory" (a word that appears a score of times in the oration). The true rewards of independence lay in the fact that the barrister, not bound into any particular structure of wealth or power, worked only for what d'Aguesseau called, with little distinction, *la société, la patrie,* and *le public.* In fact, the barrister formed the principal link between the public and the "throne of justice." In return, the public gave him its plaudits, one of the few things in France that could not be bought.[113]

What did d'Aguesseau mean by "the public"? The sociologist Lucien Karpik, noting that the king and God have almost no place in the oration, argues that d'Aguesseau's use of the word foreshadowed its late eighteenth-century meaning: a "supreme power" that occupies the discursive space once occupied by the monarchy itself.[114] Such a reading, however, is a little anachronistic. D'Aguesseau himself (as will be seen in the next chapter) was anything but an incipient democrat. In fact, evocations of "the august tribunal of the public" formed a significant part of the ceremonial language of the *parlement* in the late seventeenth and early eighteenth centuries without ever connoting a challenge to royal authority.[115] The magistrates mentioned the public more often than the king for the simple reason that the court existed to render justice to and for this public. In d'Aguesseau's oration, the "public" consisted in the first instance of barristers' clients.[116]

Nonetheless, the insistent use of the words *virtue, liberty, independence,* and *patrie* in an early modern European context can hardly fail to recall the political tradition known as republicanism. The classical republican ideas revived in the Italian Renaissance, and further developed in seventeenth-century England, stipulated that states could only function properly if composed of free, independent, patriotic citizens protected from luxury and corruption. As if to underline his debt to these ideas, d'Aguesseau concluded the oration by telling his audience of their duties to their "fellow citizens" (*concitoyens*)—words not always expected from a largely faithful follower of Bossuet.[117] As d'Aguesseau hardly wanted to encourage overt political participation by barristers, one can only conclude that he was advocating a sort of "depoliticized republicanism" for them. (D'Aguesseau also wrote a discourse on "the love of country" that explicitly attempted to adapt classical patriotism to Christian monarchies.) In essence, he was asking them to behave with the pure morals of classical Roman citizens in the midst of the "general subjection" of monarchical France, and to reap the same reward as Cincinnatus, namely, the high regard of their compatriots.[118]

The success of the oration shows that in an era of growing disillusion with religious "enthusiasm," the image of barristers as virtuous Romans perhaps seemed more useful than the image of barristers as priests for describing and justifying the unique, exalted, noncorporate nature of the legal profession. In this vein, moreover, d'Aguesseau's sophisticated invocation of republican language clearly worked better than Biaroy's simple nostalgia for Rome. But could republicanism be stripped so easily of its political content? Or, in offering to the members of the French bar this potent political vocabulary, was d'Aguesseau opening his own political Pandora's box? In the early seventeenth century, Etienne Pasquier had rejected "Ciceronianism," excoriated the barristers who had put their pens at the service of the Catholic League, and pledged the legal profession to the defense of the monarchy. Was d'Aguesseau, unwittingly, reversing course?

In fact, in a less charged political atmosphere, it is quite possible that d'Aguesseau's depoliticized republicanism would have remained compatible with Bossuet's brand of divine right political theory. Barristers might have contented themselves with a diminished role in the French state, ensuring themselves of the proper respect from magistrates by staging the occasional *querelle de préséance*, and seeking additional gratification by playing peaceful Ciceros to adoring courtroom audiences. After the year 1713, however, the political atmosphere of the *Palais de Justice* was not merely charged, but explosive. Following the proclamation in that year of the papal bull *Unigenitus*, a feeling of despair descended over the bar such as had not been known there for over a century. This bull, solicited by Louis XIV in order to extirpate the current of Catholic thought known as Jansenism, seemed not merely to erode the political and religious traditions cherished in the Palais, but to put them in mortal danger. In response, the leaders of the Order of Barristers—and particularly the combative Claude-Joseph Prévost—felt they had no option other than, like the orators of antiquity (and the reviled pamphleteers of the Catholic League), to appeal directly to the "public." From then until the end of the Old Regime, they would use the privileged resources of the Order not merely to augment their own social status, but to effect political change.

3

"A Sort of Absolutely Independent Little Republic at the Center of the State"

The barristers are an entirely spoiled Corps, and as they are usually more learned than the run of the magistrates, they have seized the ascendancy over them and have become the absolute masters of the parlement. *The license taken in their speeches and writings, which we have unfortunately tolerated for a long time, has increased their audacity, and as they are a free company in that they only work as much as and for whom they want, they regard themselves as entirely independent.* *

Cardinal Fleury to Pope Clement XII, October 23, 1730

Throughout the seventeenth century, the barristers' anxieties over the "decadent" status of their profession had two distinct sources: the fragility of their own place within the legal system, and the broader political and religious changes affecting this system. Until 1713, with the brief exception of the Fronde, it was the daily snubs and vexations of life in the courts that preoccupied them. After the promulgation of the bull *Unigenitus,* however, the quarrels between king and *parlement,* Jansenists and Molinists, all came to the fore with a vengeance.

As a consequence of this shift, from 1713 onwards the political and institutional histories of the Order of Barristers became almost indistinguishable. The link should hardly be surprising, given the difference a protected institutional niche could make under the Old Regime for keep-

*AAE CPR 715, fols. 406–7.

ing authors out of the Bastille. After 1713, the leaders of the Order cared as much about possessing such a niche as about advancing the socioeconomic interests of their membership. Their nascent Order therefore evolved from a professional association into what might be called an *organisation de combat*, determined to make its voice heard on the political scene, and to push constitutional debate to the very limits of what the crown deemed acceptable. In the process, the barristers rejected earlier strictures about the self-effacement demanded of orators in a Christian monarchy, and also the general model of the barrister as essentially a behind-the-scenes counselor and theoretician.

From a modern perspective, it seems strange that a papal bull condemning 101 propositions taken from a work entitled *Moral Reflections on the New Testament* could have had such an impact on the barristers (and on French society in general). But to the influential group of Frenchmen known to their enemies as Jansenists, the bull *Unigenitus* seemed the greatest disaster to befall France since the Wars of Religion (to the more extreme among them, it was "the greatest event the Church has seen since Jesus Christ").[1] And nowhere, outside the church itself, did the Jansenists have such strong support as within the Paris bar.

The Problem of Jansenism

Although rooted in subtle and esoteric theological distinctions, Jansenism was probably the most divisive political issue of Louis XV's reign. Originally concerned with the nature of salvation and grace, it led to a debate on the nature of political sovereignty. Otherworldly and contemplative at first, its most radical form was an extraordinary, violent movement marked by "miraculous" cures and sadomasochistic rituals: the "convulsionaries" of St. Médard. Not surprisingly, historians have interpreted this motley phenomenon in many different ways: as the "degeneration" of a more respectable religious current; as a "veiled" political crusade; as an occult and psychopathic deviation; as a millenarian movement; and much else.[2]

Jansenism began as none of these things, but rather as a reaction against certain theological tendencies of the Counter-Reformation. Tridentine theologians such as Luis Molina (themselves reacting against Jean Calvin's radical denial of human free will) stressed the limits of man's corruption and the ability of everyone to achieve salvation through good works and the help of the church. Other Catholics felt that these efforts went too far in denying the importance of God's grace, particularly as discussed by Saint Augustine. This "Augustinian reaction" culminated in 1640 with the posthumous publication of the massive treatise *Augustinus* by the Flemish theologian and bishop Cornelius Jansen (or Jansenius), who emphasized man's total corruption, and the need for efficacious grace to overcome it. Jansen and his allies projected an extraordinarily pessimistic view of the human condition, warning (unlike the Calvinists) that even those possessed of grace might lose it at any time. They also stressed the importance of the direct relationship between the individual and God, and thus the need for constant reflection, meditation, and even "retreat" from the world (another notion alien to Calvinism).[3]

Despite his Flemish origins, Jansen's work had its greatest resonance in France, where it attracted some of the leading minds of the day including Pascal, Racine, and the mathematician Pierre Nicole. The "Jansenists," from their stronghold in the abbey of Port-Royal, became a crucial force shaping French literature and philosophy in the "classical age." Their thought was hardly monolithic: it ranged from the relatively moderate Augustinianism of Antoine Arnauld to the despairing "tragic vision" of Martin de Barcos and later Pascal, who asserted that since God had removed himself entirely from the corrupt world, his intentions (including natural law) could not be discerned by men. Broadly speaking, however, the term *Jansenist* came to connote a pessimistic view of the world, and a cool, austere, precise style of expression.

Despite its popularity in intellectual milieux, French Jansenism was persecuted from the very start. In 1653, Pope Innocent X issued the bull *Cum occasione* which condemned as heretical or false five propositions "extracted" from Jansen's *Augustinus.* Four years later, the French Assembly of the Clergy demanded that all French clergymen sign a "formulary" endorsing this condemnation.[4] Thereafter, the Jansenists enjoyed only a few respites. Louis XIV detested the movement, which he called "republican," and in the last years of his reign he delivered a particularly cruel blow, dispersing the remaining sisters at Port-Royal, exhuming the bodies buried there, and razing the abbey itself. In response, the Jansenists adopted the mantle of martyrdom to which their theology so well suited them, ostentatiously sacrificing opportunities for worldly success and directing a flood of hate-filled treatises at the Jesuits, whom they identified as the source of their troubles. According to Catherine Maire, their leading theologians began using the lens of "figurist exegesis" to interpret contemporary events as reenactments of biblical ones.[5]

By soliciting *Unigenitus* from the willing Pope Clement XI in 1713, Louis XIV hoped to eradicate Jansenism once and for all, but in fact this theological blunt instrument produced the opposite effect. The problems began with the text itself, which, in condemning 101 propositions taken from Pasquier Quesnel's *Réflexions morales,* seemed to judge unexceptional examples of Catholic doctrine as heretical.[6] Even the *parlement* of Paris, long bullied into submission by Louis, balked at registering the bull, and finally did so only under enormous royal pressure. Louis's death in 1715 did little to reduce tensions. Over three thousand members of the French clergy "appealed" *Unigenitus* to a future ecumenical council, and claimed its effects should remain "suspended" until the council had acted. In 1720, however, the regent Philippe d'Orléans issued a declaration ordering obedience to the bull, and imposing a "law of silence" on the subject. While meant in part as a conciliatory move, the *Parlement* of

Paris, newly aggressive since Louis's death, initially refused to register the declaration, and gave in only after several months of complicated maneuvering.[7]

Unlike the passions of the Wars of Religion and of the Revolution, this intermediary episode of Franco-French hostility today seems curiously difficult to understand. The Jansenists, unlike the Protestants, did not threaten a religious schism—in fact, they rejected the label "Jansenist" and insisted on their identity as good Catholics. The Jansenist emphasis on individual faith was certainly troubling to the church hierarchy ("one can be damned for following the advice of one's confessor," wrote Quesnel), and Pascal's radical view of all authority as essentially "arbitrary" hardly jibed with divine-right theories of monarchy.[8] Still, the often abstruse and difficult content of Jansenist doctrine severely limited its appeal, and Quesnel's call for the utter subordination of the church to the state in secular matters should have had a positive appeal to the Bourbon kings. To solve the puzzle, some historians have stressed Jansenism's links with other potentially subversive currents of thought: *Richerism* (which stressed the rights of the lower order of the clergy against the bishops), and *conciliarism* (a belief in the superiority of ecumenical councils over the pope). In the eighteenth century, each could and did serve as a template of sorts for secular protodemocratic ideas. These later links, however, fail to explain why, as early as the 1630's, Richelieu had written of a leading Jansenist: "M. de Saint-Cyran is more dangerous than six armies."[9]

Royal hostility to Jansenism probably had most to do with the horrible resonance—in early modern ears—of the word *schism*. In 1700, the terrible carnage of the Wars of Religion lay only a century in the past. Schism had wrought havoc in French society and resulted in the assassination of two French kings. As far as the crown was concerned, the Jansenists could be as abstruse and otherworldly as they liked, but if their doctrines caused splits in the French church, civil strife might well follow as it had done so often before.[10]

The crown had another reason to hate Jansenism as well. While it flourished in several secular milieux, nowhere did it enjoy greater prestige than in the Palais de Justice, the self-proclaimed bulwark against excessive royal power. One could practically say that the Palais gave birth to French Jansenism, as the great Jansenist theologian Antoine Arnauld, and his sister Angélique, abbess of Port-Royal, were descended from several generations of barristers (and fervently Gallican barristers, at that). Another member of the family, Antoine Le Maître, shone brilliantly as a barrister for a brief time, before ostentatiously abandoning a promising career in high government circles for a life of contemplation—a move that enraged Richelieu.[11]

The debate over why Jansenism flourished in *parlementaire* milieux (among magistrates and barristers alike) is an old one, best known for Lucien Goldmann's Marxist interpretation of the Jansenist "tragic vision" as an expression of the magistracy's frustration at their eclipse by a new royal bureaucracy.[12] Goldmann's thesis itself has not stood up well to empirical criticism, and subsequent scholarly efforts have tended to emphasize more mundane factors: the appeal of subtle and learned Jansenist theology to the cultivated families of the robe, and particularly the *parlements'* devotion to the Gallican liberties of the French Catholic church.[13] The magistrates had always numbered among the strongest adherents of Gallicanism because of their belief that the church's claim to independent secular powers within France threatened the royal courts' monopoly on the administration of justice. The various anti-Jansenist papal bulls aroused all their slumbering anxieties about the Holy See trying to impose its decisions on French Catholics by fiat. It therefore led them to embrace the Jansenist cause as a bulwark against "arbitrary despotism" (in this case, of the pontifical variety).

Beyond these familiar arguments, Marc Fumaroli's study of the "age of eloquence" has recently offered an interesting new perspective on the question. Fumaroli's work, while centered on the subject of rhetoric, shows that the sixteenth and seventeenth century *parlement* constituted an enclosed and self-sufficient culture. Moreover, this culture defined itself increasingly in opposition to the competing "absolutist" culture of the royal court.[14] If the royal court was mannered, sumptuous, sensual, and open to the full power of pagan Roman eloquence, the *parlement* was plain, austere, morally stern, and strict in terms of the sorts of speech it allowed in its hallowed precincts. Both competing cultures traced their origins to Renaissance humanism, but the *parlement*'s brand remained infused with a deep Christian distrust of human nature. Good *parlementaires*—Etienne Pasquier is a perfect example—thus viewed the Jesuit order, Molinist theology, ultramontanism, mannerist painting, and the sensuality of the royal court as different facets of the same fundamental error. From this perspective, the rise of Jansenism is linked to the eclipse of *parlementaire* culture. The movement took hold at the precise historical moment that the monarchy successfully imposed its authority on French cultural life in general through institutions such as the Académie Française, and made cultural inroads even within the *parlement* itself. The moral rigidity and otherworldliness of Jansenism, Fumaroli argues, took the culture of the *parlement* to its logical extreme, while also offering escape, consolation, and the martyr's sense of moral superiority.[15]

Fumaroli's analysis itself can be taken a step further with regard to French political life. The *parlementaire* distrust of human nature, which reached new levels of intensity among the Jansenists, lent support to the magistrates' political claims very directly. The classic works of *parlementaire* political theory, stretching back to Claude de Seyssel's *The Monarchy of France*, stressed the need for restraints on royal rule to protect the kingdom from the "imperfections of [all too human] monarchs."[16] The royal cult that developed in the seventeenth century implicitly challenged these notions by raising the king above the common run of humanity to a semi-divine status (in *both* a Christian and imperial Roman sense). Jansenism, with its lugubrious emphasis on concupiscence and the imperfectibility of man, offered the ideal foil to this cult, and a useful justification for the maintenance of the traditional restraints on the monarchy—including, of course, the *parlements* themselves.

While Jansenism in the *parlement* as a whole has received copious attention, its particular strength in the bar has not. Yet bar and bench had very different relations to the movement. While the Jansenist magistrates remained a small group in the lower and middle ranks of the court who guided and manipulated their colleagues rather than commanding them, Jansenists entirely dominated the Order. Particularly before the year 1732, when the *parlement* began to intervene actively in the ongoing religious quarrels, the Order in fact served as the Jansenists' principal secular ally. The beleaguered Jansenist bishop Jean Soanen put it as follows in a letter to the Order: "You are almost the only profession which has preserved the ability freely and wisely to make heard the complaints and make known the wounds of Church and State."[17] On this issue, barristers could even set the agenda for the magistrates—hence, Cardinal de Fleury's assertion, writing to the pope in 1730, that the barristers had become "the absolute masters of the *parlement*."[18]

Measuring the exact strength of Jansenism in a particular social group such as the barristers makes for a difficult task. Most such movements tend to inflate their own numbers while their opponents deflate them, but here the reverse is true. "Jansenists" categorically refused any label, proclaiming themselves simply good Catholics. Writers skeptical of the movement, meanwhile, saw Jansenists under every Parisian cobblestone.[19] Dale Van Kley has developed the surest method for counting Jansenists in an analysis of the magistrates, reserving the term for the men who appeared in a Jansenist "necrology" or who received special praise for their piety from the illicit Jansenist newspaper, the *Nouvelles ecclésiastiques*.[20] While restrictive, the method distinguishes between active Jansenist leaders, among whom a frankly conspiratorial atmosphere prevailed, and a much larger and nebulous group of sympathizers who could be found, if not under every cobblestone, then in a good many bourgeois and noble households.

Using this method, an analysis of the available sources produces a list of sixteen incontrovertibly Jansenist barristers in the period 1700–60, to which the addition of the notoriously Jansenist Le Paige, Maultrot, and Mey (who died after the publication of pre-revolutionary necrologies) yields a total of nineteen.[21] This figure seems small. However, both by position in the bar and by family connections, these nineteen men dominated their colleagues in a way that the *parlement*'s *parti janséniste* did not. Jacques-Charles Aubry was generally considered one of the three great oratorical talents of the first half of the century. Both his son and son-in-law served as *bâtonniers*. Louis Chevallier was mentor to Aubry and other renowned orators, and a famous barrister in his own right.[22] Georges-Claude Le Roy belonged to the powerful legal clan founded by his father Georges (whom we met in Chapter 1), which also included two *bâtonniers*. The clandestine Jansenist newspaper praised the entire family for its "probity, uprightness and love of the public good." Henry Duhamel, elderly and blind, played the role of a sage to younger barristers, and helped d'Aguesseau compose royal ordinances.[23] The mercurial Claude-Joseph Prévost, whom the diarist Barbier called a "grand janséniste" on more than one occasion, had particular power as the unofficial "secretary" of the Order. The Jansenist question clearly took up much of his attention, for at his death in 1753, forty percent of his large collection of books fell under the categories of theology, church history, and canon law, with a particular emphasis on questions of grace.[24]

Why did the Order prove so peculiarly receptive to Jansenism? After the Revolution, the Jansenist magistrate Pierre-Augustin Robert de St. Vincent, himself the grandson of a barrister, offered a simple explanation. He observed that from the 1650's onwards, a great number of men refused to enter the Faculty of Theology because of the requirement that they sign the anti-Jansenist *formulaire*. "The Paris bar," he continued, "[thus] became the refuge for a very large number of those who found themselves no longer able to enter the Church."[25] This explanation seems plausible for some men, including Prévost, whom a protégé curiously described as "although not a priest, living in celibacy," as well as the Jansenist mastermind Louis-Adrien Le Paige.[26] Yet Robert's insight does not explain why so many others in the Order sympathized with their Jansenist colleagues, and indeed incurred royal displeasure by putting their names on Jansenist *mémoires judiciaires*. To resolve this second question, the broader cultural factors discussed earlier must be considered. If the Order proved more hospitable to Jansenism than the *parlement* did, it was arguably because barristers remained more attached to the "culture of the *parlement*" than the magistrates themselves. While magistrates could marry into the sword nobility, adopt the manners and habits of the court, and rise to high administrative positions, barristers found no such opportunities under the Bourbon monarchy. Thus they held fast to the older, more puritanical, more austere life-style championed by Pasquier and Loisel, which provided them with a certain honor, dignity, and status.

Entering the Fray

It is important to remember that although it was the bull *Unigenitus* that turned the Order into an *organisation de combat*, French barristers had hardly remained aloof from political activity before 1713. In fact, from the very development of the printing press they had taken naturally to political pamphleteering. Barristers were by definition literate, and in a "judicial monarchy" where social and political conflicts of all sorts were

frequently expressed in legal language, they had the appropriate professional expertise. During the Reformation and Wars of Religion, members
of the bar had thrown themselves eagerly into the political rough-and-
tumble. Even Etienne Pasquier, despite his structures concerning the
proper conduct of orators in a Christian monarchy, wrote numerous
pamphlets in defense of the royalist cause.[27] During the Fronde, members of the bar again numbered among the most prolific authors of political pamphlets. In general, with the important exception of the Catholic
League, barristers mostly entered the political arena as hired pens, working directly for great nobles, prelates, or for the crown itself.[28]

Even with powerful patrons offering to hire barristers to engage in
political polemics, Pasquier's strict injunctions about self-effacement remained a powerful disincentive. In the seventeenth and early eighteenth
centuries, however, just at the moment when Jansenism became a convulsive issue, these injunctions began to lose their force in the profession. In
their place arose an explicit "Ciceronianism" that jibed far more easily
with direct appeals to an audience outside the courtroom. The avowedly
Ciceronian Olivier Patru, who succeeded the Jansenist Antoine Le Maître
as the most revered Parisian legal orator, well illustrates this shift. Not
only did Patru serve as a principal hired pen for the Cardinal de Retz during the Fronde, he also became a member of the chosen royal forum
for Ciceronian oratory, the Académie Française.[29] The shift away from
Pasquier's ideas also manifested itself in the manuals for aspiring barristers
published under Louis XIV. An anonymous *Introduction to the Bar*, published in 1686, defended the proposition that poetry, as well as stern,
scientific logic, had an indispensable place in legal oratory. Pierre Biaroy
de Merville's 1711 manual of legal practice (discussed in the last chapter)
made no attempt to distinguish between oratory in democracies and in
monarchies, but declared straightforwardly that eloquence was "one of
the most important parts of politics, reigning in sovereign fashion over
the hearts and wills of men."[30]

The traditionalists did make one attempt to resist the trend. Just two
years after Biaroy's book appeared, François Fiot de la Marche published
a work which seems at least partly a rebuttal, entitled *Eulogy and Duties of
the Barrister's Profession*. Unlike Biaroy, Fiot felt that standards of eloquence had fallen since ancient times, and in presenting past masters of
rhetoric, he held up Quintilian over Cicero and Demosthenes.[31] He specifically challenged the notion that oratory could play the same role under
a monarchy that it had played in ancient republics, and quoted Pasquier's
admonition: "The barrister must be more of a dialectician than a rhetor
. . . and more of a man of business and judgment than of great and long
speeches. . . ."[32] These stern lessons, however, apparently had far less appeal to barristers than Biaroy de Merville's overt Ciceronianism. It was
Biaroy's work, thrice republished, which became the standard issue primer
for barristers, while Fiot's effort quickly faded from sight. The stage was

therefore set for barristers to protest the persecution of the followers of Port-Royal.

Barristers had spoken out in favor of persecuted Jansenists in a sporadic way as early as the 1650's. In 1657, Antoine Le Maître himself composed a *Letter from a Barrister in Parlement to One of His Friends*, urging the *parlement* to reject Pope Innocent X's condemnation of Jansen. In the 1670's, Jean Barbier d'Aucour, a barrister and minor poet (who never quite escaped from the "literary underground" of the *grand siècle*) wrote Jansenist pamphlets, as well as some of the most stinging verse ever devoted to theological controversy.[33]

The bull *Unigenitus*, however, marked the point at which barristers went beyond these occasional ventures to engage in what can only be called systematic campaigns of publicity. It marked the first time since the Catholic League that barristers began publishing political works on a large scale independently, rather than at the behest of a powerful patron or party. Moreover, it marked the first time ever that the leaders of the bar threw themselves with virtual unanimity into these sorts of activities. The issue of Jansenism, in short, was now forcing the barristers into unknown political territory.

The pretext for the campaign arose in the years 1714–16 when certain bishops hostile to Jansenism began to punish clerics for refusing to accept the bull, and the men and women in question invoked the writ of *appel comme d'abus*, which gave secular courts appellate power over church courts. Thus, a number of cases came to trial in the friendly precincts of the *Parlement* of Paris. The barristers seized on the opportunity to address not only the judges, but the "public" inside and outside the courtroom, both in their speeches, and their printed briefs. Once again the tendency for all important conflicts to end up in the law courts of the "judicial monarchy" had put barristers in a key position.

These cases were extraordinary ones for several reasons. First, in an effort to uphold the *parlement*'s jurisdiction against possible royal interference, the barristers—including Claude-Joseph Prévost—made arguments that directly anticipated the radical constitutional theories advanced by the high courts in the constitutional struggles of the 1750's and 1760's. The cases thus reveal a sharp ideological divide separating barristers from the *parlement* itself, which still hesitated to challenge the crown on such matters. Second, in presenting the cases the barristers did not hesitate to turn from legal argument to highly personal "professions of faith." By doing so, they effectively invented a powerful new style of legal advocacy that highlighted not only the case in question, but the barrister's own role as a defender of the oppressed. Third, the barristers made full use of the most powerful political weapon at their disposal: the printed legal briefs called *mémoires judiciaires*, which were immune from censorship. Barristers had routinely printed and distributed these briefs for more than a century—sometimes in thousands of copies.[34] They believed that although trial verdicts obviously remained in the hands of the judges, the publicization of cases through *mémoires* guarded their clients against intrigue and conspiracy. Until now, however, they had not attempted to use these briefs in a concerted manner for political purposes.

The most important case concerned six clergymen from Reims who, in 1714, ran afoul of their ambitious duke-archbishop, François de Mailly, for their opposition to the bull. Three of them fled the city, but Mailly hauled the others up in front of an ecclesiastical court which suspended them from their duties as priests and as teachers in the university. All six clergymen then appealed the case to the *parlement*, using the *appel comme d'abus*. Louis XIV blocked the move by "evoking" the case to his own council, but a year later Louis was dead and Philippe d'Orléans, regent to his infant successor, allowed the *parlement* to hear the case after all. The barristers, Prévost and Louis Chevallier, immediately went to work, and the evidence is strong that they worked hand in glove with the clerics then organizing the "appeal" to the future ecumenical council.[35]

The surviving documents leave no doubt about the barristers' strategy. "My task," Prévost declared brazenly in his principal speech, "will be less to persuade the judges I have the honor of addressing, than to make our adversaries blush. . . ." Taking a favorable verdict for granted, he and his Jansenist colleague Louis Chevallier composed their briefs and speeches essentially for the purpose of publicizing the case and thereby generating opposition to the bull. Within the space of a year, they produced twelve separate pamphlet-sized publications, all portraying the Jansenist defendants as exemplars of piety and virtue, and martyrs to a wicked Roman conspiracy.[36] The principal Jansenist history of the events, published in 1723, as much as admitted that the case had been fought with the educated public's reaction in mind. It devoted much of its summary not to the arguments, but to the "prodigious crowd of listeners," the "numerous audience," the applause which constantly interrupted the speakers, and in general to the case's impact on what it called "the public." Its authors also made certain to stress that the *mémoires* "were the first pieces produced *openly* in which the Bull was clearly spoken against" (emphasis mine).[37]

The case incidentally provides a unique glance into the birth of Jansenist opposition journalism, for in their haste to publish, it appears that the printers did not even wait for clean copies of the scrawled, much revised drafts from which the barristers spoke. Instead, they published reconstructions of the oral arguments based on notes taken by courtroom spectators.[38] *Avocat général* Guillaume-François Joly de Fleury, who summed up in favor of the Jansenist clerics, was aghast at the reconstruction of his own speech. A marginal note on his personal copy reads: "There are few writings with as many typographical errors as these, and there are even more errors of judgment (at least in the speech attributed to me). I don't know how they could have made me speak so badly."[39]

The style of the speeches seems to have been as innovative as the manner of their publication. A historical dictionary published in 1759 called Louis Chevallier "the father of this free and energetic style of speaking that does not subject itself to the constraints of cold composition," and cited his speeches in the Reims affair as a case in point. The author probably had in mind Chevallier's personal "profession of faith" in which he repeated the basic tenets of Gallicanism and conciliarism. Prévost, in conventional fashion, cited myriad legal precedents, but Chevallier did not, preferring outbursts of "Ciceronian" rhetoric that would have made Etienne Pasquier shudder. "We are not slaves," he thundered to the spectators. "We do not lie under the yoke of blind obedience. We are children of a free woman [i.e., the church], and we hold this freedom from our divine master." Prévost did not entirely abstain from such language, and likewise attacked the "deluge of abuses which have drowned my clients' trial."[40]

As to the content of the speeches and briefs, it could almost serve as a blueprint for the eighteenth-century ideological current now called "Jansenist-*parlementaire* constitutionalism." Taking advantage of the newly relaxed political atmosphere of the Regency, Prévost and Chevallier staked out positions that the *parlement* itself would only adopt towards the middle of the century. The speeches principally addressed the old and vexed question of the church's secular powers, following the unbending Gallican line set forth by Pasquier Quesnel. Churchmen, no less than laymen, Quesnel had argued, owed absolute obedience to their prince. Their own authority was therefore purely spiritual.[41] Chevallier similarly declared that "the particular powers which are in the church are only there to edify, and not to destroy," and added that Catholics enjoyed certain "liberties," guaranteed by the laws of France, that no act of ecclesiastical authority could infringe.[42] The *parlement* itself did not take such an uncompromising stand on the issue of ecclesiastical authority until the mid-century. Even during the tempestuous years 1730–32 it remained more cautious.

The *mémoires judiciaires* in the Reims case, and particularly one written by Prévost in 1715, also addressed broader constitutional issues. In dying, Louis XIV had posed a knotty legal problem: although he had taken the Reims case out of the *parlement*'s hands, he had departed to face his own judge before his privy council could decide it. Did the case now revert to the *parlement* or not? The question touched on the very nature of French kingship, and to answer it the erudite Prévost did not hesitate to rummage around in the storage attic of French constitutional theory for ideas the crown had rejected more than a century before. In the Renaissance, jurists had drawn a distinction between the physical bodies of kings, and a larger royal "dignity" which never died, and which enveloped the principal institutions of the monarchy. Apologists for the

Bourbon dynasty later recast the images to present the king as metaphorically encompassing the entire realm within his own body, but Prévost preferred to revive the older language, redolent of a time that accepted far greater limits on kingship than Louis XIV had allowed:

> ... the evocation having been made to the late King's own person, and not to a Court, which does not die with the King, it must be presumed to have ended with his life; and things must be supposed to remain in the invariable and perpetual order of the Kingdom, which is independent of the life and death of Kings.[43]

Throughout the brief he repeated the phrase "the King's own person," as if to underline the difference between individual kings and the greater royal *dignitas*.

Prévost also argued that even if the king had not died, "evocations" to the privy council were still bad policy, for the *parlement* properly had near total jurisdiction over the administration of royal justice. To make this point, he described the high court in the following terms: ". . . the *parlement* of Paris, true *parlement* of the Kingdom of France; Court of Peers, august Tribunal, born with the State, and whose founding is connected with, and adjacent to that of the Monarchy itself."[44] In 1716, the theory that the *parlement* and monarchy had simultaneous origins, that the latter had not created the former, was radical indeed. Sixteen years later, when opponents of Louis XV published a pamphlet called *Judicium Francorum* that made similar points, the *parlement* ordered it suppressed without a moment's hesitation.[45] The high court only embraced the theory of common origins after Louis-Adrien Le Paige had articulated it at length in his classic statement of Jansenist-*parlementaire* constitutionalism, the *Lettres historiques sur le parlement de France*, published only in 1753. Nor, until the 1750's, did the *Parlement* of Paris ever challenge royal evocations as directly as Prévost had done.[46]

Had Prévost expounded his ideas systematically in a treatise or pamphlet, instead of haphazardly in a *mémoire judiciaire*, they might have had an immediate impact on the development of French constitutional debate. Had the regent's government brought attention to the brief by condeming it, the result might have been the same (in a show of uncharacteristic shrewdness it did not).[47] Instead, these theories about the history of France remained for the time being mostly locked within Prévost's cluttered and disorderly mind. Yet his work eventually had an impact, for Prévost was not merely colleague, but mentor to Louis-Adrien Le Paige, and clearly directed the thinking of the notorious Jansenist *éminence grise*. It was Prévost who, in order to "get a true idea of what the 'court of France' or '*parlement* of the Kingdom,' as it was called at the time, really was," first began researches in the ancient registers of the *parlement* (the "*olim*"), which also provided the basis for Le Paige's important *Lettres historiques*. It was Prévost who first sketched out the argument, later elaborated by Le Paige in a well-known pamphlet, that the ceremony of the *lit de justice* (in which the king presided over the *parlement* in person) originally had a legislative function.[48]

In addition to experimenting with venerable Gallican, conciliar, and *parlementaire* arguments, the men who fought the Regency cases also adapted Jansenist theology itself to political purposes. According to Catherine Maire, Jansenist barristers were responsible for taking the idea that certain interpreters of scripture formed a "depository of truth" within the church, and translating it into secular terms, presenting the *parlement* as the depository of the principles of French law. Maire points to the "affair of the Council of Embrun" of 1727 as the moment for this shift, but already one of Prévost's 1716 speeches described the high court as a "temple," "sanctuary," and "altar" in which "respectable doctrine" was "deposited." A 1718 brief for another Reims priest held that ". . . the *parlement*, depository of public authority . . . holds sovereign jurisdiction over all members of the state, both clerical and lay." In this way, the barristers added a distinctive Jansenist flavor to traditional *parlementaire* constitutionalism, and put down foundation blocks for the ideological constructions of the mid-century.[49]

During the Regency, the barristers did not limit their activities on behalf of *parlementaire* constitutionalism to court cases. This was the period in which the *parlement* of Paris itself, following the death of the imperious Louis XIV, slowly began recovering its venerable habits of opposition. The barristers rushed to support it, often with more enthusiasm than was shown by the magistrates themselves. In September 1718, for instance, after the *parlement* had tried to form a coalition among the sovereign courts against the financial innovations of the Scottish financier John Law, the regent blocked the move and, to reinforce the point, had three magistrates arrested. The magistrates limited their own protests over the arrests to a two-day "closure" of the Palais de Justice, but the barristers decided to stop working, not merely in the *parlement*, but in all the myriad Parisian courts.[50] They refused to end what amounted to their strike until the *premier président* personally asked the *bâtonnier* to intercede, and even then many barristers balked at returning to one jurisdiction staffed by royal *maîtres des requêtes*. In 1720, after two more years of squabbling over both financial and religious issues, the furious regent "transferred" the *parlement* to the nearby town of Pontoise, and once again the barristers refused to practice until the crisis had ended.[51]

The barristers' vaunted "independence" made them indispensable auxiliaries for the *parlement* in these actions. As they were not officers of the crown, and had no royally chartered corps, the crown had no legal means of forcing them to appear in court. In 1720, *Procureur général* Joly de Fleury frantically searched without avail for legal means to compel them to practice before the exiled magistrates.[52] As for the 1718 strike, Edmond Barbier claimed in his journal that when the regent heard of the Order's action, he exclaimed: "What, these bastards are getting involved too?!" His informant then allegedly replied: "Monseigneur, these are the ones it is hardest to subjugate, for it is permitted to silence a barrister, but impossible to make him speak against his will."[53] By proving themselves indispensable in this manner, the barristers incidentally made it more difficult for the *parlement* to restrain their other activities in favor of Jansenists.

While these work stoppages clearly gave the Order new leverage over the magistrates, they also put the new organization's cohesion to the test. How did the Order actually take decisions, and what happened if a determined group decided to defy the majority? Since the barristers eschewed the more formal deliberations characteristic of corporate bodies, and since the *bâtonnier* possessed few established powers, in this period the Order governed itself principally through informal "general assemblies," which followed no fixed rules and possessed no stated authority. In one sense, these rather chaotic gatherings made the Order a uniquely democratic institution. In practice, however, a small number of militants managed, through a mixture of persuasion and intimidation, to impose their views on the others. The diarist Edmond Barbier complained in the early 1720's that six or seven arrogant orators, all between thirty and thirty-five years old, had effectively "taken control" of the entire Order. Barbier added that "everything takes place in a tumultuous assembly of forty or fifty, and there, these men have no regard or feeling for their elders."[54] Barbier and his barrister father, following the lead of their patron, the *lieutenant général de police*, had little love for the Jansenist-*parlementaire* leaders of the Order.[55] Nonetheless, the description correlates well with portraits of the bar from a little later in the century. Consider this passage from a 1735 journal:

> Sometimes we assemble in great numbers. If [the subject of the meeting] concerns the general interest of the Order, or the possibility of taking some dramatic action, the *bâtonnier* is scarcely left the liberty to speak. M. Prévost, or some other zealot proposes an action. Half a dozen elders at most formally support it; if someone tries to make an opposing remark, either he is jeered or interrupted, or strongly spoken against after he has finished.[56]

Its author, Louis-Adrien Le Paige, hardly suffered from a prejudice against the *parlement*.

When possible, the "zealots" did not hesitate to enforce conformity with severe applications of corporate discipline. In 1720, a barrister named Sevale dared to practice before the exiled magistrates in Pontoise, while several of the barristers who habitually practiced in the courts of the Châtelet, led by Barbier's father, also defied the strike.[57] These defections had little effect on the course of the crisis, but the Jansenists perceived them as a danger nonetheless. Sevale was struck from the *Tableau*, and when the Châtelet barristers later came to argue cases at the Palais de Justice, the group of talented young orators denounced by Barbier refused for a time to appear against them, making their cases impossible to try.[58]

More broadly, the need to preserve unanimity in the bar during strikes put renewed pressure on the leaders of the Order to bring about the "purification" of the ranks that Prévost and others had long desired. The flood of men into the Order, which did not abate during the Regency, only increased the pressure: by 1725, the membership count had reached 573, an all-time high. For several years thereafter, Prévost did not get his wish because the *parlement*, perhaps piqued by the continuing *querelles de préséance*, made one of its last attempts to exercise some control over the bar and refused to recognize several disbarments.[59] In 1727, however, the leaders of the Order abased themselves and appealed to the magistrates directly for a new ruling confirming their disciplinary powers. The magistrates, possibly hoping to bring the *querelles de préséances* to an end, concurred; the *querelles* indeed ceased for nearly a decade thereafter. Prévost and *bâtonnier* Abraham Grosteste then took the 1725 *Tableau* and started crossing off names, ending up with a provisional total of 157, or twenty-seven percent of the Order.[60] One victim was Nicolas-François Fessart, who had defended the archbishop of Reims in the 1716 case.[61] In the end, some of the victims won reinstatement, but the Order still lost fifteen percent of its membership.[62]

This sort of "government by intimidation" practiced by the Jansenists, while perhaps inherently unstable, did offer a practical solution to a fundamental dilemma. As d'Aguesseau and successive *bâtonniers* had insisted, all barristers were equal; none had the right to dominate the others. Yet the peculiar form of collective action used by the Order—the strike—was useless without virtual unanimity, particularly since it took relatively few barristers to keep the courts functioning. Faction thus meant instant defeat. Survival depended in practice upon a small, indefatigable and militant minority either persuading or browbeating their colleagues into cooperation. This peculiar political dynamic, dictated by the nature of the Order itself, allowed a theoretically loose association of "men of letters" to function as a cohesive *organisation de combat* not only in the 1720's, but throughout much of the century. It may even have contributed to the political dynamic of the barrister-rich assemblies that ruled France after 1789, which felt a similar tension between democracy and the need for unanimity.[63]

Barristers into Pamphleteers

The events of the Regency created a model for a new form of political action by barristers. Over the next thirty-five years, Prévost, Chevallier, and their successors would fight a large number of cases similar to the Reims one. Each involved Jansenist clergy facing sanctions from the church hierarchy (supported after 1718 by the full resources of the French state).[64] Each featured an *appel comme d'abus* by these clergy to the *parlement*, and in each, the Jansenist barristers followed much the same strategies as before. During the 1720's and 1730's, the cases came

The Brigandage of Embrun, illustrating the church council at which Bishop Jean Soanen was stripped of his functions on account of his Jansenist beliefs. The case provoked the barristers' most successful early foray into opposition pamphleteering. Photo courtesy of the Bibliothèque Nationale, Paris.

before the *parlement* with such regularity that *mémoires judiciaires* virtually became a form of opposition journalism. Only a handful of men actually appeared in court and wrote the *mémoires*, but hundreds of other barristers actively supported the effort by adding their signatures to the briefs. With the Order already accustomed to stopping work in unison in support of the *parlements*, this development marks what can only be called the politicization of the Parisian legal profession, and the moment when its relationship with the "public" turned from d'Aguesseau's depoliticized republicanism into something altogether more dangerous to the monarchy.

Barristers were not the only group in the early years of Louis XV's reign to put new emphasis on publicity as a means of achieving political goals, and to invoke the "public" as a legitimate interest the king could not ignore. Rather, a triad of groups did so, combining to shift the center of gravity of French politics towards the illicit printing presses that serviced them all. First among them was the Jansenist clergy, even more desperate than barristers over the bull *Unigenitus*. In a carefully coordinated movement, they poured forth at least a thousand books and pamphlets during the Regency alone, denouncing the pope's machinations and publicizing their appeal to a future council of the church. Their works not only attacked the validity of the bull; as Catherine Maire has shown, they also popularized the "figurist" notion that a small group of the faithful could, like the prophets of the Old Testament, lead an erring nation back to the true creed. The late 1720's also marked the birth of the most successful clandestine newspaper published under the monarchy: the Jansenist *Nouvelles ecclésiastiques*.[65]

The *parlements*, newly active after Louis XIV's death, and eager to prevent further enchroachment on the judiciary by the royal administration, added their voices to the chorus. When the regent effectively removed the magistrates' muzzles in 1715, he did not grant them any new powers. The high courts could now remonstrate at length when the crown proposed legislation, but they had no authority to veto, or even to modify it.[66] The king could personally force registration of new laws in the ceremony known as the *lit de justice*, and could also exile recalcitrant magistrates to Pontoise or even less amenable locations, as in 1720. The magistrates had no legal means to resist. Yet they could and did print their remonstrances and distribute them illicitly in the capital and beyond. These learned documents probably appealed only to a relatively small, educated audience. Still, according to one study, they convinced the chroniclers of the period to view the magistracy with more sympathy. In the remonstrances, the *parlements* cast themselves as the public's mandatories, humbly offering its wishes to the crown even as they "represented" the will of the crown before the nation.[67]

The barristers formed the third, and in many ways the most original part of the triad. Unlike the Jansenist clerics, who produced their works from behind a thick veil of secrecy and risked imprisonment if caught, the barristers operated openly and enjoyed an important degree of institutional autonomy. The Order itself proved a powerful shield, thanks to the independence hard won in the first years of the century, and the *mémoire judiciaire* provided it with a privileged organ for publicizing its opinions. The barristers also took a very different approach from the *parlements*, who like them operated openly. The very form of the *parlementaire* remonstrance (a "humble appeal" to the king) and the caution of the non-Jansenist majority among the magistrates acted as powerful restraints on the high court until the middle of the century. Jansenist barristers, on the other hand, had the recklessness born of desperation.

In the 1716 case, this recklessness had expressed itself particularly in Claude-Joseph Prévost's precocious constitutional theories. In the 1720's and 1730's, however, these theories largely faded into the background (perhaps because Prévost ceded the writing of the principal *mémoires* to others). As a result, direct confrontation over these most sensitive of issues was postponed for a time. Still, the barristers continued their ideological innovations along two other lines. First, in a continuation of the arguments used in the Reims case, they defended a severe and uncompromising version of Gallican doctrine: the church, while possessing the spiritual authority needed to guide souls towards heaven, possessed no secular power whatever. All use of coercion, even in matters of ecclesiastical discipline, ultimately rested with the state alone—meaning, in this case, the *parlement*.

Second, in dealing with issues of ecclesiastical government, the barristers drew on a range of ideas wholly outside the pale of secular politics—and thereby helped introduce these ideas into French political language. Particularly since Bossuet, the arbiters of political orthodoxy in France had rejected any notion that the legitimacy of royal rule rested on a contract, or on a transfer of "rights" from individual subjects to the monarch. Even the total and irreversible transfer of rights envisaged by Thomas Hobbes was anathema to Prime Minister Fleury and to Chancellor d'Aguesseau. Religion, not reason, imposed the duty of obedience to the king. Yet in a rather delicious irony, theologians did not accord the pope the same divine sanction as the king. The powerful tradition of conciliarism, developed in large part by the medieval Sorbonne, subordinated the pontiff to "general councils" of the church, while the controversial seventeenth-century theologian Edmond Richer had advocated a greater degree of democracy among the clergy. In the context of church government, therefore, barristers could raise such notions as "contracts," and even the "imprescriptible rights" of "citizens" (as opposed to the all-too prescriptible rights granted by the king to subjects). These rights took precedence over any possible act of sovereign authority, and were thus particularly useful for an embattled minority struggling against the full resources of church and state.

It is surely no coincidence that these ideas surfaced just as the barristers began addressing themselves explicitly to a "public." It was the individual members of this public who possessed "imprescriptible rights" (at least in their capacity as Catholics). Identifying these rights was therefore the first step in seeing the "public" itself—as opposed to particular institutions acting in its name—as a restraint on sovereign political action. Through the lens of the barristers' writings, in other words, the "public" now came to appear more than merely as an interest to be placated. It had a form of legitimacy.[68]

The barristers' interventions followed the ebb and flow of the Jansenist crisis. For a time in the early 1720's tensions over the bull *Unigenitus* subsided, as the regent and his successors became increasingly preoccupied with factional struggles at Versailles. In 1726, however, Louis XV's elderly tutor Cardinal de Fleury emerged as the surprise victor of these struggles and immediately combined the formidable resources of church and state to begin what contemporaries called an anti-Jansenist "inquisition." The *parlement* proved surprisingly docile during this campaign, and even suppressed a number of Jansenist works itself, thereby encouraging the anti-Jansenists.[69] The crusade came to a climax in 1727 when Fleury convoked the Council of Embrun to hear charges against one of the four bishops who had signed the Jansenist "appeal" against *Unigenitus*: the vulnerable commoner Jean Soanen of Senez. After predictably slanted hearings, Soanen was sent into internal exile. Fleury's actions also harmed the ability of Jansenist theologians to mobilize large numbers of clerics in their defense; an attempt to launch a new "appeal" in 1727 garnered less than a third of the signatures collected under the Regency. They thereby undercut the original Jansenist publicity effort, the success of the *Nouvelles ecclésiastiques* notwithstanding, and put the barristers in an even more crucial position.[70]

Even before the Council of Embrun completed its business, twenty Parisian barristers gathered to sign a *consultation* (a form of *mémoire judiciaire*) in Jean Soanen's favor. Its author (most likely Pierre-Salomon Pothouin) argued that the appeal to an ecumenical council had not lost its validity, and therefore could not become grounds for Soanen's suspension. He called on the "secular power" to prevent an unjust condemnation and warned that any action taken at Embrun would amount to attacks on Gallican liberties. The *consultation* represented an important innovation for the Order, because it spoke to a matter that had not yet even entered a secular court (let alone a Parisian one).[71] The identity of its twenty signatories, meanwhile, demonstrates the depth of support for Jansenism in the Order. Only five were Jansenists themselves (by the criteria discussed earlier), although five others were close relatives of Jansenists. Moreover, the twenty stood at the social and professional pinnacle of the bar. Fully eight were noble, and nine had held positions in the councils of the houses of Orléans, Conti, and Condé. Another was *avocat général* to the queen. Jacques-Charles Aubry and Henry Cochin numbered among the most respected legal orators of the century.[72]

After the Council of Embrun ended, Aubry prepared a second, more extended, and even more provocative *consultation* in collaboration with the abbé Boursier, a Jansenist theologian. In careful and often difficult language the two men challenged both the allegations against Soanen and the council's jurisdiction.[73] They also offered a radical contrast between the powers of princes and popes, and then laid out a vision of church government based not on God's will, but on "rights":

> A temporal Prince, whose authority is independent, can command absolutely; he is accountable to God alone for his government. The pastors of the Church cannot do the same. . . . Our Liberties in essence consist of obeying legitimate pastors, but under the protection of certain imprescriptible rights, and certain immutable principles. . . . And what are these immutable principles and these imprescriptible rights? The power that Jesus Christ has granted to the Church and to his Pastors is a purely spiritual power. The spiritual power, in all its plenitude, resides only in the Universal Church, in the body of the pastors, and in the General Council which represents the Universal Church. . . . The government of the Church is not a despotic or arbitrary one.[74]

A clearer statement of Gallican and conciliar theory, phrased in the language of rights, cannot be found. Fifty barristers signed the document (which became known as the "*consultation des cinquante*"), including seventeen who had signed its predecessor. The other thirty-three, according to Barbier, were younger barristers hoping to ingratiate themselves with the Order's powers-that-be.[75]

As in 1716, the Jansenist barristers displayed a flair for bringing their work to the eyes of the "public." The new, illegal Jansenist newspaper, the *Nouvelles ecclésiastiques,* carefully prepared the ground for the *consultation*'s reception, with apparent success; Barbier and the barrister Mathieu Marais both noted in their journals that Parisians could not wait to read it.[76] In reaction, despite the laws allowing publication of *mémoires judiciaires* without censorship, the police forbade the printing of the work on pain of death, and seized two thousand copies in Chartres. The barristers, however, easily switched to clandestine publication, using the channels already used by the *Nouvelles ecclésiastiques.*[77] The ministry might have gone further and actually arrested the signatories, but here it came up against the institutional strength of the Order of Barristers. According to Barbier, leading magistrates told Fleury "that there were no concrete measures to take against members of this corps, who would immediately cease all their activity in the bar and even in their offices." Barbier later commented that the signatories "believed that they were the only ones who had the right, *thanks to their independence*, to declare the great truths of the Church" (emphasis mine).[78]

By all surviving accounts, the *consultation* had enormous, unprecedented success. It eventually went through four separate editions, and according to Mathieu Marais, a barrister with literary ambitions who disapproved of his colleagues taking part in political squabbling, "the paving-stones are crawling with copies." Soanen himself thanked the Order for its help, and sent Aubry a valuable present.[79] A dozen bishops—spurred to action, according to Barbier, by the barristers' courage—soon published their own condemnation of the Council of Embrun, while popular songs mocked their anti-Jansenist colleagues. Copies of the *consultation* found their way out of France, and a translation into Dutch even appeared for the Jansenist communities in the Netherlands.[80] The *Nouvelles ecclésiastiques* remarked on two occasions that the work had particularly impressed the magistrates, confirming the fact that the editors saw the docile *parlement* as a less enthusiastic and reliable ally than the Order.[81]

In general, this reception also showed that despite the small percentage of Jansenists in the population, warnings about "arbitrary despotism" had considerable resonance outside legal and clerical circles. Why they did so is difficult to explain, since so few readers have left traces of their reactions. Yet it may be that non-Jansenist readers saw in these cases a warning for themselves. After all, if the king or pope could override the Jansenists' established "liberties" by fiat, what was to prevent them from doing the same to some other group? Anyone with a stake in the system of privilege, which of course depended on the king respecting privileges he had granted, had reason to fear overly bold assertions of royal or clerical prerogatives. Jansenist barristers could thus count on a receptive audience for their efforts.

Whatever the case, because of its unprecedented success, the *consultation* became a major crisis for Fleury's administration. The cardinal's papers show that he paid painstaking attention to Aubry's arguments, and even acknowledged their soundness on several points.[82] Eight pamphlets appeared attacking the barristers (at least one allegedly sponsored by an anti-Jansenist cardinal).[83] Several bishops formally condemned the work, in *mandements,* as did the pope himself in a harsh papal brief that threatened Aubry's readers with excommunication. According to the *Nouvelles ecclésiastiques,* the administration even attempted to solicit a competing *consultation* from other barristers, but without success.[84] In the spring of 1728, Fleury assembled nearly thirty bishops at the Louvre to issue a definitive condemnation of the *consultation,* and then had the royal council formally suppress it.[85] The damage, of course, had already been done.

The *consultation des cinquante,* besides scoring a remarkable success in its own right, marks the transformation of *mémoires judiciaires* into a form of regular opposition pamphleteering. (Anti-Jansenist publicists would later call 1728 the year when the bar became an "uncommon and illicit tribunal.")[86] In 1730, when the long-standing truce between the ministry and the *parlement* broke down over Fleury's decision to make the bull *Unigenitus* a law of the French state, the barristers built on their earlier example with zest. In the first eight months of the year, they composed no fewer than ten *consultations* on topics ranging from the suspension of Jansenist clerics to an anti-Jansenist thesis presented in the

Sorbonne. Again, actual authorship seems to have rested with a "hard core" of twenty-four barristers who signed all or nearly all of the *mémoires* from the period. Still, fully twenty percent of the Order signed at least one brief.[87] As in Aubry's *consultation*, the authors restricted themselves to matters of church government, and did not put forth constitutional arguments of the sort Prévost had advanced in 1715. One might almost say a tacit rule had developed, whereby in exchange for this restraint, the ministry took no legal action against the barristers themselves.[88]

The Profession in Question

The sensation caused by Aubry's brief, while illustrating the ongoing changes in French political culture, did not fail to provoke a lively debate over the barristers' involvement in French politics. Indeed, for a while the Order appeared in some danger. For the first time since François de Montholon and his colleagues had begun to form a separate association in 1660, the legitimacy of its activities was called into question, not just by magistrates concerned with maintaining their own prerogatives, but by a royal administration that now saw the bar as seditious. In response to the attacks, the Order had to stake out more clearly than ever before its own definition of the barrister's place in political life.

During the period 1728–30, the Order actually drew attacks from two different directions. One set came from Fleury and other anti-Jansenist prelates who challenged the right of barristers to comment on religious affairs. These critics, in the pamphlets mentioned earlier, called for strict controls over *mémoires judiciaires*, and an end to the professional independence that allowed them to proliferate. The second set of criticisms came from within the Palais de Justice itself, from victims of the 1727 purge who called for an end to the Order's autonomous control over its own membership. The two attacks complemented each other nicely, and thus the Order suddenly found its two most precious assets—political and professional independence—in jeopardy.

The pamphlets sponsored by Fleury and his allies in the church had two themes. First, and most simply, they accused Jacques-Charles Aubry of hypocrisy because in his brief he had dredged up old charges of simony against Soanen's prosecutor, the Cardinal de Tencin, archbishop of Embrun. Who had Tencin engaged as a barrister during his trial on these charges seven years before? Aubry himself.[89] By the standards of the day, such a reversal indeed amounted to flagrant professional misconduct, and Aubry's opponents made the most of the fact.[90] Aubry retorted unconvincingly that he had only recently changed his mind on the case, but he could not undo the damage.[91]

The principal charge against the barristers, however, was more fundamental, namely that they had exceeded their professional "competence" in turning from matters of law to theology and politics. "It does not suit you or me to dogmatize on such matters," a self-styled "provincial barrister" told Aubry in an open letter.[92] Another author, posing unconvincingly as a simple cobbler, stated that barristers had no greater right to comment on the Council of Embrun than he did. Some of the popular songs on the affair picked up on this theme, joking that thirty barristers now outranked the pope, and the charge also found its way into Fleury's *arrêt de conseil*.[93] Its most detailed exposition came in an eighty-six page pamphlet that the *Nouvelles ecclésiastiques* attributed to a certain Poisson. "The profession of the barristers is limited to defending by oral or written arguments the rights of individuals in litigation," this pamphlet insisted. "It does not embrace affairs of state."[94] In an echo of Etienne Pasquier, Poisson emphasized the difference between monarchical and democratic societies and accused the *consultation*'s signatories of seizing a political mantle appropriate to orators only in the latter. France, he said, was not ancient Greece or Rome, where orators might express themselves freely on political questions. As for the barristers' "liberty," to which he devoted an entire chapter, Poisson asserted that "to speak precisely, there is no profession less free." He concluded by warning against the barristers' ability to "seduce" the common people, and urged that they "be deprived of the means of perverting the public."[95]

In fact, the pamphlet amounted to a detailed challenge to the Order's cherished notions of "independence." Poisson displayed an extensive knowledge of the bar's structure and history, including the terms of barrister's oath, the strike of 1602, and even a 1688 *querelle de préséance* with the *procureurs*.[96] He also contended that all professions were nothing but "links" in a greater social whole, and that if barristers overstepped the boundaries of their own profession they could disrupt all the rest. In effect, Poisson was arguing for a return to the *status quo ante* of 1660, and for the barristers' confinement within a narrow occupational compartment alongside the other *corps* of the state—precisely what the barristers themselves had so fiercely resisted by rejecting official incorporation.[97]

Poisson's challenge affected the Order seriously enough to elicit several replies. One pamphlet, written not by a barrister but by the Jansenist theologian Jérôme Besoigne, bore the straightforward title: *A New Question: Does One Have the Right to Accuse the Barristers of the Parlement of Paris of Exceeding their Powers, and Dealing with Matters Beyond their Competence in the Famous Consultation. . . .*[98] This defense of the Order began cautiously enough, suggesting that Aubry's *consultation* had merely commented on an aspect of canon law and hence fell firmly within the professional competence of a barrister. However, the author could not resist pointing out that wherever a case had even the *potential* to enter the law courts—wherever it merely *touched* on a question of law—barristers had the right to issue a *mémoire*. "In a word," Besoigne declared, "the Barrister can consult wherever the Magistrate can decide."[99] At one fell swoop, this assertion extended the barristers' field of activity from actual cases pending in the courts to nearly all aspects of French life. It is difficult indeed to imagine a subject in the highly legalistic, litigious society of the Old Regime which did *not* involve a question of law. Other pamphlets echoed these claims, if less eloquently. Dominique Favier wrote that "our profession has no limits; the most elevated subjects are our concern once they enter our domain."[100]

The criticisms of the Order thus forced the barristers to redefine d'Aguesseau's "independence" as a political, rather than just a professional quality, incorporating not just their freedom from "subjection," but their ability to comment on affairs of state. In a sense, the criticisms had forced them to lay claim explicitly to something unheard of under the *ancien régime*: free speech. To be sure, they conceived of this free speech as a peculiar condition of their own profession, and did not propose extending the privilege to a wider public. They did, however, suggest that the freedom of the bar was vital to the proper functioning of the legal system, and thus to the preservation of the French "liberties" which that system embodied.[101]

If Fleury's publicists criticized the Order's political independence, the victims of Prévost's purge attacked its very existence. For the most part, these ex-barristers did not contest the Order in print. Rather, they bombarded Fleury with petitions that condemned Prévost's "despotism." Fifty-three of them also signaled their readiness to replace their obstreperous ex-colleagues at the bar.[102] Their arguments did, however, find full public expression in one crucial document: an inflammatory 1729 *mémoire judiciaire*, written by several victims of the purge and signed by Guillaume Fericoq de la Dourie, which drew sufficient attention to be cited in a pamphlet sixty years later.[103] Fericoq not only indicted Prévost and *bâtonnier* Abraham Grosteste for ruling tyranically over the other barristers, he also put forth a vision of legal practice diametrically opposed to the one the Order had elaborated since 1660.

Fericoq focused on the crucial question of whether barristers were "public men." The Order, in eschewing the status of a *corps* had gone to great length to deny any "public" character to the legal profession. Barristers were mere "men of letters," simple individuals defending other individuals before a court. They had no official public rank or functions, and the Order itself amounted to no more than a loose association charged with maintaining the confidence of potential clients. Fericoq branded such arguments a sham: "When the Graduate presents himself in the Sanctuary of Justice to be admitted to the ranks of the barristers, the Magistrate confers on him a new Order and a Public character which associates him, so to speak, with the magistracy." For this reason, Fericoq continued, only the *parlement* or the crown could judge and disbar barristers. The *bâtonnier* had no legal authority to "censor" barristers, and the sacrosanct *Tableau* had no purpose except to determine seniority. Comparing a legal vocation to a religious one, Fericoq demanded that all qualified postulants be admitted. The petitions to Fleury echoed this view of the legal profession, one calling the bar "a public academy where all must be welcome to serve their prince."[104]

These attacks on the legal profession left an important legacy. From then on, Frenchmen had two different, opposing models for conceiving of the relationship between barristers and political life. On the one side stood the quasi-republican language of "independence" developed by d'Aguesseau and further refined in the late 1720's by Besoigne and other pamphlet-writers. On the other stood the language of submission to public authority articulated by Fericoq, and complemented nicely by Poisson's calls for barristers not to exceed a narrowly defined "competence." For the rest of the century, the Order itself would naturally continue to defend the first set of ideas. Its enemies, however, could now seize upon the second in response. Fleury's ministry was the first to do so, in 1731, when it briefly tried to reform the legal profession. Later, certain *philosophes* who instinctively distrusted all exclusive intermediary bodies that came between the sovereign and individual citizens would do so as well. Fericoq's arguments would thus reappear in the pamphlet literature of the 1770's and 1780's, and ultimately triumph in the revolutionary legislation that finally abolished the Order.

The Affair of the Barristers

Despite the barristers' provocations, and the new justifications for radical restraints upon the profession, the ministry initially pursued a policy of patience. In 1730, it let pass the first nine consultations, and also an unsuccessful attempt by the elderly, blind Jansenist Henry Duhamel to lead a strike of the Order following the April *lit de justice* imposing *Unigenitus* as a law of the state.[105] Fleury's allies in the church, however, did not take such a benign attitude. In 1730, anti-Jansenist preachers attacked barristers by name in their sermons, and even tried to block them, their relatives, and servants from entering the confessional—an eerie prelude of the "refusal of sacraments" that would cause such havoc twenty years later.[106] Such attacks only helped the most zealous voices within the Order, and increased the likelihood of an eventual showdown. In the fall of 1730, it occurred.

For a document that would ignite a major political and religious crisis, paralyzing both the ministry and the Parisian courts, the *Brief for Messieurs Samson, Curate of Olivet, Couët, Curate of Darvoi and Gaucher, Canon of Jargeau in the Diocese of Orléans*, looked remarkably unprepossessing.[107] Like most *mémoires judiciaires* it was a short (seven pages), poorly printed, unbound pamphlet that bore a long, unappetizing title and mostly featured dry, legal prose. Written by the barrister François de Maraimberg in defense of three Jansenist priests who had fallen afoul of their bishop, and whose case was in danger of evocation to the royal council, it seemed at first glance to differ little from earlier *mémoires* produced for similar cases. In fact, Maraimberg largely based it on a *mémoire* written for the Reims priest Le Cointre in 1718. While he reiterated the familiar Quesnelian argument that the church's authority was wholly spiritual, this point hardly sufficed to provoke a scandal.[108]

Where the brief *did* differ from the earlier ones was in its shift of emphasis from ecclesiastical to constitutional matters. Like Prévost in 1715, Maraimberg purported to uphold the *parlement*'s competence to review the rulings of ecclesiastical courts, not only against the claims of the church, but also against those of the king's council. In two places, moreover, he used remarkably incendiary language. "According to the Constitution of the Kingdom," he asserted, "the *parlements* are the Senate of the Nation, charged with rendering Justice to the subjects of the King, who is its chief." He also declared, in language that seems somewhat unbelievable for 1730: "All laws are contracts [*conventions*] between those who govern and those who are governed."[109]

Taken in the proper context, Maraimberg's *mémoire* was actually not so radical. Claude-Joseph Prévost later had no difficulty convincing a general assembly of the Order that Maraimberg had not intended to make "republican" arguments. Even the terms "chief" and "senate," he pointed out, had long-standing precedents in French law. In general, Maraimberg drew only on conventional legal sources. As for the phrase concerning the nature of laws, taken in the context of the brief, it designated only those laws agreed upon between church and state. More neutral commentators agreed with this assessment. Mathieu Marais quipped in a letter to a Dijon magistrate that the signatories hardly imagined themselves the successors to Junius Brutus, Buchanan, or Hotman.[110] Nevertheless, as all parties were aware, the inflammatory phrases could all too easily be read *out* of context. Moreover, in the aftermath of the Council of Embrun, barristers' briefs had become a highly sought after form of opposition journalism, so Maraimberg's effort could hardly be ignored as Prévost's own 1715 foray into constitutional theory had been.

Even interpreted in the most "orthodox" possible sense, Maraimberg's *mémoire* also violated the tacit rule that had grown up since 1727 whereby barristers refrained from taking the state as an object of their critical efforts. The rule had prevailed in part because the authors of the key briefs belonged to the Order's inner circle, and had close personal connections with leading figures in the ministry and in the *parlement*. Significantly, Maraimberg himself came from outside this circle. The brother of a pious Jansenist eulogized in Cerveau's "book of saints," he had only entered the law after a short stay in the Oratory. According to Barbier he was "a great Jansenist," who had impressed the leading barristers by the strength of his religious convictions (the caustic diarist added that Maraimberg was "as ugly as a devil, and has the face of a madman").[111]

Had Maraimberg produced the *mémoire* by himself, the Order might have yet managed to dismiss it as the work of a lone eccentric. But in addition to his own signature, thirty-nine other names were signed at the end of the brief, including those of Aubry, Cochin, and four members of the Le Roy family. In point of fact, the presence of these renowned names on the brief had come about through a series of farcical errors. Originally, Maraimberg had intended only to reprint the more moderate 1718 brief for the Reims priest Le Cointre, and solicited other signatures with this idea in mind. The printer, however, feared that Maraimberg had technically violated the complicated laws governing the publishing trade, and refused to go to press. In a panic, the barrister quickly composed a new brief that supposedly did nothing more than paraphrase the earlier one, although it now employed more inflammatory language. By the time Maraimberg had finished rewriting, however, most barristers had left Paris because of the *parlement*'s annual fall vacation. Fearing the imminent evocation of the case to the king's council, he did not wait for them to return, but ordered the new brief printed immediately, bearing the thirty-nine signatures he had collected before. Their presence made the *mémoire* impossible both for the Order to disavow, and for the ministry to ignore. Equally provocative was the fact that the printer made three thousand copies—a large figure for a time when the average book sold less than two thousand.[112]

The aged Cardinal Fleury, exhausted by his battles with the *parlement*, had no desire for a conflict with the barristers at this point. He had arranged for the royal council to evoke Maraimberg's case during the vacation precisely to avoid a fight over the issue. But the *Brief for Messieurs Samson . . .* crashed into his politics of compromise like a wrecking ball. Already convinced by the events of the previous three years of the barristers' overweening ambition, the leading figures in the ministry saw in Maraimberg's hasty and ill-considered lines a challenge to the very essence of the state, one that could not go unanswered. It was at this moment that Chancellor d'Aguesseau wrote the highly prescient lines cited at the beginning of this book, when the archbishop of Paris, Charles-Gaspard-Guillaume de Vintimille du Luc, expressed his fears to Fleury that Louis XV might suffer the fate of England's Charles I, and when Fleury himself wrote to the pope about the barristers dominating the *parlement*.[113]

Given these reactions, the royal council did not hesitate to violate in its turn the tacit rules concerning *mémoires judiciaires*. In an eloquent ruling (*arrêt du conseil*) drafted by d'Aguesseau himself and issued on October 30, 1730, it not only condemned and suppressed the *mémoire*, but also demanded that all forty signatories either disavow or retract it on pain of permanent disqualification from legal practice. The ruling, of which fully eight thousand copies were printed, caused a sensation, gathering comments not only in the journals of barristers and magistrates, but also in the French-language Dutch press. At a swoop, the barristers thus found themselves the protagonists of a major French political crisis.[114]

Like most eighteenth-century *parlementaire* crises, this so-called *affaire des avocats* was labyrinthine in the extreme. It involved countless feints, bluffs, and secret negotiations, the precise details of which have survived in the archives, but which need not concern us here. (I have tried to unravel the threads as clearly as possible elsewhere.)[115] The official documents that are its most obvious relics cannot be read in a straightforward manner. Rather—as Christian Jouhaud has cogently argued in the case of seventeenth-century polemical literature—they must be seen as gestures, moves in a game of textual chess played by men who belonged to the same elite and understood the same codes. The ultimate goal of both sides was to develop statements of basic political and religious principles that all parties could agree on, and thereby avoid costly direct confrontations. At issue, therefore, was once more the sensitive and ambiguous political vocabulary of the Old Regime. What was the precise meaning of terms such as *puissance spirituelle, constitution,* or *pouvoir absolu*? Who had the authority to "fix" these meanings? The negotiations took place on such a microscopic level that "victory" for one side or the other could lie in the successful placement of a single word.[116]

At first glance, the sides in this game of textual chess seemed ridiculously mismatched. On the one hand stood the highest-ranking servants of the French crown; on the other, mere men of the law. Yet the barristers did hold one important trump card: their well-honed abilities with the printing press. As the private observations cited in the Introduction so eloquently testify, the leading figures in the ministry feared nothing more than that the debate over the *mémoire* would escape from the Palais de Justice and infect what they saw as the shifting, elusive, irrational currents of "public opinion." These men knew full well that the power of the French monarchy, ordained by God himself as it might be, nonetheless depended *in practical terms* on the consent of the population. They therefore dreaded the moment when this population might, as d'Aguesseau put it, come to speculate on "the source and true nature of all human power," and thereby expose its "weakness."[117]

The first stage of the crisis perfectly illustrates these general points. Despite the uncompromising demands of the *arrêt du conseil* of October 30, the ministry was willing to settle for less in the hope of avoiding a strike that would shut down the Parisian courts, embarrass the king, and further revive the sputtering conflict over the bull *Unigenitus.* The following month therefore saw frantic negotiations between *bâtonnier* Guillaume Tartarin, Chancellor d'Aguesseau, *procureur général* Joly de Fleury, and Cardinal Fleury. The goal was to produce a statement of loyalty by the Order that would satisfy the crown without appearing to humiliate the barristers, but each side postured, stalled, tried to anticipate the other side's moves, and generally made the process long and painful.[118] Sentiments in the Order itself varied widely, from a willingness to surrender born of dismay at Maraimberg's "treachery," to fury at the ministry's attack on the Order's "independence." Some barristers practicing before the *Grand conseil* even took part in an abortive strike. Prévost and *bâton-*

nier Tartartin managed, in a series of heated assemblies, to rally the Order behind a lengthy draft declaration of loyalty written by Aubry and Cochin. D'Aguesseau, however, rejected it as insufficiently apologetic, and angrily broke off negotiations altogether after a hundred clandestine manuscript copies began to circulate through Paris (probably at Prévost's behest). The situation was saved, however, when the *garde des sceaux* Chauvelin, a former *parlementaire* with strong ties to the bar, stepped in and took over the talks himself.[119]

The next stage of negotiations involved not Tartarin, whose early willingness to compromise had lost him the confidence of the Jansenists, but two other barristers: his son-in-law, Jean-Louis Julien de Prunay and Alexis-François Le Normand. Neither were Jansenists, but both had firm Gallican sympathies and both belonged to the "hard core" of barristers responsible for the earlier wave of *mémoires*. Socially, both belonged to the upper reaches of the Third Estate. Le Normand, son of a wealthy *procureur*, was a successful orator who had become a client of Chauvelin, a counselor to the Duc d'Orléans, and was notorious for his waiting room full of noble ladies, his extravagant personal tastes, and his 50,000 *livres* per year in *rentes*. Julien de Prunay, who left an invaluable narrative of the affair, was an ambitious young barrister who had also cultivated friendships at court, notably that of Maurepas, the rising secretary of state for the navy.[120]

With these pragmatists in charge, the negotiations, now removed to Versailles, proceeded rapidly. Maraimberg and his cosignatories, it was decided, would issue a one-page declaration of loyalty that Tartarin would endorse to mark the Order's interest in the matter. There would be no attempt to justify Maraimberg's *mémoire*, but in exchange, all talk of disavowal or retraction would be dropped. The royal council would then issue a new declaration, incorporating the barristers' text and acknowledging the members of the Order as "good and faithful subjects." There was also a secret condition: Maraimberg himself would be disbarred at the first opportunity.[121]

The composition of the barristers' declaration itself was a delicate process. Since the final text would have the seal of approval of an *arrêt du conseil*, Le Normand and Julien found themselves in the odd position of effectively dictating royal policy. For this reason, Chauvelin wrangled with them over the text phrase by phrase. The problem did not lie with the *mémoire*'s alleged "republicanism," which the Order had already taken pains to deny. Indeed, the final text of the declaration addressed the king, God's "living image," in breathlessly obsequious phrases lifted straight from Bossuet.[122] It was the ecclesiological questions that proved difficult to resolve, for here Le Normand and Julien held fast to the bar's Gallican and Richerist traditions. The intricacy and flavor of the negotiations can be grasped from the following vignette. Le Normand had proposed writing, with regard to the clergy in general, that "they hold spiritual power uniquely from Jesus Christ and his Church." But in place of the word "they" Chauvelin tried to substitute "the bishops." Julien de Prunay's friend Maurepas warned him of this change, and Julien reacted as follows:

> I cried: "What, Sir, you have not understood the difference between the word 'they' and the word 'bishops'? The word 'they' designates all the ministers of the Church, those of the second as well of those of the first order, and in this way the right of curates and other ministers of the second order of the clergy is conserved.... The phrase 'the bishops etc.' ... would allow the bishops to say that we, and the King as well, have recognized that only they hold their spiritual power from Jesus Christ, and that for this reason, the ministers of the second order only hold their power from the bishops."[123]

The two barristers firmly refused to accept any changes on this point, and when the news reached Paris, several colleagues again raised the possibility of a strike.

Fleury, however, possibly out of sheer exhaustion, did not wish the conflict to drag on. He not only accepted "they" (asking only that the barristers subsequently articulate their position on the bishops more fully at a later date), but also language that might have been taken straight from Quesnel. The final text read, in flagrant contradiction of the bull *Unigenitus*: "Even excommunication, as dreadful as it is when pronounced for legitimate reasons, cannot break the sacred bond between Subjects and their King." It also stated: "The ministers of the Church hold from Jesus Christ alone the spiritual power whose purpose is the salvation of souls, and which is enforced by spiritual sanctions. But it is to your Majesty alone that they owe the exterior jurisdiction that they enjoy in your states." With these passages ticking away like a time bomb, on November 25 the council published a remarkable 15,000 copies of the finished *arrêt* and proclaimed the affair at an end.[124]

"The Order has triumphed," wrote Mathieu Marais to a correspondent in Dijon. The barristers had survived the confrontation with honor, and Julien de Prunay even received a pension of 2,000 *livres* from Maurepas in recognition of his services. Popular songs mocked anti-Jansenist bishops for a defeat at the hands of mere advocates. Thanks to Fleury's haste to make peace, however, the triumph was far too complete to stand. The octogenarian cardinal, by seeming to endorse a declaration that contained such strong Gallican and Richerist accents, had committed a blunder that would keep the *affaire des avocats* running for another year, putting one in mind of de Gaulle's expression, "old age is a shipwreck."[125]

Thanks in part to the French-language Dutch newspapers, the *arrêt du conseil* containing the barristers' declaration received international attention. One copy soon arrived in Rome, and according to the French ambassador there, it so upset the new pope Clement XII that "great tears dropped from his eyes" as he read it. In France itself, the anti-Jansenist bishops could not contain their rage. "They screeched like eagles," the

Marquis d'Argenson wrote in his journal. The archbishop of Paris, Vintimille, by no means a "zealot" (to use the contemporary term) like his episcopal colleagues at Embrun or Laon, begged Fleury's permission to issue his own condemnation of Maraimberg's *mémoire* as heretical. In short, the cost of Fleury's tenuous peace between the ministry and the bar seemed to be an open breach between France and Rome.[126]

There now began another lengthy period of posturing and negotiation. Fleury gave Vintimille permission to issue a *Pastoral Letter* condemning the barristers, and upon reading it, they "screeched like eagles" in their turn. After some disagreement on strategy, and more talk of a strike, the Order decided to ask for the suppression of the *Letter* by the *parlement* by means of an *appel comme d'abus*. Knowing that the magistrates would not take such an action without the ministry's tacit approval, the Order also decided to use a bluff: unless the ministry gave in, it would sue the archbishop for slander, thereby giving the case maximum publicity.[127] Julien de Prunay wrote candidly: "To intimidate our adversaries, we spread the rumor of a lawsuit against the archbishop." The gambit worked: the *procureur général* himself was soon convinced that unless the Order were appeased, the "zealots" would prevail over the "moderates" in the Order, and he persuaded Fleury to strike a deal. Once again, the indefatigable Le Normand set off for Versailles, and once again he reached a compromise. On March 5, 1731, the *parlement* suppressed Vintimille's *Pastoral Letter*, and in return the Order agreed to refrain from any further complaint or strike.[128] To outside observers (and some latter-day historians) it appeared as if the magistrates had come to the barristers' defense for ideological reasons, but in fact the *parlement* had only played an auxiliary role. Julien de Prunay noted with satisfaction: "This *arrêt* was not the work of the *gens du roi* alone. It was worked out with the government and is in fact an agreement between the government and us . . . although the government did not openly appear to take part."[129]

In the wake of this second defeat, Fleury seized upon a well-worn tactic of men whose political theory told them that politics, properly speaking, did not exist in an absolute monarchy. On March 10, he summarily imposed silence on all matters concerning Maraimberg's brief. Yet despite an accompanying royal letter designed to mollify the anti-Jansenist bishops, his move predictably failed to have the intended effect. Vintimille continued to protest to him, the more ardent of the bishops continued to rage against Maraimberg's *mémoire*, and the barristers themselves remained insultingly unrepentant. Throughout the spring of 1731, the political situation therefore remained highly unstable.[130]

Gradually, as summer approached, two factors pushed Fleury towards taking more decisive steps against the Order. First, there was the phenomenon of the "convulsions." In 1727 an ostentatiously humble Jansenist deacon named François de Pâris, brother of a magistrate, died and was buried in the Parisian cemetery of St. Médard. Soon afterwards his tomb became the site of "miraculous" healings, convulsions, speaking in tongues, and assemblies of Jansenist pilgrims—exactly the sort of "popular" demonstration that Fleury dreaded. The Jansenist leaders of the Order numbered among those who flocked to the tomb, and they also offered legal assistance—along with the publicity of *mémoires judiciaires* —to beneficiaries of "miracle cures" suffering harassment from church authorities. The growth of the phenomenon in 1731 drew Fleury closer to the anti-Jansenist bishops, and stoked his anger against the barristers.[131] Second, the Order itself experienced a bout of internal strife that seemed to weaken it substantially. In May, in accordance with the secret agreement made six months previously, the outgoing *bâtonnier* Guillaume Tartarin tried to strike Maraimberg from the *Tableau*. Prévost, predictably, exploded in anger upon hearing the news, and convened a general assembly that voted to overturn the decision. Songs circulated accusing Le Normand and "Julien the Apostate" of treason. Tartarin, however, refused to yield to the majority, and the result was a conflict that continued to smolder, unresolved, long after the *bâton* had passed to a combative member of the Le Roy clan, Pierre Le Roy de Vallières (in fact, no new *Tableau* appeared until 1736).[132]

Fleury did not hesitate to exploit this turn of affairs. In early July, he gave the police strict orders to arrest anyone found reading Maraimberg's *mémoire,* and when Vintimille formally appealed to him to overturn the *parlement*'s condemnation of his *Pastoral Letter*, he readily assented. In other words, despite previously praising the barristers as "good and faithful subjects," the royal council now concurred in judging the *Brief for Messieurs Samson* . . . as heretical.[133] Fleury knew that his decision would cause an uproar. He delayed publication of the new *arrêt du conseil* for weeks, and prevented it from being cried out in the streets and distributed in public. Nonetheless, he had finally taken a decisive stand, abandoning the endless search for compromise in favor of direct confrontation.[134]

The Order, and Claude-Joseph Prévost in particular, did not shy away from the fight. From the moment that news of Fleury's decision reached the Palais de Justice, barristers began to declare that as "heretics" they could hardly appear in court as usual. By August 19, the normally optimistic Le Normand was writing to Chauvelin that "the blaze is horrendous; I am looking for ways to put it out."[135] On August 23, three hundred barristers assembled in the Palais to hear Prévost harangue them at length. "The bishops want to make themselves the absolute masters in the state," he warned. Two days later the Order unanimously ceased work in all the Parisian courts, paralyzing them and causing tremendous inconvenience to litigants (some of whom, given the *parlement*'s vast jurisdiction, had traveled hundreds of miles).[136] Although the *parlement* did not directly support the barristers, it issued remonstrances over Fleury's decisions, and provoked a small crisis of its own by attempting in its turn to define the proper relationship between church and state.[137]

Although the Order had directed countless strikes against the *parlement* in *querelles de préséance*, they had not done so against the crown, and their action, while expected, caused consternation. The royal council itself was divided. Maurepas, Julien's friend, urged patience. The Maréchal de Villars, as we have seen, proposed his combination of exile, *embastillement*, and execution. Fleury, as usual, finally chose to split the difference. On August 30, ten barristers, including Prévost and Le Roy de Vallières, received *lettres de cachet* exiling them from Paris (before leaving they went to the cemetery of Saint-Médard and thanked François de Pâris for letting them suffer for the faith).[138] Still, Fleury and Chauvelin also began considering a more radical, permanent solution. Under their direction, two young advisers to the ministry, Luc Courchetet d'Esnans and the Marquis d'Argenson, had already drawn up reports arguing that the autonomous, noncorporate status of the Order made it impossible to control and therefore a threat to the state. D'Argenson, in his striking phrase, called the Order nothing less than "a sort of absolutely independent little republic at the center of the state."[139] Fleury now considered promulgating a law abolishing the Order of Barristers. The proposal would call for opening the profession to all law graduates, putting the barristers under the direct control of the administration, and forbidding all meetings of three barristers or more.[140]

For a time, Fleury kept these plans in abeyance. The *parlement*'s annual vacation began at the start of September, and thus the barristers' strike had little immediate effect on the high court, although it did paralyze the rest of the Parisian legal system. *Procureur général* Joly de Fleury, aided by Le Normand, made several efforts to mediate a compromise, but achieved little (Le Normand, because of the fracas over Maraimberg's disbarment, had lost much of his influence in the Order). As the deadline of the *parlement*'s mid-November return approached, Joly's letters grew more and more desperate. On November 12, the magistrates duly marched in their splendid procession to the Palais de Justice and assembled to render the king's justice to his subjects. But for the first time in centuries, no barristers followed them, no barristers presented themselves to take their oath of service, and no barristers answered the calls to plead cases.[141]

It was probably at this point in the affair that someone intimately familiar with the political contours of the affair composed a remarkable pamphlet entitled *The Barristers' Imaginary Heresy, Or the Jeremiahs of Our Day*, published in December.[142] Written in the form of a passion play, it showed that, thanks to the barristers, the most extreme *parlementaire* theory and the most extreme Jansenist theology had now come together to form a potent elixir. A helpful *dramatis personae* identified the barristers as vengeful Old Testament prophets haranguing the erring People of God, while likening the Jansenist magistrate Pucelle to Judas Maccabeus, d'Aguesseau to a fearful Pilate washing his hands of his erstwhile protégés, and the bishops to a deadly, hissing hydra. The name given to the chorus—"le peuple"—is especially striking, for in the eigh-

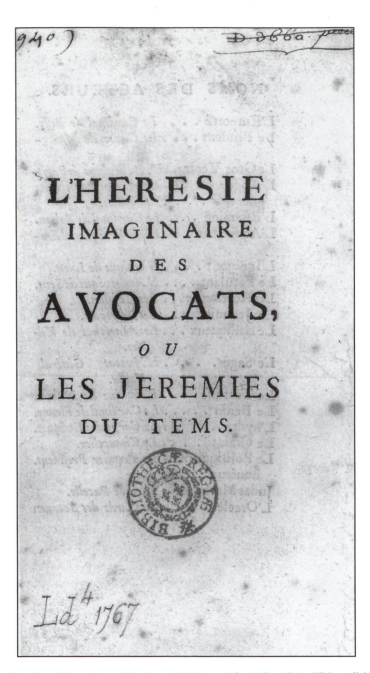

The Barristers' Imaginary Heresy, or the Jeremiahs of Our Day. This political passion play, written to defend the striking barristers of 1731, likened the members of the bar to prophets, the French episcopate to a hydra, and concluded: "This is all serious for the Third Estate." Photos courtesy of the Bibliothèque Nationale, Paris.

NOMS DES ACTEURS.

L'Emporté . . . . *Le Cardinal de Biffy.*

Le Prudent . . . . *Le Comte de Maure-*
pas.

Le Gros Ventre... *L'Archevêque de Paris.*

L'Ange du Sei- *Chauvelin, Maître des*
gneur . . . . . *Requêtes.*

L'Effeminé . . . *Le Cardinal de Rohan.*

L'Audacieux . . . *L'Archevêque d'Em-*
brun.

L'Ignorant . . . . *L'Evêque de Laon.*

Le Pétulant . . . . *L'Archevêque de Sens.*

Les Réprouvés ... *Les Jefuites.*

Les Jeremies . . . . *Les Avocats.*

Le Belliqueux ... *Le Maréchal de Vil-*
lars.

Le Sage . . . . . *L'Avocat Général*
Voifin.

Le Tartuffe . . . . *L'Evêque de Nifmes.*

Le Benin . . . . . *Le Cardinal de Fleury.*

L'hydre . . . . . *Le Corps des Evêques.*

Le Craintif. . . . *Le Chancelier.*

Le Politique mal- *Le Premier Préfident.*
heureux . . . .

Judas Machabée... *L'Abbé Pucelle.*

L'Oracle . . . . . *Le Garde des Sceaux.*

teenth century the word generally designated the lower, irrational seg-
ments of the population. Here, the author clearly drew on the biblical
phrase "*le peuple d'Israël*"—a usage which, while archaic, also anticipated
the later revolutionary transformation of the word. The pamphlet, with
its explicit parallels between biblical and contemporary events, also provides a rare popular expression of "figurist exegesis."[143]

In addition to this scriptural message, the pamphlet defended the
Order's independence and promoted a radical Jansenist, *parlementaire*
agenda. "Obey the King," it instructed its readers, "but out of love,
never out of constraint; never against the Law; never against the rights of
his crown, nor to the prejudice of the tenderness of your CON-
SCIENCES" (note the distinction between "king" and "crown").[144] A
particularly florid passage saw in the barristers' departure from the Palais
de Justice the death of justice and the ruin of the entire kingdom, and
ended on an oddly prescient note:

> In fact, since the disappearance of the Jeremiahs of our day, there is no
> longer a Defender of the Peoples' Cause; there are no more Judgments and
> confusion reigns. Lebanon is in a horrid state, the Earth is in tears, the wine
> weeps and the vine withers. . . . The waves are rising and swelling. Does any-
> one stop to consider these truths? This is all serious for the Third Estate.[145]

These images, like those in Prévost's 1715 brief on evocations, leave no
doubt that a number of barristers had adopted the principal tenets of the
parlementaire ideology of mid-century long before the actual constitutional crises of this period.

The end of the *affaire des avocats* took place in the same atmosphere of
posturing and confusion that had characterized it from the beginning. In
mid-November, infuriated by the humiliation of the *parlement*'s *rentrée
manquée*, Cardinal Fleury seems (the archival evidence is somewhat ellip-
tical at this point) to have set in motion his plans for abolishing the
Order. While trying to implement the draconian new law on the legal
profession, however, he ran into unexpectedly determined resistance from
procureur général Joly de Fleury, who threatened to resign his office unless the cardinal retreated. Fleury knew that Joly enjoyed the overwhelm-
ing support of the magistrates, and he probably feared that his resignation would only exasperate the paralysis of the judicial system. Whatever
the case, the cardinal finally did not act on the draft *déclaration du roi* and
so the Order escaped a *coup de force* and the loss of everything it had created over the previous seventy years. Whether or not because of this episode, it was now that Fleury and d'Aguesseau, faced with the prospect of
an indefinite stalemate, finally decided to abandon the path of confrontation and seek another negotiated settlement.[146]

Meanwhile the barristers, unaware of their close shave, were themselves feeling increased pressure to bring the affair to an end. The strike
had meant a total loss of income since September, and despite collections

taken up by the wealthier members of the Order (Aubry even sold his silver), the effects of the walkout soon made themselves felt. A song that circulated in the Palais put it succinctly: "Starving to death, they said, / is much worse than being heretics." Under these circumstances, the "zealous" course of action advocated by Prévost seemed less attractive, and Le Normand, the advocate of accomodation, came back into favor (it helped that Fleury had sent Prévost and nine other *zélés* into internal exile).[147]

For one last time, Alexis Le Normand returned to Versailles, entered into negotiations with Chauvelin, and agreed on a compromise. Once again, the solution involved an *arrêt du conseil* defining what all the parties to the dispute had meant to say, and ordering an end to all discussion. Unlike in 1730, however, the participants consciously agreed to leave the language as ambiguous as possible, rather than trying to impose their own meanings. To quote Le Normand on the subject (writing to Joly de Fleury): "We have to be able to say to the Bishops that we understand the point in this way, and to leave the barristers the freedom to understand it in another way, so as to lead them to the desired outcome."[148] In fact, the new *arrêt* tried so hard for ambiguity that, strictly speaking, it made no sense. On the one hand, it stated that the crown stood by its earlier recognition of the barristers as "good and faithful subjects" while on the other hand, it confirmed its approval of the archbishop's *Pastoral Letter*, which had called the barristers heretics. To the exhausted negotiators, however, peace finally mattered more than either sense or linguistic authority.[149] On November 25, cagily avoiding the turmoil of a general assembly, Le Normand called together fifty senior members of the bar and convinced them to accept the agreement. They, in turn, quickly persuaded the others. The next day, therefore, the Order returned en masse to the Palais de Justice, and soon afterwards, in response to a rapidly drafted *mémoire*, the council duly issued its final declaration. Within a week the exiles returned and the long *affaire des avocats* was definitively over.[150]

As the final *arrêt* allowed Vintimille to continue distributing his *Pastoral Letter*, some historians have concluded that in the final analysis, the affair ended in humiliation for the Order.[151] Contemporary observers, however, thought otherwise. On the fast-changing political scene of 1731, Vintimille's condemnation already seemed ancient history, and overall, it was clear that the Order profited from the crisis in two ways. First, it had managed to keep the question of the bull *Unigenitus* unsettled. Cardinal Fleury, drawn into conflict with the barristers because of an obscure *mémoire judiciaire*, had soon found himself trapped in a political morass which distracted him from all other concerns of state. Again and again he finally chose to impose an ambiguous silence rather than provoke further conflict. Second, the Order had preserved its professional independence, and by doing so in a confrontation with the crown had immeasurably increased its prestige. Barbier, who often ridiculed his overheated colleagues during the affair, nevertheless acknowledged this point: "It is always very honorable for a corps consisting of simple individuals to bring the King to look for pretexts and excuses. . . . The satisfaction the King has given them . . . is entire." The Order itself would regard the events of 1730–31 as a source of pride for many years. One undated entry in its registers spoke of "the great elevations of glory in which the bar of the *parlement* of Paris found itself in 1731, when it so distinguished itself by reviving ancient and forgotten times, to support the rights of the crown and the state."[152] In the ministerial camp as well, the affair was seen primarily as a humiliation. Consider only the dramatic admissions by Chauvelin, d'Aguesseau, and d'Argenson as to the strength of the barristers' opinions in "the public." The affair may even have left a bitter taste in the mouth of Louis XV himself. According to an (admittedly unreliable) journalist, Chancellor Maupeou said in 1771 that the king "would never forget that under the Ministry of the Cardinal de Fleury, at the time of the affairs of Jansenism, a famous barrister, called Le Normand, forced him to retreat."[153]

These dramatic admissions underline the real significance of the affair of the barristers. For one of the first times in French history a group largely composed of commoners, without powerful noble patrons and without violence, caused the monarchy to lose face in a political confrontation. Their success vividly demonstrated the growing importance of their two chief sources of influence—the ability to form an autonomous association capable of independent action within the structure of French institutions, and especially their ability to appeal to the new and nebulous force of public opinion. Far from "strangling this monster in the cradle," as the Marquis d'Argenson had advised, the affair only strengthened it.

More broadly, the events also foreshadowed the emergence of a Third Estate led by lawyers into organized French political life. It is no accident that the most radical pamphlet of the affair, *The Barristers' Imaginary Heresy*, hailed the members of the Order as "defenders of the peoples' cause," stressed the king's subordination to the law, and declared that "all is serious for the Third Estate." The transformation of the legal profession from an association of learned jurists into a politicized *organisation de combat* was now complete. Voltaire, a man with very little sympathy for barristers, nevertheless could not help admiring their actions in 1730–31. In a bilious passage of his *History of the Parlement*, which mostly mocked the Order for its pretensions, he also gave what amounted, in his lexicon, to the highest praise: "Simple citizens triumphed," he wrote, "having no arms but reason."[154]

4

The Seminary of Publicists

The barristers of our parlements *are full of enlightenment, equity and religion ... and as they seek for nothing but natural equity and the public good in the Laws and the application of rules, the* Patrie *and* Justice *themselves do not speak truly except through the mouths of these worthy barristers.*

De la nature de la Grâce ... dédié à Messieurs les Avocats
du Parlement de Paris*

Histories of France customarily divide the reign of Louis XV into two halves, the first placid and prosperous, the second buffeted by the winds of intellectual turmoil, financial crisis, constitutional stalemate, and military defeat.[1] This generalization may be valid for most of French society, but as the previous chapter makes clear, for a small but important minority of the French, the early years of "*Louis le bien aimé*" seemed anything but placid; in fact, they seemed to be years of a deadly twilight struggle for the very soul of the kingdom. In the eyes of the Jansenists, France was undergoing not a slow recovery from the famine and defeat that marked the last years of Louis XIV, but a slide into corruption and spiritual poverty parallel to the decadence of Biblical Israel and Judah. The mood was not one of contentment, but of desperation.

As we have seen, however, this desperation led those Jansenists who belonged to the Paris bar to experiment both with new political ideas and with new means of disseminating them. They challenged the rights of the bishops and the crown and pursued confrontation with both parties aggressively—far more aggressively, in fact, than their supposed "masters"

*(n.p., 1739), p. 6.

in the *parlements* did. After 1715, therefore, the former "seminary of dignities" was transformed increasingly into a seminary of publicists, a breeding ground for authors who wished to use compelling rhetoric in the legal pursuit of political goals. The rank and file of the Order of Barristers followed their Jansenist leaders, not only out of fear of disbarment, but out of common concern for the survival of the "judicial monarchy."

The events of the three decades that followed the "affair of the barristers" did not do much to alleviate the apocalyptic mood among Jansenists. The royal administration, hand in hand with the church hierarchy, continued systematically to root them out from clerical positions and to enforce recognition of the bull *Unigenitus*. In response, the Jansenist barristers kept up their campaign of *mémoires judiciaires*. In the period from 1732 to 1749, in fact, as the *parlements* mostly avoided confrontation with the crown and the last Jansenist bishops died or were replaced, the Paris bar became not simply the principal secular ally of the Jansenists, but also a principal source of licit opposition to royal policies.

After 1749, thanks to the full-scale constitutional crisis that began with the controversy over the refusal of sacraments to Jansenists, the political initiative passed clearly to the magistracy. Nonetheless, barristers continued to produce the most important political texts during this crucial period in which, to quote Keith Baker again, "French politics broke out of the absolutist mold."[2] Moreover, the crisis of the 1750's brought the travails of the Jansenist minority to the attention of much larger numbers of educated Frenchmen than before, so that the barristers' writings began to create ripples far beyond the walls of the Palais de Justice. The Order itself, however, enjoyed no immunity from the general climate of criticism that it was helping to foster, and during this period, the very qualities that made it an effective *organisation de combat* also made it the object of considerable controversy.

Hubris and Humiliation

Although the Order continued to function as a Jansenist *organisation de combat* during the late 1730's and 1740's, it no longer did so in the same confrontational, highly visible manner that had characterized its activities in the previous decade. It no longer produced declarations, defied ministries, or attempted to dictate royal policy. Its most effective members now operated quietly, behind the scenes, rather than trying to draw the attention of the continent to their actions. The change occurred because of a showdown between the barristers and a *parlement* no longer willing to tolerate their free-wheeling tactics.

Following the imposition of *Unigenitus* as a law of the state in 1730, the minority of active Jansenists among the magistrates finally convinced their colleagues that Fleury's anti-Jansenist "inquisition" posed a serious threat to French liberties. As a result, the high court abandoned the quiescence it had shown in the 1720's, and became embroiled in its most serious conflict yet in the century with the crown.[3] For several months, the magistrates took the leading role both in defending persecuted Jansenists, and in upholding the prerogatives of the judiciary against the crown. Inevitably, given the high court's prestige and institutional strength, the barristers found themselves moved off the center of political life, and obediently followed the *parlement*'s lead. They cooperated with it on several work stoppages, and as in 1720, their help proved crucial in blocking royal measures aimed at restructuring or emasculating the court. After all, without barristers (and without most *procureurs*, who also joined the strikes), even a replacement *parlement* simply could not function.[4] In 1732, the Jansenist barristers also helped the *parlement* plot its moves in the delicately choreographed confrontations with the ministry. According to the journal kept by one magistrate, the judicial strike of May 1732 was planned in "secret conferences" with "skilled barristers," and the final resolution to strike was taken at the house of the Jansenist barrister Nicolas-Claude Visinier.[5] In these ways, the barristers rehearsed the role of *éminences grises* that Louis-Adrien Le Paige and others would play so successfully in the 1750's and 1760's.

The magistrates had now clearly expressed their intention not to be upstaged by mere barristers. Had they then continued their own aggressive political behavior, even the most "zealous" members of the Order probably would have followed them without demurral. The confrontation with the crown soon came to a compromise ending, however, and according to Jean Egret, the threat of drastic royal action against the high court left the magistrates "stupefied" and unwilling to provoke further troubles.[6] Then in 1733, the brief War of the Polish Succession broke out, and, as often occurred in periods of war under the Old Regime, the *parlement* toned down its opposition even further in the name of patriotism.[7] In this atmosphere, many of the "zealots," above all Claude-Joseph Prévost, once again attempted to take the lead and behave, in the Marquis d'Argenson's words, as a sort of "second magistracy."[8] The conditions for a major confrontation between the bar and the bench were thus in place, and in 1735, it occurred. The events are worth considering briefly, for they show that despite the affair of 1730–31, French society was not yet ready to tolerate members of the Third Estate negotiating as equals with ministers and chancellors.

The stresses between the Order and the *parlement* festered particularly in two areas. First, between 1730 and 1735, the leading Jansenists in the Order became increasingly involved in the controversy swirling around the convulsionaries' "saint," François de Pâris. Church authorities imposed sanctions on beneficiaries of his "miraculous" cures, once again giving barristers the chance to appeal to secular courts via the *appel comme d'abus*. One group of ten barristers, all belonging to the elite "hard core" of 1727–30, published *mémoires judiciaires* in these cases with particular intensity.[9] Several more (notably Prèvost) publicly affirmed their belief in the phenomenon. Prévost's young protégé, Louis-Adrien

Le Paige, soon became the "secretary" of the convulsionary movement, a position he held throughout much of the eighteenth century.[10] Yet in defending the convulsionaries, these barristers seemed to go far beyond the pious, erudite Augustinianism traditionally associated with Jansenism. They identified themselves with men and women, frequently from the artisanal classes, who twitched, screamed, spoke in tongues, and sometimes punished themselves in gruesome, sadomasochistic fashion.[11] While a few magistrates also joined the "cult of St. Médard," most of them rejected what they saw as a grotesque perversion of religious faith. The *parlement*'s refusal to support the convulsionaries drove a wedge between them and the leaders of the Order.[12]

Even more divisive than the leading barristers' increasingly zealous and hermetic religious faith was their perceived new arrogance. In 1735, the Marquis d'Argenson advised Fleury that "the haughtiness of this order has reached an extreme degree. Everyone with business in the Palais de Justice has suffered from it continually during the last four years. The barristers boast of nothing less than . . . of having protected the *parlement*." Verthamon, presiding magistrate of the *Grand conseil*, who had criticized the Order for its conduct in 1731, declared in open court in 1735 that "the barristers want to make themselves the masters of all the tribunals." The Order ironically confirmed the point by threatening a strike unless Verthamon apologized. Barbier, as unsympathetic as ever to his colleagues, wrote that "there is now much presumption and interest in the members of the corps, something that was not true formerly." Louis-Adrien Le Paige wrote darkly in his journal that "one is never closer to a fall than when one stands the highest."[13]

The anti-Jansenist party did all it could to heighten this reputation for arrogance, for it thereby strengthened its case that the Order should not speak out on matters beyond its "competence." During the 1731 events, a series of widely publicized anti-Jansenist pamphlets portrayed *avocat général* Pierre-Paul Gilbert de Voisins as a mere tool of the Order.[14] Later, the Jesuit publicist Guillaume-Hyacinthe Bougeant ridiculed barristers in two well-known anti-Jansenist plays. *The Lady Theologian*, which mocked the fashion for Jansenism among Parisian women, featured two signatories of the *consultation des cinquante* who insisted on censoring theological treatises while neglecting their real clients. *The Saint Exposed*, directed against the convulsionaries, presented a group of barristers who claimed with temerity that they secretly determined all the *parlement*'s decisions. These broadsides, of course, underscored the Order's new prominence even as they attacked it.[15]

In 1734–35, the issue of the barristers' arrogance crystallized in three separate controversies. The first erupted over a booklet by the Dijon barrister François-Bernard Cocquart entitled *Letters or Disserations in Which it is Shown that the Profession of Barrister is the Most Beautiful of All Professions*, addressed in theory to his son.[16] Unlike previous works on the profession, Cocquart made no mention of the "laborious" and difficult elements of legal practice. He devoted all his efforts to praising the bar, and in so effusive a manner as to make even the effusive Biaroy de Merville sound half-hearted. No profession, Cocquart insisted, was more honorable, more useful to the public, more noble or more virtuous than the law ("the profession of barrister," he asserted rather implausibly, "is a very sure route to heaven"). He slighted the *procureurs*, and more provocatively claimed that venality of offices had "tarnished" the glory of the magistracy.[17] This work soon drew a biting *Response of a Son to his Father*, written by an aggrieved *procureur*, which alleged that barristers were mere mercenaries, a quality which placed them far below the magistrates.[18] This work was so pointed that many barristers concluded (it seems, inaccurately) that Cocquart's original work had been nothing but a *persiflage*, written by an enemy of the Order to elicit the cutting response.[19]

The second controversy involved the Académie Française. Ever since its founding, the Académie had traditionally invited one or two distinguished legal orators to take their place among the immortals, and in 1733, it proposed to bestow this honor on the eloquent and aristocratic Alexis-François Le Normand. Yet admission to the Académie required that candidates pay ceremonial visits to their future colleagues to plead for endorsements. Some members of the Order (possibly aiming to punish Le Normand for his excessive moderation in 1730–31) complained that such "begging" was below the dignity of the legal profession, and under this pressure, Le Normand declined the honor. His gesture set off another flurry of pamphleteering in which several writers attacked the Order's hubris.[20]

The final controversy proved the most serious, for it involved both Jansenism and the *parlement*. In early 1735, the aged bishop of St. Papoul suddenly and dramatically retracted both his submission to the bull *Unigenitus* and his condemnation of the *consultation des cinquante*. According to Le Paige, a number of barristers felt that the Order itself should salute the bishop for his courage. Prévost in particular supported the idea, shouting "we must, we must, and right away" in one meeting with his hesitant colleagues. At his insistence, a letter was composed and printed, along with an introduction which compared the Order favorably to the episcopacy and praised its earlier actions in favor of the church.[21] Le Paige commented that the boastful and intemperate text scandalized most barristers, who feared it might lead to another "affair." The *parlement*, however, forestalled any interference from the ministry by suppressing the letter itself. It also defused any possible complaints from the Order by first consulting with several respected senior barristers. Prévost and the Le Roy clan sulked: "They turned their backs; they said . . . the Order was not what it had been in 1731, it had lost its touching religious convictions."[22]

In May 1735, the growing tension on the fault-line between barristers and magistrates finally produced an earthquake. It began as a simple dispute over *préséance*, similar to those in which the barristers had earlier defended their social status: When one of the king's *avocats généraux* (roughly, "solicitors general") argued a case against a barrister, should the court recognize his status as a magistrate by letting him stand inside the magistrates' enclosure, separated from the rest of the courtroom by a heavy bar? A quarrel on this point between several young magistrates and the Jansenist barrister Georges-Claude Le Roy led to a boycott of the chamber in question (the fifth *chambre des enquêtes*) by the Order.[23] The quarrel dragged on into early July, delighting the Marquis d'Argenson, who wrote to Fleury that the "two magistracies" were devouring each other. D'Argenson, who throughout his career saw the *parlement* as a dangerous source of unbridled English-style democracy, even compared the magistrates and barristers to moderate and radical Tories.[24] Le Normand tried to resolve the dispute over a cozy dinner with the *parlement*'s *premier président*, in which he accepted a compromise on the question of *préséance*, but he only made matters worse. The young magistrates crowed that they had forced the Order into submission, while the young barristers jeered Le Normand as a "traitor." Soon afterwards, between four and five hundred robed barristers marched to the residence of the *premier président* to declare themselves "dishonored," and a strike against the *parlement* began.[25]

Once again, the courts of Paris ground to a standstill, but this time the Order was in poor shape to carry out a protracted work stoppage. The controversy over the letter to the bishop of St. Papoul had already exacerbated the divisions, dating back to 1731, between Prévost's "zealots" and Le Normand's "moderates." Moreover, in the spring of 1735, the divisions had grown deeper still thanks to the still-festering issue of François de Maraimberg. Ever since 1731, the Order had failed to issue a new *Tableau*, so as to avoid the vexing question of Maraimberg's disbarment. Yet without a new *Tableau*, no new barristers could begin to practice, and over three hundred *stagiaires* were now pressing the Order to resolve the stalemate. *Bâtonnier* Louis Froland, a rich Norman known for his ostentatious dress, attempted to prepare a new list, but the Jansenists, fearing that he was planning to sacrifice Maraimberg, prevented him from doing so. Acrimonious accusations flew from all sides, and in the end, no *Tableau* came out until 1736, when the Order finally acquiesced in Maraimberg's disbarment. In his valedictory speech to the Order in April, Froland warned despairingly that without "unity" the barristers would "succumb to their plentiful enemies."[26]

Ultimately, the strike did indeed prove a great blow to the *organisation de combat*. Despite repeated efforts at mediation by the *premier président*, the so-called zealots, led by Prévost, remained determined to satisfy their honor.[27] Early on, a majority of the Order decided to return to work nonetheless, but they changed their minds when the young magistrates issued an intemperate internal ruling (*arrêté*) mocking the Order for its rapid "submission."[28] It took several more weeks for the so-called moderates to grow so frustrated that they became willing to swallow a portion of "dishonor," if by doing so they could end the affair and embarrass Prévost. Jean-Louis Julien de Prunay, the sober and responsible negotiator of 1731, particularly resented the way that Prévost and the Le Roy clan had dominated the Order throughout the decade, dragging it into one debilitating and expensive conflict after another.[29] In late July, he and his friend Nicolas-Robert Huart convinced twenty colleagues (including the Jansenist but conciliatory Aubry) to return to work without waiting for a decision by a general assembly. The group, with a median thirty-one years's membership in the Order, represented the well-established, middle-aged bar, now belatedly rebelling against Prévost and his youthful coterie.[30] Following this break in the ranks, fifty other men, including Barbier (eager to revenge himself on Prévost's "cabal") hastened to return to the courts as well. This desertion effectively broke the strike, for seventy barristers sufficed to take care of the *parlement*'s daily business.[31] Prévost and his allies initially refused to give in, but as the magistrate Delisle recorded, by the end of July even his zealous followers had begun to mock him, "for his heatedness, his great exclamations, his rages and his useless speeches against the *parlement*."[32] Finally, in August, he too returned to practice.

The strike's ridiculous origins and embarrassing conclusion combined to make the Order an irresistible target of satire, a "public laughingstock," as Le Paige and Barbier both put it. A number of comic pamphlets on the subject quickly appeared, and were distributed "under the cloak" by a Palais de Justice bookseller, attracting considerable attention.[33] These works, at least one of which was composed by *procureurs'* clerks, ridiculed the barristers not only for the strike, but for the very idea of claiming to enjoy a special "independence" and a special right to defend the public. A mock salute from the Pont-Neuf's satirical "Regiment of the Skullcap" saluted "these rare men who have dared struggle against the sovereign himself, and wished to deal with him as equals." The author claimed, in an echo of d'Argenson, that the barristers had established, "in the most monarchical State of Europe, a small republic composed of men who, under the pretext of exercising a free profession, pretended to depend on no authority and who in fact recognized none." A fake "letter of pardon" to the barristers (strikingly signed by "the public" in place of the king), purported to forgive them for the crime of overweening pride and took yet another jibe at "this poorly understood liberty which resides only in the imagination."[34] Popular songs bid farewell to Le Roy and "Prévost the Great" and warned that without barristers to bore people to sleep, the price of opium would surely rise. A placard nailed to the door of the barristers' library read: "Dispersit superbos."[35]

The strike of 1735 thus marked a turning point for the barristers of Paris. It damaged the unity that was a necessary precondition for collective action and showed that the Order could not always count on the support of the "public" it had taken such care to cultivate. For these reasons, the events somewhat curtailed the prestige and political power that the barristers had accumulated since 1727, and brought an end to dramatic actions such as the strike of 1731. They also brought an end to the dominance of the extraordinary—and extraordinarily eccentric—Claude-Joseph Prévost, a man whose drive and personal force might have placed him alongside Mirabeau had he not been born seventy-five years too early. In 1735, having lost the confidence of his colleagues, the sixty-three year old "bear" retired into a decent obscurity, from which he would write tomes on criminal law and charity and a bizarre thousand-page defense of the *consultation des cinquante* of 1728 which he never completed. Although duly elected *bâtonnier*, he never entered office.[36] His precocious theoretical innovations would only bear fruit in the hands of his protégé Louis-Adrien Le Paige, that great *éminence grise* of the end of the old Regime. He died in 1753.

The events of 1735 did not, however, bring an end to the barristers' efforts on behalf of Jansenist-*parlementaire* constitutionalism. In Le Paige's heyday, the Order remained an *organisation de combat*. It simply functioned, so to speak, in a different key. It no longer expressed itself through collective action, but it still remained a tightly run, well-protected refuge from which Le Paige and others could produce pamphlets and *mémoires*, and formulate *parlementaire* strategy with impunity. The Jansenist leaders maintained their draconian rule, but less to preserve the unity needed for strikes than to prevent barristers from using their talents and privileges in the service of the wrong patrons. The Order's new posture meant a loss of visibility, but this loss had the advantage of diverting criticism from the Order, and suited Le Paige's own predilection (shared by Maultrot and Mey) for working quietly behind the scenes while leaving to the magistrates the honor and burden of speaking for the "nation." The days of self-styled "Jeremiahs" declaiming from the hillsides were over.

The Long March of the Jansenists

The disastrous 1735 *querelle de préséance* certainly did nothing to staunch the flow of *mémoires judiciaires* in which members of the bar provided a caustic, running commentary on the ill fortunes of the Jansenist faithful. Over the next twenty years (including the lull in domestic strife due to the War of the Austrian Succession), at least forty-seven "political" *mémoires* appeared, several running into hundreds of pages.[37] It is true that the authors of these works attempted few conceptual innovations, preferring to remain within the intellectual framework erected by Aubry and his colleagues in the 1720's. They took care to avoid any repetitions of the dangerous "affair" of 1731. Perhaps for these reasons their efforts have received little attention from historians. Nonetheless, they were indispensable to the Jansenists, particularly during the period 1733–49, when the *parlement* itself refrained from a directly confrontational stance. Indeed it was the Order which—in the absence of other legal centers of opposition such as a national press or representative bodies—served as a principal link between the constitutional radicalism of the 1730's and that of the 1750's. Certainly Cardinal Fleury's fear of the barristers did not abate during this period. He wrote to the *procureur général* in 1739, for instance, that their conduct had "dangerous consequences for the state."[38] When the magistrates did begin to assert themselves once more, they built upon the Order's achievements, and depended heavily upon its Jansenist leaders.

In general, the publication of Jansenist *mémoires* followed the pattern established in 1727–30. The driving force behind them remained a small group of Jansenist barristers, descended from the "hard core" of 1727, and now centered around Prévost's protégé Le Paige.[39] It held regular meetings in barristers' homes to discuss the *mémoires*, and the atmosphere was heated: the participants took for granted the existence of a plot by the Jesuits to subjugate the king to the "triumphant chariot of religion."[40] Whether through intimidation or inspiration, the group attracted considerable support within the Order. In the single case of a priest suspended by the bishop of Cambrai in 1740–41, 126 barristers (out of 699 then listed on the *Tableau*—and perhaps 350 in active practice) affixed their signatures to at least one *mémoire*.[41]

The character of this *parti janséniste* within the Order changed as Le Paige's influence grew. A member of a family that had given Paris generations of successful barristers, *procureurs*, and priests, Le Paige—who entered the bar in 1733 but soon abandoned active practice—came naturally to the leadership which the outsider Claude-Joseph Prévost had struggled to achieve.[42] He had all his mentor's boundless energy, but whereas the elder man tended to expend his forces in useless quarrelling and quixotic adventures, the cool and methodical Le Paige was capable of awesome concentration. Convinced that the government's anti-Jansenist campaign marked a repetition of Biblical persecutions (a conviction rooted in "figurist" exegesis), he strove to bear witness to the new travails of the faithful by collecting as much information about it as possible. He assembled notes, pamphlets, correspondence, and engravings and bound them into hundreds of folio and quarto volumes. Despite his participation in the often gruesome, sadomasochistic "*séances*" of the convulsionaries, Le Paige instinctively followed a path of conciliation in his political dealings, and remained on good terms with members of the ministry. His stature in the bar was such that successive *bâtonniers* deferred to him on the wording of the Order's official statements.[43] His most important collaborator was the barrister Gabriel-Nicolas Maultrot, son of a wealthy notary, who, according to one biographer, wrote "a countless multitude of *mémoires*" for priests of the second order. Both men worked so tirelessly that they went largely blind by late middle age.[44]

As in 1727–30, the *mémoires judiciaires* produced by Le Paige and his colleagues functioned as a sort of opposition journalism. They did not come out at regular intervals, but clustered around particularly dramatic episodes such as the attempt to reintroduce the seventeenth-century "formulary" in the diocese of Montpellier, or the refusal of sacraments to Jansenists which began in Paris in the late 1740's. At times, the pace of composition was frenetic. In the Cambrai case, eighteen separate *mémoires* appeared in the space of little more than a year, totalling well over two hundred pages.[45] At a revealing moment in 1756, Guy-Charles Aubry wrote to Le Paige as he might to a strict taskmaster, begging for more time to finish a *mémoire* on the refusal of the sacraments: "it has been physically impossible for me to go faster."[46] In nearly every case, the barristers took as their pretext for intervention an *appel comme d'abus* filed by persecuted Jansenist clerics. Their efforts focused on the "abuses" of a few dangerous prelates, particularly Languet, archbishop of Sens. The barristers thus provided much less comprehensive coverage of Jansenist affairs than the *Nouvelles ecclésiastiques*, but whereas the *Nouvelles* depended on a precarious clandestine network of editors, printers, and *colporteurs*, constantly in danger of arrest, the *mémoires* were legal and circulated openly.[47]

It is difficult to judge the effect produced by the *mémoires*. Certainly, Jansenist clerics greeted them as rapturously as they had Aubry's earlier efforts. One of the few surviving Jansenist bishops wrote to the barrister Pierre Soyer that the Order's collected *mémoires* had provided the most precious possible aid to his cause.[48] The *Nouvelles ecclésiastiques* continued to trumpet each *mémoire* as it appeared, paraphrasing them at length and sometimes reprinting them in their entirety. Another Jansenist author went so far as to dedicate his treatise on the nature of grace to the barristers, telling them that God "has put the Church of Jesus Christ itself among your clients."[49]

The *mémoires* had sufficient effect that considerable efforts were made to suppress and refute them. A 1739 attack on Bishop Languet drew a flurry of responses from him and other members of the episcopacy. The *mémoires* in the 1741 Cambrai affair drew condemnations from the bishop, the Council of Mons (like Cambrai, in the Austrian Netherlands), and the Vatican, which placed it on the Index.[50] In 1742, the king's council suppressed a series of *mémoires* against the bishop of Montpellier for their "spirit of revolt," and the same fate awaited four more efforts produced during the 1749 crisis over the refusal of the sacraments.[51] These acts by the council did not, however, lead to protracted "affairs," for they imposed no penalties on the authors, and made no charges of heresy. The tacit rules of 1727–29 had come back into force. For their part, the barristers again restricted their (highly visible) *mémoires* to ecclesiastical affairs, and left constitutional speculation to illegal pamphlets.

As in the earlier periods, the very idea of barristers using a legal means of publicity to promote their Jansenist agenda raised considerable controversy. The 1739 dispute with Languet makes a good case in point. It began when the zealous bishop promulgated a catechism that ignited Jansenist outrage (it offended chiefly by its "lax" teachings on usury and marriage, and even its approval of abortion early in pregnancy to save the life of the mother—a practice the Jansenists abhorred). A catechism would not seem an obvious subject for legal commentary, but twenty-five members of the Order stretched Jérôme Besoigne's maxim "where the magistrate can decide, the barrister can consult" to the limit.[52] In the second of two *mémoires* on the controversy, Le Paige argued that since catechisms influenced the "spirit of the People," they were a legitimate concern of the public authorities and therefore susceptible to *appels comme d'abus*. This reasoning was tendentious enough to revive the debate on the profession begun in 1728. Several anonymous pamphlets raised the familiar theme of the profession's "competence" while stigmatizing the Order as "a party which admires the most infamous convulsions."[53] The Order's intervention in the 1741 Cambrai affair seemed even more outrageous to critics as the case took place in the Austrian Netherlands, beyond the reach of French law altogether. The bishop of Cambrai accused the barristers of creating "a tribunal which their Sovereign himself does not recognize as belonging to him."[54]

The Crisis of the Mid-Century

The barristers' solitary vigil ended in 1749, when the conflict over the crown's attempt to impose new taxation, and then the outbreak of the "refusal of the sacraments" controversy, set the stage for what Jean Egret has called a "*rentrée en scène*" by the magistrates.[55] In this controversy, orthodox priests, directed by Archbishop Vintimille's aggressive successor Christophe de Beaumont, denied the last rites to alleged Jansenists. The magistrates, in turn, ordered the priests to perform the rites, and arrested them if they refused. The barristers helped justify the *parlement*'s intervention in a string of *mémoires judiciaires*, but the magistrates now occupied the spotlight.[56] In subsequent years, as the *parlement* defied royal attempts to restrain its intervention in church affairs, the religious crisis grew into a full-fledged constitutional one and the barristers found *mémoires judiciaires* eclipsed by more direct forms of political writing. The primary exception came in the spectacular 1761 trial of the Jesuits before the *parlement*, in which Le Paige and his allies once again used briefs to marshal evidence against their archenemies and, in the words of the magistrate Robert de St. Vincent, to "fix public opinion" on the subject.[57]

In general, however, the political reinvigoration of the *parlement* led the Order's *parti janséniste* to adopt new strategies in addition to *mémoires*. Its members produced masses of pamphlets and books developing the *parlement*'s constitutional theories. They helped coordinate and direct the *parlements'* strategies, and collaborated on the most important remonstrances. They exploited their positions in Parisian institutions and great noble households to help the Jansenist cause. Finally, they ensured the Order's crucial cooperation in the judicial strikes that dotted the decade.

Of these activities, pamphleteering was by far the most important. Even a casual look at the ideological debates of the 1750's and 1760's reveals the barristers' tremendous overrepresentation in the authorship of polemical writings. Of sixty-four key works cited by Carroll Joynes in his thesis on "opposition theory in the *parlement* of Paris," fully forty-three came from the pens of Parisian barristers, particularly the prolific Jansenist trio of Le Paige, Maultrot, and Claude Mey.[58] Le Paige's *Lettres historiques sur le parlement de France*, which attempted at great length to demonstrate a continuity between the earliest assemblies of the Frankish nation, which had supposedly elected the king, and the eighteenth-century *parlements*, was particularly important. In it, Le Paige argued that the *parlements* in fact composed different branches (or *classes*) of a single, national assembly, and his work (backed by research in the archives first explored by Prévost) provided the principal theoretical background for the high court's remonstrances for many years.[59] Dale Van Kley writes of Le Paige, Mey, and Maultrot that "it was they who, to a much larger extent than the magistrates, laid the legal foundations upon which the parlement's positions on the religious and ecclesiastical controversies of this period were erected."[60] These barristers in fact helped the *parlement* produce its remonstrances, sometimes composing parts of the texts.[61]

These men's commitment to polemical writing was not exceptional for the Paris bar, however. Many other barristers tried their hand at composing pamphlets, notably Edme-François Darigrand and Olivier Pinault. As soon as a young barrister demonstrated any polemical skills at all, the *parlement* sought to recruit his services. Jacob-Nicolas Moreau, who later abandoned the *parlementaire* cause, recalled that after he published a short pro-Jansenist pamphlet, "many of the magistrates at the head of the [Jansenist] party sounded me out about writing for them, since they were then distributing brochures with unparalleled prodigality."[62] Clearly, the magistrates could not do without the bar's polemical skills and legal expertise.

When the crown finally gave up on its attempts to silence the growing opposition, and joined the ideological battle, it relied on barristers almost as heavily as the *parlement* did. Its decision to appeal to public opinion in the first place came on the advice of Moreau, who remained on the *Tableau* until 1764.[63] Moreau also wrote the royalist *Lettre du Chevalier de *** à Monsieur ***, Conseiller au Parlement, ou Réflexions sur l'arrest du Parlement du 18 Mars 1755*, which sold ten thousand copies (an immense figure for the time) and was reprinted in the French-language Dutch newspapers. According to Le Paige, this work did the most damage to the *parlementaire* cause of any single royalist pamphlet.[64] The barrister Daniel Bargeton wrote propaganda for Controller General Machault during the controversy over new taxation, while Louis Coquereau defended the bull *Unigenitus*. Later in the century, the barristers

Blondel, Gin, Bouquet, and Linguet all became prolific authors of anti-*parlementaire* propaganda. After throwing the pro-*parlementaire* Darigrand into the Bastille, the royal authorities later tried to hire him for themselves.[65]

The barristers' position as the intermediaries of choice between the Palais de Justice and the larger reading "public" comes across best in a story recounted by the magistrate Pierre-Augustin Robert de St. Vincent. During 1753, a committee of magistrates charged with preparing a series of important remonstrances asked the barrister Claude Mey secretly to write the text for them an—indication, in itself, of his importance in their councils. Mey, however, refused: "He told us that the *parlements* had in these matters a tact, a unique diction, and a choice of expressions appropriate for the tone the *parlement* should take vis-à-vis the King. It would be overly bold of him to wish to put himself in the place of those who should do the work."[66] In this comment, Mey implied that if the magistrates had the proper "tone" for addressing the king, he himself—a barrister—had the right one for speaking to the public.

Recent studies of Le Paige, Maultrot, and Mey have tried to show the importance of their works not only to the crises of the mid-century, but to the ideological origins of the French Revolution as well. It has been suggested, intriguingly, that if Jansenist-*parlementaire* works have attracted little interest in this area compared to those of the Enlightenment, the reason lies not only in their relatively parochial subject matter, but in the selective memory of the men of 1789. The leaders of the revolutionary assemblies had no desire to acknowledge the importance of austere, pious Jansenists in the unraveling of the Old Regime. For them, the only possible ancestors of their own revolutionary program lay among the *philosophes* whom they rushed to inter in the Pantheon. Yet the ideas of national sovereignty which proved crucial to the Revolution, it is argued, first reached a wide-scale audience not in the works of Rousseau, but in tracts such as the *Lettres historiques*.[67]

While this is not the place to undertake a full-scale evaluation of these hypotheses, a consideration of works such as the *Lettres historiques* within the broader context of eighteenth-century legal practice does suggest a degree of caution. As the previous chapter argued, after 1713 barristers produced books and pamphlets in order to have an immediate effect on those legal cases that stood at the heart of the ongoing religious conflict. Although they made innovative use of the ideological tools at hand, challenging the theoretical foundations of the regime mattered less than evoking an immediate reaction in the "public." Indeed, as the story of Maraimberg's 1730 *mémoire* reveals, barristers could severely misjudge the reaction their works would elicit, and find themselves accused of a "republicanism" they actually found repellent. Because Jansenist theorists like Le Paige purposefully operated in a zone of legal and linguistic ambiguity where phrases such as "laws are contracts" could have multiple meanings, varying interpretations of their writings were inevitable—even desirable, to an extent. A properly ambiguous text might raise the specter of rebellion (helping to frighten the ministry into compromise) while still allowing the barristers to argue that they had meant to express nothing but the purest orthodox sentiments.

For these reasons, it is important not to put undue stress on apparently "radical" passages in these polemical works. It is also important to remember that these members of the legal elite enjoyed annuities from princely houses, were treated as equals by the highest magistrates (remember the letter from Durey de Meinières to Le Paige, cited in Chapter 1), and generally occupied enviable and privileged positions in society. Like the *philosophes* of Robert Darnton's "High Enlightenment," these men had few material incentives to wish for a fundamental upheaval in the sphere of French government. Calls for national sovereignty could serve more as a bluff or a threat than as a simple reflection of their political convictions.

Take the *Lettres historiques* as an example. As Dale Van Kley has written, the work had a very clear, immediate purpose, namely to justify the *parlement*'s conduct in the refusal of sacraments controversy 1751–53.[68] Above all, Le Paige hoped, through his discovery of the *parlement*'s full "rights," to defend its defiance of royal orders, and its determination to prosecute anti-Jansenist priests. His arguments about the simultaneous origins of *parlement* and crown (presaged by Prévost in 1716) can of course still be read as a justification for the ultimate sovereignty of the nation. But even then, what did he understand by the concept? A consideration of the book as a whole reveals a tremendous gulf between Le Paige's notion of the "nation" and the one invoked by the National Assembly in 1789. For one thing, Le Paige maintained a discreet silence on many of the most important features of French government.[69] He did not challenge the institution of monarchy itself, or the existence of a privileged nobility. He did not introduce the notion of a "contract" into his discussion of the "nation," and did not raise the notion of individual rights. In his view, the French nation possessed rights as a corporate whole, not as an assembly of citizens. Nor did Le Paige endorse an individual right to resistance except in the most ambiguous and limited way (a subject might passively refuse a king's command, but not raise up arms in revolt).[70]

The most audacious arguments in the *Lettres historiques* came in the book's evocation of a "primitive and essential" French constitution. The phrase carries obvious echoes of the "primitive church" so dear to the Jansenists. Yet Le Paige no more hoped for an actual return to this "primitive" state than Rousseau desired a return to the "state of nature." He explicitly introduced it not as a political ideal, but rather as a starting point for an essentially legal argument. Unlike another author of the period concerned with distinguishing between "true monarchy" and "despotism"—Montesquieu—Le Paige had little interest in considering laws "in general," or the question of which laws best suited different nations.[71] Le Paige did not care which laws might, in the best of all possible worlds, suit the French kingdom. He cared only about which laws France actually possessed—its legal inheritance from its misty beginnings on the Champ de Mars.[72]

In this respect, the *Lettres historiques* bears all the hallmarks, and limitations, of its author's narrow, untheoretical legal training in the University of Paris, and his subsequent career in the law. Indeed the genre it best fits is neither political theory, nor history (it has few formal features in common with most historical works of the period), but rather the *mémoire judiciaire*. Le Paige's purpose was to establish the validity of a legal claim—the claim of the "nation" to certain rights in the legislative process—and he proceeded in precisely the manner he would have used to prove a title to a piece of land. First, in thirty-odd pages, he described the legal relationships between the different parts of the French nation in its "early infancy," at the time of Clovis. Then, at vast and tedious length, he showed how these same relationships remained essentially unchanged, generation after generation, even as words changed and structures evolved, for over a thousand years. At each juncture, the critical fact was continuity, as one title succeeded another, and continuity, not "reason" or "nature," constituted proof of legitimacy: "The authority of the *parlement* . . . is today, Monsieur, precisely what it was at the time of Clovis."[73] It is a classic lawyer's argument.

Le Paige's French "nation" itself was in some ways a concept born out of analogy to legal structures familiar to lawyers. It did not consist of rational individuals possessed of certain inalienable rights; indeed, it did not really consist of individuals at all. It was a collectivity, similar to the corporate bodies that the French law cherished. The *parlement*, moreover, "represented" this nation not in the way that the English parliament represented its electorate, but in the way legal guardians represent their wards (whatever the theological origins of the idea of the "repository of fundamental laws," surely this legal concept had just as much importance to those Jansenists who were also barristers).[74] This legal language was very useful in making the case for a "judicial monarchy" that revolved around the legal system. It sufficed to reassert the rights of a larger national community, for which the judiciary provided the sinews, against the encroachments of the crown. It even had the potential to jostle the foundations of the prevailing Bossuetian orthodoxy, and thereby send tremors into the heart of the regime. But Le Paige did little to advance positively the principles upon which the Third Estate would declare itself the "National Assembly" in 1789. Other, younger barristers, who despised nearly everything Le Paige stood for—including the Order—would do more in this respect.

For all the immediate importance of the *Lettres historiques* and the other polemical works stemming from the Order, Le Paige and his allies also

contributed to the *parlements'* cause through their role as behind-the-
scenes strategists. Dale Van Kley has described these barristers' crucial
role in the crisis of 1753–54 and in the trial of the Jesuits in the early
1760's.[75] In each case, they helped determine the *parlement*'s moves, for-
mulated the magistrates' legal arguments, and served as a nerve center—
particularly for communications with the other *parlements.* In 1753, when
the crown exiled the Parisian magistrates and sought to replace them with
a so-called *chambre royale,* Le Paige single-handedly led the drive to keep
other courts from recognizing the new tribunal's authority.[76] The barristers received no public credit for their contribution, but then, the magistrates could hardly award such credit without tarnishing their own image
as a fount of judicial wisdom. Thus the magistrate Lambert praised Le
Paige as "a person so useful to the public, *although in secret*" (emphasis
mine).[77] The Jansenist magistrates even kept the barristers' role hidden
from their own colleagues. While Claude Mey initially refused to write
the "great remonstrances" of 1753, he nonetheless ended up drafting
several sections of the final text. However, Robert de Saint-Vincent and
his colleague Roland d'Erceville both recalled that when the remonstrances were presented to the *parlement* as a whole, two magistrates
"passed for" the authors of these sections. D'Erceville himself treated
Mey with a degree of envy and resentment.[78]

The barristers also promoted the interests of Jansenists through their
positions in influential institutions and noble households. For instance,
since the beginning of the century Jansenist barristers had made up at
least a fifth of the board of the *Hôpital général,* an ecclesiastical institution that numbered over a thousand personnel and over five thousand
patients.[79] The *hôpital* undoubtedly owed much of its reputation as a
stronghold of Jansenism to board members such as the barristers Philippes
Guillet de Blaru, Henry Duhamel, Nicolas-Claude Visinier and Augustin
Denyau—all members of the Jansenist "hard core" of 1728—who ensured the appointment of Jansenist clerics to its staff. Meanwhile, Jansenist
barristers sat in the councils of the leading princely households: Aubry,
Le Roy, and Chevallier in the house of Orléans; Cochin, Guyot de Chesne,
and Robert in the house of Condé; Duhamel, Gerbier, Pothouin, and Le
Paige in the house of Conti.[80] The princes, who despite their supposed
emasculation by Louis XIV never entirely forgot the lost splendor of their
houses and remained active in court politics, undoubtedly found congenial the services of these men whose work did so much to diminish the
sweep of royal authority.

The position of the barristers in the *Hôpital général* took on new importance in 1749, when Archbishop de Beaumont decided to wrest control of the institution from the Jansenists.[81] The chief opposition he faced
on the board came from Charles Arrault (son of the stern 1717 *bâtonnier*
of the same name), who urged the Jansenist clerics in the *hôpital* to resist
the archbishop's incursions. A showdown occurred in July, when the
Jansenist mother superior fled Paris and Beaumont imposed his own can-

didate, Mme. de Moysan (the widow of a financier), over the board's objections. In response, Arrault convinced nineteen out of twenty-two administrators, including four other barristers, to resign.[82] Arrault and Le Paige also used the tight networks among barristers and *procureurs* to dig up damaging rumors about Mme. de Moysan, and put their formidable propaganda machine into action to discredit her. The crown scrambled to select a new board, including two non-Jansenist barristers: Etienne-Adrien Dains and Pierre Le Merre (who was already on retainer to the archdiocese).[83] But the Order threatened disbarment if they accepted the offer, and they bowed to the pressure.[84] The inclusion of barristers on the board remained a sore issue between the *parlement* and the crown for years.[85]

The barristers' influence in the princely houses depended entirely on the political goals of the prince. In 1756, as a result of complicated court maneuvers involving the king's secret diplomacy, the Prince de Conti moved closer to the *parlementaire* opposition, and chose Le Paige as his virtual chief of staff. In March 1756, he appointed the barrister *bailli* of the Temple, the gloomy fortress in northern Paris where Louis XVI would spend his last days, which belonged to his domain. The Temple, like the Orléans family's Palais Royal, fell largely outside the jurisdiction of the Parisian police: "Here one lived under one's own laws. . . . It was like being in a foreign country yet in the heart of one's own land," wrote one contemporary. Le Paige immediately transformed it into a refuge for Jansenists and a home for illicit printing presses. When the police did stage an unexpected visit in 1757, they found a fully equipped printing shop with several Jansenist pamphlets in various stages of production.[86] Le Paige also developed an extraordinarily close relationship with Conti, sending him long, intimately phrased letters advising him on political strategy. Robert de St. Vincent wrote about Le Paige that as early as 1757, "everything led to him when one wanted to deal with the Prince."[87]

Conti's sponsorship afforded the barristers not only increased range for their activities, but also increased protection in a political atmosphere that was turning progressively more polarized and dangerous. In 1757, after Damiens attempted to murder Louis XV, the barrister Jean-Baptiste Le Gouvé, a frequent signatory of Jansenist *mémoires*, was accused of remarking at a dinner that France "needed a blood-letting." It took Conti's direct intervention to keep Le Gouvé out of prison. The prince also kept Le Paige out of trouble, both after the police raid in 1757, and several years later, when a minister threatened legal action against the barrister for printing a book without a royal *privilège*.[88] This protection, when added to the Order's ability to defend its members by going on strike, in fact made barristers almost immune to arrest. Between the short exile of 1731 and Maupeou's coup of 1771, only one barrister felt the hand of the law, and he was the exception who proves the rule. Edme-François Darigrand, a man who ran afoul of his colleagues numerous times, raised the specter of bloody civil war in the preface to a lengthy attack on financiers and the royal administration (the book also repeated Le Paige's thesis about the "union des classes").[89] Le Paige himself never went to such extremes, and in the aftermath of Damiens's failed assassination attempt, the ministry found itself wholly unable to tolerate such threats. After tracking Darigrand down through the Jansenist distribution channels of his book, the police arrested him and sent him briefly to the Bastille.[90]

The final weapon used by barristers in the 1750's was also the most direct: the strike. At three points in the 1750's the magistrates staged lengthy work stoppages. Each time, barristers, and *procureurs* as well, closed their offices in sympathy (some *procureurs* had Jansenist sympathies, but in general the group seems to have been motivated more by corporate solidarity with the *parlement*).[91] As in 1720 and 1732, these auxiliary strikes, along with parallel actions in the Paris Châtelet and the provincial courts, proved crucial to the survival of the *parlement*. The royalist barrister Gin later wrote that if the barristers had not supported the magistrates, "the *parlement* would have had to ask the offended Monarch for mercy." In 1770, one magistrate allegedly claimed that the magistrates could go on strike "in all safety, because it was quite certain that the barristers would hold fast."[92] In 1753–54, Barbier commented that his colleagues' actions "were the hope of the parlement."[93]

These actions also posed problems for the Order, however. Not only were they frequent, but in contrast to the 1720 and 1732 periods of inactivity, they now lasted months or even (in 1753–54) more than a year. During these periods, barristers who had little outside income suffered badly.[94] Barbier alleged in 1756 that the majority faced disaster because of the repeated interruption of their work, and were only stopped from resuming practice by fear of disbarment. Jacob-Nicolas Moreau wrote that the stress hastened his father's death, citing the elder man's "grief over the exile of the *parlement*, whose end no one could then foresee. . . . He thought my future lost, for he had never imagined another for me."[95] Nonetheless, as in Prévost's day the ranks of the barristers held.

Repression and Dissent

The 1735 humiliation of the Order did not affect the draconian system of discipline implemented by Claude-Joseph Prévost. Indeed, the Order's new, less theatrical political incarnation demanded just as strict a degree of conformity from its members. Without this conformity, work stoppages in support of the *parlement* would have had no chance of succeeding. Without it, the Jansenists could not have controlled barristers serving on the boards of institutions such as the *Hôpital général*. Worst of all, without it even more non-Jansenist barristers might have begun putting their services at the disposal of the crown, rather than the *parlement*. In eighteenth-century France, very few men combined a flair for polemical writing with the sort of in-depth legal expertise needed to unravel the complicated issues over which "magisterial" and "ministerial" camps fought. It made sense for the Jansenist leaders of the Order to keep close watch over their own pool of talent. After 1735, therefore, the Order's leadership sought less to end the blatant intimidation practiced by Prévost and his allies than to replace it with more subtle tactics. They also sought to repair relations with the magistrates, lest more squabbling inadvertently harm the *parlement*'s cause.

Thanks to the rise of Le Paige and others who enjoyed close personal relations with magistrates, repairing relations proved the easier of these tasks, and after 1735, *querelles de préséance* ceased almost entirely (a somewhat different state of affairs prevailed, however, in the provinces).[96] In 1762, it is true, a judge in the Châtelet harshly admonished a barrister in open court, provoking the barristers who practiced there, led by the touchy and self-aggrandizing Nicolas-Daniel Phelippes de la Marnières, to go on strike. The affair dragged on for three and a half weeks, but rather than encouraging his colleagues, *bâtonnier* Jacques Merlet (a Jansenist) remained aloof, stayed in touch with the *premier président* of the *parlement*, and arranged a quiet settlement.[97]

The *parlement* did not fail to take notice of the barristers' new willingness to cooperate, and in return acted to protect the Order's "independence." In 1739, for instance, Cardinal Fleury once again challenged the Order's jurisdiction after a victim of disbarment appealed to him directly for reinstatement. In a bilious letter to the *procureur général*, which showed the extent to which the Order continued to trouble him, Fleury wrote:

> Does the *bâtonnier* of the barristers claim to be the Sovereign judge, beyond all appeal, of the reputation of his colleagues, providing no other reasons for his judgments than his own whim. . . ? I confess to you, Monsieur, that I am tremendously scandalized by such conduct. . . .[98]

The *procureur général*, however, vigorously defended the Order's structure, stressing its prudence and "delicacy" and assuring the cardinal that the barristers posed no threat to the state. Faced with this firm riposte, Fleury took no further action.[99]

The *gens du roi* and the *parlement* defended the Order with particular enthusiasm during the 1750's. In 1753 and again in 1756–57, royalist writers sought to undermine the Order by publishing *persiflages*: pamphlets allegedly written by barristers which in fact propounded anti-Jansenist, anti-*parlementaire* theses.[100] In each case, the *parlement* immediately suppressed the offending text, praised the barristers effusively, and gave the *bâtonnier* a forum to vent the Order's collective spleen in speeches duly included in the printed copies of the *parlement*'s rulings.[101] In 1757, Le Paige and Maultrot wrote the speech delivered by *bâtonnier* Etienne Pons, and used the chance to put the Order as a body on record supporting the tenets of *parlementaire* constitutionalism (which they themselves, of course, had largely devised!). By contrast, the less combat-

ive *parlement* of 1730 had refused to condemn a similar pamphlet, and
even prevented the Order from issuing its own public denunciation.[102]

The peace with the *parlement*, however, did not help the leadership
of the Order control two perennial problems: numbers, and the presence
of "unsuitable" members who allegedly tarnished the prestige of the profession. Between 1735 and 1750, the Order expanded at an unprecedented pace, largely because of two factors beyond its control. In 1738,
a dispute between Chancellor d'Aguesseau and the barristers in the king's
council over a new code of procedure led all 170 members of this separate company to lose their positions.[103] After the dust settled, at least 66
of them, including Le Paige's father, found refuge in the Order. The
period also saw a new influx of *procureurs'* clerks who had found that
thanks to a loophole in the regulations, spending two years in the bar
gave them the right to buy a venal office without completing the usual
ten-year apprenticeship.[104] The Order's numbers had already crept back
up from 500 after the 1729 purge to 619 in 1735. Now they ballooned
to 684 in 1738–39, and 712 in 1744, a record for any single bar association under the *ancien régime*. New entries into the bar, which had averaged only 19 per year between 1710 and 1715, jumped to 28 per year
between 1740 and 1745. Barbier, reflecting the Order's traditional anxieties about social status, grumbled about the presence of "men without
wealth and employ, who, to maintain their station, are obliged to do
many things unworthy of the profession."[105] It would also seem reasonable that the crowding increased competition for clients.

The problem of numbers, coming on top of the need to preserve
unanimity during strikes and the threat of internal dissent, made a new
"purification" inevitable. In 1748, the leadership used large-scale disbarments to prune the numbers to 638.[106] In 1751, it sought the *parlement's* sanction to institute even more thorough reforms, and the magistrates concurred. In a new *règlement* they extended the two-year *stage*
to four, and also authorized the *bâtonnier* and his deputies to investigate
prospective barristers before issuing certificates of approval.[107] As in
1727, the ruling gave the signal for an extended purge, which forced
more than a hundred men to leave the bar.[108]

While these actions were exceptionally harsh, the Order acted as an
increasingly strict censor throughout this period. The unwritten code of
conduct it had enforced since the beginning of the century became
increasingly severe, and men who had acquired even the faintest taint of
suspicion received swift "justice." Fleury, in 1739, sarcastically referred to
"that fine and severe morality which the barristers trumpet in their writings but belie by their actions."[109] The Order disbarred Jacques Charpentier for suing to recover promised honoraria—an action deemed to
derogate from the nobility of the profession. It charged the struggling
Louis Babille with "normally keeping a young woman with him." Charles-
François-Jean Bidault ran afoul of the Order for a conflict of interest (taking on a case against former clients), while Henri Hulot was accused of

moonlighting as a tutor in the law faculty. According to Malesherbes, the Order also readily expelled anyone who incurred the displeasure of powerful magistrates.[110]

As it had since the seventeenth century, the Order also kept close watch over barristers' courtroom behavior. Thus speeches and *mémoires judiciaires* which used an "indecent" style, or slandered other barristers, constituted grounds for expulsion.[111] In 1740, the Order disbarred a certain Chesnel de la Charbonnelais because of a *mémoire* deemed insulting to the *premier président* of the *cour des aides.* In 1751, Jean-Baptiste-François Grimont met the same fate after *Avocat général* d'Ormesson accused him of writing a *mémoire* slandering an *intendant des finances.*[112] *Avocat général* Gilbert de Voisins insisted on the first of these occasions that the barristers observe strict discretion: "May they know the limits which must distinguish the legitimate defense they owe their clients . . . from the Excesses into which one can fall under this pretext, in alleging facts which are extraneous, useless, insulting and which attack people's honor and reputation."[113]

In addition to miscreants who violated its standards of morality or decorum, the Order also punished men whose infractions were of a more questionable—or more political—nature. It struck Charles-Nicolas Daunard off the *Tableau* for having attempted to practice during the 1731 strike. In 1739, a certain Jamoays lost his place for allegedly holding an "incompatible" post—namely, a minor judgeship attached to the Sorbonne—despite the fact that many eminent barristers held similar positions. Jamoays claimed that the Order really wanted to punish him for holding anti-Jansenist opinions.[114] In 1749, the Order threatened quite openly to disbar Pierre Le Merre and Etienne-Adrien Dains if they accepted Archbishop Beaumont's offer to replace Jansenist barristers on the board of the *Hôpital général.* Thus the Order effectively reserved the "liberty" of the profession to those who conceived of liberty in the correct terms.[115]

The Order's increasing severity was accompanied by the institution of an important new structure: a governing council, called the *députation.* It is uncertain exactly when this body came into being. Once again, Falconnet's quip about the Order's oral tradition, "even more versatile than imperfect," comes to mind. The records of the 1660's make occasional reference to "deputies of the benches," but it does not seem that these men met regularly or exercised any real authority, and Alexis Durot's 1770 description of the Order describes the *députation* of his own day as a recent innovation. It may have had its origins in 1751, when the *parlement*'s new *règlement* gave the power to certify *stagiaires* to "a small number of senior Barristers chosen by the *bâtonnier.*" It certainly existed by 1755, when it voted to disbar Jacques Charpentier and Louis Babille. By 1763, its members were listed in the *Tableau*, and it had become an established part of the scene in the Palais de Justice, the ancestor of the present-day Conseil de l'Ordre.[116]

The *députation* gave the Order a greater degree of corporate structure than it had ever possessed—certainly more than its founders had envisaged in the 1660's. It consisted of two representatives from each of the barristers' twelve "benches" in the Palais de Justice, elected (generally in order of seniority) for two-year terms. According to Durot, it served as a court of first instance in disciplinary matters and had the responsibility, under the *bâtonnier*'s supervision, for preparing the *Tableau*. Individual barristers could still call for a general assembly, but Durot claimed that since the establishment of the *députation*, none had done so. The *députation*, Durot argued, conducted its business in "a much less tumultous manner."[117] Thus the great meetings so vividly described by Barbier and Le Paige became things of the past. Incidentally, the creation of the new council gave the benches themselves much greater importance, and called attention to the imbalance among them (some had as few as 8 members, others over 150).[118]

The increasing rigidity of the Order may have helped maintain conformity, but it also paved the way for increasing criticism. The institution of the *députation* in particular amounted to something that the barristers theoretically rejected—increased corporatism—and thus exposed them to charges of hypocrisy. The end of the general assemblies, meanwhile, signaled a decrease in what one might call "direct democracy" in the Order. For all the intimidation that had so often characterized these meetings, the general assemblies had at least fostered the perception that the Order's destiny lay in the hands of the membership as a whole. The very sight of hundreds of black-robed men assembling in the halls and corridors of the Palais de Justice, deliberating over tactics or indignantly announcing a strike, created a striking sense of transparency. Like the citizens of Rousseau's ideal republic, the barristers could *see* their general will taking shape. By contrast, the *députation* conducted its business out of sight, making charges of cabals and conspiracies—so much a part of eighteenth-century French political culture—all the more plausible. Soon, dissident barristers would be attacking the "secrecy" of the Order as vehemently as the Order itself attacked the "secrecy" of the administration.[119] Yet to the Order's leaders, extremism in the pursuit of "purity" was no vice. It was not only a means of preserving their political effectiveness, but a sign of adherence to the noblest traditions of the world of the law.

The Order made matters worse for itself by treating the emerging specter of "philosophy" as intolerantly as it treated Jesuitism. In 1761, the barrister François-Charles Huerne de la Mothe defended a woman whom the church had excommunicated for becoming an actress in the Comédie Française. In his briefs in the case, he borrowed from the lexicon of the *philosophes*, asserting that his client was struggling against ignorance, superstition and misplaced zeal.[120] His words aroused a fury in the clergy. Yet far from protecting Huerne, the *bâtonnier* himself denounced his works to the *parlement*, which suppressed them, and confirmed Huerne's disbarment, already pronounced by the *députation*. "Our attachment to the true maxims and our zeal for religion, have not permitted us to remain silent or passive on the subject of [this] pernicious book," the *bâtonnier* proclaimed with all the gravity of a royal censor.[121] According to a newsletter, the *Mémoires secrets* of Bachaumont, a similar incident occurred in 1769, involving the barrister Le Blanc, who had defended a monk seeking release from his vows.[122] These attitudes did the Order little good at a time in which the reading public it cherished was coming to look critically upon all examples of "privilege," "secrecy," and "intolerance." The Order's practices had already received plentiful criticism from men who did *not* challenge its fundamental religious and political ideas. How must they have appeared to readers who drew greater inspiration from d'Alembert than from d'Aguesseau?

In the end, the Order's rigidity only succeeded in spurring the dissent it was designed to squelch. Consider the career of the royalist pamphleteer Moreau, originally a barrister from a Jansenist family. While hardly a man of the Enlightenment (he invented the notorious label of *cacouacs* for the *philosophes*), in the 1750's Moreau shared the growing distaste of cultivated Frenchmen for religious excess of all sorts. His poor opinion of his convulsionary colleagues led him to write his notorious pamphlet *Lettre du chevalier*, in which, as he later recalled, "I treated with more or less equal ridicule both the fanaticism which the *parlement* had adopted over Unigenitus, and that of the [anti-Jansenist] theologians." The pamphlet itself urged the French away from religious "chimeras" towards their proper pursuit of "glory and the arts."[123] Inevitably, it drew sharp criticism from Le Paige and the *Nouvelles ecclésiastiques*, and Moreau soon found himself estranged from his colleagues. In response, he devoted himself wholly to producing propaganda for the ministry, ending up historiographer royal.[124]

For the moment, few other barristers dared follow the route Moreau had taken. Nonetheless, there is evidence that some secretly shared his opinions. During the brief 1762 *querelle de préséance* at the Châtelet, certain magistrates proposed setting up their own, separate Order to replace striking barristers. The Jansenist *bâtonnier* Jacques Merlet quickly rejected the idea, and his reasons for doing so are instructive. In a private note, he observed that a separate company of barristers might well attract opponents of the *parlement* prepared to practice during judicial strikes, thereby making the Châtelet "a ready-made *chambre royale*"—a reference to a court created by the ministry to replace the *parlement* during the crisis of 1753–54.[125] Clearly, Merlet believed that a number of his colleagues would support the crown if given the chance.

By the early 1760's, therefore, the Order of Barristers was clearly riven by a number of contradictions. It had taken the lead in encouraging constitutional debate in France, and yet it was repressing debate within its own ranks. It had made itself into a uniquely successful, privileged platform for presenting uncensored ideas to a broad reading public, yet at the time of the greatest intellectual flowering in French history, it was trying to keep that platform in the hands of a narrowly sectarian movement. In works such as the *Lettres historiques*, its leaders had asserted the rights of the "nation," and appealed to a sociologically indistinct "public." Yet in the very same works, they defended a traditional social structure and a form of "representation" (by the *parlement*) that more closely resembled legal guardianship than elective government.

These contradictions were directly related to the transformation the Order had undergone since the beginning of the century. To the extent that the leading barristers became publicists, and addressed themselves to the new, figurative "tribunal of public opinion" rather than to real tribunals, their stake in preserving the existing judicial system had inevitably decreased. To earlier generations of barristers, who envisaged themselves primarily as the sober and self-effacing technicians of the "judicial monarchy," the prestige and prosperity of the bar had depended on a specific institution—the *parlement*—not merely hearing, but deciding all important social and political conflicts (subject only to the rare correction of the monarch). To these men, the political autonomy of the high courts was a matter of the highest importance. For their eighteenth-century successors, however, what mattered most was that a few, emblematic cases came to trial, giving them the chance to present their arguments to a broad reading public. The identity of the judges, and even the final verdict, was no longer of paramount importance. Indeed, in a perverse way a negative verdict could even serve the cause better, by arousing public outrage (in this way, the Jansenist barristers of the eighteenth century foreshadowed the liberal barristers of the early and mid-nineteenth century). In effect, these men were now treating the legal system primarily as a vehicle, not as an end in itself. By doing so, they unmoored the legal profession from its ideological origins.

These developments had potentially unpleasant political consequences for the Order's Jansenist leaders. Barristers such as Moreau, who derived their status and income from their polemical skill, had no intrinsic reason to support the *parlements* over the crown. To them, the Order's strict code of conduct seemed not a necessary guarantor of "purity," but a straitjacket. They might fear royal "despotism"—which in its extreme version threatened to extinguish *all* public debate and put an end to *all* court cases—but they also feared the obscurantist "liberty" defended by their sectarian colleagues. In sum, the end of absolutist politics in the mid-eighteenth century was bringing a day of reckoning not only for the crown, but for this leading force in the opposition as well.

5

The Profession Transformed

When in 1770 the parlement *of Paris was dissolved . . . the leading members of the Bar practicing before the* parlement *. . . shared its fate, relinquished all that had assured their prestige and prosperity, and, rather than appear before judges for whom they had no respect, condemned themselves to silence. In the history of free nations I know of no nobler gesture than this; yet it was made in the eighteenth century, and in the shadow of the court of Louis XV.*

Alexis de Tocqueville, *The Old Regime and the Revolution*

Two dramatic and well-known judgments, close together in time, mark an end of one era in the history of the French legal profession and the start of another. On August 6, 1761, the *parlement* of Paris, following a long campaign masterminded by Louis-Adrien Le Paige, voted to close all colleges, associations, and seminaries of the Jesuit Order in France. Within three years, Louis XV himself reluctantly agreed to the *parlement*'s decision, and the Jansenists' greatest enemies were summarily expelled from French soil. Jansenists continued to suffer some vestiges of persecution, and Le Paige continued to detect Jesuit conspiracies in every shadow. Still, the turmoil caused by the Bull *Unigenitus* had effectively come to an end. By the 1780's, Le Paige was actively cooperating with the *lieutenant général de police* to squelch conflicts over Jansenism, and even drafting *arrêts de conseil* to suppress hostile proclamations by anti-Jansenist bishops.[1]

Meanwhile, on March 9, 1762, the *parlement* of Toulouse passed sentence on Jean Calas, a Protestant wrongfully accused of having murdered his son to prevent him from adopting Catholicism. The judges

*Translation by Stuart Gilbert (New York: Doubleday, 1955), pp. 116–17.

ordered the public executioner to extract a confession by stretching Calas's limbs and forcing him to drink vast quantities of water, then to end his life by binding him to a cartwheel and shattering his bones with iron bars. The sentence was carried out the next day. Within weeks, the case had come to the attention of a horrified Voltaire, who seized upon it as an emblem of the evils of religious intolerance. He immediately began a campaign to have the verdict overturned, aided by barristers from both Toulouse and Paris. In a flurry of pamphlets and *mémoires judiciaires*, he succeeded in turning Jean Calas into the prototypical martyr of the "*infâme*," and transformed the struggle for the man's posthumous reha- bilitation into the greatest *cause célèbre* of the French Enlightenment. Within three years Calas had been vindicated.[2]

The two judgments, and their aftermaths, could not present greater contrasts. The first, as Dale Van Kley has shown in his meticulous study of the Jesuits' expulsion, formed part of the great conflict waged between *parlements* and the leaders of the French Catholic church. In the second, *parlements* and church joined forces as defenders of the faith. The first came after a campaign to influence public opinion in which barristers and magistrates stood together against traditional adversaries in the name of (Gallican) liberty and French law. The second provoked a campaign to influence public opinion in which barristers and men of letters criticized magistrates and laws alike. The first marked the apotheosis of Jansenist barristers and their *organisation de combat*. The second marked the be- ginning of their decline, and the transformation of the French legal pro- fession into a raucous forum open to all manner of legal and political reformers.

Given the strict discipline enforced in the Order of Barristers, this transformation might have dragged, painfully, over many years. The ad- vocates of change, however, found some very unlikely allies in the form of royal ministers, whose campaign to silence the obstreperous *parlements* reached a climax in 1771. While very few barristers managed to shed their suspicion of "arbitrary despotism" altogether, as Jacob-Nicolas Moreau had done, many took advantage of the opportunities presented by Chan- cellor Maupeou's 1771 "coup" against the high courts to free themselves from the less arbitrary despotism of their Jansenist colleagues.

"Joining Philosophy to Jurisprudence"

Needless to say, Louis-Adrien Le Paige and his Jansenist allies in the bar did not return to a life of contemplation after their carefully engineered victory over the Jesuits. Throughout the 1760's they sedulously pursued Quesnel's goal of restricting the church's secular authority. Le Paige's protégé, the barrister François Richer, took the familiar argument to new lengths in his 1766 work *De l'autorité du clergé*, claiming that since men and women did not need to live in society to fulfill their religious duties, religion was a wholly personal concern. The state therefore should retain jurisdiction over all outward manifestations of religion—including church property and the administration of the sacraments.[3] Skirmishes over the continued harassment of Jansenists also continued throughout the decade, and when the crown and *parlements* came to grips over the conduct of the royal governor of Brittany, d'Aiguillon, the Order's *parti janséniste* again advised the increasingly defiant magistrates.[4] To this extent, nothing had changed.

Nonetheless, during the 1760's, it was Voltaire's efforts to exonerate Jean Calas, well-known to students of this period, which became the model for barristers seeking to build careers. Voltaire himself had little respect for the legal profession, but he recognized its importance to his campaign. He wrote to a correspondent that *mémoires judiciaires* "take the place of judicial rulings, and direct those of the judges."[5] In order to combat the Toulouse *parlement*, he engaged the services not only of a local barrister, Théodore Sudre, but also of barristers in the king's council and the Parisian Jean-Baptiste-Jacques Élie de Beaumont. The *philosophe* himself wrote parts of several *mémoires*, notably a melodramatic narrative purporting to come from the hand of Calas's son.[6] The texts he solicited from the barristers (including a *consultation* signed by fifteen of Élie's colleagues) did not raise any novel legal points nor propose reforms in the law: they simply criticized the courts of Toulouse for not following the proper rules. Still, they pleased Voltaire. He credited Élie de Beaumont with convincing the "public" of Calas's innocence, and thanked him for having "joined philosophy to jurisprudence." When a Montpellier court seized copies of several briefs in 1763, the *philosophe*'s concern for the independence of the legal profession matched that of any jurist: "if barristers lose their right to make arguments then there will be no law or justice in France."[7]

The importance of the Calas case for shaping the legal profession can be seen in the careers of three barristers who first rose to fame in the 1760's, and dominated the bar until the end of the *ancien régime*: Élie de Beaumont, Guy-Jean-Baptiste Target, and Pierre-Jean-Baptiste Gerbier. Like their predecessors at the pinnacle of the legal profession, Le Normand and Cochin, they each accumulated large fortunes, moved in exalted social circles, and, in the cases of Gerbier and Élie, capped their careers with entrance into the nobility. Unlike their predecessors, however, all three came to see the appeal of fighting cases that could electrify the "enlightened" reading public throughout Europe. Each one started out as a staunch *parlementaire*, but each felt the temptation to lend their services to the ministerial party at various points; indeed, Gerbier finally succumbed to temptation and ended his days as a publicist for *Contrôleur-général* Calonne. One might say that each felt a tension between two irreconcilable realms: the "public sphere" in which they made their reputations, in which individual authors spoke to a socially indistinct "public"; and the world of the *parlements*, in which magistrates still pursued the explicit goals of preserving a traditional social hierarchy and limiting any sort of "representation" to their unelected selves.[8]

Of the three, Target, the son of a barrister, has attracted the most attention from historians (among other achievements, he helped draft the Declaration of the Rights of Man and the first French constitution). He first gained the spotlight in 1762, at the age of 29 years, as one of the barristers who prosecuted the Jesuits before the *Parlement* of Paris.[9] He continued to appear in Jansenist cases throughout the 1760's, but in 1769 he also took on a typical *cause philosophique*, representing a client who had challenged the right of his father, a *fermier général*, to imprison him through the use of a *lettre de cachet*. Although Target defended the *parlements* vigorously until the very end of the Old Regime, he did not ignore their faults. In a pamphlet series called *Lettres d'un homme à un autre homme*, written during the Maupeou crisis of 1771–74, he admitted that the magistrates too often held their own interests above those of the public, and that venality of offices brought too many "mediocre" men into the magistracy. In 1771, he visibly hesitated before finally deciding to cast his lot with the courts against the ministry.[10]

Élie de Beaumont, son of a minor royal officer in Normandy, was a close friend of Target. A slight, sickly man whose health did not allow him to speak in court, he made his reputation instead as an *avocat consultant*, earning high praise for the elegance of his *mémoires judiciaires*. He had a personal interest in the Calas case because his wife, a novelist and *salonnière*, came from a Protestant family (throughout his career Élie fought for the legitimization of Protestant marriages). At his comfortable château in Normandy, he played the role of Enlightenment squire, setting up Italianate gardens studded with neoclassical sculpture, tinkering with scientific devices, and even sponsoring a "philosophical festival."[11] After his success helping to exonerate Calas, he answered Voltaire's call once again in 1765 in the case of another Protestant accused of murdering his child, Pierre-Paul Sirven. His principal brief for the accused man adopted a thoroughly Voltairean style, denouncing "fanaticism" as a "monster" that roamed France thirsty for victims.[12] Voltaire (despite some private reservations about Élie's skills) praised the barrister on this occasion in terms guaranteed to intoxicate him with visions of European fame: "I will send your *factum* to all the princes of Germany who are not bigots. . . . I wish to be the first trumpet of your glory in Saint Petersburg and Moscow. . . ."[13] Élie remained loyal to the *parlements* between 1771 and 1774. His private papers, however, contain a plan, drafted during these years, for a special "plenary court" to handle the registration of laws. It is a project which the *parlement* itself would have angrily rejected, and which foreshadowed the ministry's plan to emasculate the high courts in 1788.[14]

It was Gerbier, "the eagle of the bar," who enjoyed the greatest prominence in the eighteenth century. Indeed, before the Revolution a veritable cult grew up around this "French Cicero." The *Gazette des tribunaux* hardly exaggerated in its claim that "he enjoyed, while alive, a portion of his immortality." Gerbier was the son of a Jansenist barrister, always carried a pocket edition of Pascal, and was suspected by the police of Jansenist sympathies himself. However, he lived in a distinctly un-Jansenist high style, circulating among the high aristocracy and even inviting the Prince de Conti and the Duchesse de Chartres to his country home. His tall, spare figure commanded immense fees, and spectators flocked to hear his speeches in the Palais de Justice as they would to see a great actor.[15] Like Target, Gerbier shone in the trial of the Jesuits, whom he blamed for hounding his father from a post in the *Parlement* of Rennes. He achieved his apotheosis, however, in 1768, when chosen for the greatest honor available to a barrister—presenting the letters of office of a new chancellor to the *parlement*. Before an audience that included the King of Denmark, he delivered a long-remembered oration, beginning with the grandiose opening lines, "*Montez, montez au capitole!*" that was interrupted over twenty times by applause.[16]

Both through their links to the *philosophes*, and the unprecedented celebrity they enjoyed, Target, Élie, and Gerbier epitomized an increasingly important figure in the world of the law: the barrister as *homme de lettres*. The line separating jurists from literary men had always been thin, of course. Olivier Patru's explicit adoption of "Ciceronian" oratory in the seventeenth century already signaled a convergence of legal oratory and "literary" genres, and Patru himself entered the showpiece of the crown's cultural enterprises, the Académie Française. The more barristers addressed themselves primarily to the "tribunal of public opinion," however, the more it made sense for them to imitate prevailing literary styles, particularly when, in the 1760's, barristers and *philosophes* began to collaborate on *causes célèbres*. Voltaire's own contributions to the *mémoires* for Calas spurred a host of imitations, notably from Alexandre-Jérôme Loiseau de Mauléon, who joined with Élie in the defense of Sirven. According to Bachaumont, Loiseau "regarded his profession more as that of orator than of jurist" and produced *mémoires* which "read like novels."[17]

The perception of growing similarities between barristers and *hommes de lettres* was only heightened by a steady flow of aspiring poets, novelists, and playwrights into the bar. Just as would-be Jansenist priests had found refuge in the legal profession fifty years before, now this growing class of men—some fitting the profile of the "poor devils" famously caricatured by Voltaire—swelled its ranks after finding that purely literary fame was eluding them. When the police inspector Joseph D'Hémery compiled files on known Parisian writers between 1748 and 1753, roughly ten percent of his total was composed of lawyers, would-be lawyers, or law clerks (including 14 men listed on the *Tableau*). Of the 540 barristers listed on the *Tableau* of 1770, at least ten percent published works on topics other than the law.[18]

These developments further highlighted the contrast between the

Order's narrow, sectarian goals and the legal profession's position in France's rapidly changing political culture. The more that leading barristers came to see themselves primarily as *hommes de lettres*, the more they demanded to write on topics of their choice, and not to remain constrained within limits set forth by a group of aging Jansenists. Yet the leaders of the Order rejected these claims, and registered their disapproval of *avocat-écrivains* in no uncertain terms. Five of d'Hémery's fourteen author-barristers disappeared from the *Tableau* in the great purge of 1751, while Loiseau de Mauléon left the Order in 1768. Élie de Beaumont skirted disbarment in 1765 and on several subsequent occasions.[19] The Order tolerated Élie's daring briefs for Calas and Sirven primarily for one, rather fortuitous reason: the Jansenists, partly due to their belief that religion was a personal matter, supported Protestant emancipation.[20]

Despite their "philosophical" temptations, Target, Élie, and Gerbier never challenged the Order itself, either in its political aims or its organization. In the 1760's, however, a handful of *avocat-écrivains* began to do exactly this. Barristers, they insisted, should not paper over the contradiction between their status as "public men" addressing an entire nation on the one hand, and the Order's privileges and narrow agenda on the other. They called for the bar to open its ranks to all applicants with a bare minimum of legal knowledge and thus effectively tried to dissolve the distinction between barristers and *hommes de lettres* entirely.

Of these men, by far the most important was Simon-Nicolas-Henri Linguet, whom one biographer has called "the first modern lawyer."[21] Born in 1736, the son of a Jansenist schoolteacher, he spent a troubled youth traveling and trying to establish himself as an author. In 1764, after many failures, he enrolled as a *stagiaire* of the Order. "I have never respected the profession of barrister," he allegedly wrote, "but I am going to enter it. That is because one must do something in life. One must make money, and it is better to be a rich cook than a poor and unknown savant."[22] Even before entering the bar, Linguet anonymously published a blistering attack on French law which called the entire idea of a legal profession into question. Why should certain men have the exclusive right to appear for others in court, he asked? In ancient Rome, a man had needed no special privilege, but only genius, a good voice, and "the art of touching hearts" to speak in public. "One demanded much spirit of him, and very little knowledge." In France, by contrast, true genius quickly suffocated under the mountain of laws, ordinances, and rulings which barristers manipulated to preserve their own privileged position.[23] Carrying on the tradition pioneered by Sudre and Élie de Beaumont, Linguet first made a name for himself defending the Chevalier de la Barre, a young nobleman gruesomely executed for sacrilege whose case had been taken up by the *philosophes*.[24] He expressed his philosophy of legal practice quite succinctly in a letter to a client: ". . . your judges will be, even without realizing the fact, compelled or restrained by the Public, by the most widely spread opinion. It is thus the Public we must instruct, convince, and win over."[25]

Ambroise Falconnet echoed many of Linguet's opinions. Born in 1742, he too failed in a literary career and enrolled as a *stagiaire* in 1769.[26] In his *Essay on the Greek, Roman and French Bar*, published in 1773 but almost certainly composed earlier, he argued that the Order of Barristers was not inherently evil, merely corrupt. Legal eloquence had flourished in ancient times, and in France as well until the Renaissance, but had subsequently deteriorated. Venality of offices had delivered the greatest blow, for it blocked barristers' advancement and thus destroyed their greatest incentive to shine.[27] Like Linguet, Falconnet called for the abolition of venality and a complete overhaul of French law. He also shared Linguet's disdain for legal erudition, arguing that the first requirement of eloquence was "*une belle âme*" and the second, "*un coeur sensible*." While Falconnet acknowledged that oratory played different roles in classical democracies and monarchies, he suggested that it could reach equal heights in both: "Glory," as well as "liberty," he argued in an unconscious echo of Richelieu's "Ciceronians," provided fertile ground for true eloquence to flourish.[28]

The most unlikely of the new orators was Pierre-Louis-Claude Gin, born in 1726. His father had belonged to the Order for nearly sixty years, and signed many Jansenist *mémoires judiciaires*. Gin himself inherited sufficient capital to purchase an ennobling office of *secrétaire du roi* at age twenty-seven years.[29] Unlike Linguet and Falconnet, he did not display literary ambitions until middle age (in the 1780's, he published translations of classical authors), but his text *The Eloquence of the Bar*, published in 1767, had much in common with the other men's works.[30] Gin cast it as a practical manual for lawyers, an updated version of Biaroy de Merville. He found more to praise in the modern bar than Linguet and Falconnet, but like them he promoted an ideal of legal oratory that minimized the importance of juridical learning and stressed "genius" and sentiment. A barrister, he argued, needed an inherent sense of natural law—itself reducible to the golden rule—far more than he needed technical expertise. As for oratory: "All the rules can be reduced to a single principle: feel vividly, and you will express yourself vividly as well." Despite a few passages on church law that retained traces of his Jansenist upbringing, Gin drew mainly on secular thinkers for inspiration, and singled out for praise Buffon, d'Alembert, and even (while deploring his "Pyrrhonism") Rousseau.[31]

Linguet, Falconnet, and Gin's ideas broke dramatically with the conventional wisdom of the Order of Barristers. Their common emphasis on nature, genius, sentiment, and simplicity indicated the extent to which they had abandoned earlier notions of oratory and absorbed the new aesthetic ideas promoted by the *philosophes*.[32] If Patru and his followers had rejected Pasquier's preference for legal learning over artful rhetoric, Linguet and the others went a step further by practically rejecting legal learning altogether. If Prévost and Aubry had waged cases before the "tribunal of public opinion" as well as before actual tribunals, Linguet and the others scorned the courts in which they practiced and counted "public opinion" for everything. If Cochin and Le Normand had tried to balance the temptations of classical oratory with the demands of a Christian monarchy, Linguet and the others effectively ignored the fact that they practiced under a Christian king and behaved as if they were speaking in the forum or the *agora*. Not for them the "depoliticized republicanism" of d'Aguesseau's great oration: like Rousseau they were wholly republican, at least in spirit.

Needless to say, these men's ideas represented a challenge to the very existence of an Order of Barristers. Only Linguet made the challenge explicit, but much the same conclusions followed logically from Falconnet and Gin's work as well. If legal oratory depended less upon mastery of the details of an archaic legal system, and more upon simple "feeling" and an inherent grasp of natural law, then why have a legal *profession* in the first place? In direct anticipation of revolutionary reforms, Linguet argued that if the law were sufficiently simple, and the judges sufficiently enlightened, then no lawyers were needed at all, only eloquent citizens.[33]

Before 1771, Linguet, Falconnet, and Gin had little effect on legal practice. If they disapproved of the Order, the Order returned the favor, almost disbarring Linguet in 1770.[34] Only a few isolated figures at the top of the profession, men such as Élie de Beaumont and Loiseau, had much latitude to experiment with a more self-consciously literary approach to the law, and even then only in certain, approved cases. Lesser barristers who imitated them could easily incur charges of breaching legal decorum and find themselves struck from the *Tableau*. Despite the unprecedented freedom enjoyed by *mémoires judiciaires*, barristers were still subject to censorship by the Order itself.

The immediate significance of the three men's ideas lay less in the legal sphere than in the political one. Their hostility to the legal system dominated by the *parlement*, and to the *parlement*'s allies in the Order, naturally drew them, as it had drawn Moreau, towards the political positions of the crown. Linguet dared take on the defense of the notorious Duc d'Aiguillon in the Brittany Affair. Gin secretly advised the ministry on strategies to use against the *parlements*. Together with a small number of barristers whose religious opinions had led them to defend the Jesuits, they therefore made up a small but real *parti du roi* within the bar.[35] Furthermore, their aversion to the exclusive and privileged position of the Order intersected with the critique of the bar advanced since the 1720's by dissidents such as Fericoq de la Dourie (who wanted the profession to become a "public academy"). Fericoq and his allies, writing in 1729, could supply few arguments to bolster a case born of personal resentment. Gin, Linguet, and Falconnet, drawing on currents of thought that stigmatized all varieties of privilege, had arguments in abundance. In 1771, moreover, they were given a chance to put their theories into practice.

Simon-Nicolas-Henri Linguet, who led a revolution in French legal practice during his tempestuous career at the bar. Engraving by Delattre. Photo courtesy of the Bibliothèque Nationale, Paris.

The Showdown of 1771

The so-called Maupeou Revolution of 1771–74 is one of those Janus-faced events that have always fascinated historians: the greatest political upheaval in France since the Fronde, it also foreshadowed the much greater Revolution to come. For three years, Louis XV and his chancellor, René-Nicolas-Charles-Augustin de Maupeou, succeeded in breaking the power of the *parlements*. They exiled the stubborn magistrates and replaced them with more pliant men who did not demand a role in the national legislative process. Upon the king's death in 1774, his grandson Louis XVI reversed the measures, but in the intervening years much had changed. In particular, a newly cohesive and radical opposition, calling itself "patriotique," had taken shape, voicing demands that would only be met in 1789. Not surprisingly, scholars have long hunted among these confusing and tortuous events for signs of a "traditional" politics shedding its husk to reveal a "new" politics in birth.[36]

Despite the fact that Maupeou's "reforms" primarily affected the legal system, nearly all the scholarship on the crisis has focused on what would now be considered its overtly political aspects: the effects on royal authority, the development of political ideologies, the forms of political organization. Historians have devoted far less attention to its impact on the legal system itself, and the culture of the law courts, perhaps because the *structural* changes Maupeou wrought did not endure beyond Louis XV's death.[37] Still, if it had little effect on the formal aspects of the legal system, the Maupeou Revolution nonetheless had a profound impact on the nature of legal practice in France.

The crisis began dramatically in late 1770 in the wake of the Brittany Affair. First the chancellor tried to issue a new edict greatly restraining the *parlement*'s political role. The magistrates went on strike, as they had many times before in the century, and stayed on strike despite royal orders to resume work. As in the 1750's, the barristers and *procureurs* loyally closed their offices in sympathy. In January, the crisis took a new and decisive turn: Maupeou exiled the magistrates to remote villages and replaced them with the *conseil d'état*. Law clerks and other Parisians, in mobs numbering up to seven thousand, greeted these substitute magistrates with a storm of abuse. Soon the Paris courts settled into the familiar rhythm of judicial strikes, with sessions adjourned as soon as they had opened for lack of lawyers to argue cases.[38]

Unlike his predecessors, Maupeou recognized that the key to replacing the *parlement* successfully lay in finding men to argue cases before his replacement court, and he initially concentrated much of his energy on this goal.[39] In a challenge to the Order's monopoly on legal representation, he invited law graduates who did not belong to the Order, particularly barristers in the king's council, to plead before his judges. Crowds of spectators, however, shouted down the few men who accepted the invitation.[40] Maupeou also hoped to win over the *procureurs*, whose indebtedness and status as royal officials made them an easier target.[41] After initial blandishments had little effect, he threatened to strip them of their offices and even to try them for mutiny. Most procureurs remained unconvinced that the chancellor's reforms would endure, however, and continued to defy him.[42] As a result, Maupeou's endeavors remained for the moment an embarrassing failure, a "phantom of a jurisdiction," as the *procureur* Regnaud put it in a never-published, violently anti-Maupeou account of the crisis.[43]

Here the crisis might have remained, eventually petering out as so many had before, but Maupeou had greater daring than earlier ministers, and faced with stalemate, he plunged ahead with more radical reforms. In February, he broke up the jurisdiction of the *Parlement* of Paris, creating six new appellate courts (*conseils supérieurs*) to handle the bulk of its caseload. This action, besides addressing long-standing complaints about the irrationality of French judicial boundaries, had the important effect of making many Parisian lawyers redundant. At the same time, he decided gradually to abolish most of the *procureurs'* offices as their owners died or retired.[44]

The final elements of the Maupeou Revolution in Paris came in April, when, in a dramatic break with the past, the chancellor created an entirely new *parlement* to replace the exiles. At the same time he did away with both the notorious fees paid to magistrates (*épices*) and, most impressively, venality of offices in the high court. Merit, not wealth would once again govern appointments there, he claimed. This last reform was aimed partly at wooing barristers to his side, for Maupeou invited leading members of the Order to become judges, even offering Gerbier the coveted position of *avocat général* (Gerbier declined, but many men hinted at their availability).[45] In the end, nine members of the Order gained positions on the bench, including two who had made their royalist sympathies clear before the coup: Gin and the criminalist Pierre-François Muyard de Vouglans.[46] The chancellor's opponents hastened to describe all the new magistrates as lowborn opportunists, accusing Gin, for instance, of selling his services for 40,000 *livres*. Yet as Joël Félix has recently shown, the new magistrates did not differ terribly from their predecessors in social background, training, or competence (five of the nine barristers named, for example, were noble or in the process of ennoblement).[47]

Even with a *parlement* in place, Maupeou still needed lawyers to make it function, and lacking leverage over members of the Order, he began a fresh assault on the *procureurs*. In late April, he spread rumors that he was about to suppress 300 of their offices immediately, and thereby panicked 130 of them into volunteering their services.[48] He then suppressed *all procureurs'* offices, and simultaneously created 100 new venal positions combining the functions of *procureur* and barrister. The new officers would hold the title *avocats du parlement* (in contrast to the

Order's *avocats au parlement*) and would be organized into a "company" under strict royal supervision. Maupeou distributed 87 of the posts to his 130 volunteers, and the rest to barristers in the king's council.[49] There would therefore be no need for the Order of Barristers at all.

This reform, the most drastic ever undertaken of the French legal profession, matched the audacity of overhauling the magistracy. Like the new *parlement*, the new "company" of barristers in theory represented an "enlightened" move to improve the cumbersome legal system. With the jurisdiction of the *parlement* greatly diminished, the Parisian courts had no need for close to a thousand barristers and *procureurs* haunting their corridors. Nor was there any particular reason not to combine all the functions of legal representation in a single profession, as in modern France and America. But the edict spelled disaster for the Order, and utter ruin for more than three hundred *procureurs*.[50] The partisans of the old *parlement* thus rushed to tar the hundred new "barristers" with the same brush they had used on the new magistrates, calling them opportunistic, lowbred, incompetent scoundrels. They even alleged (incorrectly) that a quarter lacked law degrees, necessitating an emergency trip to the notoriously lax law faculty at Reims.[51]

Did Maupeou intend, by this decision, to abolish the Order of Barristers itself and banish its members from the law? In fact, despite appearances, the chancellor merely hoped to provoke it into ending its strike. His substitute barristers, while they might possess the requisite legal knowledge, lacked experience in oratory and legal writing, and could not easily fill the robes of experts like Target and Élie de Beaumont. Regnaud wrote that the chancellor still longed for advocates with "luster," and the preamble to the edict invited all "matriculated barristers—meaning members of the Order—to argue cases alongside the new *avocats du parlement*. Only one practicing barrister, a man who had defended both the notoriously anti-Jansenist abbé Luker and the Duc d'Aiguillon, actually reopened his office for consultations.[52] The others remained on strike, even as the "*avocats du*" began to appear in court and Maupeou's *parlement* began to function.

Why did the Order continue to hold out? It would be a mistake to attribute its continuing resistance entirely to ideological conviction. Even in mid-1771, it still appeared unlikely that Maupeou would persevere with his audacious reforms. The old *parlement* had survived many previous royal assaults. Surely the former magistrates would soon return in triumph to the Palais de Justice, rewarding those who had remained faithful and wrecking the careers of turncoats. As Malesherbes observed, the *parlement* was "a powerful corps, whose slow vengeance is always terrible." Edme-François Darigrand (the author of *Antifinancier*) wrote to Le Paige that according to the "experience of a thousand years," the crown could not hold out against *parlementaire* resistance for more than six months.[53] Soon, the Order would return to work, dealing harshly with any renegades who had defied it.

* * *

Despite Darigrand's assuredness, the Order's leaders knew that Maupeou's achievements would not collapse by themselves. They also dreaded even the possibility that he might consolidate them. For one thing, the dissolution of the old *parlement* meant that the archbishop of Paris now had free rein to recommence the refusal of sacraments and other anti-Jansenist measures. The "coup" might even open the door to the return of the Jesuits to France.[54] Beyond these immediate Jansenist concerns, the chancellor's act also represented the climax to the crown's long campaign of encroachment on the judiciary. It eliminated the *parlements'* effective role in the legislative process, and significantly curtailed the place of the courts in resolving social conflicts—to the advantage of the hated royal administration. It also seemed to deprive the "nation" and "public opinion" of any means of self-expression, particularly since Maupeou was simultaneously attempting to intensify royal censorship operations.[55] In all these ways—not even considering the effects of the sharp reduction in caseload caused by the creation of the new appellate courts—the "coup" directly threatened the prestige and livelihood of all the inhabitants of the world of the law.

For these reasons, in the spring and summer of 1771, the chancellor's opponents launched a propaganda barrage of unprecedented dimensions against him. Well over a hundred pamphlets and broadsides, ranging from calm, closely argued constitutional treatises to quasi-obscene lampoons emerged from hidden presses. As in the 1750's and 1760's, Parisian barristers wrote the lion's share of this material, again confirming their position as the master polemicists of French politics.[56] Le Paige and his Jansenist colleagues did much of the work, but several of the younger barristers who kept their distance from Port-Royal also contributed, including Target and Élie de Beaumont. Maupeou sponsored a counter-offensive of at least ninety pamphlets, and barristers contributed heavily to it as well, notably Pierre Gin.[57]

As in the 1750's and 1760's, the composition, printing, and distribution of the pamphlets against Maupeou was a carefully managed affair. In fact, like most Old Regime propaganda campaigns, it was the product of that favorite bugbear of eighteenth-century political writing—an organized conspiracy.[58] Louis-Adrien Le Paige himself probably directed one set of operations from his stronghold in the Temple, from which the Parisian police were banned. One early biographer claimed that Le Paige *personally* wrote most of the material, and the evidence of his own library proves that he certainly composed, edited, and distributed a substantial number. Le Paige himself commented in 1788 that "it is to be hoped that what was done in 1771 is done again, and that nearly everything is passed under the same eyes before being used, so as to assure the unity and truth of the principles." Records from the Bastille, meanwhile, hint that Le Paige's protégé André Blonde worked in concert with former Chancellor Lamoignon on the "printing, smuggling and publicity of these writings."[59] Certainly the police believed that the printing press they had uncovered in the Temple in 1757 was still functioning. Le Paige himself, in several letters, denied playing any role, but he later marked at least one of them "*lettre ostensible*," meaning written for the eyes of the police. In 1772, after being subpoenaed to testify in the ongoing police investigation into the pamphlets, Le Paige fled into hiding outside of Paris.[60]

This conspiratorial activity led the *parlementaire* publicist Pidansat de Mairobert to write, in a much-quoted passage, that Jansenism, "having lost its true interest [with the expulsion of the Jesuits] . . . has turned itself into the party of patriotism."[61] It is too simple, however, to attribute the entire campaign to the efforts of the *parti janséniste*. Many sources hint at an important role for the Duc d'Orléans, who led the Princes of the Blood in producing a sensational "*protestation*" against Maupeou (also attributed, inaccurately, to Le Paige).[62] A client of the prince, Jacques-Mathieu Augeard, later boasted that he had personally commissioned the pamphlets by Blonde, Target, and Élie de Beaumont. Augeard himself wrote one important series of pamphlets. In 1776, meanwhile, the bookseller Hardy recorded in his journal the rumor that the famous secret printing press had been located not in the Temple, but at the château of a member of the Orléans family, the Comte d'Eu.[63] Nor did many of the men and women involved in the campaign need Jansenist beliefs in order to hate the chancellor. By abolishing *procureurs'* offices and drastically reducing the caseload in the new *Parlement* of Paris, Maupeou had created a small army of unemployed lawyers and law clerks, who stood to gain both revenge and money from the sale of illicit pamphlets.[64]

Beyond the pamphlets' varied origins, their contents as well displayed considerably less "unity" than Le Paige claimed for them. It is true that Le Paige's own contributions amounted to little more than restatements of his *Lettres historiques*. Many others continued his practice of considering the nation a collective "corps," and even revived, as Prévost had in 1716, the idea that the "body" of royal sovereignty extended far beyond the physical person of the king.[65] Target and Élie de Beaumont, on the other hand, tended to provide pragmatic, ahistorical justifications for the *parlement*, and did not strain to excuse its faults. Target in particular had many harsh words for venality, the old magistracy, and corporatism. Even more importantly, he (and many other authors) claimed that the true "representatives" of the French nation lay not in the *parlements*—who filled the role only by default—but in the long-dormant Estates General.[66] One need only read the opening lines of his *Lettres d'un homme*, with their clear foreshadowing of revolutionary patriotism and "fraternity," to gauge their distance from Le Paige's lawyerly proofs of historical title:

> The French are all ranked, and each have their own occupations; they have a corporate spirit and hardly any other. Wherever you travel you will find priests, financiers, army officers, magistrates, merchants, but hardly ever citi-

zens. . . . I prefer to see a single nation, a single family, brothers who at heart have the same interests and the same rights.

Furthermore, unlike Le Paige, who generally spoke only of the nation's *collective* rights, Target forthrightly attributed rights to individuals, and spoke of a social contract. The barristers of the *parti janséniste* would not come around fully to these positions until all immediate hope of reversing Maupeou's reforms had been lost.[67] Their original "political language" no longer held exclusive sway over a legal world which was becoming, so to speak, politically polyglot.

Even as the most politically active barristers were adding to the already lengthy bill of indictment against Maupeou, the chancellor was intensifying his efforts to bring their colleagues back to work and thereby consolidate his initial victory. During the summer and fall of 1771, his writers directed a large number of pamphlets explicitly at members of the Order.[68] Some of these works, particularly Pierre Gin's *Entretien d'un militaire et d'un avocat*, took the tone of a father gently scolding overzealous children. They spent relatively little time justifying Maupeou's reforms, and more appealing to the barristers' sense of duty to needy clients. They also emphasized the horizons opened up by the abolition of venality in the *parlement*.[69] In case the barristers did not respond to this flattery, however, Maupeou also employed simple intimidation. The pamphlet *Pensez-y bien* ("think well about it," a phrase from the French catechism), changed its tone dramatically halfway through the text. After first dropping respectful pleas for the barristers to return to its bereft "public," it suddenly began taunting them as "cowards" driven by "the blackest and most indefensible malice." It threatened the Order with economic ruin and warned that the opportunity to return would not last forever. Another pamphlet literally raised the specter of starvation in the form of the ghost of a barrister's wife who had not survived her husband's new spell of unemployment.[70] Maupeou's pamphlets worried the leaders of the Order sufficiently to elicit a number of responses, including the predictably titled *Nous y pensons*. Yet these counterattacks—which mostly appeared too late to help—took a surprisingly tepid, defensive stance. They freely admitted the defaults of the old *parlement* and spoke less of the polity as a whole than of the need to preserve the Order's hard-won independence.[71] Clearly, Maupeou's arguments were making an impact.

The pressure on the barristers grew critical as the autumn vacation dwindled and the *rentrée judiciaire* of November 11, 1771 began to loom. Having received no income for nearly a year, the barristers had become more vulnerable to economic pressure (particularly since a partial bankruptcy engineered by the Abbé Terray had cut deeply into their *rentes*).[72] Rumors also began to circulate that the king would soon bar all barristers and their descendants from holding any royal office. In late October, a group of twenty-eight met secretly to discuss returning to work. They were, for the most part, a colorless group, the workhorses of the bar. Typical of them was Louis-Claude Rimbert, who lorded over the early morning sessions in which the *parlement* treated "*causes ordinaires.*" Yet the group also included Claude-François Thevenot d'Essaule, advocate of the Jesuits and d'Aiguillon, Pierre Bouquet, who later composed historical works justifying the chancellor's reforms, and C.-G. Coqueley de Chaussepierre, a royal censor and confidant of the *lieutenant-général de police.*[73]

The formation of this group—like the formation of Julien de Prunay's coterie in 1735—spelled the end of the strike. The twenty-eight men initially offered to trade their services for repeal of a proposed new code of legal procedure, which curtailed lucrative "*procès écrits,*" but Maupeou, now confident he had the upper hand, refused to discuss any possible deal. After meeting for a second time, on November 6, the group sent the chancellor four delegates. This time he received them, and although the delegates feebly attempted to defend the independence of the Order, in the end they agreed to return to work without conditions.[74] News of their submission soon reached the Palais de Justice, and as it did, hundreds of other barristers were, to cite Regnaud, "possessed by a sort of vertigo." Some worried that if they did not submit to the chancellor immediately, they would lose their careers. Others feared that with the *parlement*'s caseload so much lower than before, "*les vingt-huit*" (as they soon became known) might actually monopolize all pleading themselves. Thus on St. Martin's day, around two hundred barristers, joined by the new *avocats du parlement,* assembled in the Palais de Justice to take their oath.[75]

Even after this victory, Maupeou continued scheming to win the cooperation of the remaining holdouts, who included many prominent orators. He did so by announcing that he would strike from the *Tableau* all members of the Order who did not formally register their submission by November 24. The chancellor put particular pressure on Gerbier, who was deep in debt (Terray's partial bankruptcy reportedly cost him 200,000 *livres*), and desperate to keep his sister, a Jansenist whom the police had arrested for pamphlet-smuggling, out of prison.[76] The grandiose orator soon succumbed. In a letter to his patron, the Prince de Conti, he insisted he would "put his head on the block" if asked, but argued that continued resistance served no purpose. On Le Paige's advice, he did demand one small concession in return for his collaboration, namely that Maupeou give up his plans to alter the *Tableau,* thus keeping the Order at least theoretically intact.[77] Still, Gerbier's return dismayed the holdouts, for it gave many others an excuse to return as well. Even Target briefly flirted with returning to work before retreating into a stern resistance which earned him the monicker of "the virgin Target."[78] All in all, precisely fifty percent of the Order eventually collaborated with the chancellor, giving his new courts the "luster" he had wanted. The other fifty percent remained on strike, although many eventually opened their offices for consultations.[79]

The decision to defy the Order and return to work was a wrenching one, even for those barristers who secretly approved Maupeou's reforms. For the first time, the crown had managed to break a strike, and therefore called into question the independence the barristers had struggled so hard to achieve. Needless to say, those men who remained on strike rained abuse on their "turncoat" colleagues, issued a formal "Protest of the Order of Barristers," and declared all the "*rentrants*" disbarred.[80] Songs, verses, and satirical prints denigrated the "four beggars" who had negotiated with the chancellor, and all who followed them.[81] In several cases, meticulously publicized by the chancellor's opponents, this opprobrium caused deep psychological wounds. The young barrister Jean-Baptiste-Oudart Jobart, convinced that he had forfeited his manhood by returning to practice, allegedly castrated himself, and committed suicide two years later.[82] Claude-Louis Chanlaire boasted wildly that he would erase the record of his collaboration by shooting Maupeou, although he was discovered and safely incarcerated before he could do so.[83] If nothing else, these incidents demonstrate the depth of loyalties that the Order of Barristers still commanded.

The Order Divided

Why did some men agree to practice before the so-called *parlement Maupeou* while others went on strike? Historians discussing this question have traditionally followed the *parlementaire* pamphleteers of 1771, who blamed the "return of the barristers" wholly on a combination of financial need and unscrupulous opportunism.[84] Yet was this the case? Thanks to a *parlementaire* pamphlet entitled *Le palais moderne*, and the printed *Tableaux* of the Order, it is possible to determine precisely which barristers returned to practice, and which remained on strike. An examination of these lists yields some unexpected conclusions.[85]

First of all, age seems to have played an important part in determining whether or not to return. Among barristers who had entered the Order before 1720, only 22 percent returned to work. Of those who joined between 1720 and 1740, 37 percent returned, and of those younger men who became barristers after 1740, fully 56 percent returned. There are two possible explanations for this pattern. First, barristers who had joined before 1740 had more probably accumulated moderate fortunes by 1771 and reached the point of retirement (particularly from the strenuous life of an *avocat plaidant*), leaving them with less to lose from remaining on strike.[86] Yet younger barristers may also have had a greater attraction to the sort of ideas propounded by Linguet, Gin, and Falconnet. Incidentally, the same age pattern prevailed in Besançon, where a majority of barristers supported Maupeou (overall, the situation of barristers in the provincial *parlements* varied widely).[87]

As to financial status, the archival evidence unfortunately does not permit definite conclusions. Many of the barristers practicing in 1771 died during or after a Revolution which scattered them throughout France and drastically affected their economic circumstances. Estimates of their wealth (most readily made from post-mortem inventories) are therefore difficult to obtain, even without asking about the effects of Terray's partial bankruptcy. One fact, however, suggests that financial pressure did not count for as much as *parlementaire* publicists claimed: in 1770–71 the barristers returned to work after less than a year. In the 1753–54 crisis, by contrast, they had managed to remain on strike for fifteen months.

What about political conviction? For those barristers who remained on strike, this factor—along with calculations that the old *parlement* would eventually return—was obviously decisive. But what of those men who returned or who joined Maupeou's new magistracy? At least three of them, Linguet, Gin, and Thevenot d'Essaule (whom Maupeou named a magistrate in one of his new appellate courts), had all showed a clear preference for crown over *parlement* in the 1760's. Did other *rentrants* share their beliefs? Determining the loyalties of barristers before 1771 might seem impossible, but one important source does open a wedge into the subject: *mémoires judiciaires*, which listed the legal teams on each side of several ideologically fraught cases. While some members of these teams probably served only as window dressing, for the most part barristers gravitated to clients they found sympathetic.[88] Let us consider three important cases, all of which engaged the *Parlement* of Paris in the late 1760's.

The first case is the most clear-cut. In 1769, a conflict arose between the Jansenist nuns of the Hôtel-Dieu, and a clerical inspector, the abbé Luker (whom Maupeou later named a magistrate in his *parlement*). Two teams of barristers rushed to publish lengthy *mémoires judiciaires* in the case. Those supporting the nuns included Le Paige, Maultrot, Mey, Aubry's son, and several other Jansenists. Luker's advocates included Maupeou's future magistrate, Muyard de Vouglans, and two of *"les vingt-huit"*—the men who had initiated the return of the barristers. What decisions did all these barristers make in 1771? Only one of the nuns' eleven counsel resumed practicing before the *parlement* Maupeou, but all ten of Luker's counsel did so.[89]

The legal duels of the so-called Brittany Affair, climaxing with the trial of the Duc d'Aiguillon before the *Parlement* of Paris, provide an almost equally straightforward example. The affair produced an enormous flurry of *mémoires*, but the teams of barristers remained mostly constant from 1767 to 1770.[90] Le Paige, Maultrot, Mey, and other known Jansenists led the charge against d'Aiguillon, who had become a symbol of royal "despotism." Appearing in the duke's defense were Linguet, and two members of *"les vingt-huit,"* including Thevenot d'Essaule. Once again, in 1771 the teams split along ideological lines. All seven of the surviving barristers who signed *mémoires* against d'Aiguillon remained on strike, but ten of the duke's twelve surviving counsel returned to practice. It is true that Laurent-Jean Babille, a barrister close to Le Paige, also defended d'Aiguillon. However, Linguet, in a letter to the duke, spoke of Babille's inclusion as a deliberate ploy.[91]

The final case presents in some ways the greatest interest. Unlike the first two it was not directly political, and is most familiar to historians of the book. In the 1760's, a literary speculator named Luneau de Boisjermain bought up the *privilèges* (roughly, "permits to publish") of a number of classics of French literature, and attempted to print them on his own, thereby cutting out the guild members who theoretically enjoyed a monopoly on publishing under the *ancien régime*. The guild then seized Luneau's stock, setting in motion a lengthy legal tussle that, in one form or another, dragged on for over a decade and produced at least forty-one *mémoires judiciaires*.[92] While historians have generally interpreted the case as a step in the development of modern ideas of literary property, it also had clear political overtones.[93] Linguet, Luneau's principal advocate, defended his client by launching a harsh attack on the corporatism of the book guild. He defended Luneau's "literary property rights," but he also argued that those rights only existed within the bounds set by the system of royal *privilèges*. To Linguet, the case thus represented a battle between corporatism and royal authority.[94] Linguet's team included Jean-Pierre Reymond, who became one of Maupeou's magistrates, and two of "*les vingt-huit*." Meanwhile, the chief defender of the *libraires* was Nicolas de Lambon, who as *bâtonnier* helped lead the strike against Maupeou. Where did these men turn in 1771? Of the nine barristers defending Luneau who were still alive, all but one resumed practicing before the new *parlement*. All the members of the other team remained on strike.[95]

All in all, these three cases thus yield a striking pattern. Of the barristers still alive in 1771, a total of twenty-two had taken the *parlementaire* side in the cases, twenty-four the anti-*parlementaire* side.[96] Among the first group, all but six defied Maupeou and remained on strike, while in the other camp, all but two returned to practice. Should the *rentrants* then still be dismissed as opportunists? Before 1771, if anything, some of them seemed to put conviction above ambition, considering the Order's hostility to royalist views (the real opportunists in the bar before 1771 *supported* the *parlement*). To be sure, these *anti-parlementaires* represented only a small fraction of the Order. Then again, the *parti janséniste* was also very small, and the only evidence that *it* enjoyed widescale support comes from *parlementaire* publicists—hardly an unbiased source. Remembering *bâtonnier* Merlet's 1762 fears about a "ready-made *chambre royale*" existing within the Order, it seems reasonable to suppose that the *anti-parlementaires* had at least a small following, especially among the readers of Linguet, Falconnet, and Gin. It therefore also seems reasonable to conclude that political motivations played a role for *both* sides in the division of the Order in November 1771, and that even if few barristers could wholly shed their fears of "arbitrary despotism," there were many who feared it considerably less than Le Paige did.

*   *   *

Whatever factors prompted the decisions, the return of the barristers marked a crucial moment in the continuing battles of *parlements* and kings. For the first time in the century, the crown had overcome the resistance of the lawyers, and thus succeeded in banishing the obstreperous magistrates without bringing the Parisian courts grinding to a halt. As Linguet later wrote about the new *parlement*: "The barristers did much to affirm it. . . . They argued cases there, and the public began to realize it could be judged by men who had not bought their offices."[97] Even the largest propaganda campaign ever seen under the Old Regime failed to block the reforms. But the new court system was not simply the old one with the politics left out. In destroying the old *parlement* and leaving its most enthusiastic supporters in self-imposed exile, Maupeou had fundamentally altered the legal and political terrain.

Lawyers into Demagogues

The Maupeou crisis marked a fundamental turning point in the history of the French legal profession, affecting its political stance, the nature of legal practice, and the culture of the law courts. For the supporters of the old *parlements*, the return of half of the barristers and the apparent success of Maupeou's new courts brought a sense of gloom and dismay comparable only to that which fell on the bar after the destruction of Port-Royal and the promulgation of the bull *Unigenitus*. Just as it seemed, in 1713, that the crown was trying to create an "arbitrary despotism" in the church, now it seemed to have taken the same step in the state. Indeed, some of the pamphlets subsidized by the chancellor treated the very notion of "fundamental" laws as nonsense, and asserted that the king could rule precisely as he pleased. To a Jansenist, the similarities of 1713 and 1771 seemed obvious, and Le Paige even sketched out a pamphlet entitled "State Molinism" to prove the point.[98] But how could he and his allies fight against this new *acte d'autorité*? The appeal to public opinion had brought no apparent results; indeed, some sources suggest that the population of Paris generally approved of Maupeou's reforms. By late 1772, the campaign against the chancellor fizzled out. Even before Le Paige himself fled Paris, he wrote despairingly to a long-time correspondent that "the state has reached such a degree of illness, because of the abuses which have corrupted its sound constitution, that its ruin is almost inevitable."[99]

As in 1713, despair brought about some fundamental changes of attitudes and tactics. Whereas the *purs et durs* Jansenists in the bar had previously held up the magistrates as the legitimate and best ramparts against "arbitrary despotism," after 1771 they began to realize that the magistrates were not sufficient: only the nation itself, through its representatives in the Estates General, could defend its rights and preserve justice and equity. Le Paige admitted as much in his correspondence, and put the ideas into a never-published third volume of his *Lettres historiques*. Maultrot, Mey, and several other barristers similarly gave the *parlements* a much-reduced role in their massive *summa* of *parlementaire* constitution-alism, the *Maximes du droit public françois*, which they compiled during the crisis and which stayed influential until the Revolution. In sharp con-trast to Le Paige's works—and like Target's earlier *Lettres d'un homme*—the *Maximes* put much less emphasis on the collective rights of the nation. Instead, drawing heavily on such un-Jansenist authorities as Harrington, Locke, Pufendorf, Grotius, and Burlamaqui, as well as more familiar French conciliarist thinkers, the authors devoted considerable space to in-dividual natural rights, and the limits on sovereign political power, strain-ing to make these notions compatible with traditional French jurispru-dence.[100]

This shift away from the *parlements* and the collective rights of the nation ultimately made it easier for Maupeou's different opponents to unite under a single banner. While it may be going too far to assert, as one scholar recently has, that the Maupeou crisis welded Jansenist and Enlightenment currents of opposition together, it did allow the *parle-mentaire* camp to expand into a broad-based opposition calling itself *patriotique*.[101] Those pamphlets that appeared after 1772 increasingly included not only traditional *parlementaire* fare, but also Rousseauian, republican works such as the Bordeaux barrister Guillaume Saige's *Caté-chisme du citoyen*, and the Parisian Martin de Mariveaux's *L'ami des loix*. This second treatise condemned the "despotism" of Louis XV, forth-rightly asserted the superiority of the nation to the king, and declared baldly that "the French nation has a social contract."[102] The restored *parlement* wasted no time banning both pamphlets in 1775. Still, their appearance symbolizes the waning of one phase of *parlementaire* constitu-tionalism, aimed at restoring an idealized Catholic, corporate judicial monarchy, and the start of a new phase, which was at least potentially revolutionary.

While historians have paid considerable attention to these ideological de-velopments, they have neglected another set of developments triggered by Maupeou's "coup" which ultimately proved just as destructive of the Old Regime. These developments took place not among the *parlementaires*, but among those who defied them by returning to work, and it took place not in the realm of explicit ideological debate, but rather in the realm of legal practice: the trying of cases and the writing of *mémoires judiciaires*. What form would legal business take under the new *parlement*?

As barristers began to practice again in 1772, they found themselves facing a peculiar question: What had happened to the Order? During the tumult of the autumn, rumors had spread about its possible suppression by a newly aggressive ministry. According to a correspondent of Le Paige, Maupeou apparently considered formal legislation to abolish the Order.[103] Like Fleury before him, the chancellor never put such measures into ef-fect. Unlike Fleury, however, he effectively achieved his goal nonetheless.

When the Order split in November 1771, the faction that refused to return included the incumbent *bâtonnier*, Nicolas de Lambon, and a large majority of the *anciens avocats* (barristers of twenty years standing) who had traditionally directed the organization. Insofar as the Order existed as an institution, therefore, it was still on strike, and the holdouts emphasized the point in their formal statement of protest, which ludicrously declared over two hundred and fifty men disbarred. Maupeou's hundred *procureur*-barristers had a corporate body of their own, but its jurisdiction did not extend to the established barristers, who generally despised these former *procureurs*.[104] Thus the barristers who returned to active practice found themselves operating in a vacuum. If one of them violated any of the unspoken rules that had formerly governed the practice of law, there no longer existed a mechanism to punish him. Certainly, he could no longer be struck from the *Tableau*, for the *Tableau* itself was no longer being published.[105] In any case, would the *Tableau* itself still have any validity? The royal declaration of June creating the one hundred *procureur*-barristers seemed to render the printed list superfluous: it stated that all "matriculated barristers" could practice—that is, everyone who had taken the barrister's oath, not only members of the Order. This clause had the effect of allowing thousands of men to practice before the *parlement* if they wished, and in point of fact, many barristers not listed on the *Tableau* of 1770 soon began to do so. Among them was Ambroise Falconnet, a mere *stagiaire* at the time of the coup, who soon became one of the most prominent orators in the new *parlement*.[106]

In other words, the Order of Barristers had indeed effectively ceased to exist. As Regnaud wrote: "It can presently be said that this Order, formerly so famous, has been annihilated, or, if one prefers, is preserved only in that small number who remain peacefully at home, not to reappear until happier times return." Pidansat de Mairobert's anti-Maupeou *Journal historique* later agreed that "the Order having been dispersed during the absence of the *parlement*, was in theory suspended from its functions throughout the duration of the [Maupeou] Revolution." Barristers returning from the *rentrée* ceremonies in November declared that "the King had destroyed the Order."[107]

This eclipse of the Order had two important immediate consequences, which have attracted very little attention from historians.[108] First, it put an end to the exclusivity of the legal profession. Now, anyone who could afford to go through the charade of acquiring a legal degree at Reims could practice before any law court in Paris. Maupeou had made the profession a "public academy" open to all, just as Fericoq de la Dourie and his allies had demanded in 1729 (and just as the Revolutionary authorities would do in 1790). Second, the unwritten code of conduct that the Order had imposed on the courts had now ceased to function. All the multitudinous sins that its Jansenist leaders had so strictly repressed in the name of a lost "purity," from irreligion to breaches in courtroom decorum, were sins no more.

All of this made possible profound changes in the nature of French legal practice. In 1772, according to many contemporary observers, the Parisian courts became the arena for a succession of sensational trials and the presses released a flow of *mémoires judiciaires* more inflammatory than any previously seen. On March 4, 1772, for instance, the newsletter called the *Mémoires secrets* commented that "the bar is heating up more than ever before." A year later it added: "Never have the tribunals resounded with so many singular and scandalous cases."[109] In late 1773, the critic Jean-François de la Harpe complained of the tedium prevailing in the theater, but added that "in compensation the bar has become a well-known arena which draws the attention of all of France. . . . The scenes which take place there and the actors who gain distinction there are equally worthy of interest."[110] Looking back on events in 1813, Jean-François Fournel recalled that "by a bizarre conjuncture of circumstances, there was a flood of new cases which, by their singularity, and the talent of the counsel, came to occupy public attention and curiosity."[111] The *procureur* Regnaud commented voluminously on the sudden flood of "*causes d'éclat.*"[112]

The cases to which these authors referred ranged across the spectrum of French law. In one, Luneau de Boisjermain continued his vendetta against Parisian *libraires*. In another, a Demoiselle Camp took the Vicomte de Bombelles to court over the validity of a Protestant marriage they had contracted. The Duchesse d'Olonne waged a suit against her former lover, the Comte Orourcke (rumor had it that Linguet, her barrister, replaced Orourcke in her bed, and that Falconnet later succeeded Linguet in both legal and amorous capacities).[113] In a particularly spectacular case, the humble Véron family sued the Comte de Morangiès for nonpayment of a debt, in a conflict that would divide partisans along class lines. The playwright Beaumarchais went to court against the magistrate Goezman, savaging him, and the new *parlement*, in a series of brilliant *mémoires* that inspired many imitations.[114] Many of these cases featured the flamboyant Linguet, and each drew hordes of spectators to the *parlement* to watch the fireworks. A claque of three hundred noblemen consistently hissed and jeered François-Michel Vermeil, one of the Véron's barristers (Falconnet was another), while Linguet, appearing for Morangiès, strode through the Palais de Justice with a bodyguard of sixty nobles. In the case of the Duchesse d'Olonne, so many onlookers crowded the Palais, cheering the barristers, that the magistrates had to triple the guard in the main hall.[115]

What was it that made these cases so particularly "scandalous"? Certainly, each contained ample sources of titillation and outrage, but observers tended to put the blame particularly on one factor: the conduct of the barristers. No longer content to act merely as the mouthpiece for their clients, barristers, it seemed, had suddenly become *dramatis personae* in their own right, treating trials primarily as showcases for their rhetorical talents and as opportunities to continue long-running duels. Pidansat de Mairobert, writing of *mémoires judiciaires*, quipped: "The aim of these writings now seems less to shed light on the case and to work for the justification of the clients, than to avenge the private quarrels of the Barristers, who tear into each other without shame, and with sharp teeth."[116] Regnaud repeatedly bemoaned the "delirium" and "stupor" into which the bar had fallen, and vented his spleen on the subject in a passage of bitter, bilious eloquence:

> It seems . . . that the bar has become an arena where barristers, suddenly transformed into gladiators, advance with their eyes gleaming with rage, seize hold of each other, tear into each other, throw each other down, and make the success and merit of their case depend on the passion and the sort of rage with which they fight it. This was not the way that the sublime Patru, the eloquent Cochin, the famous Normant and the honest Doucet spoke and wrote. These men paid attention to their station in life. They did not amuse themselves . . . composing Novels, periodical works, or Philosophical Letters. They had gone gray in the study of the law and knew what it meant to fight a case.[117]

Similar charges issued from the pen of a former *procureur*, Louis Groustel, in a *mémoire judiciaire* directed at Falconnet, counsel for the Vérons: "At present, several [barristers], who are more Novelists than Jurists, recognize no leader and no discipline. In a sort of stupor, driven by avarice, with their eyes closed they strike out at every object they come across."[118] If Linguet, Falconnet, and Gin had called for an elision of the distinctions between barristers and *homes de lettres*, and the replacement of a trained legal profession by simple "eloquent citizens," it now seemed to horrified traditionalists that they had achieved their goals.

Undeniably, two of these observers—Regnaud and Pidansat de Mairobert—had axes to grind in their descriptions of the courts. As fanatic opponents of Maupeou who never missed an opportunity to impugn him, it obviously suited them to depict his new courts as a circus in which justice ceded to sensation. The portrait fitted in well with their vision of the new magistrates as incompetent opportunists and the *rentrants* as corrupt turncoats. Groustel, however, had no such obvious prejudices; indeed, he and Linguet stood on the same side of the Véron–Morangiès case, whereas Falconnet, his *bête noire*, was sometimes identified with the chancellor's opponents.[119] As for Fournel, he only joined the bar in 1775, and recorded his impressions long after the events of 1771–75 had become ancient history.

Further evidence for the changed climate in the courts comes from the tension that quickly developed between the barristers and the royal administration. In theory, Maupeou should have acted indulgently towards those barristers who had permitted his new court system to function normally. In practice, he and the magistrates he had chosen soon found them intolerable. In early 1773, the barrister Jean-Joseph Léon and several colleagues used a *mémoire judiciaire* to contest a published decision of the new *parlement*, and emphasized their conclusion by putting the word *"injuste"* in oversized capital letters. In response, the *parlement* exiled Léon from Paris. Next October, it did the same with four more barristers who had offended it—including, temporarily, Linguet.[120] Linguet, not surprisingly, earned the wrath of the new court on many occasions, and by 1773 had become involved in daily quarrels with the new *avocats-généraux*.[121] Matters came to a head in 1774, when the new *parlement* tried to disbar him, but was stymied by the *conseil du roi*, where he still had connections.[122] Maupeou's magistrates, who were still having trouble establishing their own authority, never made a systematic attempt to impose a new code of conduct on the bar (Maupeou himself sometimes restrained the magistrates out of fear that they might provoke a new barristers' strike).[123] The ministry itself, however, in 1774 issued a strict *déclaration du Roi* on *mémoires judiciaires* which, after condemning the new "excesses" in the genre, limited the printing of *mémoires* to the actual period in which cases were judged, and banned their sale until considerably after the judgment.[124]

Did these developments really represent a break with pre-1771 practice? The Paris Palais de Justice had, after all, witnessed sensational courtroom scenes before. Unfortunately, courtroom decorum is not a subject that lends itself to easy quantification. Nor is it much use to compare pre-1771 and post-1771 *mémoires judiciaires*. Sarah Maza has amply demonstrated the increasingly autonomous and subjective *personae* adopted by barristers in their post-1771 writings. But how can one prove the *absence* of this motif in the tens of thousands of pre-1771 *mémoires* that flood the shelves of Parisian libraries? "Scandal," and the transformation of men into "public" figures, is always a matter of perception. For this reason, the best indication that a significant new form of legal practice developed under Maupeou is the undoubted belief of contemporaries that such a thing occurred.

The question remains how many barristers actually adopted the new style of fighting cases. After all, to a large extent one man deserved the credit for the changes—Linguet, who appeared in nearly all the important trials of the *parlement* Maupeou (in 1773 alone, he claimed to have appeared in seventeen, winning thirteen).[125] Yet at the very least, Linguet served as an influential role model. As Le Paige wrote in 1775, in unwitting echo of Regnaud: "He is said to have spoiled the taste of the young men there, who have begun to imitate his manner of tearing into both litigants and counsel. The bar is said to have become nothing more than an arena of gladiators who tear into each other with sharp teeth."[126] The irresistibility of Linguet's example showed through most clearly, however, in the case of a not-so-young barrister: Gerbier. Before 1771, Gerbier's grandiose oratory had put him very much in the tradition of Cochin and Le Normand. He never parted ways with the Order's *parti janséniste*. Yet in 1771–74, Gerbier became nearly as notorious a figure as Linguet himself. Regnaud included him—or more precisely, he included "the new

Gerbier"—in a list he compiled of the most outrageous barristers.[127] Gerbier and Linguet generally appeared on opposite sides of cases, and developed a mutual antipathy of astounding proportions that constantly interfered with the needs of their clients. By early 1774, the *Mémoires secrets* could summarize their relationship in the following piece of doggerel: "It is a great shame, you say. They are mad, these haughty barristers who, in writings full of rage, tear to pieces each other's robe and each other's honor."[128] In the person of Gerbier, the more traditional segment of the bar effectively gave up the fight to preserve the old code of conduct, and accepted the new norms of legal practice.

It is easy to see why Linguet's freewheeling style proved so attractive in the Parisian bar. With the arrival of the *parlement* Maupeou, barristers could take on cases that would receive the maximum amount of attention, and fight them in the most visible possible manner, all without worrying about the reactions of their stern, disapproving Jansenist leaders. For the first time, their unique privilege of publishing without censorship was not offset by the Order's own internal censorship. Thus, an author of briefs that read like novels could compete in the expanding literary market as a sort of *philosophe*, and pose not merely as the public's defender, but as its spokesman, a modern French version of the orators who had harangued the citizenry in ancient Greece and Rome. After living all their lives in the shadow of the magistrates, barristers suddenly outshone them, not only because of the diminished status of Maupeou's placemen, but because the new literary market made them into celebrities: the press discussed them and their scandals as avidly as it discussed the theater and the world of letters. Along with notoriety, of course, came larger honoraria, and quite probably substantial income from the sale of *mémoires judiciaires*.[129]

Supporters of the old *parlement* generally condemned these changes in the practice of law, and reviled everyone concerned (especially Linguet). It is true that they were not above making use of *causes célèbres* themselves when they spied an opportunity to discredit Maupeou. Thus, while the dramatist Beaumarchais wrote *mémoires judiciaires* without even belonging to the bar, and indulged in precisely the same "licentious" tactics that Maupeou's critics generally anathematized, these same critics applauded his wickedly satirical treatment of the magistrate Goezman. Similarly, the publicist Pidansat de Mairobert slanted his coverage of the Véron–Morangiès trial violently in favor of the "humble" Vérons, and treated their struggle against the "arrogant" Morangiès as a parable for the battle between the magistrates and the crown (Pidansat also had a personal animus towards Morangiès's barrister, Linguet).[130] Nonetheless, most supporters of the old *parlements* never quite lost their distaste for these cases, and the barristers who fought them. Regnaud, whose *parlementaire* zeal matched Pidansat's, treated the Vérons' barristers with the same contempt he showed towards others who appeared before the new *parlement*: "The Linguets, *the La Croix, the Vermeils, the Falconnets,* the Caillards, the La Gouttes and the new Gerbier are men whose names will one day rank with the Goezmans, covered with equal infamy" (emphasis mine). Falconnet, who in any case also worked for clients tied to the ministry, derived no benefits from his apparent flirtation with the *parlementaire* camp. Even after the end of the Maupeou crisis and the return of the striking barristers, the Order refused to list him on the *Tableau*.[131]

It would, of course, be overstating matters to attribute the explosion of sensational trials and the new role adopted by barristers in the 1770's simply to the circumstances of the Maupeou crisis. During the 1750's and 1760's, the French press had undergone spectacular growth, with an expanding pool of writers putting ever more works before a seemingly voracious public. The *parlementaire* conflicts of the same years had focused the attention of readers—particularly newspaper readers—on the courts, and accustomed them to legal language.[132] Malesherbes wrote in 1774: "Has anyone reflected on the gradual progress that printed *mémoires* have made on minds over the past twenty years? Women who once read only novels now read them." Linguet himself pointed to yet another possible factor: new legal procedures established for Maupeou's *parlement* which gave a greater weight to oral, as opposed to written arguments, thereby highlighting the role of the barrister.[133]

Before 1771, however, the Order of Barristers had stifled such developments, acting as the censor of the Palais de Justice. Younger barristers in particular could not risk publishing *mémoires* that might affront their easily offended Jansenist elders. Only with the end of this unofficial form of censorship could they take advantage of the features that made the *mémoire judiciaire* a natural vehicle for reaching the expanding reading public: its link to sensational *causes célèbres*, its freedom from royal censorship, and its ability to function as a sort of occasional journalism. The Order probably could not have maintained its icy grip on the profession indefinitely. Nonetheless, its sudden and complete disappearance in the Maupeou crisis gave the transformation of legal practice an explosive, vertiginous quality, and allowed it to proceed in particularly radical directions. In a sense, the Maupeou crisis represented for legal advocacy what the freeing of the presses in 1788–89 would represent for publishing.

Restoration and Reckoning

Had Louis XV lived a few years longer, his reforms of the court system might have become permanent, and the united opposition fostered by those reforms might have continued to develop. But the king's Achilles heel—the Achilles heel of any ruler who seeks to concentrate power in his own person—is that he made his policies hostage to his own physical survival. On May 10, 1774, Louis XV succumbed to smallpox, and his most radical reforms soon followed him into oblivion. His young successor,

Louis XVI, influenced by the aging counselor Maurepas and eager to cement his sudden popularity with a spectacular gesture, exiled Maupeou and recalled the old *parlement* within months. He also rescinded all the legislation passed since 1771, including the abolition of the *procureurs*, the creation of the *avocats du parlement*, and the royal declaration on *mémoires judiciaires*.[134]

For the barristers, the situation was chaotic. Since 1771, the way in which cases were fought had changed drastically. The Order's leaders had adopted broad-based *patriotique* positions in light of which the rigid Jansenist morality they had once foisted on their colleages seemed fanatical and archaic. Yet suddenly, the *status quo ante* had apparently returned (the edict abolishing the *avocats du parlement* specifically declared that barristers could now practice as they had before 1770).[135] The Order's former leaders returned from their long strike and prepared to take up where they had left off in 1770. Nicolas de Lambon resumed his functions as *bâtonnier*, and Élie de Beaumont, in a speech before the *parlement*, praised Louis XVI for "restoring to the bar, too neglected, its former constitution." In January 1775, the *conférences* in the Barrister's Library resumed, and Pierre-Paul-Nicolas Henrion de Pansey delivered an oration that proclaimed the continuity of the Order in particularly grandiose terms.[136]

Yet not everyone wanted the Order restored to its previous state. Notable among the figures acknowledging the benefits that had accrued since 1771 was the staunch *parlementaire* Malesherbes, *premier président* of the *cour des aides*, who had close ties with many members of the Order, notably Target and Élie de Beaumont. Today, Malesherbes is best known for his protection of the *philosophes* as director of the book trade in the 1750's, for his passionate writings on freedom of the press, and for his courage in defending Louis XVI before the Convention. But this epitome of the enlightened magistrate was also a keen observer of the existing French legal system. After the suppression of his office in 1771, he wrote a series of essays on the subject, including one on the barristers which he revised after Louis XV's death at the request of his friend Turgot, newly appointed to the ministry.[137] This essay on the barristers contained many of the arguments, and even some of the phrases, that Malesherbes would soon put into his great attempt to reconcile *parlementaire* thought with the Enlightenment, the remonstrances of the *cour des aides* of May 1775 (which, incidentally, praised *mémoires judiciares* as the only form of free expression left in France).[138] It never led to legislation, but it deserves to be recalled nonetheless, for it shows how drastically representations of the legal profession had changed since the 1750's. It also provides additional evidence of how, in a nation lacking a free press or true representative institutions, the legal profession provided a crucial bridge between the political culture of the dying "judicial monarchy," and the proto-revolutionary one that succeeded it.

LE RETOUR DU PARLEMENT

The Parlement's Return, illustrating Louis XVI's 1774 decision to annul his grandfather's sweeping reform of the French judiciary. The engraving shows the Palais de Justice as it existed at the time. Photo courtesy of the Bibliothèque Nationale, Paris.

In the first draft of the essay, composed under Maupeou, Malesherbes expounded the principles that had guided him during his career as director of the book trade: "the liberty of speaking, writing, and above all printing is the only dike remaining to us in France against despotism." Of course, he noted, most Frenchmen did not possess freedom of the press. But one group did—barristers, in the limited form of *mémoires judiciaires* —and thus they constituted nothing less than "the last rampart of national liberty." This liberty, he added later, amounted to "but a portion of the liberty that is natural to all men, which other men have been deprived of, and which only barristers have conserved."[139] Foreshadowing his later remonstrances, he asserted that only with full freedom of expression and "publicity" such as existed in the judiciary, could monarchical government function appropriately and avoid the pitfalls of arbitrary, clandestine rule.

To this extent, the argument tallied somewhat with the self-glorifying ethos propounded by the Order since the start of the century. But Malesherbes defined the "liberty" of the profession in a very different way from d'Aguesseau and his imitators. In the Order's lexicon, liberty meant not only the liberty of individual members of the bar, but also the liberty of the barristers as a whole—as an Order—to manage their affairs without interference. Malesherbes, by contrast, was concerned only for the rights of individuals. He particularly disapproved of the Order's procedures for disbarment, which he called "an arbitrary justice . . . more dangerous, more abusive, more destructive of liberty" than anything else. While he did not call for the Order's abolition, he proposed that, at the very least, all disbarments be voted by its general assembly, and preferably left to the *parlement*.[140]

Malesherbes did not share Regnaud and Pidansat de Mairobert's antipathy for the changes in the nature of legal practice that had occurred under the *parlement* Maupeou. In fact, he argued that outrageous conduct by barristers might be necessary when fighting powerful opponents. Libel and slander were best punished after the fact, by an open and independent judiciary. He admitted that barristers had a tendency for "insolence," but added that "there is no comparison between these particular abuses, and the enormous inconvenience of restraining the liberty of the defenders of the public." He even praised "the perhaps frenetic, but salutary liberty used by Linguet," and condemned the attempts of the Maupeou *parlement* to suspend him.[141]

Malesherbes cast the second draft of the essay, written after Louis XV's death, as an argument against a proposal apparently floated by several of the new king's advisors to ban barristers' strikes. Although he condemned the Order's "riots and tumultuous assemblies" more strongly than in his first draft, he also noted that "it was to these abuses that we owed the salutary liberty of barristers, the independence which this corps had, or believed it had from all powers which make other citizens tremble."[142] He alleged that those calling for limits on the independence of the profession really wanted to protect their own private interests against barristers' criticism. The crown should thus take no actions other than to deprive the Order of its power to disbar, so that the public, rather than the *députation*, could judge the probity and talent of individual barristers. He also took pains to emphasize that for the moment, the barristers' freedom to condemn abuses of power represented the last vestiges of French liberty: "The sole salvation of citizens, the sole resource of the weak and oppressed against despotic boldness and violence, the sole rampart of our proprieties."[143]

All in all, Malesherbes's thinking on the bar had far more in common with that of his contemporaries Linguet, Falconnet, and Gin than with that of d'Aguesseau or Prévost. Strikingly, for a magistrate, he saw "publicity," rather than legal expertise, as the essence of the legal profession. It was not a barrister's principal function to guide judges to correct decisions through his learning, so much as it was to make the facts of cases widely known, thereby preventing judges and administrators from abusing their powers. The "liberty" incarnated by the bar was no longer simply the liberty to criticize and restrain an absolute monarch, but the freedom of speech which, ideally, belonged to all the citizens of a nation.

*   *   *

In the end, Turgot did not implement any of Malesherbes' suggestions, and the Order was left to its own devices. However, the changes that had occurred under the Maupeou *parlement* nonetheless made a return to the *status quo ante* considerably more problematic than the leadership believed. The Order's noncorporate status, and its lack of written rules, both of which had proved so convenient before 1770, made matters particularly difficult. The *parti janséniste* could rely neither on royal legislation, nor on written precedents to reimpose their code of conduct. Rather, they had to appeal for the cooperation of colleagues who had, since 1771, discovered the professional advantages to be reaped from a policy of laissez-faire.

The ceremonies marking the return of the old magistrates showed that even those barristers who had remained on strike now wished to fashion a more visible political role for themselves than the Order would have deemed appropriate before 1770. In various Parisian courtrooms, seven opponents of Maupeou used the occasion of their first appearances in four years to deliver forceful paeans to the old *parlement*, the texts of which were printed and distributed in the city.[144] These speeches had no precedents in previous exiles of the *parlement*, and constituted a sort of impromptu ritual in which the barristers explicitly adopted the mantle of spokesmen for the "nation" they had defended during the strike. Jean-Baptiste Darigrand (brother of Edme) declared: "The profession of barrister gives me the priceless right to be the organ of the People of whom you are the protectors." Target, meanwhile, gave a speech that cogently summarized the skeptical attitude taken by self-styled *patriotes* towards the magistrates: ". . . in a Nation *that has no other spokesmen*, you are its necessary organs" (emphasis mine). In language that the *Maximes du droit public* was helping to popularize, he also called for "the preservation of the rights of man."[145]

While Target contented himself with this declaration of autonomy from the magistrates, another speaker demonstrated that he knew the potential rewards to be reaped from courtroom controversy. Jacques-Claude Martin de Mariveaux, a mere *stagiaire* at the time of the coup, who had published the Rousseauian pamphlet *L'ami des loix*, was accused of harboring ambitions to become the *patriote* version of Linguet.[146] In a speech in the Châtelet, he virulently insulted the late king, causing a scandal which allowed him to issue an angry "supplement" accusing his detractors of jealousy and hypocrisy.[147] Clearly, he felt that regardless of the restoration of the old *parlement*, success at the bar still lay in attracting attention through ostentatiously outrageous behavior.[148]

Another sign that the changes of 1771–74 would not easily disappear came from the leadership's attempt to settle accounts. In late 1774, when the old *parlement* returned, those barristers who had remained on strike desired nothing more than revenge on Linguet and the twenty-eight "traitors" of 1771. Yet the influence of several magistrates eager to avoid further strife (particularly Malesherbes) and the need to avoid alienating the hundreds of *rentrants*, prevented large-scale disbarments.[149] The *députation* eventually voted to strip *"les vingt-huit"* of their seniority and to disbar one of the deputies who had negotiated with Maupeou.[150] Even this limited punishment, however, provoked a grass-roots revolt among the *rentrants*, who forced a rare meeting of the Order's general assembly to decide the issue. By a vote of 105 to 78, the defendants were let off with nothing but a light reprimand.[151] Thus, while the mechanisms established in the 1750's and 1760's resumed functioning, the leaders of the Order nonetheless found their authority effectively limited.

Thus stymied, the leadership then decided to focus its efforts on the one man who symbolized all the corruption and depredation of the *parlement* Maupeou: Linguet. Disbarment proceedings began immediately, with the charges including disrespect for Roman and French law, and outrageous behavior in court—charges that were clearly true, and encapsulated a large part of the new form of legal practice that Linguet had pioneered. The leadership did not count, however, on the resistance it would encounter.[152]

Linguet knew he had made too many enemies to expect mercy from his colleagues, so he decided to lose his case as flamboyantly as possible, and then win reinstatement on appeal. He also used the proceedings as a forum to advance his own vision of the legal profession and to call for the Order's abolition. Barristers were not private individuals (*particuliers*), he argued in a series of briefs and pamphlets, but rather their opposite in the eighteenth-century lexicon: *hommes publics*. Thus only the "public" itself, or its representatives, could judge them. On this basis, he condemned the anomalous status of the Order, arguing that if it were a "corps" it should submit itself to "public authority"; otherwise it had no basis for existence whatsoever. The Order as it stood was an illicit, subversive organization, "a republic which runs itself according to an uncontested tradition rather than well-recognized principles." In language typical of the *philosophes*, he seductively juxtaposed the "secrecy" and "darkness" of the barristers' deliberations to the "light" of public scrutiny.[153] Thus, instead of answering the bill of indictment drawn up by *bâtonnier* Lambon, Linguet put his own prosecutors on trial before the same public to which he appealed as his own judge.

In this new sort of trial, one waged before the "tribunal of public opinion," the Order found itself cruelly mismatched. Even its most experienced pamphleteers could not equal Linguet's skill with the press and courtroom theatrics, the tools of publicity. He greeted every turning in the battle with a new brochure, writing feverishly to bring each event to public attention within days of its occurrence.[154] The writings he produced for the case, mostly written within a two-month period, fill a 300-page volume. And at the climactic moment, Linguet made sure that the public would hear him by supplying the public himself. On February 3, 1775, when the Order convened a general assembly to rule on his case, the barristers arrived in the Chambre St. Louis of the Palais de Justice to find it occupied by hundreds of Linguet's followers. When the barristers trouped away to find another meeting-place, the crowds followed. It took the intervention of armed guards, sent by the *premier président*, to ensure a closed meeting. Only after this spectacle did the Order manage to vote, but the grand *metteur en scène* had made his point and was already preparing his next appeal.[155]

For a time, it seemed as if Linguet's entreaties to "public authority"—which meant, in practice, either the *parlement* or the royal council—might actually succeed. Both the restored magistrates and the council repeatedly intervened in the affair, alternately confirming Linguet's disbarment and sending the case back to the Order's general assembly.[156] The magistrates in particular, perhaps influenced by Malesherbes, seemed eager to reclaim the supervision of the Order that they had abandoned in the early years of the century. To some barristers, the threat to their sacrosanct "independence" seemed grave indeed, as shown by a remarkable letter Target wrote to Le Paige on January 29, 1775:

> We have all agreed to defend our ancient discipline, which is our most precious inheritance. I see all of us rightly determined never to give it up. Yet people are talking a great deal about ferment in the *parlement* which may yet result in some spectacular gesture . . . and then . . . we will no longer exist. . . . It would be terrible if an interminable affair dragged us down along with M. L[inguet] in his fall.[157]

Target concluded by asking Le Paige to beg his patron, the Prince de Conti, to intervene with the *parlement*. In March 1775, some barristers even threatened a strike if the *parlement* did not let them disbar Linguet.[158]

Target himself did not limit his efforts in defense of the Order to these backstage maneuvers. He also composed a pamphlet, called *La censure*, aimed at justifying the Order's right to judge its own membership. In it, he reiterated all the old claims to the "independence" of the bar, and, in a somewhat chilling phrase, praised the Order's unwritten code of conduct as "*ce merveilleux despotisme des moeurs*."[159] Like earlier defenders of the Order, Target insisted that it was not a "public" body, but simply a loose association of private individuals (*particuliers*) engaged in a common pursuit, and that actions such as elimination from the *Tableau* represented nothing more than an expression of no confidence in one of their number. Target further bolstered his arguments by comparing the Order's discipline to the "censorship" of morals by the community that had supposedly existed in ancient Rome—an example familiar to readers nourished on the classics, and one recently popularized by Montesquieu and Rousseau. There was a strong distinction between censorship and formal justice, Target argued. While formal justice could lead to the deprivation of liberty and honor—and thus necessarily placed the burden of doubt on the accuser, and was subject to appeal—"censorship" placed the burden on the accused, and was final. After all, the bad reputation of a single man could bring discredit upon an entire corps or profession. Thus, the Order's decisions could not be overturned.[160]

In essence, this argument amounted to the Order's familiar attempt to distinguish itself from chartered corporations, now dressed up in the mantle of the Roman Republic. It is interesting, however, that just like d'Aguesseau in his oration on the "Independence of the Barrister," Target found he could best justify the Order's claim to a special place in the polity by resorting to the language of classical republicanism. The pamphlet even juxtaposed the image of "nations where all orders of citizens are subjected to Censorship," to that of "bodies which exercize a particular Censorship over their members," thereby offering an implicit comparison between the Order and classical republics.[161] Perhaps for this reason, *La censure* had greater success than any other work on the profession since d'Aguesseau, both in Paris and in the provincial *parlements*. "Censorship" became a key term in the Order's lexicon during the remainder of its existence, ranking with d'Aguesseau's "independence."[162]

In the end, the Order seemed to escape the fate Target had imagined in his letter to Le Paige. Spurred less by *La censure* than by what they saw as Linguet's insufferable arrogance, the magistrates finally decided to let his disbarment stand.[163] Summing up the case, *Avocat général* Barentin conceded that the barristers had the right to discipline themselves as they saw fit, and that no court had the right to interfere in their affairs.[164] This decision, in which the *gens du roi* again surrendered their claims to supervisory power over the *Tableau*, represented an important gain for the Order. Still, the barristers had barely escaped disaster, and their victory was a precarious one. By waging the battle as he had, Linguet managed to submit the workings of the Order to a scrutiny it had never before known. In addition to his own works, news-sheets such as the *Mémoires secrets* covered the proceedings in lavish detail.[165] Suddenly, terms such as *députation* and *bâtonnier* became known outside of the Palais de Justice. Linguet made sure to identify himself as an author as well as a barrister, so that the Order's grievances against him would seem the prejudice of a benighted and privileged cabal against men of letters.[166] As the next chapter will show, his campaign left the Order with its legal authority intact, but its moral authority in tatters. As for Linguet himself, he used his newly heightened notoriety to launch a career as one of the most successful political journalists of the Old Regime.[167]

Linguet's disbarment represented the farcical finale to a decade that had seen the legal profession turned upside down. In 1765, the Order had been at the height of its power and influence, bolstered by the victories of its dominant *parti janséniste*. Yet it failed to resolve the tension between the essentially democratic nature of its political tactics, and the rigid, sectarian, and inegalitarian nature of its leaders' political goals. Many individuals felt this tension, and during the Maupeou crisis, it helped tear the bar asunder. In 1775, despite the rhetoric about a glorious restoration, the Order was in disarray. The strict system of censorship that had prevailed before 1771 had collapsed. Many individual barristers (including Gerbier) had undergone an apprenticeship in a new sort of legal practice, one which recognized only "the public" as an overarching source of authority. Barristers no longer presented themselves as intermediaries between the public and the ancient, inviolable institutions of French government, but as members of that public, debating before it and acting as its spokesmen.

As a result of these changes, the Order of Barristers was no longer the cohesive, disciplined *organisation de combat* that Claude-Joseph Prévost had struggled to build in the early years of the century, and that Louis-Adrien Le Paige had continued to guide. Instead, it had become something of an open forum where free and critical discussion of "public" issues could take place, with the results communicated to a growing readership through *mémoires judiciaires*. It is precisely this sort of body which Jürgen Habermas has associated with a "civic public sphere" in which criticism of the existing regime could develop. Habermas himself associates this sphere primarily with "literary" institutions outside the precincts of state authority such as salons, coffeehouses, German *Tischgesellschaften*, and the periodical press. In France, however, where literary institutions were weak, and often subject to censorship or police surveillance, it is natural that if the type of bodies Habermas described emerged, they would do so more easily within the ambit of the sprawling, divided French state, in protected, autonomous enclaves such as the Order of Barristers.[168]

Whether the Order would have become such a place without the political crisis of the early 1770's is difficult to answer. Possibly the Jansenist leadership would not have managed to maintain control over an increasingly restive membership for many more years. They never had the chance to conduct the experiment, however. Instead, the transformation took place both more quickly, and as a result, more intensely, and the credit belonged largely to the one man who would have wanted it the least: René-Nicolas-Charles-Augustin de Maupeou. In his misguided attempt to strengthen royal authority, the chancellor had not only fostered the metamorphosis of the old *parti parlementaire* into a more supple, less sectarian *parti patriote*; he had also assisted at the birth of one of the most potent forums for opposition the monarchy had ever known: an Order of Barristers filled with men hoping to defend the next Jean Calas. For this reason, the experience of the "Maupeou Revolution" shows that a new, contestatory politics did not simply emerge out of the general social transformation of eighteenth-century France, outside and independent of what Habermas calls the "representative public sphere." It was born out of that sphere, out of the most "traditional" politics of the Old Regime.

6

The Vanguard
of Reform

*I resolved to write only on matters of the sort that belonged particu-
larly to the* philosophe *or literary jurist; to lift these cases, as much as
I could, to their true dignity, and when they bore on a possible reform
of the laws, to examine the law itself along with the case, and to amass
the materials for improved legislation. . . . In point of fact, I was
hardly a barrister except in name.*

Pierre-Louis Lacretelle, "Un Barreau Extérieur à la fin du XVIIIᵉ siècle*

If Pierre-Louis Lacretelle was "hardly a barrister except in name" in the
waning years of the Old Regime, he was in good company. While the
majority of Parisian lawyers continued to go about routine business,
the elite of the profession concerned themselves with what can only be
called politics. Every case they fought had two audiences, the judges and
"public opinion," and two purposes, the vindication of their clients and
the implementation of enlightened reform. In some respects, these goals
were not materially different from Élie de Beaumont's at the time of
the Calas affair. The idea was still to join "*philosophie,*" in the eighteenth-
century sense of the word, to jurisprudence. The context, however, had
changed drastically. For one thing, following the Maupeou crisis and the
fiasco of Linguet's disbarment, barristers no longer had to fear the censo-
rial disapproval of the Order. Furthermore, the broader political realm
itself had grown more sympathetic. In the late 1770's and 1780's, the
word "reform" issued from every lip, including the king's, like an incanta-
tion, yet royal indecision and institutional inertia conspired to stymie the

*In Pierre-Louis de Lacretelle, *Oeuvres de P. L. Lacretelle aîné*, 5 vols. (Paris, 1823–
24), I, p. 123.

structural changes that the regime needed most desperately. Louis XVI and his ministers (like some twentieth-century reformers) therefore found it easiest to act on those issues where "reform" meant simply ending archaic practices such as judicial torture or official religious intolerance at the stroke of a pen.[1] No issues were better encapsulated in heart-wrenching individual tales of injustice, and no issues were thus better suited to the ferocious ambitions of "*philosophe*-jurists."

This new context greatly benefited the legal profession, giving it a degree of status and visibility it had not known since Etienne Pasquier's day. At the same time, however, it drew barristers even further from their professional and political roots than the Maupeou crisis had done. A Prévost or a Le Paige had treated French law as quasi-sacred, consistently worked to restrain the scope of royal legislation, and struggled to place bodies of immovable magistrates at the keystone of an immemorial French constitution. Men like Target and Lacretelle (who first made a name for himself defending the rights of Jews in his native Lorraine) thought differently. They were more likely to treat French law as a Gothic palimpsest in need of thorough revision, to press for more ambitious royal legislation—sometimes, hand in hand with ministers—and to see the *parlements* as obstacles to reform as well as bulwarks against despotism. They shared, albeit in a more tactful vein, Linguet's hostility to the broad traditions of French jurisprudence, and agreed with Malesherbes that their own calling consisted less of interpreting imperfect laws than in exposing injustice to the glare of publicity. From this perspective, there was indeed little distinction between barristers and simple "eloquent citizens," and little distance to travel from encouraging legislation through *causes célèbres* to debating it in a National Assembly.

The Order in Decline

One simple statistic testifies to the weakened status of the Parisian Order of Barristers between 1775 and its dissolution in 1790. Over these fifteen years, only five barristers were disbarred, in comparison to the scores struck from the *Tableau* in the preceding decades and the hundreds purged in 1727 and 1751. Infractions of the bar's unwritten code of conduct, once punished by "civil death," now resulted, at best, in reprimands or brief suspensions.[2] The Order kept two barristers on its lists even after the *parlement* demanded their disbarment for having written "licentious" *mémoires*—one of which denounced the "barbarity" of French jurisprudence.[3] The Jansenist warhorse Gabriel Maultrot remarked grumpily in 1783 (after a humiliating run-in with a younger colleague) that more than one barrister who deserved disbarment several times over was still happily ensconced on the *Tableau*.[4]

The new leniency did not result from any softening on the part of the Order's traditional leaders. To the contrary, between 1774 and 1789 they attempted with all their might to restore the old discipline and unwritten

code of conduct. In 1778, in an echo of Prévost, *bâtonnier* Jean-Prosper
Duvert d'Emalleville went so far as to say that barristers should judge their
colleagues "not according to the narrow rules of the law courts, which can
only take action against specific infractions, but on the basis of a pure austerity that puts even the *absence of virtue* on trial [emphasis mine]." He
warned that without a strong Order, whose "liberty is intimately linked to
the public interest," barristers would lose the courage necessary to their
calling.[5]

Meanwhile, other barristers raged against the "unworthy" men now
sullying the corridors of the Palais de Justice. Echoing the criticisms of the
Maupeou period, they paid particular attention to the blurring of lines
between barristers and men of letters, and to the practice of appealing to
public opinion over the head of the judges. In 1776, for instance,
François Chavray de Boissy warned his colleagues against following Linguet's example:

> Reject these vain and superficial Reasoners, these feeble creatures who . . .
> give the impression they know everything without having to study. . . .
> [T]hese men are always swollen with metaphysical and erroneous ideas, with
> carefully-studied antitheses; they have exaggerated declamation, and voices
> which better are suited to our Theaters.[6]

Three years later, *bâtonnier* Pierre-Henri Caillau de Courcelles, in his valedictory speech to the Order, denounced "*mémoires* written less to instruct
than to amuse" and also "the malignity which has entered into the
speeches of young barristers, which distills the spleen of slander and
calumny . . . and turns the public into both spectator and judge." Such
charges continued to resound throughout the 1780's.[7]

The antics of the barristers also continued to elicit harsh criticisms
from outside the Palais de Justice. The Duc de Nivernois, in a speech to
the Académie Française in 1785, criticized the undue "vehemence" and
"passion" that now typified most legal oratory.[8] The *Mémoires secrets*
repeatedly decried the "license," "disorder," and "indecency" of Parisian
courts, and the "wars of insults" between barristers that took up more
energy than the cases themselves.[9] The *parlement* was so unhappy with
matters that it made its own, hesitant attempts to restore discipline in the
bar. In 1777, it issued a secret internal ruling that warned the Order to
"keep the barristers within the bounds of moderation, and not to permit
irrelevant or insulting facts to enter into their writings." In 1780, and
again in 1787, the *bâtonnier* and leading magistrates consulted on possible new regulations restraining the tone of *mémoires judiciaires*.[10]
Avocat général Séguier, summing up one notorious *cause célèbre* in the
late 1780's, denounced the frivolity and irreverence of *mémoires judiciaires* in very much the same language used by the leaders of the Order.[11]
His very need to complain, however, testifies to the stubborn persistence
of the problem.

As if in conscious mockery of these critics, throughout this period barristers continued to cause "scandals" in court—now more or less with im-

punity. In the summer of 1775, for instance, Martin de Mariveaux, fresh from his debacle at the Châtelet, accused *Avocat général* d'Aguesseau of culpably withholding information in a case the two were contesting. Urged to retract the allegation, Martin duly visited the *premier président*, but instead of apologizing, he tore off his cravate, his robe, and his barrister's hat (*bonnet carré*) and threw them down in the magistrate's courtyard in a gesture of Roman self-sacrifice. Even these theatrics led only to a brief suspension, although Martin's stormy career did eventually end in disbarment.[12] A similar dispute erupted in 1780 between *Avocat général* Séguier and Jean-Baptiste Treilhard, and Treilhard's position in the bar did not suffer in the least. He went on to become a deputy to the Third Estate and the Convention, and a member of the Directory in the late 1790's.[13]

Needless to say, the great public *causes célèbres*, the scandalous, crowd-pleasing dramas of the *parlement* Maupeou, continued as dramatically as ever in the final fifteen years of the *ancien régime*. Lacretelle later recalled: "Never were there seen as many extraordinary cases as in the last years of the monarchy." As the Véron–Morangiès case faded into memory, it was replaced by others: the case of the *Présidente* Robert de St. Vincent; the case of the "fille Salmon"; the Kornmann trial; the case of the Comte de Sanois; and most spectacular of all, the case of the Queen's necklace. Each trial received vast publicity, in news-sheets like the *Mémoires secrets*, in the periodical press, and in specialized publications such as the *Gazette des tribunaux* (founded in 1775 by Mars, an *avocat au conseil* under Séguier's protection).[14] Moreover, each unleashed a flood of *mémoires judiciaires*, in which counsel often singled out each other for particular insult, as they had under Maupeou. Some barristers took to composing their *mémoires* in highly personal fashion, such as in Lacretelle's defense of the Comte de Sanois, which began with a first-person narrative by the barrister of how he came to meet his client in piteous circumstances. Sarah Maza, who has studied these cases closely, writes that in the 1780's, the circulation of *mémoires* began rising "vertiginously," sometimes reaching a level of 20,000 or more copies.[15]

As a result of these cases, the leading barristers achieved the sort of celebrity hitherto reserved for *philosophes*. Target, whose wax image appeared in Curtius's famous museum, was certainly better known than any magistrate.[16] In 1785, he became the first barrister since the early years of the century to join the Académie Française. After defending a certain Damade Beller, who had had his arms slashed by three nobles for not showing proper deference, Élie and Target became the subjects of a grandiose engraving (reproduced on the cover of this book) depicting them as the servants of divine justice.[17] The *Gazette des tribunaux* regularly serenaded the leading barristers with adoring, if generally execrable verse, and in 1785, Target and Lacretelle were among only eleven Frenchmen named honorary citizens of New Haven, Connecticut.[18] No longer fearful of having to defend themselves against charges of irreligion, they and other leading barristers became highly visible members of "philosophical" salons and Masonic lodges (all in all, 128 members of the Paris bar joined lodges).[19] To young barristers, the newfound prominence of the bar was electrifying. "I am young, and everything looks beautiful to me in the career I have chosen," the twenty-one-year-old Jacques Godard wrote to his cousin Jean Cortot (also a barrister) in June of 1783. "I believe there is no finer station in life than ours."[20]

Although the leaders of the Order failed in their attempts to reverse the developments of the Maupeou years, they did manage to make their influence felt in two areas: recruitment of new members, and the *députation*. Recruitment, unlike disbarment, remained in the hands of the *"anciens"* (barristers of twenty years' standing), so it was the traditionalists' most important line of defense. In the last years of the Old Regime, more men than ever hoped to join the profession (some provincial bars doubled in membership between 1750 and 1789).[21] The traditionalists, however, hauled out Prévost's old dictum that the Order should insist on the "purity" of all candidates, and between 1775 and 1786 they managed to keep numbers well under the records achieved in the 1730's.[22] Critics charged that they excluded an astonishing range of candidates: all ex-*procureurs*, priests, officeholders of any sort, teachers, secretaries, and also anyone who did not possess a sufficient library and 1,500 *livres* of *rentes*, or was over thirty years of age.[23] In general, the available evidence supports these charges. The decision to ban *procureurs*, for instance, led to a squabble between the two branches of the legal profession which ended in the barristers' formal withdrawal from the ancient "Community of Barristers and *Procureurs*" (which now became the corporate body of the *procureurs* alone in name as well as in practice).[24] Among the victims of the new policies was Ambroise Falconnet, whose flamboyant practice prejudiced the *anciens* against him despite his efforts to please the "patriots" in the early 1770's.[25]

The *députation* too remained firmly in the hands of older barristers. Until 1781, its members lacked credibility as representatives because the Order's thirteen traditional "benches"—each of which named two deputies—varied greatly in size, from less than 10 to more than 150 members. In 1781, however, *bâtonnier* Marc-Antoine Laget-Bardelin replaced the benches with ten "columns" of equal size. He also stipulated that the deputies would henceforth be chosen from each column in order of seniority—a move designed to reinforce the influence of the *anciens* even more.[26] This change did little to make disbarment easier, however, since the membership as a whole retained a veto over the *députation*'s decisions.[27] Quite possibly as a result, the deputies therefore generally settled for punishing barristers with fines and suspensions, rather than risking assemblies in which miscreants might be entirely exculpated.

With a generally more relaxed climate prevailing among the barristers, criticism of the Order might have been expected to die down. In point of fact, however, the reverse occurred. The Order's very existence seemed no less a monstrous "abuse" in 1780 than it had in 1765 to those men who adhered to the ideas first developed by Linguet, Falconnet, and Gin. The organization's decrepitude, meanwhile, made it safer for "enlightened" critics to press their case, while the leadership's grip on recruitment and the *députation* gave them continuing grist for outrage. In a flood of brochures and articles, the critics thus continued to denounce the Order, and sought to erase not merely the line between lawyers and *hommes de lettres*, but, more fundamentally, the line between lawyers and citizens. Drawing obvious sustenance from both the physiocrats and Rousseau, who shared a hostility to all intermediary bodies between individuals and the state, they demanded that all qualified men have access to the courts, subject only to the restraint of "public authority." The specific arguments ranged over a number of areas, most importantly history, legal education, legal writing, and eloquence. Many of the critics were not members of the Order themselves, but rather victims of the new recruitment policy. Nonetheless, their broadsides had a powerful effect on the Order, and found support within its ranks.[28]

The most telling criticisms were on the subject of the Order's history. In 1778, Antoine-Gaspard Boucher d'Argis had published his slim *Abridged History* of the Order, which attempted to legitimate the current organization of the bar by tracing its origin back into the mists of the Middle Ages. While Boucher was hardly a benighted Jansenist (he had contributed heavily to the *Encyclopédie*), he believed passionately in the Order's importance and utility, much as Target did.[29] In his history, he thus played down the importance of the changes introduced since 1700. The *Tableau* and *députation*, he argued, were simply new names for old concepts; the barristers' right to self-government was not recently acquired, but an inheritance from time immemorial. Ambroise Falconnet, drawing upon materials from the Barristers' Library, demolished this "invented tradition" in a 1785 *mémoire judiciaire* that defended the right of a man named Morizot to plead his own case in the *parlement*. Falconnet showed that before the 1660's, recruitment and discipline had remained largely in the hands of the magistrates. He remarked (in an obvious dig at Target) that even in 1693, the date of the *parlement*'s important regulation on the *Tableau*, "neither Censorship, nor Censors had been imagined." He concluded that an avaricious "cabal" had usurped for itself the right to argue cases that properly belonged to anyone with rudimentary legal training. Thus, the bar had become a *corps*, and worse, one which submitted to none of the controls that regulated other *corps*.[30]

Falconnet's work echoed loudly through the Palais de Justice. The *Mémoires secrets* reported that other barristers attempted to denouce it to the *parlement* as a slanderous *libelle*. In 1788, a ferocious pamphlet urging the Estates General to sweep out the Augean stables of the legal profession drew heavily on its historical arguments, giving them even wider currency. A year later, someone (probably Falconnet himself) expanded the brief into a hundred-page booklet, deleting the sections about Morizot, spicing up the text, and urging the Estates General either to replace the "inquistorial" Order with venal officers whom the state could control, or simply to abolish it altogether.[31] "Should one," it asked, "in a Monarchy, tolerate a Tribunal where the oppressed have no defenders, where the most absurd and extravagant despotism operates to the disadvantage of the Public [and] litigants . . . ?"[32]

The critics also attacked the traditional program of post-university legal education, which the Jansenist Armand-Gaston Camus had recently updated, and which remained the base for the barristers' training program.[33] In a series of articles for the *Gazette des tribunaux*, Pierre-Louis Lacretelle (who did not wish to do away with the Order entirely) ridiculed the idea that legal training was synonymous with slow and dreary progress through the "sea of the *coutumes.*" The "science of law," he argued, had been "suffocated under a swarm of writings." He suggested that would-be "*philosophe*-jurists" study only small selections of particularly valuable works, and rely less on their book learning than on their own innate qualities. "Before turning to the Author," he wrote, "let us penetrate the Law ourselves. . . . Let us adopt nothing without proof, nor on anyone's word; it is reasons, and not authorities, which must be final for us."[34] Similar observations came from the future revolutionary Jacques-Pierre Brissot, who spent a short and unhappy time as a *stagiaire* in 1780–81. In a pamphlet recounting his tribulations as "an Independent in the Order of Barristers," Brissot ridiculed the faculties of law and condemned the leading jurists for ignoring the study of modern rhetoric and metaphysics.[35]

The subject of legal writing gave rise to some of the sharpest debates. In 1775, both Falconnet and Jacques-Vincent Delacroix—reacting to the criticism of the bar during the Maupeou period and to the chancellor's abortive 1774 declaration on *mémoires judiciaires*—undertook to defend the genre's newly "literary" form.[36] Falconnet began conventionally enough by portraying *mémoires* as absolutely necessary to keep the facts of a case, and the relevant laws, from being ignored or willfully distorted. Still, he continued, one could hardly expect people to read *mémoires* attentively without good reason. A *mémoire* would only succeed if it managed to "attact glances, stir curiosity, keep attention, excite interest and capture support." Authors also needed to persuade the public of their passion for glory and hatred of iniquity. Thus, "in the profession of barrister one can not be a bad writer without committing a crime."[37] Delacroix argued along similar lines, stressing the role of public opinion as a "censor" of the powerful, and the importance of exposing injustice. He underlined the need for authors to write in a style appropriate to their subject matter, even if that style was "furious." Implicitly, both authors seemed to share Malesherbes' conviction that publicity, not legal argument, lay at the heart of the barrister's vocation.[38]

Oratory was yet another battlefield. Brissot expressed himself most forcefully on this point, bemoaning the dryness and pedantry, not to mention the hostility to the Enlightenment, that characterized the French bar. Far from abhorring the theater, he called on the barristers to embrace it: "The French theater is the only school in which the barrister can find decent models. Orators and actors work in the same domain: the passions of men, the collision of their interests, their crimes, their virtues." While Brissot admitted in passing that oratory could not attain the same heights under a monarchy as it had in the ancient republics, he made the admission with particularly bad grace, and called on orators to do their best regardless. They should imitate not only Demosthenes and Cicero, but John Wilkes and Edmund Burke as well.[39] Brissot's obsession with "republican" eloquence made a telling contrast to the attitude of the traditionalist Chavray de Boissy, who in his 1776 oration had warned against democracy's tendencies toward chaos and tyranny, and the superiority of the French monarchy to the "overproud liberty and ornate ostentation of a republican State."[40]

Although the critics of the Order did little but expound upon ideas already outlined in the 1760's by Linguet, Falconnet, and Gin, the debate served to draw the lines between the two sides more starkly than ever before. The traditionalists defended the Order as a fragile society's bulwark against anarchic, irreligious attacks. In 1783, they even published a pamphlet entitled *Le triomphe de Thémis* (Themis being the muse of law), which directly associated attacks on the Order with "this philosophical boldness, which [has] already partly torn away the holy veil of Religion."[41] They also continued to treat barristers as an elite, above and removed from the rest of society. *Le triomphe de Thémis* remarked derisively, for instance, that "the common people are always the common people, and let themselves be blindly carried off by the prejudices which seduce them." Chavray de Boissy disparaged "this vague and dispersed multitude" and praised "the small, learned number, the enlightened part of the Public, that which thinks, which reflects. . . . "[42]

The critics, on the other hand, reversed these images. They depicted the Order not as a rampart of, but as an obstacle to justice and enlightenment. They emphasized not the separation between barristers and other citizens, but the links between them. They defined the Order not as a meritocratic elite, but as a group of desperate and greedy men trying to keep undeserved privileges and thereby prevent the development of true eloquence in a reborn *agora*. "Every barrister is a citizen before being a barrister," Brissot stressed. Falconnet wrote boldly: "What is the barrister? The voice of the nation."[43]

Like Linguet and Gin before them, the critics' distaste for *parlementaire* constitutionalism and their opposition to corporatism of all sorts drew them surprisingly close to the ministerial party. Brissot, in language one would have expected more readily from Calonne, asserted that "the state should not tolerate the existence of a corps which can cause and which has caused dangerous troubles." The 1789 version of Falconnet's brief for Morizot blamed the Order for sapping the foundations of the French monarchy and alleged that its very existence was "a revolt, a crime of lèse-majesté." The 1788 *Thémis dévoilée* ("Themis unveiled") asked indignantly, in terms reminiscent of the Marquis d'Argenson's description of the Order as a "republic": "Shall there exist a democracy within a monarchical state? . . . [The Order] eclipses even royal authority, since it is freed from all authority."[44] The language suggests that the critics looked favorably on the idea of an all-powerful, unitary sovereign power that tolerated no intermediary bodies between itself and individual citizens. They might have preferred a reborn Roman republic to the French monarchy, but they certainly preferred an "enlightened" monarchy to *parlementaire* "aristocracy."[45]

It should be emphasized that the critics' hostility to corporatism was uniquely a feature of the Order of Barristers, and had little resonance elsewhere in the world of the law. Once again, the *procureurs* provide a useful point of comparison, for until the very end of the Old Regime, their unabashedly corporate community remained strong and unchallenged. Thus, while the ministry reduced the number of *procureurs* from four hundred to three hundred after the end of the Maupeou crisis, the community's expenses remained largely constant from 1751 to 1789.[46] In the 1780's, the community also attempted to give new muscle to its ethical guildelines by cracking down on "solicitors": *procureurs* who actively sought out clients, or even stole clients from their colleagues.[47] The community's leadership positions remained highly sought after, and on one occasion the competition led to a bitter lawsuit in which one *procureur* alleged that his rival had tried to bribe his way into a post by holding banquets for his colleagues.[48] In general, therefore, the barristers' experience should be seen as an exception, not a challenge to David Bien's contention that "the order of privilege was not moribund, but remained alive, functioning and useful until 1789."[49]

What were the broader effects of the debate over the Order? The pamphlet wars alone make clear that the traditionalists found themselves on the defensive, for they published at least two pamphlets in direct response to their critics.[50] Within the Order itself, the critique seems to have been fully accepted by the only barrister of the period to leave a detailed journal: the elderly Claude-Rigobert Lefebvre de Beauvray. In this work, devoted mostly to political affairs, Lefebvre condemned the traditionalists both for disbarring members out of spite and for displaying "a patriotic zeal that is sometimes pushed to enthusiasm and even to fanaticism." In 1787, he called colleagues striking on behalf of the *parlement* "proud mortals who preach against despotism in the most despotic of tones."[51] The critique also left its mark on the young barrister Jacques Godard, who left a valuable record of life in the Order in letters to his cousin Jean Cortot. Godard was a protégé of Target, and thus might have been expected to accept his mentor's defense of "censorship." He did share Target's predilection for classical Roman analogies, but in 1788 he gave Cortot a rather caustic description of the Order, and had particularly harsh words for the *députa-*

tion, "this newly created aristocracy, which, in the times of despotism, set itself up in the midst of a republic of free men."[52]

The critics' message also received wide and favorable diffusion from the network of self-consciously "enlightened" publicists that existed in the 1780's. The newsletter the *Mémoires secrets* greeted Brissot's *Un indépendant à l'ordre des avocats* with a long, favorable review that condemned the Order's "barbarous" practices and decried Linguet's exclusion. Louis-Sébastien Mercier's popular *Tableau de Paris* castigated the Order for expelling its only decent orator, Linguet, and mocked the barristers—particularly the more senior members—for treating old "authorities" as more important than human reason. "This corps which calls itself free," he commented, "is in thrall to a swarm of prejudices. . . . Any name which seems to shine too brightly upon the *Tableau* will be inexorably struck off." Mercier argued for the convergence between men of law and men of letters more explicitly than any other eighteenth-century author: "The profession of letters should be indispensably linked to the profession of barrister; or rather the two should be, as in ancient times, one and the same estate."[53] Yet another echo of the critics came from Linguet himself, in his successful *Annales politiques, civiles et littéraires du dix-huitième siècle*, which he published from 1777 onwards.[54] Incidentally, these stinging and witty, though utterly partisan portrayals have had an understandably devastating effect on the barristers' historical reputation.

By the late 1780's, the criticism of the Order seems to have taken such a heavy toll that the organization lost even more of its earlier authority. In the so-called Kornmann affair, a sensational adultery trial that preoccupied Parisians on the eve of the Revolution, men not listed on the *Tableau* published *mémoires judiciaires* without incurring the slightest penalty either from the Order or the *parlement*. Notable among them was Nicolas Bergasse, a would-be *philosophe* known primarily for his tireless activities in favor of the pseudo-scientific Mesmerist movement, who had taken a law degree and published essays on legal reform, but never actually practiced law. Bergasse's enemies (including Beaumarchais) protested in vain against his briefs, which they claimed had been "fraudulently printed under the title of *Mémoire*, without the author's name or that of a barrister. . . . "[55] Even before the revolutionary legislation of 1790, in other words, the courts were opening up to educated men outside the elect cicle of the Order, and its monopoly on legal practice was crumbling.

The most telling fallout from the dispute lies in the debate immediately preceding the convocation of the Estates General. In Paris, as elsewhere in France, the elections to the Third Estate yielded a gigantic overrepresentation of lawyers. A number of pamphlets appeared criticizing this result, and they clearly drew heavily on the arguments put forth by the critics.[56] A typical such work declared, in the name of the "people":

> You [the barristers] are suspect to us, because you are slavishly devoted to
> the *parlement* . . . because the spirit of your Corps stifles all public spirit in

you. . . . Decreed: that every man may enjoy the natural right to defend himself before the Tribunals, and to defend his fellow men there, without needing to borrow the voice or the signature of a barrister; and that the exclusive right which the corporation of this Capital, known under the name of *Order of Barristers*, arrogates to itself in this regard will be abolished as unjust and contrary to the proper order of things.[57]

Here, cogently summarized in a few lines, were nearly all the themes advanced by the critics of the Order since the 1760's.

For the old guard of the Order, then, the late 1770's and 1780's were a bitter time. The "pure austerity" championed by barristers from Pasquier to Prévost to Duvert d'Emalleville had seemingly vanished, replaced by a riotous, theatrical atmosphere. Instead of effacing themselves, barristers made spectacles of themselves, justified the practice in a flood of writings, and were rewarded for doing so by attention in the press and a host of cases. This was not merely the triumph of Ciceronianism, but Ciceronianism gone wild. If the bar was still a "little republic at the center of the state," it was no longer one in which dignified barristers spoke in an orderly way about the virtues of the judicial monarchy, but an anarchic one in which sensational *causes célèbres* combined with the profession's special privileges to put barristers in the vanguard of reform and allowed them to behave, some years before 1789, as if France itself were already a Republic.

Paving the Way for Legislation

Although Élie de Beaumont severely criticized the magistrates of Toulouse in his briefs in the Calas and Sirven cases, he never called the laws they enforced into question. As the second dragged on into the 1770's, however, a young barrister from Toulouse named Pierre Firmin de Lacroix persuaded Voltaire to let him take part in the defense as well. Lacroix appears in Voltaire's correspondence as a young man hungry to establish a literary reputation at all costs, and particularly to outshine Élie's earlier efforts. His brief in the case, published soon before the suppression of the *Parlement* of Toulouse in 1771, certainly seems designed to attract attention. It presented Sirven as the victim, not of a particular abuse of power, but of a legal system that was itself arbitrary and unjust. Seeking to explain why Sirven had fled to Geneva, Delacroix wrote: "Our criminal laws, more worthy of Draco's Code than of the Code of a gentle and polite nation, will terrify the most virtuous man. . . . We must live with a secret inquisition, that only treats clever or powerful defendants well." Lacroix also excoriated the French for "habitually regarding as just whatever is authorized by unjust laws," and warned that "the time will come, and it is surely not far off, when this shocking contrast between our manners and our laws will cease."[58]

During the course of the 1770's and 1780's, it was no rarity for barristers to follow Lacroix's example in their discussions of French law—and even to exceed him in severity. Lacretelle, who contributed his share of such writings, defended them by reference to the general thirst for reform: "It is today, especially, when all minds, turning to the study of legislation, are inviting barristers to a broader view of things . . . that their works should be treated with greater tolerance. . . . "[59] It may seem odd that criticism of existing laws found its way directly into *mémoires judiciaires*, since the cases in question would be judged according to the existing laws. The barristers' willingness to behave in this manner thus shows how high they had come to estimate the force of public opinion in practice, as well as in theory. Like Linguet before them, they now counted on public reactions rather than legal arguments to influence the judges.

What were the political implications of this new, critical attitude towards the jurisprudence that previous generations of barristers had venerated? Sarah Maza, who has charted a great upsurge in calls for judicial reform in the *causes célèbres* of the 1780's, has written that the phenomenon marks a shift of emphasis on the barristers' part from the possible abuses of social and political power (as in Élie's brief for Sirven), to the very foundations and legitimacy of that power. She also argues that attacks on the "absolute" authority of judges became, by a sort of political metonymy, an attack on absolute authority of all kinds. Thanks to the barristers' new aggressiveness on these matters, Maza concludes that they displaced men of letters as leaders of the prerevolutionary ideological crusade in the crucial years before the outbreak of the Revolution.[60]

While Maza's analysis of the *mémoires judiciaires* is penetrating, the notion of an "ideological crusade" suggests a high degree of conscious radicalism on the part of the leading Parisian barristers. Did this really exist? While a few barristers—Martin de Mariveaux or Bergasse, for example—certainly favored drastic, Rousseauian changes in French society, their more established colleagues had decidedly more limited notions of what constituted "reform." Target, for instance, while eager for a new criminal code, religious toleration, and an end to *esprit de corps*, could barely conceive of a fundamental alteration of the forms of government. Consider this passage from a pamphlet he wrote in the winter of 1788–89, discussing problems that might arise in the forthcoming Estates General:

> It is to be feared, one hears tell, that the representation of the common folk will become overwhelming, that the leading orders will be annihilated, and that the kingdom (truthfully, I have heard this said) will degenerate into a democracy. Nothing of the sort is to be feared. . . . Democracy in a nation of twenty-five million, under the government of a monarch! I confess in good faith that I have no idea what this means. . . . [61]

There is little evidence that a Lacretelle, an Élie de Beaumont, or a Gerbier would have dissented from this point of view. Secure in their positions in society, eager until the end for grants of nobility (Élie and Gerbier both ended their lives as members of the Second Estate), these men sought to correct the imperfections of an existing system, not to displace it root and branch.

These increasingly strident calls for judicial reform are probably best analyzed not in terms of the as yet barely imaginable revolutionary upheaval, but rather within the more immediate political context of the pre-revolutionary decades. Both they, and the fracturing of the Order after the Maupeou crisis, signaled the imminent breakdown of the long-running division between *parlement* and crown which had governed French high politics throughout so much of the eighteenth century. Political historians generally locate the collapse of this division (also referred to as a split between "magisterial" and "ministerial" parties) much later, at the moment in September 1788 when the *Parlement* of Paris appeared to thwart the ambitions of the Third Estate by limiting its representation at the forthcoming Estates General. At this moment, so it is argued, magisterial and ministerial "discourses" coalesced into a single, revolutionary discourse.[62] Late 1788 may indeed have been the moment when this fusion appeared openly in the political pamphlet literature, but the events of the 1780's reveal a process of ideological erosion which, by 1788, had left the venerable camps little better than facades, riven with cracks and liable to collapse at the smallest breeze.

One historian has recently explored the divisions within the "ministerial" camp in the 1780's. On the one side, his work suggests, stood the "king's faction": men committed to the preservation of Bourbon absolutism, but generally amenable to its enlightened reform along the lines proposed by the reforming minister Turgot in the mid-1770's (the current of ideas that Keith Baker has labeled "administrative" thought). Many of them had no particular commitment to privilege as a principle, or to existing institutions, and showed a postive hostility to corporatism, hoping to eliminate all autonomous powers between the crown and individual subjects. On the other side was a "queen's faction," grouped around Marie-Antoinette, and including supporters of former Foreign minister Choiseul. These figures favored the institution of a frankly aristocratic constitution, of the sort advocated earlier in the century by Saint-Simon. Choiseul, significantly, while a great noble of the sword, had shown more sympathy to the *parlements* than any of Louis XV's other ministers.[63]

The old *parlementaire* camp was also clearly prey to divisions, in this case between those magistrates and barristers who had fully adopted the "patriotic" position during the Maupeou crisis, and those who remained committed to a Catholic, corporate constitution with the *parlements* as its keystone. Typical of the first position were not only the Linguets and Falconnets of the bar, but also Target, Élie, Gerbier, Lacretelle, and the authors of the *Maximes du droit public françois*, with its heavy borrowings from Locke and natural law theorists. To take Target as an example, his pamphlets during the Maupeou crisis, and his speech to the returning magistrates in 1774 made clear his conviction that the *parlements* constituted merely the best bulwark against despotism available. The most vociferous magistrates, however, including Robert de Saint-Vincent, Duval d'Eprémesnil, and *Avocat-général* Antoine-Louis Séguier, continued, in their remonstrances, to defend a variety of the political doctrine espoused by Le Paige thirty years before. The *parlements*, they held, were an integral element of the ancient French constitution, and had an inalienable right to represent the French people. The idea of reviving the Estates-general remained highly controversial in the high court as late as 1787, and even its promoters showed no desire to curtail their own constitutional prerogatives. As Bailey Stone has shown, most magistrates also retained a firm commitment to a corporate vision of society, as embodied most memorably in Séguier's description of the different *corps* of the kingdom "as the links in a great chain."[64] These magistrates had allies among those traditionalists in the Order of Barristers who wanted to restore the *status quo ante* of 1770.

The differences between these two very different strands of the *parlementaire* tradition, already visible within the Order itself, surfaced to a certain extent in the dramatic *causes célèbres* of these years. Just as the *parlementaire* Élie de Beaumont had found himself opposing the *Parlement* of Toulouse in the 1760's, so other barristers found themselves opposing the Paris *parlement* in a number of later cases. The most famous involved three alleged thieves from Champagne who had been sentenced to death on the wheel in 1785 (the so-called *trois roués*). Convinced of the men's innocence, a famous Bordeaux magistrate and legal reformer, Charles-Marguerite Dupaty, published a blistering *mémoire* in which he criticized the great Criminal Ordinance of 1670 in detail and called on Louis XVI to take heed of "the bloody shoals of your criminal legislation."[65] Although Dupaty had distinguished himself on the *parlementaire* side during the Maupeou crisis, his new work horrified figures in the *Parquet*, one of whom (most likely *Avocat-général* Séguier), in a page-by-page commentary, expressed shock that a magistrate would dare speak so freely to "the sacred person of the king." The commentator wrote severely that the authors of the seventeenth-century Criminal Ordinance had been learned jurists, not barbarians.[66] At Séguier's instigation, the *parlement* suppressed the *mémoire*, and the traditionalists in the Order then expelled the Parisian barrister who had cosigned Dupaty's brief, Louis-Auguste Legrand de Laleu (with their typical post-Maupeou leniency, they reinstated him two years later).[67]

Similar divisions arose in the case of the Comte de Sanois, whom relatives had imprisoned by use of a *lettre de cachet* ("royal arrest order"). Pierre-Louis Lacretelle's massive brief in the case not only drew on a wide range of literary motifs to depict the comte as a piteous victim deserving of restitution, but also contained a long attack on the institution of *lettres de cachet* itself, arguing that it violated both established traditions of French jurisprudence and also natural law. "I speak," Lacretelle proclaimed in the brief, "for the rights of man, and for those of the citizen."[68] According to Lacretelle, the traditionalists in the Order, who disapproved of his career as a "*philosophe*-jurist," instructed his opponent in the case to act as their "avenger." In one of the last attempts to uphold Etienne Pasquier's ideal of oratorical self-effacement and moderation, this barrister, Guillaume-Alexandre Tronson du Coudray, wrote that the Palais de Justice should reject "the language of enthusiasm and the vagaries of passion," and "restrain Orators within the bounds of a simple and methodical discussion."[69] He also criticized Lacretelle for daring to use a *mémoire judiciaire* to discuss matters of state. To those who remembered the days of Cardinal Fleury it must have been a delicious irony: the formerly "seditious" Order had now abandoned the Jansenists' old motto "where the magistrate can decide, the barrister can consult," and was calling on barristers not to exceed their professional competence. It was the critics of the Order—themselves linked to elements in the ministry—who had now taken up the motto and were calling for barristers to enjoy extensive freedom of speech.

In some ways, it is arguable that these splits in the "magisterial" camp echoed those within the ranks of the "ministerial" party. Intellectually, a Target or a Lacretelle had far more in common with a reforming minister like Turgot than with a Séguier. Turgot had more in common with them than he did with those courtiers who wanted to revive the glory and power of the high nobility. A detailed study of high politics in the reign of Louis XVI might well prove that between roughly 1785 and 1789, both the ministerial and magisterial parties divided and then recombined into two new camps: one (including both physiocrats and "*patriotes*") favoring toleration, sweeping judicial and financial reform, some sort of participation for the governed in government, the abolition of privileged bodies, and the principle of national sovereignty; the other (including high aristocrats of both the robe and sword, and the traditionalist barristers) favoring strict Catholicism and censorship, preservation of existing privileges, an aristocratic constitution, corporatism, and royal sovereignty. Obviously, in these two new camps could be seen the lineaments of revolutionary and counterrevolutionary parties.

Unfortunately, such a study of Louis XVI's reign remains to be written.[70] However, a consideration of events taking place within the microcosm of the Order of Barristers do suggest that the idea of such a "crossover" is not far-fetched. In the 1780's, as the great *causes célèbres* became more explicitly involved with the drive for reform, the barristers who fought them became more closely involved with reforming figures in the ministry. Ministers such as Calonne and Malesherbes knew the importance of the sensational trials that often seemed to monopolize the attention of French readers. Thus, they took the trouble to respond in print to barristers, and even made use of briefs to advance their own legislative projects.

Consider the relationship, for instance, between Lacretelle and several ministers. In 1786, the barrister argued a case before the *parlement* against the French East India Company at the behest of the abbé Morellet and certain unspecified court factions. The *Contrôleur général des finances* Calonne, who supported the company, himself composed a short work in response.[71] The same year, Calonne also penned an anonymous defense of *lettres de cachet* in response to Lacretelle's brief in the Sanois case. Unlike even the other barristers in the case, Calonne did not describe the barrister's attack on *lettres de cachet* as illegitimate, but simply presented his own reasoned arguments in their favor.[72] Lacretelle also served as an informal assistant to Malesherbes for several years, and drafted pieces of legislation for him. Before publishing his brief in the Sanois case, Lacretelle submitted it to Malesherbes for his approval. In early 1788, Loménie de Brienne, Calonne's successor, asked both men to work on legislation regulating the use of *lettres de cachet*.[73]

Just as striking as these relationships was Target's role in the restitution of civil status to French Protestants. Target helped compose the Edict of Toleration itself, but Malesherbes and the baron de Breteuil, chief promoters of the project, characteristically valued the barrister's literary skills more than his legal expertise.[74] Target, they felt, could serve the cause best by rousing public concern in a trial brief, if possible featuring a sympathetic litigant. In fact, Target had the perfect vehicle at hand, in the case of the Marquise d'Anglure, whose relatives had challenged the legitimacy of her birth—and thus her inheritance—on the grounds of her father's Protestantism.[75] Malesherbes summed up his strategy in a letter to Lacretelle:

> I beg you tell M. Target that I beg him please to hurry the printing of the brief for Mme. d'Anglure, because I foresee that this brief will provide the occasion for advancing the general case, and I think this quite necessary because in this country we are so overwhelmed by pressing matters that we are quite slow to make up our minds about objects of legislation.[76]

The *Mémoires secrets* agreed with this view of the case: "Me. Target has not flattered himself that he can win for the comtesse d'Anglure a case clearly judged by the Law. His broader and more patriotic object is to abrogate this law, this absurd and barbaric fiction that there are no Protestants in France."[77]

Target soon complied with Malesherbes's request. Drawing on secret government documents supplied to him by Breteuil, he composed a massive, masterly brief, which first tried to establish "natural" laws of marriage, and then proceeded to examine the actual laws on Protestant marriage which supposedly made the marquise a bastard. He arrived at a double conclusion, first that the current laws contradicted nature, and second, that they also contradicted basic principles of French jurisprudence. It followed that French civil law had "abandoned" French Protestants, leaving them in a legal vacuum.[78] Target therefore called on the king to intervene in the case, invoke natural law, and rule in the marquise's favor. "This affair . . . essentially belongs to the Legislator" he asserted. He furthermore expressed confidence that "in this time of enlightenment, zeal and reform," the king would actually change the law and grant Protestants civil status.[79] The next year, the king did precisely that.

In addition to demonstrating the cozy relationship that had grown up between reforming ministers and reforming barristers, the case of the Marquise d'Anglure also revealed a fundamental shift in the way reforming barristers like Target now conceived of the French polity. The high courts, still wary of the royal administration's encroachments on the judiciary, had never ceased to defend the venerable line that without an autonomous, powerful judiciary, justice and equity could not be assured. Target, however, was now arguing something of the reverse: that an autonomous, powerful judiciary was a potential *obstacle* to justice and equity because individual judges might let their private interests and prejudices govern their decisions. Only a public authority responsible to the entire nation could truly guarantee the rule of law. "Judicial decisions on matters of such high importance," he stated in his brief, "determine public happiness or unhappiness, and so are for this reason alone necessarily subject to revision by the sovereign. It is on such great occasions that principles, obvious justice, and above all utility for the People and the tranquility of citizens become, when the written law hurts them, the truest and most powerful means of oversight."[80] While earlier generations of barristers could scarcely have denied the legitimacy of royal oversight, they stressed not the king's ability to intervene, but rather his responsibility to abstain from doing so in all but the most dire circumstances.

In taking this line, Target did not depart greatly from the prevailing orthodoxy on the subject. In a survey of works on criminal law reform, many written by practicing barristers (including Lacretelle and Legrand de Laleu), David Jacobson sees as a principal theme the desire to restrain the power of judges, notably by instituting trial by jury, limiting the secrecy of judicial proceedings, and minimizing magisterial discretion by setting out clear and inflexible penalties for each crime. These texts—which themselves became the basis for much revolutionary legislation—drew heavily on Cesare Beccaria, whose vastly influential work *Dei delitte et delle pene*, popularized by Voltaire, argued that the more leeway a judge had to interpret the law, the more arbitrary and unjust his decisions.[81] One of the most prominent reformers, the liberal Grenoble magistrate Michel de Servan, wrote that judges should not be active, autonomous "depositories" of law, but rather automata mechanically applying the rules laid down by a legislator.[82] Still, it is significant that these ideas found a far warmer reception in the Paris bar than in the *parlement*, where figures like Servan were the exception, not the rule.

To be sure, even this growing hostility to a powerful, autonomous judiciary did not convince the leading barristers to embrace the idea of "enlightened despotism" promoted by men such as their former colleague Moreau. Their collaboration with the ministry had its limits, as illustrated in the story of Chancellor Lamoignon's abortive attempt to carry out a complete overhaul of the French criminal code in 1787–88. Just as Louis XIV's ministers had drawn on the expertise of the Paris bar in preparing their great ordinances in the 1660's and 1670's, so when Lamoignon decided to replace these ordinances he sought help from the same source, particularly his secretary Jean Blondel, Lacretelle, and a six-member *conseil de législation* which included Target and his Jansenist colleague Louis-Simon Martineau. Their proposals, which owed much to Beccaria and his French followers, met with opposition from the *parlements*, who predictably objected to the diminution of their own powers. It is true that the barristers did not flinch from taking the ministerial side in this dispute. They did balk, however, when, as part of the ongoing struggle over finances, Lamoignon decided to imitate Maupeou and abolish the *parlements* altogether in May 1788. As we will see, the barristers' deeply inculcated reactions to the threat of "arbitrary despotism" kept nearly all of them from approving of this explicit *coup de force*. Soon after the so-called May Edicts, the members of the *conseil de législation* handed in their collective resignation.[83]

Nonetheless, despite this final rallying to the side of the *parlements*, it is clear that barristers such as Target and Lacretelle no longer looked upon the high courts the way Prévost or Le Paige did, and could not be counted on to stand with the more recalcitrant magistrates in the face of less harsh reforms. Despite the ideological legacy common to bar and bench, the former no longer saw a quasi-independent court as the best safeguard of justice and individual rights, and its members no longer expressed much Jansenist suspicion of the sovereign power. It was precisely this power, acting in an "enlightened" manner for the good of the nation, which could most effectively guarantee justice and rights. Moreover, barristers, as spokesmen for the nation, could help, serving as auxiliaries to the sovereign himself, both directly and through the publicity of *causes célèbres*.

The Pre-Revolution

From a modern perspective, the awakening of the Third Estate in late 1788 and 1789 appears a dramatic act of self-assertion, but at the time, to many inhabitants of the world of the law, it seemed almost a form of treason. After centuries of dedication to the *parlements* and the ideal of the judicial monarchy, the barristers suddenly seemed to switch camps, flocking behind the banner of the abbé Sieyès and a host of other pamphleteers, notably Guy Target, who chided the magistrates for their "aristocratic" prejudices. In the early 1790's, the aged magistrate Pierre-Augustin Robert de Saint-Vincent, writing his memoirs in lonely German exile, saw in this desertion ample justification for his Jansenist suspicions of human nature:

> Who would not be confounded by the capriciousness of the human spirit upon seeing [that] men who enjoyed public esteem in the profession of barrister . . . put themselves at the head of the Revolution of 1789? Here the human mind is seized with stupor . . . for how can the feelings of respect for religious principles and for monarchical authority, of which the older barristers were always the principal defenders and buttresses, be reconciled

with this sudden effervescence which caused an entire order of citizens, known for their wisdom, prudence, learning, experience and maturity, to fly off the handle [*sortir de ses gonds*]?[84]

In a similar vein, the most senior *procureur* in the Palais de Justice, Jean Le Maître, excoriated barristers serving in the National Assembly in a series of venomous 1790 pamphlets, comparing them to the men who had treacherously returned to practice in 1771. Indeed, Le Maître ludicrously belittled the Revolution as nothing but the latest exile of the *Parlement* of Paris, and predicted it too would come to an end with the traditional Red Mass marking the magistrates' return.[85]

Whereas these men, still caught up in the tremendous emotions of the Revolution, could only view the barristers' actions with stupefied incomprehension and hostility, today we can look for explanations in a more detached spirit. In a nation lacking a free press or true representative institutions, barristers, given the special privileges of their Order, were in a unique position to exploit the growth of literary markets and the nebulous phenomenon of "public opinion." At first they exploited them for purely political purposes, on behalf of the Jansenists and *parlementaire* ideology, in order to restore an idealized judicial monarchy (in which barristers would hold an honored, if subordinate place). Later in the century, however, more and more men came to see the relationship between barristers and the "public" not as a means to this end, but as an end in its own right. The prestige they garnered as "voices of the nation" and as the vanguard of reform legislation appeared far more attractive to them than the "painful and laborious" path to office followed by a Pasquier or Loisel. Thus, while their ideas remained heavily influenced by *parlementaire* constitutionalism, their commitment to the *parlements* as institutions frayed, particularly in the 1780's.

Despite these tensions, in the period that Jean Egret has called the "pre-Revolution" an open break in the "magisterial" party took time to appear. Barristers discounted neither the continuing dangers of "arbitrary despotism" (which threatened to silence "public opinion" once and for all), nor the magistrates' ability to wreak vengeance on opponents who still depended for their livelihood on the court system.[86] Thus for a time, the final battles between *parlement* and crown during the "pre-Revolution" of 1787–88 seemed to follow the venerable pattern established earlier in the century, with remonstrances, *lits de justice*, strikes of all judicial personnel, and so forth—although now the high court also made a point of calling for the Estates General. In 1787, when Calonne tried to force the *parlements* to register his proposed land and stamp taxes (following the failure of an Assembly of Notables set up to approve them), the magistrates went on strike and the barristers followed their example as automatically as they had in the 1750's and, initially, in 1771. When the king banished the *Parlement* of Paris to Troyes, the *bâtonnier*, Nicolas Samson, declared that the barristers would follow the magistrates into exile if called upon to do so (the *premier président* begged them to remain in Paris).[87]

In the fall, the barristers and magistrates returned to work together in triumph.

A year later, with the stalemate over taxation still unresolved, Louis XVI, his chief minister Loménie de Brienne, and Chancellor Lamoignon attempted, like Maupeou before them, to vanquish the "magisterial" opposition once and for all. Following a brutal coup in which royal troops surrounded the Palais de Justice and arrested two magistrates, the king issued the May Edicts which abolished the *parlements* outright, transferred their responsibility for registering laws to a new "plenary court," and created a series of new appellate courts called *grands bailliages* to handle judicial business. As in 1771, barristers and *procureurs* alike refused to practice before the new courts. Once again, they contributed heavily to a flood of pamphlet literature attacking the new system and calling for the restoration of the old *parlements*. Much of this literature emanated from a coterie of barristers around Target, but, according to Louis-Adrien Le Paige, it did not have the conspiratorial cohesion of the anti-Maupeou efforts. Such cohesion was not necessary, however, for with the literal bankruptcy of the French state impending, the crown could not hope to persevere in its reforms. Within months, the king reversed course, recalled the magistrates, and convoked the Estates General for the first time since 1614.[88]

During these events, the degree of real enthusiasm for the *parlements* varied widely in the bar, and overall did not approach even its 1771 levels. At one end of the spectrum stood the remnants of the Order's *parti janséniste*. Although Le Paige, Maultrot, and Mey were now aged and infirm (Maultrot was entirely blind, and Le Paige, nearly so), they had found a handful of enthusiastic successors in the persons of Armand-Gaston Camus (a future member of the Convention), Henri Jabineau, and Pierre-Jean Agier. These younger Jansenists kept up the tradition of defending rebellious lower clergy and drafting defenses of the magistrates until the very end of the Old Regime.[89] Jabineau wrote remonstrances for the *Parlement* of Paris, and when he was caught smuggling the printed "complaints" of the *Parlement* of Rouen into Paris, was briefly detained in the Bastille.[90] As for Agier, he remained wholly devoted to the corporate, organic "nation" that Le Paige had championed in the 1750's (although like Le Paige himself, he now considered the Estates General, not the *parlements*, its proper representatives). In his pamphlet *Le jurisconsulte national*, he took this idea to new, quasi-republican lengths, calling upon the Estates to reclaim their sovereign legislative power from the king. Calonne, in a pamphlet of his own from 1789, numbered Agier's work among the eight most seditious printed during this period.[91]

At the other end of the spectrum, however, a number of barristers followed the earlier example of Linguet, Gin, and Muyard de Vouglans in forthrightly supporting the crown. The most surprising of these "royalists" was Gerbier. Despite his abject explanations to Le Paige and the Prince de Conti, many members of the Order never forgave him his "treason" in returning to practice in 1771. Following accusations of corruption in 1774 and 1775, many barristers even called for his disbarment.[92] Clearly, these charges rankled, and helped drive Gerbier into the opposite camp, for the year 1787 found him working as a publicist for Calonne. Indeed, it was Gerbier who reputedly drafted the minister's notorious "Preamble" to the report of the first two sections of the Assembly of Notables, advancing the case for the land and stamp taxes.[93] Among other barristers to advance royalist opinions was the blind Lefebvre de Beauvray, who, in his detailed journal of events between 1784 and 1787, forcefully criticized the *parlements* for attempting to establish an English-style regime.[94]

The single most important pro-royalist barrister was probably Jean Blondel. Originally a supporter of the *parlements* and a friend of Target's, he shifted his loyalties when Lamoignon named him to a position in the Chancery in the mid-1780's. Jacob-Nicolas Moreau later described him as "very *parlementaire*, but *parlementaire* in my way"—which is to say of course not *parlementaire* at all.[95] Just before the *parlement*'s exile to Troyes in 1787, Blondel probably published a highly successful short pamphlet entitled *Observations of a Barrister on the Ruling of the Parlement of Paris of August 13, 1787*, which stated the ministry's case in forceful terms and condemned the *parlement*'s call for the Estates General.[96] Like many of the criticisms of the Order, this pamphlet combined *anti-parlementaire* royalism with a surprisingly democratic tone. "If the Estates General were to be formed according to the ancient usages," it argued, "a great share of the most enlightened subjects of the King would be excluded." While Blondel cautioned that any "new arrangement" of the Estates would be illegal, his argument clearly foreshadowed later attempts by the crown to reach out to the Third Estate over the *parlement*'s head.[97] The work appears to have terrified the magisterial party, for it responded with no fewer than five violent ripostes, and also called for Blondel's disbarment. The *parlement*'s allies in the Order may also have been disturbed by the fact that, according to Jacques Godard, Blondel had a number of "very zealous partisans" within the bar.[98]

Until the fall of 1788, only these two points of view, magisterial and ministerial, made themselves heard in the ongoing pamphlet debate. They did not, however, necessarily reflect the prevailing opinions in the bar. The ambivalencies among barristers in the "magisterial" party can be better gauged in the continuing correspondence of Godard and Cortot.[99] Following the May Edicts, Godard spent much of his time in classic *patriote* fashion, collecting materials for a projected collection of remonstrances, protestations, and other criticisms of the Edicts from all over France—a kind of *Lamoignoniana*, parallel to the earlier *Maupeoueana* and *Calonniana* (in the end, it seems never to have materialized).[100] Unlike the *patriotes* of 1771, however, Godard paid as much attention to the declarations of barristers and other men of the law as he did to formal protests of law courts.[101] His letters become most excited when describing incidents where barristers showed greater fortitude than magistrates, as in this comment on events in Pau, written on July 4, 1788: "At the moment that the magistrates, forced by the people to go to the Palais de Justice, sat down in their places, the Syndic of the barristers presented himself and pleaded the cause of the people. Here is a superb moment which brings back among us the fine days of Rome and Athens."[102]

The language Godard used in reference to the *parlements* is particularly revealing. On May 29, he wrote to Cortot that "there are now in Paris and in the whole of the Kingdom the names of three parties: that of the royalists, that of the *parlementaires* and that of the Nationals. These latter two have made common cause; the Nationals hope that this alliance will be long, and that at its return the *parlement*, instructed by this crisis, will remain attached to the good principles."[103] A few days later he began a sentence "If today the King were allowed to deprive the *parlement* of its privileges . . . ," only to correct himself: "or rather, to deprive the nation of its right to have *parlements*. . . . "[104] After the *parlement*'s restoration, and its ruling of September 25 which gave the Third Estate only minority representation in the upcoming assembly, he commented sadly that "*parlementaire* prejudices . . . are not extinguished" and might "harm the interests of the nation."[105] In these passages, Godard explicitly expressed the convictions that had pervaded many of Target's writings since 1771: the *parlements* were at best allies of circumstance to patriots—and not terribly trustworthy ones, either. Barristers, far more than magistrates, were the true voices of the nation.

The end of the Godard–Cortot correspondence demonstrates this point with particular force. In early February of 1789, Godard criticized his cousin for not supporting the Third Estate in its attempt to win greater representation against the privileged orders. He also reported two "lively altercations" between himself and the *parlementaire* leader d'Eprésmesnil on the same subject, and mentioned several pamphlets he had written as well. Only by the "collision of opinions," he insisted, would the truth emerge.[106] Cortot, who had previously applauded his cousin's "patriotic fervor," now replied in an angry and sarcastic vein:

> Go ahead and write, since this matters so much to the sort of reputation you want to make for yourself . . . Write, to justify the murders that your perfidious system has already led to in Brittany, and which some men have dared to threaten us with here in terrible notices tacked onto our doors. . . . It hardly suits a man of your age to have lively arguments with a Magistrate such as M. d'Eprémesnil, to dare to fight with a man who could crush you with a single word.[107]

Whereas Cortot retained an instinctual deference towards noble magistrates, his cousin now saw d'Eprémesnil not as a partner in the institutions of a judicial monarchy, but as an obstacle to the will of the nation.

The Godard–Cortot correspondence shows that the final break between most barristers and the *parlement* in 1788 was by no means abrupt or fortuitous. When the high court ruled that the three estates should each have equal representation in the Estates General, and that voting should proceed by estate, rather than by head, it defended its action by arguing that were the Third Estate to have a majority vote, the despotic ministry might well suborn or manipulate the inexperienced deputies to achieve its own nefarious purposes.[108] Thirty years before, this echo of Jansenist-*parlementaire* constitutionalism might well have held sway over Parisian barristers. By 1788, however, while certain aspects of the magisterial tradition remained vital and important, this particular argument had lost its power to convince. Meanwhile, the new suspicion of "aristocracy" and "*parlementaire* prejudices" had primed the members of the Paris bar to see in the high court's action an attempt to deprive the "national party"—and beyond it, the nation itself—of its well-deserved victory.

Despite Godard and Target's frenetic activities, it might seem that in 1788–89 the Paris bar showed remarkable passivity in comparison with some provincial ones.[109] During the summer of 1788, at least five major Orders of Barristers—Bordeaux, Aix, Toulouse, Perpignan, and Rennes— issued one or more formal protests against the May Edicts (Louis-Adrien Le Paige probably wrote one of the Breton texts).[110] During the elections to the Estates General, these and other Orders featured prominently in the debates on representation. In Rennes, the bar association engaged in several dramatic altercations with the *parlement* over the issue. In Paris, however, the Order itself hardly attracted any attention at all. Admittedly, in Paris the elections took place by district, while in other cities they took place by corporate affiliation, but this distinction does not explain the Order's inaction at earlier moments.[111]

Yet arguably, the Order's invisibility only testifies to the Parisians' political precociousness. Provincial barristers continued to think of themselves in essentially corporate terms, but the Parisians, their Order already greatly weakened, no longer did. Even though most of them might still, as a matter of tactics, ally with the "magisterial" party against "ministerial despotism" in the summer of 1788, they no longer shared the "magisterial" assumptions about the corporate organization of society. One Rennes pamphlet tellingly described barristers as "doubly citizens, both by their identity as Bretons, and by the functions they have devoted themselves to," and stated that they therefore had a special responsibility to protest injustice. A Claude-Joseph Prévost would have applauded this sentiment but Target, with his repugnance for *esprit de corps*, might not have.[112] Parisian barristers in fact took just as large a part as their provincial colleagues in the campaign against the May Edicts, but they did so not as citizens *and* barristers, but as citizens alone. They made use of their professional standing only in a few *mémoires judiciaires* on the question of representation in the Estates General, and by the winter of 1788–89, the old system of censorship had effectively collapsed, making this familiar tactic superfluous. These last examples of the political legal brief amounted to mere wisps in the snowstorm of pamphlets that fell on France in the last months of the Old Regime.[113]

In fact, in the pamphlet debates of late 1788 and early 1789 it thus becomes difficult, if not impossible, to speak of a particular accent or coloration separating barristers from the multitude of Parisians now taking an active part in political life.[114] In a sense, it can thus be argued that the critics of the Order had finally succeeded in their goal: the forbidding, black-robed figures of the *avocats* had given way to simple, sober *citoyens éloquents* who would now wear regular clothing (or perhaps, for the more vain, togas). Target, Lacretelle, and others did make important contributions to the pamphlet literature calling for a written constitution, a permanent Estates General, the "doubling of the Third," and voting by head. Furthermore, Target's *Les Etats-Généraux convoqués par Louis XVI* bore recognizable traces of its author's political odyssey.[115] Yet with the final disappearance of "magisterial" and "ministerial" parties, whose differences were ultimately rooted in a debate over French judicial institutions, the barristers' own institutional identity ceased to have the same importance. Years later, many members of the Order would again coalesce into an identifiable (and strongly counterrevolutionary) political grouping, but those who took part in the first flush of revolutionary enthusiasm wanted nothing more than to meld themselves into the seamless body of the nation.

At only one moment during 1789 would Parisian barristers be singled out for special attention: the elections to the Estates, which they dominated to a remarkable degree. Out of 407 electors selected to vote for deputies to the Third Estate from Paris, 68 came from the Order, representing over eleven percent of its membership. When the electors convened on April 26, they named Target as president, and Camus as vice-president. Eight of the 36 electors chosen to draft the formal grievances of the city of Paris were barristers. Among the deputies finally chosen to represent the Third Estate of Paris and its suburbs, 7 of 28 came from the Order, including Target, Camus, and Treilhard.[116] Jean-Sylvain Bailly, the first mayor of revolutionary Paris, wrote in his memoirs that the barristers "were one of the most enlightened groups. They made an impression everywhere both by their numbers and by their opinions. . . . One can say that the success of the Revolution is owed to their Order, which no longer exists, and which is to be forever mourned." In July, voters chose a new group of 120 electors, who became the municipal government. Twenty-three came from the Order.[117] As in other Western societies, the barristers' practice in public speaking and familiarity with legislative issues made them the "political class" par excellence.

The list of grievances (*cahier de doléances*) submitted by the city of Paris to the Estates General, which amounted to a series of proposals for an eventual French constitution, reflected the presence of so many barristers among the electors. The surviving Jansenists, led by Camus, managed to insert the doctrine of Pasquier Quesnel squarely into the section on religion, which demanded that priests obey the laws of the state, suggested the election of bishops, and made reference to the "primitive maxims" of the church and to "Gallican liberty." In an echo of scores of *mémoires judiciaires,* the *cahier* stated firmly that "ecclesiastical jurisdiction does not extend in any way to temporal matters; its exterior usage is governed by the laws of the state."[118] The section on justice, in passages Prévost would have applauded, insisted on the independence of magistrates in judicial matters, and denounced the practice of evoking cases to the king's council. In general, however, the electors broke firmly with much of *parlementaire* constitutionalism, and endorsed the positions taken by the reforming barristers in the 1780's. Thus, despite the talk of judicial independence, the section on the constitution specifically denied the high courts a right of remonstrance, and demanded a complete overhaul of French law. One passage in particular might have come from the pen of Linguet: "A formless collection of Roman laws and barbarian customs, of codes and ordinances which bear no relation to our manners . . . cannot form a body of legislation worthy of a great nation. . . . "[119]

Not everyone in Paris was content with the tremendous overrepresentation of barristers in these various proceedings. In some electoral districts, voters complained that experience in public speaking gave members of the legal profession an unfair advantage over others. Meanwhile, as we have seen, several pamphlet-writers leveled the more serious charge that members of the Order were ipso facto traitors to the Third Estate, both because of their allegiance to the *parlement,* and because of the Order's own "despotic" nature.[120] Several barristers took the trouble to respond to these charges, arguing that if anything, their professional skills, coupled with their experience in dealing with overbearing nobles, made them more effective advocates for the Third Estate. Only rarely, however, did these responses include a positive defense of the Order's political record, or an attempt to justify the tenets of *parlementaire* constitutionalism.[121]

In fact, assertions of the barristers' continuing loyalties to the *parlements* as institutions at this late date were fundamentally mistaken. The content of the Parisian *cahiers* already suggests the inadequacy of the equation, but even stronger evidence emerges in examining the list of the barristers who actually took an active political role in 1789. It is of course impossible to examine most of these men's political attitudes in great detail—in most cases, the sources simply do not exist. Yet, for a significant fraction of them, those who entered the bar before 1770, one simple test is available: had they agreed to practice before Maupeou or not? The answer is surprising. Of 28 barristers whose careers dated to before 1771, and who became deputies, alternates or electors in 1789, fully 78 percent (22) were *"rentrants"* who had practiced before Maupeou. In contrast, among all barristers whose careers spanned the period 1771–89, only 59 percent had collaborated with the chancellor. Fully 20 percent of the *rentrants* still practicing in 1789 played an active role in revolutionary politics, but only 7 percent of the surviving strikers did.[122]

These figures cast some small doubt upon any exclusive connection between the "magisterial party" and the Revolution.[123] While *parlementaire* constitutionalism obviously contributed strongly to the development of revolutionary ideology, Maupeou's willingness to smash age-old institutions to the advantage of a strong sovereign power also presaged the events of 1789. To be sure, given their long-nurtured fears of "arbitrary despotism," most barristers had well-developed suspicions about strong sovereign power. But it was those men whose distaste for the *parlements* led them to at least flirt with the ministry's program, who rushed most enthusiastically to the banner of the nation in 1789. It was those men who led the way towards a fusion of magisterial and ministerial ideas.

Postscript: The Abolition of the Legal Professions

With the coming of the French Revolution, this story approaches its end. Yet there was one final act in the drama of the Order of Barristers: its abolition. During the first years of the Revolution, the National Assembly rushed to implement many of the most radical ideas of pre-1789 legal reformers. Going beyond the furthest imaginings of a Maupeou or a Lamoignon, the Assembly made a clean sweep of the monarchy's archaic, cumbersome, incoherent judicial system. *Parlements, bailliages, sénéchaussées*, and a millenium's worth of other institutions were in the space of months cast onto a giant dustheap labeled "feudalism." The idea of an independent judiciary, charged with guarding fundamental laws, fell victim to revolutionaries who believed that a democratic sovereign power needed no such restraints—indeed, that such restraints could only serve the needs of a self-interested minority.[124] As part of this process, the assembly also granted the wishes of the harshest critics of the Order, and did away with an organized legal profession altogether.

This action was not a curiosity of the French Revolution alone, for modern democracies generally swing between two opposing views of professional organizations. In the first, these organizations are perceived as necessary upholders of standards, guardians of the public against charlatans and crooks. In the second, they are seen as bastions of monopoly and privilege, barriers to the progress of equality. The United States illustrates this ambivalence as well as France does: it possessed a recognized legal profession at independence, but during the Jacksonian period, many states opened the practice of law to any "man of good moral character" regardless of formal education or legal knowledge. As late as 1914, not a single American state required lawyers to have law degrees.[125] Still, nowhere has the pendulum swung so fast and so far as in the France of 1789–90.

The reaction of the barristers to the overturning of the world of the law testifies to the uniqueness of their experiences during the eighteenth century, and their peculiar role as catalysts in the transformation of pre-revolutionary political culture. Most members of the world of the law responded to the overturning of their privileges with exceedingly bad grace. They denounced the National Assembly's actions as illegal and demanded extravagant monetary compensation for their offices. The barristers, however, acquiesced in the destruction of their Order with barely a murmur.[126]

The case of the *procureurs* illustrates the more typical reactions. As a venal corporation, they epitomized everything that the assembly had pledged to eradicate, and their abysmal public reputation guaranteed that their plight would elicit minimal public sympathy. The *procureurs'* conspicuously tepid enthusiasm for the Revolution did not help matters: only two sat as deputies from Paris, and only a handful more belonged to the the Paris Commune. A 1789 pamphlet already labeled them counterrevolutionaries, and the series of vitriolic counterrevolutionary pamphlets published by the dean of the Community, Jean Le Maître, could have done little to relieve such suspicions.[127] Under these circumstances, the National Assembly did not hesitate to abolish the three hundred offices of *procureur au parlement* in 1790. In their place it created new, nonvenal positions—to be held by men called *avoués*—with less stringent entrance requirements and fewer opportunities for exorbitant profits.[128] Even those *procureurs* who might have applauded the Revolution protested these actions. In particular, they railed at what they considered the unconscionably low amounts the assembly reimbursed them for their offices. In a series of pamphlets, they argued their case for higher amounts at tedious length, and, as late as 1790, praised the old system of justice and argued for its preservation.[129]

In contrast to these protests and those of other groups, the Order of Barristers seemed to vanish almost without notice. On September 2, 1790, while discussing the appropriate costume for lawyers in a new, reformed court system, the National Assembly passed the following measure: "The men of the law, formerly called barristers, not being allowed to form either an order or a corporation, will wear no particular costume in their duties." In 1791, it completed the process of destruction by allowing any citizen to become an "unofficial defender" in the courts, thereby making barristers altogether superfluous.[130] In this way, almost as an afterthought, the National Assembly succeeded where successive royal ministries had failed, and finally destroyed the "absolutely independent little republic in the center of the state."

Several historians have searched for debates over the abolition of the legal profession and found surprisingly little.[131] The first direct attack on lawyers in the assembly came on August 11, 1789 from Mirabeau. The great orator demanded that "every man be allowed to plead his own case, without having to pass his papers through the hands of these rapacious agents . . . ," by which he meant *procureurs*, bailiffs, and recorders as well as barristers. The assembly's Committee on the Constitution soon endorsed this suggestion in its report on the reorganization of the judiciary. The committee specifically proposed abolishing all Orders of Barristers, making lawyers "responsible for their conduct to the Law alone."[132] Significantly, the author of this report was Nicolas Bergasse, the Mesmerist and self-proclaimed "barrister" who never appeared on the *Tableau*, but had begun to practice anyway in the Kormmann affair. For the moment, however, his efforts did not succeed. The Assembly put the committee's recommendations aside for the moment, and thereafter the future of the legal profession received only desultory attention from this National Assembly of lawyers. Over the next year, only one barrister, Louis-René Chauveau, appeared before the Committee on the Constitution to defend the Order's existence.

The motion of September 2 itself passed with no opposition and elicited little criticism. Even Target, the great defender of the Order, did not contest it.[133] Simon Linguet, seeing his long-standing desires satisfied, commented with laborious wit on the barristers' failure to react:

> Up to this point it does not seem that this order has deliberated on the *order* of the day, and the ORDERS of the Assembly. Thanks to a rather bizarre conjuncture, its BATONNIER, Me. Tronchet, and the famous doer of things, Me. Target, and those other famous men, Me. Martineau and Me. Treilhart [sic], who were once the vilest flatterers of the *Magistratesque* order, number today are among its greatest undoers, and there is no likelihood that their *order* will oppose their orders, and their example.[134]

The only apparent evidence that *any* barristers condemned the assembly's action at the time is the series of pamphlets signed by the "dean of the barristers and *procureurs* in the *Parlement* of Paris." Michael Fitzsimmons puts some stress on them in his fine history of the Order in the Revolution. But as shown earlier, these pamphlets in fact came from the pen of a *procureur*, Jean Le Maître. Only in later years would barristers openly criticize what had been done, and lobby for restoration of their lost Order.[135]

The abolition of the Order raises two puzzling questions. First of all, why did the National Assembly, dominated as it was by barristers, take such an action at all? Barristers were not venal officers, and did not form a chartered corporation. Their free association, professedly open to all men of talent and probity, did not obviously violate the assembly's principles. Why did the deputies extend their antipathy towards privileged corporatism to this self-proclaimed noncorporate body? Second, why did the barristers greet the extinction of their Order with such resignation, as if awaiting the *coup de grâce*?

Michael Fitzsimmons has recently proposed an answer to the first of these questions. In 1789–90, he argues, the barristers elected to the National Assembly, and those who remained private citizens, were possessed by two "separate dynamics." The deputies were "gripped by a sense of the sublimity of the nation," born out of the delirious night of August 4, when the assembly seemed to put the entire "feudal regime" of privilege on the bonfire. They were driven to abolish everything that even smacked of privilege, to eliminate all potentially invidious distinctions between French citizens. The other barristers, meanwhile, remained locked into a traditional "consciousness of état, corps and ordre. They had little sympathy for or understanding of the new standard of the sublimity of the nation asserted by the National Assembly."[136] Thus for Fitzsimmons, the abolition of the profession stemmed from a revolutionary mentality that had not existed before 1789 and was alien to all those who had not experienced the night of August 4 at first hand.

This interpretation certainly helps explain why many of the barrister-deputies acted as they did. To them, September 2, 1790 represented a chance to make an "August 4-style" sacrifice of their own, even if their "corps" had a better *raison d'être* than most. Yet other, more important factors were at work. After all, the idea of abolishing the Order did not spring from the brow of Marianne in 1789, but dated back almost to the *creation* of the Order as a functioning bar association. As we have seen, Fericoq de la Dourie and others called for abolition in 1727, and found a ready echo from Cardinal Fleury and his ministerial advisors. In the 1760's, Linguet, supported at least in part by Falconnet and Gin, again proposed the effective abolition of the legal profession. Between 1774 and 1789, a debate on precisely this subject did great damage to the Order, with the critics' charges gaining support in the private musings of barristers such as Godard and Lefebvre, not to mention in highly popular works such as the *Mémoires secrets* and Mercier's *Tableau de Paris*.

Turning to what little discussion of the subject took place in the National Assembly, it becomes clear that the arguments for and against the Order did not represent a wholly new departure, but in many ways continued the debate carried on by the traditionalists and critics in the 1770's and 1780's. When Bergasse wrote that barristers should be "responsible for their conduct to the Law alone," he echoed Linguet and Brissot's call for barristers to have no authority above them but the crown—at the time the fount of all legislation. As for Louis-René Chauveau, the defender of the Order before the Committee on the Constitution, his words might have come from any of a dozen speeches by Lambon, Chavray de Boissy, Caillau de Courcelles or, Duvert d'Emalleville. "After the suppression of the Order of Barristers," he insisted, "the bar will be peopled by all those men who would have been kept out or purged by a salutary discipline." Bergasse, he continued, "has confounded liberty with license."[137] It is clear, therefore, that the barrister-deputies drew not only on the new spirit sweeping the assembly, but on long-standing currents of thought within the legal profession as well.

Did most barristers still abide by a "traditional consciousness of état, corps and ordre" in 1789? If so, then why did they, unlike the *procureurs*, show such remarkable passivity? Fitzsimmons correctly rejects the earliest explanation, given by the former barrister Jean Fournel in the early nineteenth century, namely that barristers preferred a sort of professional harakiri to practicing before a reorganized and "unworthy" judiciary (as he notes, no other sources corroborate this account).[138] Fitzsimmons himself speculates that many senior barristers had died, that others had left Paris, and that still others were distracted by their new duties in revolutionary posts. Still, only a minority of barristers served in these posts, and as for the other factors, it is perhaps sufficient to note that the *procureurs* and many other groups managed to protest their fate in no uncertain terms despite similar disarray. Beyond Chauveau's appearance before the Committee on the Constitution, there is no evidence that *any* barrister worked to save the Order.

Arguably, within the Order of Barristers, the change in "mentality" that Fitzsimmons attributes to the effects of the Revolution itself actually began much earlier. Thus if the abolition of the legal profession came as something of an anticlimax, it was because the critics of the Order had already effectively won the battle. In the 1780's their ideas seemed quite simply self-evident. Was arguing cases a right, not a privilege? Should it be open to all? Obviously. Was formal training and erudition important to effective advocacy, particularly in comparison with literary skill? Obviously not. Should advocates have the freedom to practice as they saw fit, subject only to the discipline of the highest public authority? The question answered itself. Was the Order a bastion of undeserved privilege? There was no doubt. These arguments amounted to far more than the pouting complaints of a few unsuccessful candidates for membership in the Order. They had become the conventional wisdom of a large part of the Order, particularly the younger members. It is hardly surprising, then, that when the National Assembly acted upon these arguments, the Order responded with tacit approval.

Most barristers, it is true, eventually turned against the Revolution. The former Jansenist Camus, who became a *conventionnel*, and Jacques-Nicolas Billaud-Varenne, an unremarked barrister in 1789 who became a member of the Committee of Public Safety, were exceptions, not the rule.[139] Target, the hero of the Third Estate, turned out to be a typical *monarchien* and by 1792 was offered the chance to defend Louis XVI (it was an honor he prudently—too prudently, said his enemies—declined). Those barristers who later wrote memoirs or histories of the period generally regretted their initial enthusiasm. They also regretted the abolition of the Order.[140] Yet this political disillusionment—an experience shared by millions of Frenchmen—should not blind us to the barristers' initial revolutionary sympathies. In 1789, barristers were indeed the revolutionary profession par excellence, a group among whom democratic ideas had already triumphed. Embracing these ideas may well have meant rejecting the Order's proud traditions of "independence" and autonomy. But it must be remembered that since the beginning, the Order had served as a means to an end—an instrument to preserve the social position of barristers in a society of privilege, and to defend the ideal of a judicial monarchy. By 1789, neither of these goals had much relevance to Parisian barristers, who saw vast new careers opening up before them in a democratic society. They therefore abandoned their Order, and indeed their profession, with little regret. Only later did many of them come to think better of what they had so easily given away, and to think of themselves again as barristers first, citizens second.

Conclusion

In the midst of the great turmoil, when corruption had spread every-where, when despotism had left nothing unsoiled and had forced every head to bow down, where did liberty still survive? Where were the re-straints and the barriers that tyranny's force could not overturn? Was it not the Order of Barristers which preserved its liberty together with its discipline? Did not despotism number the destruction of our privi-leges among its chosen means of destroying what remained of the citi-zens' liberty?

          Réponse d'un avocat à l'écrit intitulé les Idées d'un citoyen de Paris *

When Guy Target, in his brief for the Marquise d'Anglure, called on the legislator to act, he could scarcely have imagined that within three years he would be a legislator himself. Nor could he have dreamed that within six years, after a career spent posing as the nation's advocate against the king, he would be asked to serve as the king's advocate against a stern and unforgiving nation (or rather, against a Convention claiming to represent the nation). Such, of course, was the tremendous concentration of events and overturning of fortunes that characterized the French Revolution.

For the most part, this book has not directly concerned itself with either the origins or the subsequent course of the Revolution. As to the origins, it would be ludicrous to draw too many conclusions from the ex-periences of a single professional group, no matter how important this group later proved in the maelstrom of revolutionary politics. As to the second problem, if the warring historical factions of the past thirty years have agreed on anything, it is that the Revolution's radicalization cannot be explained in terms of the Old Regime alone (whether it depended

*(Paris, 1789), p. 4.

more on external "circumstances" or a "revolutionary dynamic" is another question entirely). This book has mostly attempted to chart some
of the changing political contours of the Old Regime, and particularly
the opening up of French public life to men of relatively little social
standing, wealth, and privilege that occurred between 1660 and 1790. It
has tried to show how, in a nation where the law courts had long fought
to establish themselves as the principal mediators between the king and
his subjects, and where a free press and elective representative institutions
were conspicuously absent, the legal profession was central to this process
of opening, and to the birth of democratic politics in France.

At this point, however, it may be worthwhile, after first recapitulating
the principal conclusions of the book, also to speculate briefly as to their
larger significance for the Revolution as well as the Old Regime. For despite the rhetoric to the contrary, the deputies to the National and Legislative assemblies, and the Convention, were not wholly "new men," that
is to say, regenerated products of a complete rupture with the past. The
Target who took the lead in dismantling the *parlements* was the same
man who had praised them fifteen years earlier as "the repositories of the
tears of the poor, the wishes of the People, the holiness of the Laws."[1]
The Armand-Gaston Camus who sat in the Convention as it attempted
to eradicate French Catholicism was the same man who had earlier sat at
the feet of Louis-Adrien Le Paige, imbibing his Jansenist verities. The lessons and experiences gained in earlier years did not simply vanish, or
cease to count. By retracing the path that barristers followed before
1789, it should be possible, hardly to explain everything about their subsequent behavior, but at least to define some of the beliefs and presuppo-
sitions that shaped their actions as they skidded down the treacherous
slope of revolutionary events. First, however, a recapitulation is in order.

Although Parisian barristers refused to keep detailed records of their
Order, the membership's exceptional loyalty and longevity (by Old Regime standards) might have been expected to ensure a high degree of
institutional continuity nonetheless. In any given year, it was not unusual
to find twenty or more barristers who had spent more than half a century
in the bar, and the median length of service rarely dropped below fifteen
years.[2] Many of the most influential barristers, including Prévost, Le Paige,
Maultrot, and Mey, all lived into their eighties, a fact perhaps not entirely
unconnected with their abstemious Jansenist tastes. In fact, the entire
hundred-and-thirty-year life of the Parisian Order of Barristers under the
Old Regime was spanned by just two men's careers. Michel Duperray,
who signed many of the early Jansenist *consultations* and corresponded
with Bishop Soanen, took the barrister's oath in 1661, just after the start
of the *conférences de discipline* at the home of *bâtonnier* François de
Montholon. He died, still active, in 1730, just at the moment when an
eighteen-year-old law graduate named Louis-Adrien Le Paige was beginning to frequent the Parisian courts as a *stagiaire*. Le Paige's own life linked

Louis XIV and Napoleon, while his career covered both the Order's zenith and its later decreptitude and abolition.[3]

Yet despite this degree of continuity, and despite well-known nostrums about lawyers' essentially conservative nature, this hundred-and-thirty-year span witnessed several drastic upheavals in the way law was practiced in Paris. Barristers familiar with the calm and decorum of the bar in the early years of Louis XIV's personal rule were astonished at the turmoil and emotion generated during the heyday of Claude-Joseph Prévost. Barristers who began their careers under Prévost blinked in disbelief when seeing what the bar had become in the time of Simon Linguet. The reasons for these transformations lie in three distinct moments of political crisis.

The first of these moments, which actually stretched out over the first half of the seventeenth century, involved both the steady encroachment on the judicial system by the royal administration, and the completion of the long process by which magistrates became the nucleus of a new nobility, the *noblesse de robe*. Barristers therefore found themselves reduced in prestige (at least relative to the magistrates) and blocked in their chances for advancement, all within a judiciary which was itself losing its central position within the French state. This loss of status, which barristers freely lamented in writings such as Loisel's *Dialogue* or Gabriau de Riparfonds' testament, finally led to the establishment of a new, independent organization: the Order of Barristers. With its founding also came a new consciousness of the bar as a separate profession, possessed of its own standards and its own honors. It was no longer primarily the "seminary of dignities," a preparation for greater things in the service of the king. It was an independent, honorable calling.

Nonetheless, the founders of the Order strenuously worked against the perception that it amounted to just another *corps* of legal practitioners, among the many that flourished in the Palais de Justice. They refused to form a chartered corporation, or to accept venal offices. In the word "order" itself, redolent of chivalry and monasticism, they underlined what they considered the unique, quasi-sacred nature of their vocation, and also the unique "independence" which, so they claimed, allowed complete dedication to the interests of their clients. In their new association, d'Aguesseau emphasized in 1698, only reason and nature would establish rankings, not the prejudices of the world. To describe the special purity of the Order, the barristers made use of grandiose analogies, comparing themselves to priests, and then, in the eighteenth century, to classical Roman republicans. When the Marquis d'Argenson called the Order a "republic" in 1735, he meant the term as a broad insult, but in fact, barristers did often envisage their Order as a sort of little republic of virtue existing amidst the decadence of modern times. Arguably, this habit of thought later made them more receptive to authors such as Rousseau, who also used elements of republican language.

This refusal to form a *corps* did not prevent barristers from imitating one when it suited them, however, particularly during the struggles they waged over etiquette (at these moments the Order bore very little relation indeed to a republic of virtue). It was through collective, corporate-style work stoppages over issues of headwear, placement in processions, and the positioning of speakers in court that the barristers forced the noble magistrates to give them that degree of ceremonial respect which they cherished almost as fervently as did the courtiers of Versailles. In addition, in order to maintain the "purity" deemed necessary to their calling, the leaders of the Order enforced a draconian discipline far stricter than what prevailed in many other corporate bodies.

These developments did not have any immediate bearing on the barristers' attitudes towards the law or the proper constitution of the French polity. In these matters, under Louis XIV they continued to uphold the views of *politique* predecessors such as Etienne Pasquier, and pursued the ideal described here as the "judicial monarchy." That is to say, they believed in strong royal power, but power mediated through, and restrained by, the institutions of royal justice. They saw the court system, guided by a spirit of equity and the magistrates' oracular interpretations of divine justice, as maintaining a proper balance among conflicting interests in French society, and also guaranteeing the property and privileges of individual subjects against the danger of royal—and even more importantly—ecclesiastical caprice. In this vision of things, barristers themselves functioned primarily as advisers to the magistrates, to their clients, and occasionally to the king himself (as in the drafting of the great ordinances of the 1660's). They remained an integral part of the institutional structure of the *parlements*, and by extension, of the monarchy. While the doctrine of radical self-effacement demanded of barristers by Etienne Pasquier lost its hold by the mid-seventeenth century, the concommitant introduction of "Ciceronian" oratory in no way led to any invasion of "republican" political values; if anything, the new style of oratory fit in far better with the "Louisquatorzian" quest for ever more elaborate glorification of the crown. Even d'Aguesseau's explicit invocation of classical republican virtues in his 1698 oration on the "Independence of the Barrister" had no political resonance for members of the Order. The association remained a vehicle for social, not political, goals.

This shunning of any active involvement in public affairs came to an abrupt end, however, in the second moment of crisis: the dying Louis XIV's final, convulsive attempts to rid his kingdom of the Jansenist "heresy." Louis's campaign, which culminated in the bull *Unigenitus* in 1713, horrified the members of the Order for two reasons. First, and most obviously, it effectively branded many barristers themselves as heretics because of their attachment to the theology of Jansenius, Saint-Cyran, Antoine Arnauld, and Pasquier Quesnel. Second, the very issuance of the bull seemed to put the livelihood of French Catholics at the mercy of the Roman pontiff, effectively nullifying the protection that the French crown and its judicial institutions supposedly offered to individual subjects through the web of privileges and particular "liberties" that pervaded Old Regime society. In other words, the form as well as the content of the bull seemed to challenge both basic Augustinian principles of restraint and moderation, and the principles of equity and justice that bound the kingdom together. The notion that an alien and capricious authority could reach into the heart of France and impose physical penalties on men and women in defiance of royal law was quickly stigmatized as "arbitrary despotism," a threat to the very constitution of the state as well as the church. If it succeeded, barristers asked, what further "enterprises" would follow? These fears were widely shared beyond the citadel of the Palais de Justice, and thus the bull raised a far greater degree of opposition than might have been predicted from the small numbers of men and women who could accurately be called "Jansenist." Yet this opposition did not initially find effective institutional expression—certainly not from the *parlements*, who offered only tepid resistance to the crown, even after they recovered their right to remonstrance in 1715.

This moment of despair in the life of the Paris bar therefore prompted its Jansenist members to take unprecedented measures. Rather than rely on the magistrates to block the bull, they decided to harness the power of the printing press and, in conjunction with Jansenist clerics, to appeal directly to the audience they called the "public." If the *parlements* would not defend ordinary Frenchmen from arbitrary despotism, they reasoned, then ordinary Frenchmen would have to be goaded into defending themselves, and into demonstrating that the bull could only be imposed at the cost of unacceptable civil strife. Barristers therefore began the familiar task of deploying their oratorical expertise in the form of polemical writings, but for the first time they did so not as hirelings of great nobles, the crown, or a Catholic League, but from an independent position, and on their own behalf. In the pathbreaking trial of the clerics from Reims in 1716, Claude-Joseph Prévost and Louis Chevallier addressed their speeches directly to the "public," and an impressive organization of printers and peddlers made their printed legal briefs—immune, like all briefs, from censorship—available to a wide readership. Thus began a half-century in which barristers' briefs, sometimes printed in 10,000 or more copies, became a legal form of opposition journalism, and one of the most effective examples of it yet seen in France.

The adoption of these new tactics not only represented a new, and more direct engagement in public life than before; it also represented a step away from the ideal of the "judicial monarchy," in which "public opinion" existed nowhere save in the *parlements'* remonstrances. It can be argued that Jansenist barristers were prepared to use impure means (in this case, demagogy) to achieve the pure end of restoring some half-mythical *status quo ante* in which printed propaganda would again have no place. Yet, in fact, barristers soon found the means too seductive to abandon with any ease. Within the context of briefs on the subject of ecclesiastical government, figures such as Aubry and Maraimberg began to elaborate notions of "imprescriptible rights" possessed by individual members of the public, and "contracts" between the rulers and the ruled —ideas which, in a secular context, would have been wholly anathema given prevailing theories on the divine right of kings. Later on, Louis-Adrien Le Paige, systematizing and expanding upon the ideas of Prévost, and adding his own inimitable talent for pamphleteering, began to adapt Catholic conciliarist ideas to secular purposes.[4] In his monumental *Lettres historiques*, he posited a "nation" that held the same relationship to the king that the church as a whole supposedly held to the pope, and whose interests were guarded by a national *parlement* born together with the monarchy. These ideas, while in no way an example of Lockean social contract theory, nonetheless were difficult to square with earlier political language which still recognized the king as sole sovereign. Although the barristers presented their appeal to "public opinion" simply as a means of calling the king back to his proper duties, in point of fact it was becoming a quest for new forms of political legitimacy.

It is crucial to recognize that this ideological evolution did not proceed independently from the evolution of legal practice itself: in fact the two were intimately linked. In the late seventeenth and early eighteenth centuries, the dominant figures in the bar were still the great orators, men such as Olivier Patru. In the 1720's and 1730's, however, their successors, men such as Alexis Le Normand and Henry Cochin, were eclipsed by the authors of "political" briefs and pamphlets. Indeed, Le Normand himself was repeatedly overruled and humiliated by his more "zealous" colleagues, who also conspired to deny him the crowning glory of his oratorical career: entry into the Académie Française. Advancement in the bar was coming to depend not only on a talent for legal analysis and public speaking, but on participation in the Jansenist *causes célèbres*. Thus, whereas d'Aguesseau had defined success in the bar as the ability to please the public, the young barristers who rushed to put their names to incendiary *consultations* now defined it as the ability to *speak for* the public. In a single case from the early 1740's, fully a third of the barristers in active practice signed a *consultation*, even though doing so could conceivably arouse the ire of the ministry.[5] From the "seminary of dignities," the legal profession had thus changed itself into the "seminary of publicists," producing most of the authors responsible for the important *parlementaire* writings that challenged the monarchy in the mid-century. Later on, many of the most important royalist writers, notably Moreau, Linguet, Bouquet, and Gin, would come out of the same milieu. These changes all acted to increase the barristers' professional distance from the magistrates. The members of the bar now acted less as an institutional part of the judicial power than as its autonomous auxiliaries.

Under these conditions, the Order of Barristers itself underwent a radical transformation, becoming what I have called an *organisation de combat*. Thanks to the draconian rule of Claude-Joseph Prévost and his fellow Jansenists, "impurity" in a barrister was redefined to mean not only those qualities which might tarnish the dignity of the bar, but any beliefs or actions which might threaten its unanimity, and thereby make a strike, waged to support Jansenists or the *parlement*, ineffective. Although the crown, in its own pamphlet campaigns, repeatedly decried the barristers' overstepping of their professional "competence," it tried only once to impose penalties on barristers for their writings lest it provoke a strike. And in this one case, the "affair of the barristers" of 1730–31, the Order stood firm, the Parisian courts ground to a standstill and the ministry finally retreated. This case so inflated the confidence of Prévost and some of his fellow "zealots" that by 1735 the Marquis d'Argenson could sarcastically describe the bar as a "second magistracy."[6] It took the humiliating *querelle de préséance* of 1735 to make the "zealots" realize that the Order's ambitions had necessary limits. Even so, once the magistrates began to intervene more actively in favor of persecuted Jansenists against the ever-present threat of "arbitrary despotism," the Order continued to provide them with a highly useful auxiliary force, ensuring that if the crown tried to cow the high courts by force, or replace the magistrates with its own pliant nominees, the legal system would cease to function. Meanwhile, the harsh discipline acted to stifle not merely any possible defections to the crown, but also any possibility of barristers using the profession's privileged position to advance causes other than Jansenist-*parlementaire* ones.

The Order as it existed in the 1750's was a formidable organization; yet in a surprisingly short period of time it fell victim to its own success. Why? One obvious reason is that the issue that had first galvanized its entry into the politics of public opinion—Jansenism—faded away after the expulsion of the Jesuits in the early 1760's, depriving the "zealots" of their most important political motive. Just as importantly, though, the political freedoms gained by barristers soon lured into the bar men who wished to do battle for issues other than the rights of Jansenists. The astonishing success enjoyed by Voltaire in the case of Jean Calas, just at the moment of the victory over the Jesuits, revealed the tremendous potential of *causes célèbres* for exposing many different varieties of intolerance and persecution. Few of the barristers inspired by Voltaire's example had even a vestigial loyalty to the ideal of the judicial monarchy, although many appreciated the role of the *parlements* as a bulwark against despotism. Nor did they think of publicity simply as a means to a specific political end: they believed that continuous, open public debate had a positive value. For this reason they also had suspicions about any organization that sought to restrict access to the courtroom and the printing presses.

For a time, the tensions engendered by these developments remained largely below the surface, despite the disbarment of a Huerne de la Mothe for his "irreligious" briefs, and the moves to inflict the same penalty on Calas's advocate, Élie de Beaumont, and the controversial Simon Linguet. Yet in the *causes célèbres* of the late 1760's, a number of barristers began to take positions consistently opposed to the interests of the *parlements.* If these men did not quite form a *parti du roi* within the Order, their presence did suggest the existence of real political divisions. Clearly, the more it became possible to base a career at the bar on a talent for polemical writing, rather than on legal expertise, the less reason barristers had to defend the prerogatives of the legal system as a whole, and therefore of the *parlements.*

The tensions finally broke out into the open thanks to the third moment of crisis: Chancellor Maupeou's coup against the *parlements* of 1771, and the creation of new courts subservient to the crown. To the leaders of the Order, this blow seemed every bit as harsh as the bull *Unigenitus* itself. They fought against it using the weapons they had so carefully honed in the previous decades, mounting the largest campaign of pamphlets yet seen in eighteenth-century France. To some in the Order, however, Maupeou's actions had a certain attraction: they represented a necessary correction to the overweening claims of the magistracy, and also, just as importantly, an opportunity for their own advancement. Thanks to Maupeou's abolition of venality, nine barristers managed to enter the *parlement* themselves. Furthermore, since the leadership of the Order refused to practice before the new courts, effectively suspending the existence of the organization, those who did return to work found that the unwritten code governing their conduct of cases had suddenly disappeared. Despite the abuse hurled at them by their striking colleagues, they not only returned to practice, but began to give free rein to their heretofore frustrated literary ambitions. Led by Linguet, they transformed one case after another into sensational *causes célèbres,* turned the spotlight on themselves as much as possible (sweeping away the last traces of Pasquier's doctrine of self-effacement) and began to draw on the full range of ideas, motifs, and vocabulary popularized by the *philosophes.* If their predecessors had brought barristers and men of letters closer together by making publicity an essential part of the profession, these men sought to erase the line altogether, and make publicity the essence of the profession (as indeed they believed it could be if the law itself were sufficiently simplified).

In 1774, Louis XV's death brought Maupeou's experiment to an abrupt conclusion, but the returning leaders of the Order, despite considerable effort, could not manage to reverse the changes of the previous three years. Their weakness resulted in the first instance from their earlier insistence on distinguishing the Order from corporate bodies. If their association indeed amounted to little more than an agreement by certain law graduates to argue cases against each other, with no formal officers, and no written charter, then disciplinary powers ultimately lay not with a handful of aged veterans, but with all the barristers gathered together in a general assembly. As early as 1735, Prévost had failed to keep the membership united against the *parlement* and so a strike collapsed. In 1771, the leadership had proved unable to prevent half the membership from returning to work. In 1775, once again, the leadership found that the rank and file simply would not support a drastic purge, or a return to the old unwritten code of conduct. The reason for this reluctance was simple: the new, freewheeling style of legal practice that had flowered during the Maupeou period was too attractive, and too profitable to abandon, particularly for the younger barristers more inspired by Voltaire than by d'Aguesseau.

Thus the cohesive, disciplined *organisation de combat* never revived, and during the last fifteen years of the Old Regime, frenetic, flamboyant *causes célèbres* continued without interruption. Barristers continued to make names for themselves through self-consciously "outrageous" courtroom behavior that would have utterly horrified a Pasquier or Loisel. The ideal of the *jurisconsulte-philosophe* popularized by Pierre-Louis de Lacretelle flourished, and Mercier's dream that men of law and men of letters should form "but a single estate" seemed to many onlookers an imminent and desirable state of affairs. Among the many critics of the bar, the very idea of an Order of Barristers—of any sort of organization that gave a privileged minority superior access to courtrooms and the printing press—came to seem self-evidently absurd and hateful.

During this period, the political atmosphere in the bar also shifted. The more radical critics of the Order, their prejudices towards the judiciary confirmed and strengthened by a flowering legal reform movement, desired nothing less than the complete overhaul of the French legal system, with all the political consequences that would flow from this event. They called for the replacement of the rickety tower of existing jurisdictions by a simple, rational set of appellate courts, and the replacement of the complex, overlapping legal doctrines by a single, simple, rational code that any citizen could understand. A privileged, aristocratic body such as a *parlement*, they now argued, had no place trying to exercise guardianship over the laws—such a role belonged only to an enlightened sovereign power. For more moderate barristers such as Target, this prescription seemed too extreme. Nonetheless, the implicit reforming agenda of their own cases often found greater favor in the ministry than in the *parlements*, and Target and Lacretelle in particular collaborated actively with Malesherbes and other reforming ministers to bring about changes in the law. Instead of *causes célèbres* exposing the abuses of the ministry to the glare of publicity, they now exposed the abuses of the judges, and indeed of the laws themselves. The barristers, rather than acting as auxiliaries of the judicial power, had therefore gone some way towards becoming auxiliaries of the legislative power, which is to say, of the crown. To be sure, fears of "arbitrary despotism" had not disappeared, and a blow such as the May Edicts of 1788, in which the king once again tried to dissolve the high courts, quickly drove most barristers back into alliance with the magistrates. But by this point, they clearly saw the magistrates not as their natural superiors, but as allies of circumstance, and untrustworthy ones at that.

Even for the remnants of the old *parti janséniste*, the political situation looked different. The *Maximes du droit public françois*, composed during the Maupeou crisis, had far more to say about individual rights than the Jansenist literature of the 1750's or before. Whereas Prévost and Chevallier had called for a temperate monarchy restrained by courts of law acting in the name of a collective nation, their successors called for a monarchy restrained by individual citizens, and they bolstered their arguments with citations drawn not only from Jansenist and conciliarist sources, but from natural law theorists, John Locke and Algernon Sydney. Nor, after the *parlements'* manifest inability to stand up to Maupeou, did the Jansenists place the same emphasis on the constitutional role of the judiciary. While defending the *parlements'* right of registration, they also argued that the Estates General was necessary fully to represent the French nation. In these ways, even the most *parlementaire* barristers established a certain distance from the magistrates, many of whom continued to defend the high courts as quasi-sacred institutions, and who still thought of the French polity as a chain of corporate bodies, not as a union of individual citizens.

In sum, long before 1789, the two languages of politics, "magisterial" and "ministerial," that had long competed within the world of the law, had come to seem insufficient to most Parisian barristers. They had not rejected *all* of what Dale Van Kley has called the "Jansenist constitutional legacy." To the contrary. They still drew on the great Jansenist publicists, Le Paige, Maultrot, and Mey, for many of their ideas, particularly the key notion of national sovereignty.[7] But once a synthesis of magisterial and ministerial ideas began to emerge during the heated debates of 1788–89, the barristers quickly rallied behind it, abandoning both *parlement* and crown for the new standard of the nation.

The consequences of this account for our understanding of the Old Regime have already been touched on in the preceding chapters. First of all, this history illuminates the central role of the French state in creating what can be called the eighteenth century's "politics of public opinion." The emergence of this form of politics of course depended on many different factors: an expansion in the market for printed works, the invention of new forums for the communication of ideas, and the transformations broadly referred to as the "desacralization" of the monarchy. These factors explain why many new and previously marginal voices were able to make themselves heard in political debate. They do not, however, go very far towards explaining why men already well-ensconced within French institutions, the sort of men who in the Renaissance had already considered themselves quintessentially "political," should have gone so far not only to embrace the printing press with fervor (their predecessors had done so on many occasions), but to redefine their very calling around the notion of "publicity."

If barristers, among the different groups who helped transform French political culture in the eighteenth century, acted in this way, it was because initially they felt they had no choice. In their minds, the crown itself was systematically violating the principles that had bound France together: reducing the power of the "depositories of the law," liberating the sovereign from all restraints, and confiding to an alien, Roman hand the key to French souls. While they remained ostentatiously loyal to what they called the "royal power," they meant by this phrase the entire sphere of the monarchy, including the *parlements*, not simply the king. As to the physical monarch, the barristers quite simply feared a terrible plot "to subjugate those who have been regarded as the images of God on earth to the triumphant chariot of religion," to quote not a pamphlet designed for public consumption, but Claude-Joseph Prévost's confidential remarks to a meeting of Jansenist barristers in 1739.[8]

It is true that the barristers' fears of despotism throughout much of the eighteenth century focused on the church, and the crown's support of the anti-Jansenist forces within it. In the barristers' minds, however (as in the minds of most of their contemporaries), what we define as religious, political, and legal issues were fused together into a single whole. Whether the issue at hand was the future of Catholic theology, the burden of taxation, or the right of remonstrance, a single scale of measurement applied, with "justice" at one end and "arbitrary despotism" on the other. Consider again the striking, apocalyptic 1731 pamphlet, *The Barristers' Imaginary Heresy*, issued in the midst of an affair that began with the trial of three Jansenists priests. It warned that if the alliance of ministry and bishops, secretly controlled by the Jesuits, succeeded in muzzling the barristers, "defenders of the people's cause" (and portrayed as "modern Jeremiahs"), then the axle of justice around which the kingdom revolved would crumble, and the entire nation would metaphorically sink beneath the waves.[9] To Le Paige, writing forty years later, the idea of "state Molinism" still came quite naturally.

Briefly put, then, Jansenist barristers first began appealing to the "tribunal of public opinion" because they felt the monarchy had broken down the political structures that had previously accommodated their interests. Had the monarchy really done this? The "plot" to subjugate France to the papacy of course had no more existence in fact than another "plot" whose discovery had momentous consequences in the eighteenth century: the one feared by the American colonists on the part of English ministers and bishops.[10] It can be argued that the barristers' view of the political scene, while coherent and sincerely held, amounted to no more than an ideological construction, an all-too-familiar attempt to contrast a lost, mythical golden age (in this case, of the "judicial monarchy") with a corrupt and dispiriting present. Yet I have contended here that the barristers' perceptions, while filtered through a number of lenses (including that of Biblical exegesis), did not arise *ex nihilo*.[11] They represented at once a response to, and an interpretation of ministerial policies aimed at extending the prerogatives of the royal administration, and freeing it from incumbrances inherited from the Middle Ages. These policies affected the barristers in a directly material way, by threatening the importance of the courts. They also derived from philosophical principles very much at odds with the barristers' cherished Augustinian notions of restraint and moderation. The monarchy of the eighteenth century was a very different creature from its mid-sixteenth century predecessor, however much the barristers may have exaggerated and mythicied the changes. It was against this new, institutionally stronger, centralizing monarchy that the barristers protested.[12]

The monarchy's role in creating the politics of public opinion did not end with its encroachment on the judiciary and its opposition to the Jansenists. As the conflict with the *parlements* grew more heated and polarized in the mid-eighteenth century, the crown began openly attempting to sweep away the existing system of restraints on royal power, to build up an unfettered administration, and to institute supposedly "rational" reforms without regard for precedent. This campaign probably developed more in the heat of political battle than according to any preconceived plan.[13] Nonetheless, it did proceed, and indeed reached new heights in the Maupeou crisis. The now explicit attack on the "judicial monarchy" had two unintended effects, however. First, it killed any hope among the monarchy's opponents that the "judicial monarchy" could be revived without fundamental constitutional changes. Even more importantly, by briefly doing away with the existing judicial order, it smashed many of the restraints that the *parlementaire* camp had imposed on itself, and on the emergence of new currents of opposition. The Paris bar as it existed between 1775 and 1789, filled with men who considered themselves heirs to the ancient Romans in a directly political sense, posed a far greater danger to the regime than its predecessor had ever done. Thus the monarchy, by attempting to kill off one opponent with whom it had lived in uncomfortable symbiosis, ended up speeding the rise of a new, far more deadly one.

A second broad consequence of the barristers' experience for the history of the Old Regime involves the role of the legal profession itself as a principal channel for the development of the "politics of public opinion." From the initial Jansenist involvement in the trial of the Reims clerics in 1716, through the affair of the Council of Embrun and the extraordinary success of Aubry's *consultation,* to the concerted campaigns of *mémoires* of the 1730's and 1740's, barristers repeatedly pushed the boundaries of what constituted acceptable levels of opposition within a theoretically absolute monarchy. It is difficult to gauge the impact of their writings, but the crown's own strenuous—indeed, sometimes desperate—attempts to silence the barristers, and to limit their activities to a narrowly defined corporate sphere, provide one crude, but important measurement. In numerous pamphlets and in projected "reforms" of the profession, the ministry repeatedly questioned the right of barristers to speak out on matters where they did not have direct professional "competence." It questioned the legality of using *mémoires judiciaires* as a form of occasional opposition journalism, and often suppressed these documents, although it dared not impose sanctions on the authors. Both Cardinal Fleury and Chancellor Maupeou hoped as well to destroy the *Tableau*, the crucial instrument that allowed the Order's *parti janséniste* to keep its troops in line. The cardinal even called the barristers the "absolute masters of the *parlement*," and noted that their severe discipline had "dangerous consequences for the state."[14] Royalist and anti-Jansenist pamphleteers took great pains to mock the barristers as buffoons stumbling into unfamiliar territory, but this very attempt to exorcise through ridicule underlined the extent to which the barristers represented a new and threatening force in French political life.

Towards the end of the Old Regime, barristers went beyond simply opposing the crown on the issues of Jansenism and *parlementaire* constitutionalism. They succeeded in turning French courtrooms into an open forum for the discussion of religious toleration, judicial reform, and the abuse of privilege—three of the issues dearest to the *philosophes*. In fact, as Sarah Maza has convincingly suggested, during this period the courts became a living theater of the French Enlightenment, where barristers prompted their clients to speak in the accents of Rousseauian sentimentality, carried on battles against the *infâme*, and exposed superstition and privilege to the glare of reason and utility. Private squabbles became metaphors for the proper conduct of public life: in a harbinger of what would become known as "revolutionary morality," barristers held up the highborn and the high-placed—even the royal family itself—to the moral standards of the intimate, domestic, private sphere. Whether, as Maza argues, barristers should be seen as the true successors to the heroic first generation of *philosophes* (better they, she implies, than pale literary imitators such as Suard or La Harpe), it is undeniable that these great *causes célèbres* marked one of the first intrusions of Enlightenment values and ideas into the sphere of French government.[15] And as many historians have observed, courtrooms offered a sort of rehearsal hall for the men who would soon have, to put Shakespeare's words into a different context, "a kingdom for a stage."

A final consequence of the changes in the bar concerns what might be cumbersomely called the explicit politicization of private social relations. While historians today like to identify the Revolution itself as the moment when Rousseau's dictum "everything depend[s] fundamentally on politics" suddenly became self-evident for educated Frenchmen, within the large section of the educated population involved in the law, the idea had been self-evident for years.[16] Even those successful orators who avoided politically sensitive cases—a Henry Cochin or a Alexis Le Normand early in the century, Gerbier towards the end—repeatedly found themselves having to decide whether to take part in a strike, to sign a controversial *consultation*, or to accept a position offered by the ministry. If they tried to trim or compromise, as Le Normand and Gerbier both did, then their standing among their colleagues suffered badly.

   It may be argued that the politicization of the bar had little impact on
the hundreds of men who stayed out of the public eye, and avoided "matters of the sort that belong particularly to the *philosophe* or literary jurist."
Yet during the heyday of the Order, these barristers' own careers depended on backing the leadership's political views, even in the case of
strikes that caused considerable financial hardship. Barristers also knew
that adding their name to the appropriate *consultation* was a quick way to
ingratiate themselves with the leadership and advance to a position of
greater visibility. In fact, both before and after the Maupeou crisis, success
in the profession depended as much on an ability to pose as a virtuous
defender of the "public" as it did on oratorical genius or legal expertise.
During the last fifteen years of the Old Regime, meanwhile, nearly every
aspect of legal practice took on political meaning. The style of legal briefs,
the manner adopted in court, the attitude taken toward the monuments
of French jurisprudence—all these things identified barristers with one
camp or another. Nor was loyalty to the Order solely a matter of calcu-
lation for the rank and file. One need only consider Charles Arrault's
anguished letters after he switched sides in the affair of the *Hôpital
général,* or Jean-Baptiste Jobart's horrifying self-mutilation after he
agreed to practice before the *parlement* Maupeou, to gauge the psychological impact of betrayal.
   It may be asked to what extent these Parisian developments, though
echoed in some of the other *parlements,* influenced barristers working in
the myriad smaller courts of the Old Regime judiciary. Certainly, most of
the men who pursued legal careers in France did not, in the course of
arguing over routine matters of inheritances and leases, conform to the
ideal of legal practice sketched out by Pierre-Louis de Lacretelle. Nonetheless, it is worth repeating the fact that the elite Parisian barristers wrote
the manuals, treatises, and dictionaries of jurisprudence that defined the
profession of barrister throughout the kingdom. It was their careers, as
reported in the *Gazette des tribunaux* and other periodicals, which served
as models, and goals towards which others might struggle. Even the men
whom Burke derided as "obscure provincial advocates . . . the fomenters
and conductors of the petty war of village vexation," had certainly read
about Target's entry to the Académie Française and learned that barristers
were the "voice of the nation," before their own election to the Third
Estate.[17]

   What, then, were some of the consequences of these changes in the world
of the law for the events that began in 1789? To answer this question, it
may be worth engaging in a brief counterfactual speculation. What if, as
the abbé Mably believed possible at the time, the crisis of the 1750's had
precipitated the calling of the Estates General?[18] What constitutional arguments would have been advanced by barristers elected to represent the
Third Estate of Paris? Obviously, an Estates elected in the 1750's would
have differed in countless ways from the real article of 1789, but on a few

specific points, the intellectual exercise can illuminate how changes within the Palais de Justice had ramifications for France as a whole.

If the pamphlets and *mémoires judiciares* of the period are any indication, these hypothetical barrister-*députés* would have insisted that any revised French constitution include at its very heart some sort of *parlement*. Whether or not they would ultimately have insisted on preserving the existing institution, complete with its combination of judicial and quasi-legislative functions, and venality of offices, they clearly believed in the utility of an autonomous "depository of the laws" capable of restraining the actions of the sovereign. Their justifications would doubtless have sounded very similar to those given by the *Président* de Montesquieu in *L'esprit des lois*, in one of his most explicit references to French politics:

> The bodies that are the depository of the laws never obey better than when they drag their feet and bring into the prince's business the reflection that one can hardly expect from the absence of enlightenment in the court concerning the laws of the state and the haste of the prince's councils.[19]

While having more in common with the "brakes" on royal power dear to the sixteenth-century jurist Claude de Seyssel than with the "checks and balances" analyzed elsewhere in Montesquieu's work and adopted by the authors of the American constitution, this notion of a "depository" nonetheless stems from one basic supposition, namely that political power is inherently dangerous. For the Jansenist lawyers of the 1750's, as for Montesquieu, and for the founders of American democracy (who still lay heavily under the influence of Calvinist political thought), political power tended to magnify the inherent defaults of human nature and therefore resulted in oppression unless relentlessly restrained.[20] Thus the need for some sort of counterbalance or bridle on the executive.

It was precisely this suspicion of the nature of political power and belief in the needs for restraints upon it that diminished so rapidly in the Paris bar between the 1750's and the late 1780's. The barristers who became deputies to the Third Estate, and then to the successive revolutionary assemblies, had far more confidence about the ability of an "enlightened" sovereign power not to succumb to the temptations and abuses of power than their Jansenist predecessors did. In fact, many of them believed that a strong sovereign power, acting in the interests of all citizens, offered the best defense against privileged, unscrupulous minorities who might subvert or distort the operations of "public opinion." In 1789, the aristocratic *parlements* themselves typified this sort of dangerous minority for the barrister-deputies. The debates over the Declaration of the Rights of Man, to which Parisian barristers contributed heavily, gave full articulation to these preoccupations. The final product, in contrast to the American Bill of Rights, sought to safeguard the rights of citizens by strengthening and delineating the power of the state, rather than restricting it.[21]

The reasons for this shift in attitudes towards political power obvi-

ously extend beyond the Palais de Justice. The fading of Jansenism, with
its lugubrious, almost Protestant insistence on original sin, and its Augustinian warnings about the spirit of "domination," played an important
part, as did other, obvious trends in French intellectual life. Yet the shift
also came about because it coincided so strongly with the barristers' interests and ambitions. As long as the bar remained essentially an auxiliary
to the judicial power, barristers themselves were necessarily subordinate to
the magistrates—in fact, given the magistrates' rising status, far more subordinate than their Renaissance predecessors had been. While a few barristers might achieve positions of real power, as Le Paige did, they could do
so only by becoming ghostly *éminences grises*—"a person so useful to the
public, although in secret," to quote Lambert's praise for the author of
the *Lettres historiques*—and thereby sacrifice worldly rewards of status and
income.[22]

The prospect of becoming auxiliaries to the legislative power, on the
other hand, using *causes célèbres* to dramatize the need for reform and
collaborating with ministers on the development of specific reform projects
—to participate, in other words, in the development and expression of
sovereign power, rather than the limiting of it—offered barristers far
more visibility, not to mention the obvious rewards showered on
"French Ciceros." Similar rewards accompanied the position of being
"spokesmen for the nation," incarnating the force of public opinion not
only for French audiences, but for European ones. It is not surprising,
then, that after Simon Linguet showed his colleagues the way in the late
1760's and early 1770's—and after Maupeou unwittingly encouraged
the process through his disruption of the Order—they eagerly followed.
It is not surprising that the profession increasingly attracted other followers. The barristers thereby took a large step towards abandoning the ideal
of the judicial monarchy, and accepting the need for an indivisible and
largely unbridled sovereign power representative of the nation as a whole.

Barristers elected to an Estates General in the 1750's would also
likely have taken a very different stand on what might be called "problems
of association." Several historians have recently begun to speculate that
the forms of association men and women engaged in under the Old
Regime, in *corps*, academies, Masonic lodges, and so on, may have had a
subtle impact on their broader political preconceptions. For instance, participation in bodies which made no internal distinctions based on social
rank may have accustomed them to certain ideas of social equality. The
growth of voluntary associations also matters for another reason. According to many social scientists, such associations are crucial building blocks
of modern civil society, defined as social institutions and a sphere for
public debate that lie outside of the control of the state.[23] Yet historians
have not considered the sort of voluntary association which probably
numbered more deputies to the Third Estate as members than any other:
Orders of Barristers.

When the subject of association in pre-revolutionary occupations arises, we still tend to think about it in the terms bequeathed to us by the eighteenth century itself, that is, in terms of polar opposites. At one end of the scale was the privileged *corps*: a body which existed by royal or *parlementaire* charter, imposed various fees and duties on its members, and possessed a monopoly on the practice of a particular occupation (at least in a given area). Entry into it depended on money, on inheritance, or on a number of other essentially arbitrary factors. This was the "ideal type" of occupational association for Colbert and other royal legislators, and it came close to the reality for many if not most French occupations during the eighteenth century. At the other end of the scale, meanwhile, was a condition of complete occupational freedom, under which anyone would have the right to practice the occupation in question with a minimum of training. Discipline and standards here would be maintained not by an autonomous *corps*, but by an ill-defined "public authority." This was the "ideal type" that lay at the heart of much reformist and revolutionary legislation, the former often abortive, as in the case of Turgot's "six edicts." It is sometimes assumed that Old Regime occupations passed directly from the first to the second of these ideal states. Neither, it might also be remarked, was very compatible with the sort of independent voluntary associations now associated with modern civil society. As far as the *corps* are concerned, their ultimate dependence on a state that sanctioned their existence (and had often been responsible for it), as well as their practice of admitting members on the basis of essentially arbitrary factors (heredity, payment, etc.), distinguished them from such associations. The proponents of complete occupational freedom, meanwhile, were positively hostile to any independent social institutions that might come between the state and its citizens.

What makes the Order of Barristers so interesting is that while it did not fit into the first of these ideal categories, neither did it anticipate the second. From the early *conférences de discipline* in the 1660's to Target's pamphlet *La censure* in 1775, barristers consistently attempted to present the Order as something that looked quite different: a truly voluntary association of "independent" practitioners, dependent on no higher authority for its charter, subject to no higher authority for supervision, and making no distinction between members other than on the bases of merit and seniority. As d'Aguesseau said in his 1698 oration, "In entering this celebrated body, men abandon the rank which prejudice attributed to them in the world, to resume the rank that reason has given them in the order of nature and truth."[24] At some moments, notably during judicial strikes, the leaders of the Order insisted that despite this loose, egalitarian organization, the Order speak with a single voice. On other occasions, however, the barristers meeting in a general assembly of the Order did not insist on unanimity, held votes, and abided by the wishes of the majority.

Most opponents of the Order before 1750 criticized it for not accepting the status of a chartered *corps*, but by 1789, most fire was coming from a different direction. Now, critics tended to stigmatize the Order

because it existed in the first place. Authors both outside and inside the
bar (the latter in seemingly blatant disregard of self-interest) insisted that
nothing less than a condition of complete occupational freedom, regulated by "public authority," would now suffice for barristers. Linguet,
Brissot, Mercier, and many others contributed to this chorus. Furthermore, their criticism, even when it did not extend to a complete condemnation of the Order, echoed far more widely and caused far more damage
than the relatively tame attacks sponsored by the ministry in the early part
of the century. It ultimately proved successful, for in 1790 the Constituent Assembly did indeed act to ban all Orders of Barristers.

Once again, exploring the reasons for this shift would obviously take
us far beyond the confines of the legal profession. They are connected
with a process of broad intellectual evolution taking place in French society as a whole. But the particular history of the legal profession nonetheless offers an insight into why the new arguments gained such an enthusiastic reception on the part of one large and influential section of the
French middle classes, and in the revolutionary assemblies they dominated. It therefore illustrates, too, the great obstacles that blocked the
emergence of an independent civil society under the old regime, even
after the absolute monarchy fell into its terminal sickness.

The crucial factor was the growing emphasis in the bar on publicity,
and the growing tendency of barristers to define themselves principally in
relation to the phenomenon they dubbed "public opinion," instead of to
the law itself. It can be argued that lawyers, who lacked a fixed position in
the constellation of French corporate bodies, naturally benefited from the
rise of a socially indistinct, noncorporate "public." Yet this transformation
did not come without strings attached. Jürgen Habermas has forcefully
reminded us that eighteenth-century ideas concerning the public derived
much of their power from the fact that they were linked with an ideal of
free, open, transparent communication—an ideal which stood in sharp
contrast to the partial, exclusive, and privileged forms of communication
native to absolute monarchies.[25] The "public," in this view, while exclud-
ing most of the population, nonetheless allowed all educated men to
make their opinions known to each other through the medium of print.
"Public opinion" therefore could only be accurately gauged if all educated
men (*not* women) had an equal opportunity to contribute to it. Yet if this
was the case, then how could lawyers be justified in creating any associations that, for whatever reasons, privileged certain members of the public
over others and gave them easier access to the presses? This was why the
Orders of Barristers received such ferocious critiques in the late eighteenth century. It was crucial to the projects of Linguet, Falconnet, and
others that, ideally, any citizen should have the right to appear for any
other before the courts, which they likened to the forum or the *agora*.
These attacks, incidentally, bore a close relation to the frenzied
denunciations of cabals and "despotism" in the Republic of Letters,
launched in the same period by the likes of Mercier, Carra, Fabre d'Églan-

tine and, once again, Brissot (in fact, many of the same names come up in the two domains). They too stemmed from the basic assumption that any attempt to allow certain people privileged access to the presses amounted to little less than treason to the public. Here, as in many other ways, the experiences of eighteenth-century men of law and men of letters (who also stood outside the traditional constellation of *corps*) resembled each other quite strikingly.[26]

It may be asked why, in France, the idea of such an absolutely free, open forum for the expression of "public opinion" exerted such force. Keith Baker has provided an important insight into this problem with his suggestion that, in France, the figure of "public opinion" had to compete with the long-standing figure of a monarch who supposedly exercised all linguistic authority in the kingdom, who ruled over all debates and made "politics" unnecessary.[27] Gaining legitimacy for the "public" in these circumstances was terribly difficult, for instance in comparison with the situation in England, where the monarchy was not so formidable and "public opinion" already had an institutional voice of sorts in parliament. The critics of the legal (and of the literary) establishment in France could best generate support for their position by making the case that only an "absolute" public, one which was pure and transparent and gave equal access to all educated men, could overcome the dangers of an "absolute" monarchy. It was for this reason that Linguet's call to smash the "despotism" of the Order of Barristers (like the attacks on the literary "aristocracy") had such resonance and success.

The particular power of these arguments among barristers may also suggest why the revolutionary assemblies heavily populated by them tried so hard to eliminate corporate and noncorporate associations alike in many different occupations, and to create what could be called an atomized society of equal citizens, subject only to the single controlling force of public authority. Just as the Order had seemingly interfered with the full and free articulation of public opinion, now there seemed a danger that *any* intermediary associations, lying in the nebulous sphere between individuals and the state, might interfere with the full and free articulation of the *nation*'s opinion, and its will.[28]

The pre-revolutionary debates over the legal profession were lively and passionate, and even today have the power to elicit strong responses. It is hard to feel much sympathy for the final, traditional defenders of the Order of Barristers, and their devotion to what can easily seem a crabbed, pedantic, and intolerant legal culture. These are the men who could disbar the poor Huerne de la Mothe for taking on the case of an excommunicated actress, and who threatened others with the same fate for the sins of daring to oppose *parlementaire* constitutional ideas or for practicing law during a judicial strike. It is all too easy, by contrast, to feel sympathy for these men's eloquent opponents, whose rhetoric even today occasionally has the power to dazzle, and whose sharp wit seemed to carry all before it. One cannot think of the protestations of the traditionalists, for instance, without remembering Mercier's devastating quip: "men of letters fight for glory; lawyers fight for glory and their soup."[29]

Yet on reflection, a few words of caution are in order. The discrediting, not merely of the *parlements*, but of the very idea of a "depository of the laws," clearly had tremendous consequences both for the Revolution itself, and for the subsequent character of French republicanism. Consider Philippe Raynaud's description of constitutional debates under the Third Republic:

> The majority of "republicans" distrusted supreme courts and a "government of the judges," which seemed to them to lead to a negation of the rights of the Parliament, and beyond this, to an arbitrary limitation on the Nation's capacity to make decisions on matters that concerned it; conversely, conservatives and liberals, who wished for the establishment in France of some sort of control over the constitutionality of laws, denounced, behind this French "legicentrism," the tendencies towards despotism which they saw very largely manifested in the legislative activity of the Convention, and later, in the anti-clerical laws of the Third Republic.[30]

These divisions clearly had roots in the weakening of support for a "depository of the laws" in the late eighteenth century, and thus in such developments as the split between barristers and the *parlement*, the weakening of the Order, and the eclipse of Jansenist barristers together with their suspicions of all political power. To the present-day heirs of Raynaud's conservatives and liberals, therefore, these earlier developments must seem a prelude to a larger tragedy: the inability of the French to develop the notion of legitimate limits on sovereign power, which in turn foreshadowed (although they did *not* determine) the Revolution's inability to remain within moderate bounds.

A similar caution applies when considering the questions related to problems of association. The radical vision of a France free of lawyers, attractive as it seemed at the time (attractive as it can still seem, in Western societies choked with litigation), did not long outlast the radical phase of the Revolution itself. As Michael Fitzsimmons has shown, the judicial system of the 1790's pleased few of the people who used it, and the "unofficial defenders" who now replaced barristers in most trials drew harsh criticism for their corruption and incompetence.[31] By late 1794, the *avocats au parlement* had already begun to regroup and plan for a restoration of the Order. They held regular meetings and even recruited new members. The process accelerated under Napoleon, and by 1806 the restoration was assured, although the emperor's distrust of lawyers delayed the actual event until 1811. This reversal of the 1790 legislation drew little criticism, even from the men who had struggled to bring it about.[32]

The Order, failed, however, to recover the autonomy it had enjoyed in its heyday. The Napoleonic legislation that henceforth governed the practice of law stipulated that barristers could only practice upon taking an oath not to "say or publish anything contrary to laws, to rulings, to morals, to the security of the State or to public tranquility." It banned unauthorized assemblies of the Order, and assured government control over disciplinary matters and the choice of the leadership.[33] Cardinal Fleury had proposed exactly such legislation eighty years before, but then the barristers had possessed sufficient strength to defy him. Now they had no choice but to submit. Thus, one key element of the critics' program and of revolutionary legislation—the subjection of the legal profession to sovereign political authority—remained in place. The barristers struggled against these restraints for the next six decades, but only with the coming of a stable, liberal democracy in the 1870's did they finally free themselves from the last vestiges of Napoleonic control.[34] When they did, it was with the understanding that the Order itself existed primarily to protect the interests of all its members and to ensure the smooth functioning of the judiciary, not to advance a particular political program. Barristers had come to accept the necessity of distinguishing between *hommes de loi* and *hommes politiques*, and recognized that a complex modern nation needs a legal profession with a degree of autonomy and exclusivity, as part of a civil society that shields citizens from abuses of power.

These cautionary notes are meant to suggest that the history of the Parisian Order of Barristers is well-suited to illuminate the curious, stumbling, passage taken by France towards a more democratic and liberal political culture. On the one hand, it shows that despite the existence of a formidable and repressive (though erratic) censorship apparatus, to some favored groups the monarchical regime grudgingly allowed extensive liberty to engage in political criticism and speculation. By the 1770's, not only had Parisian barristers won the freedom to criticize nearly every aspect of the existing government, in a real sense this project of criticism had become their principal vocation. Their devotion to it, and their embrace of the politics of public opinion, made them a true political elite. It allowed them to play a role out of all proportion to their numbers and social status in shaping the vibrant, colorful, contestatory political life of eighteenth-century France. Yet on the other hand, the decline and disappearance of the Order of Barristers was symptomatic of the regime's failure to develop the institutional structures needed to sustain a stable, moderate democratic order. The French would have to reinvent these institutions—including an Order of Barristers—before liberal democracy could take firm root. In other words, while the Old Regime allowed the barristers to hone their formidable powers of criticism, it did not prepare them for the problem of how to proceed once their project of criticism had succeeded.

Notes

ML   Siméon-Prosper Hardy, "Mes Loisirs, ou Journal d'événemens tel
          qu'ils parviennent à ma connoissance (1764–1789)," 8 vols.,
          Bibliothèque Nationale, Manuscrits Français, 6680–87.

MS   [Louis Petit de Bachaumont, Mathieu-François Pidansat de Mairobert,
          et. al.], *Mémoires secrets pour servir à l'histoire de la république des
          lettres*, 36 vols. (London, 1777–89).

NE   *Nouvelles ecclésiastiques*

PCOR   *The Political Culture of the Old Regime*, vol. I of Keith Michael
          Baker, Colin Lucas, and François Furet, eds., *The French Revolution
          and the Creation of Modern Political Culture* (Oxford: Pergamon
          Press, 1987).

Note: BCC Manuscripts 359–68 are on permanent loan to the BACA.

Preface

1. François Hotman, *Francogallia*, reprinted in Julius H. Franklin, trans.
and ed., *Constitutionalism and Resistance in the Sixteenth Century: Three Treatises by Hotman, Beza & Mornay* (New York, 1969), p. 88.

2. For two interesting studies on different parts of Europe, see Lauro
Martines, *Lawyers and Statecraft in Renaissance Florence* (Princeton, 1968), and
James Allen Vann, *The Making of a State: Württemberg 1593–1793* (Cornell,
1984).

3. William J. Bouwsma, "Lawyers and Early Modern Culture," *American
Historical Review*, LXXVIII, 2 (1973), 310, 311.

4. Keith Michael Baker, *Inventing the French Revolution: Essays on French
Political Culture in the Eighteenth Century* (Cambridge, 1990), 170.

5. For a summary of revisionist arguments on this subject, see William
Doyle, *Origins of the French Revolution* (Oxford, 1980), esp. 12–14. The found-
ing work of revisionism is Alfred Cobban, *The Social Interpretation of the French
Revolution* (Cambridge, 1964).

6. See Colin Lucas, "Nobles, Bourgeois and the Origins of the French
Revolution," *Past and Present*, 60 (1973), 84–126.

7. Baron Francis Delbeke, *L'action politique et sociale des avocats au XVIIIe
siècle* (Louvain, 1927).

8. Lenard Berlanstein, *The Barristers of Toulouse in the Eighteenth Century
(1740–1793)* (Baltimore, 1975), esp. 183–86; Michael Fitzsimmons, *The Parisian Order of Barristers and the French Revolution* (Cambridge, Mass., 1987),
esp. 193–99.

9. This work will be discussed in detail in the *Introduction*.

Introduction

1. *Mémoire pour les Sieurs Samson* [sic] *Curé d'Olivet, Coüet Curé de
Darvoi, Gaucher Chanoine de Jargeau, Diocèse d'Orleans, & autres Ecclesiastiques
de différens Dioceses, Appellans comme d'abus; Contre Monsieur l'Evêque d'Orleans
& autres Archevêques et Evêques de différens Dioceses, Intimés. Sur l'effet des
Arrests des Parlemens, tant provisoires Que Définitifs en matiere d'Appel comme
d'Abus des Censures Ecclesiastiques* (Paris, 1730), 3.

2. Quoted in Georges Hardy, *Le Cardinal de Fleury et le mouvement
janséniste* (Paris, 1924), 240.

3. See in particular Joachim-Antoine-Joseph Gaudry, *Histoire du barreau de Paris, depuis son origine jusqu'à 1830*, 2 vols. (Paris, 1864), I:138–47; cf. David A. Bell, "Des stratégies d'opposition sous Louis XV: L'affaire des avocats, 1730–31," *Histoire, économie et société*, IX, 4 (1990), 567–90 (and see later, Ch. 3).

4. BSPR LP 17, 794.

5. BSPR LP 449. John Law was a Scottish financier who led a brief and disastrous attempt to reform France's financial system.

6. AAE CPR 729, fol. 80.

7. AAE MDF 1271, fol. 301. For attribution, see René Louis de Voyer de Paulmy d'Argenson, *Journal et mémoires du marquis d'Argenson*, J.-B. Rathery, ed., 9 vols. (Paris, 1859–67), I:82–83.

8. BM 2357, fol. 257.

9. See the treatment of the notion of "opinion" in eighteenth-century France in Baker, *Inventing* (see Preface, n. 4). 167–99.

10. D'Argenson, VI:464.

11. See Sarah Maza's article "Le tribunal de la nation: les mémoires judiciaires et l'opinion publique à la fin de l'ancien régime," *Annales: Économies, Sociétés, Civilisations*, XLII, 1 (1987), 73–90.

12. The barrister in question was Jacob-Nicolas Moreau. See Keith Michael Baker, "On the Problem of the Ideological Origins of the French Revolution," in Dominick LaCapra and Steven L. Kaplan, eds., *Modern European Intellectual History: Reappraisals and New Perspectives* (Ithaca, 1982), esp. 214–16.

13. Pierre-Louis de Lacretelle, "Dernière note sur l'ancien ordre des avocats et la corporation des avocats aujourd'hui," in *Oeuvres de P.L. Lacretelle aîné*, 5 vols. (Paris, 1823–24), II:462; Malesherbes, "Mémoire sur les avocats," AN 263 AP 10, dossier 1, no. 2, fol. 20; Jean-Sylvain Bailly, *Mémoires de Bailly*, Berville and Barrière, eds., 3 vols. (Paris, 1821), I:51; AAE MDF 1271, fol. 279. Although anonymous, this report is written in the same hand as the report claimed by d'Argenson in his journal (see earlier, n. 7).

14. Wilfrid Prest, ed., *Lawyers in Early Modern Europe and America* (New York, 1981); Jean-Louis Debré, *Les républiques des avocats: La justice au XIXe siècle* (Paris, 1984); Edna Hindie Lemay, "La composition de l'assemblée nationale-constituante," *Revue d'histoire moderne et contemporaine*, XXIV (1977), 345.

15. See Lucas, "Nobles, Bourgeois" (see Preface, n. 6).

16. Besançon, which now counts fewer than 80 lawyers, had over 150 in the mid-eighteenth century, when the population was a quarter its present size. See Maurice Gresset, *Gens de justice à Besançon de la conquête par Louis XIV à la Révolution française*, 2 vols. (Paris, 1978), I:8, 39, 93.

17. Alexis de Tocqueville, *The ancien régime and the French Revolution*, Stuart Gilbert, trans. (New York, 1955), 193.

18. *Réponse d'un avocat à l'écrit intitulé les Idées d'un citoyen de Paris* (Paris, 1789), 5–6.

19. On the problem of oratory under the French monarchy, see Marc Fumaroli, *L'âge de l'éloquence: Rhétorique et "res literaria" de la Révolution au seuil de l'époque classique* (Geneva, 1980), esp. 427–92 and 587–660.

20. See Robert Darnton, "The High Enlightenment and Low Life of Literature," in *The Literary Underground of the ancien régime* (Cambridge, Mass., 1982), 1–40.

21. For an example of the first approach, see Georges Lefebvre, *The Com-*

ing of the French Revolution, R.R. Palmer, trans. (Princeton, 1967), 51–54; for the second, Delbeke, *L'action politique* (see Preface, n. 7).

22. For a summary of revisionist arguments, see Doyle, *Origins* (see Preface, n. 5). The best summary of recent work on the Enlightenment is Roger Chartier, *The Cultural Origins of the French Revolution*, Lydia G. Cochrane, trans. (Durham, 1991).

23. For a consideration of this term, see Keith Michael Baker's "Introduction" to *PCOR* xi–xxiv.

24. Keith Michael Baker, "Politics and Public Opinion Under the *ancien régime*: Some Reflections," in Censer and Popkin, eds., *Press and Politics*, 204–46, quote from 204.

25. François Furet, *Penser la Révolution française* (Paris, 1978); Jürgen Habermas, *The Structural Transformation of the Public Sphere: An Inquiry into a Category of Bourgeois Society*, Thomas Burger and Frederick Lawrence, trans. (Cambridge, Mass., 1989). The most prominent example of the "new political history" is the *PCOR* collection of essays.

26. Chartier provides the best summary of this research in *Cultural Origins*.

27. See esp. Baker, *Inventing the French Revolution*, 12–27, 167–99; Mona Ozouf, "L'opinion publique," in *PCOR*, 419–34; Chartier, 20–37; also Arlette Farge, *Dire et mal dire: L'opinion publique au XVIIIe siècle* (Paris, 1992); and Jeffrey Merrick, *The Desacralization of the French Monarchy in the Eighteenth Century* (Baton Rouge, 1990).

28. See the useful discussion of the idea of "politics" in Baker, *Inventing the French Revolution*, 4.

29. I am using the phrase "the politics of privilege" in a different way from Gail Bossenga in her excellent *The Politics of Privilege: Ancien Régime and Revolution in Lille* (Cambridge, 1992). Also, I do not mean to say that notions of natural law were absent from France before the late eighteenth century. Michael Sonenscher has shown its importance in the world of Parisian artisans in *Work and Wages: Natural Law, Politics and the Eighteenth-Century Trades* (Cambridge, 1989).

30. Quoted in Philippe Godard, *La querelle des refus de sacrements (1730–65)* (Paris, 1937), 277.

31. Sarah Maza, "Domestic Melodrama as Political Ideology: The Case of the Comte de Sanois," *American Historical Review*, XCIV, 5 (1989), 1249–64.

32. Habermas, esp. 14–26, 89–117. For a discussion of Habermas's influence on the history of eighteenth-century France, see Benjamin Nathans, "Habermas's 'Public Sphere' in the Era of the French Revolution," *French Historical Studies*, XVI:3 (1990) 620–44; See also Baker, *Inventing the French Revolution*, 168; and Chartier, *Cultural Origins*, esp. 20–37 and 67–110.

33. For programmatic statements of the two approaches, see Sarah Maza, "Women, the Bourgeoisie and the Public Sphere: Response to Daniel Gordon and David Bell," in *French Historical Studies*, XVII, 4 (1992), 935–50; and Keith Michael Baker, "Defining the Public Sphere in Eighteenth-Century France: Variations on a Theme by Habermas," in Craig Calhoun, ed., *Habermas and the Public Sphere* (Cambridge, Mass., 1992), 181–211.

34. For a useful summary, see Doyle, *Origins*.

35. Habermas, 57–67. On the press, see Censer and Popkin, eds., *Press and*

Politics. On the policing of "public opinion," see, most recently, Farge, *Dire et mal dire*, esp. 44–56, 70–74.

36. These arguments have been elaborated at greater length in David A. Bell, "The Public Sphere and the World of the Law," *French Historical Studies*, XVII, 4 (1992), 912–34. They owe much to conversations with Prof. Dror Wahrman.

37. Tocqueville, esp. 77–107.

38. See William Beik, *Absolutism and Society in Seventeenth-Century France: State Power and Provincial Aristocracy in Languedoc* (Cambridge, 1985), esp. 223–44; Roger Mettam, *Power and Faction in Louis XIV's France* (Oxford, 1990), 194–217; Sharon Kettering, *Patrons, Brokers and Clients in Seventeenth-Century France* (New York, 1986). On the formation of a "national" community in Britain, see Dror Wahrman, "National Society, Provincial Culture: An Argument about the Recent Historiography of Eighteenth-Century Britain," *Social History*, XVII (1992), 43–72.

39. See, most recently on these themes, Michel Antoine, "La monarchie absolue," and Ralph Giesey, "The King Imagined," both in *PCOR* 3–24 and 41–59, respectively.

40. Beik, 225.

41. Michael Sonenscher, "Journeymen, the Courts and the French Trades, 1781–1791," *Past and Present*, 114 (1987), 90. See also Sonenscher's comprehensive *Work and Wages*.

42. Hilton Root, *Peasants and King in Burgundy: Agrarian Foundations of French Absolutism* (Berkeley, 1987), esp. 183–93; Gresset, 730–34; Yves Castan, *Honnêteté et relations sociales en Languedoc, 1715–80* (Paris, 1974).

43. On the actual, slow replacement of law courts by administrative panels, see Antoine, "La monarchie absolue." Even so, according to a study by Colin Kaiser, one obvious measure of the judiciary's importance, namely the volume of litigation in the *Parlement* of Paris, reached its height in the late seventeenth century, and then fell fifty percent in the century before the Revolution. See Colin Kaiser, "The Deflation in the Volume of Litigation at Paris in the Eighteenth Century and the Waning of the Old Judicial Order," *European Studies Review*, X (1980), 309–36.

44. Very few historians have approached eighteenth-century politics in these terms. One exception is Jeffrey Merrick's, "'Disputes over Words' and Constitutional Conflict in France, 1730–32," *French Historical Studies*, XIV, 4 (1986), 497–520.

45. Among the more valiant attempts to build up lexicons of *ancien régime* social and political usage are William Sewell, "État, Corps and Ordre: Some Notes on the Social Vocabulary of the French *ancien régime*," in Hans-Ulrich Wehler, ed., *Sozialgeschichte Heute* (Göttingen, 1974), 49–68. For a very different viewpoint, see the works of Roland Mounsier, esp. *Les hiérarchies sociales de 1450 à nos jours* (Paris, 1969). Both Sewell and Mousnier take one particularly clear and appealing contemporary exposition of terms—Charles Loyseau's *Traité des ordres*—and present it as a sort of "standard grammar." At best, this work should be thought of as an introductory primer to one of many, constantly shifting *patois*.

46. See Donald Kelley, *Foundations of Modern Historical Scholarship: Language, Law and History in the French Renaissance* (New York, 1970), 278–83.

47. Some historians have seen this as a shift in systems of representation from the "iconic" to the "textual." See Marie-Hélène Huet, *Rehearsing the Revolution: The Staging of Marat's Death* (Berkeley, 1982). I owe this reference to Sarah Maza.

48. See esp. Chs. 5 and 6.

49. "There are societies in which men of law cannot take a position in the world of politics analogous to that which they hold in private life; one can be sure that in such a society lawyers will be very active agents of revolution. . . . Lawyers played a prominent part in overthrowing the French monarchy in 1789." Alexis de Tocqueville, *Democracy in America*, J.P. Mayer, ed., George Lawrence, trans. (New York: Harper and Row, 1988), 264–65.

50. Following his mentor Roland Mousnier, Gresset dwells particularly on barristers' resentment at the sale of offices, and the concurrent degeneration of a "society of orders" that had once supposedly offered them great chances for advancement. See Gresset, esp. 718–30 and 776–79. Tensions over venality seem to have been greater in Besançon than elsewhere in eighteenth-century France, however, because of its late introduction there. Gresset makes much of the barristers' open quarrels with magistrates, which supposedly weakened the groups' "vertical solidarity." Yet, similar disputes in Paris in the early eighteenth century had little effect on this solidarity, which later frayed without any open disputes (see Chs. 2 and 6).

51. Fitzsimmons, *The Parisian Order of Barristers* (see Preface, n. 8), esp. 193–99.

52. Lucien Karpik, "Lawyers and Politics in France, 1814–1950: The State, the Market, and the Public," *Law and Social Inquiry*, XIII, 4 (1988), 707–36; idem, "Le désintéressement," *Annales: Économies, sociétés, civilisations*, XLIV, 3 (1989), esp. 737; idem, "La profession libérale: Un cas, le barreau," in Pierre Nora, ed., *Les lieux de mémoire*, part III: *Les France*, 3 vols. (Paris, 1993), II: 284–321.

53. Michael Fitzsimmons is particularly keen on establishing the Order of Barristers's "corporate" nature (see, for instance, 3–4 and 31–32). On modern sociological views of professions, see, for instance, Magali Sarfatti Larson, *The Rise of Professionalism: A Sociological Analysis* (Berkeley, 1977), and Rolf Torstendahl and Michael Burrage, eds., *The Formation of the Professions: Knowledge, State and Strategy* (London, 1990). Lucien Karpik, in "Lawyers and Politics in France," offers a lucid summary and critique of sociological studies of the professions.

54. Jacques Revel has convincingly argued that this interpretation derives from an unjustifiably literal reading of eighteenth-century corporate rhetoric. See Jacques Revel, "Les corps et communautés," *PCOR* 225–42.

55. "Profession: La condition qu'on a choisie dans le monde, la vacation à quoy on veut s'appliquer, dont on veut faire son exercice ordinaire. . . ." *Dictionnaire de Furetière* (Paris, 1690). Larson's *The Rise of Professionalism* is a good example of the thesis that professions are a phenomenon of industrial capitalism. On the British legal profession before 1800, see the excellent works of Wilfred Prest, *The Rise of the Barristers: A Social History of the Bar in Early Modern England* (Oxford, 1986), and David Lemmings, *Gentlemen and Barristers: The Inns of Court and the English Bar 1680–1830* (Oxford, 1990).

56. Matthew Ramsey, *Professional and Popular Medicine in France, 1770–1830: The Social World of Medical Practice* (Cambridge, 1988).

57. A recent work of British history which takes for granted the existence of "professions" before the Industrial Revolution is Geoffrey Holmes, *Augustan England: Professions, State and Society 1680–1730* (London, 1983).

58. See Ch. 6.

59. Pierre-François Biaroy [or Biarnoy] de Merville, *Règles pour former un avocat* (Paris, 1711), 310.

60. Gresset; Berlanstein, *The Barristers of Toulouse* (see Preface, n. 8); Albert Poirot, "Le milieu socio-professionnel des avocats au Parlement de Paris à la veille de la Révolution (1760–1790)," 2 vols., unpublished thesis of the École des Chartes, 1977.

61. Jean-François Fournel, *Histoire des avocats au Parlement de Paris et du barreau de Paris depuis St. Louis jusqu'au 15 octobre 1790*, 2 vols. (Paris, 1813); Gaudry (see n. 3); Charles Bataillard and Ernest Nusse, *Histoire des procureurs et des avoués, 1303–1816*, 2 vols. (Paris, 1882); André Damien, *Les avocats du temps passé* (Paris, 1973).

62. Ramsey; Prest, *The Rise of the Barristers*; Lemmings.

63. See Dale Van Kley, *The Damiens Affair and the Unravelling of the Old Regime, 1750–1770* (Princeton, 1984).

64. To raise just two problems, some relatively minor cities (Douai, Colmar) had important courts, while some very major cities (notably, Lyon) lacked them, whereas some regions had estates that reduced the influence of the courts and some did not.

65 See, for instance, the queries to the Paris bar from the barristers of Lorraine and Barrois (BCC 361, nos. 97–98) and Besançon (BN JF 586, fols. 284 ff). Parisian barristers also issued printed consultations for provincial colleagues, including *Mémoire à consulter et consultations sur l'incompatibilité de la Profession d'Avocat, avec les Fonctions de Commis dans les Bureaux du Contrôle des Actes* (Rouen, 1764) for the bar of Rouen, and Honoré-Marie-Nicolas Duveyrier, *Consultation sur la discipline des avocats* (Paris, 1775) for the bar of Poitiers.

66. See particularly Jean-Baptiste Denisart, Antoine Camus, and Jean-Baptiste Bayard, eds., *Collection de décisions nouvelles, et de notions relatives à la jurisprudence, donnée par M. Denisart, mise dans un nouvel ordre . . .*, 14 vols. (Paris, 1783–1807); Claude de Ferrière, *Dictionnaire de Droit et de pratique, contenant l'explication des termes de droit, d'ordonnances, de coutumes & de pratique. Avec les jurisdictions de France*, 3d. ed. (Paris, 1749); and Joseph-Nicolas Guyot, *Répertoire universel et raisonné de Jurisprudence civile, criminelle, canonique et bénéficiale*, 17 vols. (Paris, 1784–85).

67. *MS*; *Gazette des tribunaux*, 26 vols. (Paris, 1775–89).

Chapter 1

1. See, for instance, the caricature in Michel Vovelle, *La révolution française: Images et récit*, 5 vols. (Paris, 1986), I:63.

2. De Puyseaux, *Parallèle entre le capucin et l'avocat. Quant à l'utilité publique* (Rome, 1782), 18–19.

3. On the institutions of the Old Regime, see Roland Mousnier, *Les Institutions de la France sous la Monarchie absolue*, 2 vols. (Paris, 1980); and see esp. Denis Richet, *La France moderne: L'esprit des institutions* (Paris, 1973). The extent to which jurisdictional quarrels featured in the battles over the *parlements*

emerges clearly in Jean Egret, *Louis XV et l'opposition parlementaire* (Paris, 1970).

4. Louis-Sébastien Mercier, *Le tableau de Paris*, 12 vols. (Amsterdam, 1783–88), III:1.

5. For a basic introduction to pre-1789 French law, see Émile Chénon, *Histoire du droit français public et privé des origines à 1815*, 2 vols. (Paris, 1926).

6. Simon-Nicolas-Henri Linguet, *Nécessité d'une réforme dans l'administration de la justice et dans les loix civiles en France* (Amsterdam, 1764), 95.

7. François Chavray de Boissy wrote, in *L'avocat, ou réflexions sur l'exercice du barreau* (Paris, 1777), "Thirty years of study barely suffices to train a jurist" (101–2). Similar remarks are found in Biaroy de Merville, *Règles* (see Introduction, n. 59), 57–59, and the anonymous *Réflexions d'un militaire sur la profession d'avocat, utiles au barreau et au public pour détruire les abus qui dégradent l'un et nuisent à l'intérêt des deux* (Paris, 1781), 11.

8. Pierre-Nicolas Berryer, *Souvenirs de M. Berryer*, 2 vols. (Paris, 1839), I:41–42.

9. Linguet, *Nécessité d'une réforme . . .* , 33. For a detailed description of the court system, see Mousnier, *Institutions*, II:249–404.

10. G. Durant-Farget, *La vie au palais* (Paris, 1927), 5–8. The number of courts varied slightly through the course of the century.

11. J.-François Bluche, *Les magistrats du Parlement de Paris au XVIIIᵉ siècle* (Paris, 1960; repr. 1986), 211.

12. Louis d'Orléans, *Les ouvertures de Parlemens*, cited in Fumaroli, *L'âge de l'éloquence* (see Intro., n. 19), 427–28.

13. For one of the best descriptions of the processions of the Saint-Martin, see Maupoint, *Calendrier historique, avec le Journal des cérémonies et usages qui s'observent à la Cour, à Paris, et à la Campagne* (Paris, 1737), 128 ff.

14. Habermas, *Structural Transformation* (see Intro., n. 25), 5–12, esp. 8.

15. The offices bestowed permanent noble rank upon the families that possessed them after three generations of continuous possession. For details on the organization and function of the *Parlement* of Paris, see Bluche, 9–17.

16. Sarah Hanley, "Engendering the State: Family Formation and State Building in Early Modern France," *French Historical Studies*, XVI, 1 (1989), 4–27. See also Richet, 33.

17. Michel Antoine, "La monarchie absolue" in *PCOR* 10–11; Richet, 52–54.

18. For the best comprehensive discussion of the *parlements'* claims in the eighteenth century, see Egret, *Louis XV et l'opposition parlementaire*.

19. Claude de Seyssel, *The Monarchy of France*, Donald R. Kelley, ed., J.H. Hexter, trans. (New Haven, 1981), esp. 54–56.

20. The most important recent works on this subject are Beik, *Absolutism and Society* (see Intro., n. 38); David Bien, "Offices, Corps and a System of State Credit," in *PCOR*, 89–114; and Bossenga, *The Politics of Privilege* (see Intro., n. 29).

21. For the early development of absolutist ideas, see Ralph Giesey, "The King Imagined" in *PCOR* 41–59; and Sarah Hanley, *The Lit de Justice of the Kings of France: Constitutional Ideology in Legend, Ritual and Discourse* (Princeton, 1983). See also, Roger Mettam's stimulating attack on the notion of absolutism in *Power and Faction* (see Intro., n. 38), 13–44.

22. The best treatment of the *parlements*' claims can be found in Van Kley, *Damiens* (see Intro., n. 63) 166–225. See also the still useful discussion in Élie Carcassonne, *Montesquieu et le problème de la constitution française* (Paris, 1927), esp. 25–38 and 261–96.

23. William Doyle, "The Parlements," in *PCOR* 162.

24. On early notions of national sovereignty, see Julian H. Franklin, *Constitutionalism and Resistance* (see Preface, n. 1).

25. The most comprehensive recent sociological study of lawyers is Richard L. Abel and Philip S.C. Lewis, *Lawyers in Society*, 3 vols. (Berkeley, 1988–89). See also the important critique by Mark Osiel, "Lawyers as Monopolists, Aristocrats and Entrepreneurs," *Harvard Law Review*, CIII, 8 (June, 1990).

26. ADCO E 642, Godard to Cortot, June 19, 1783. Godard's first name is not given in these letters; however, in the letter of the same date Godard indicated that he had just joined the Order of Barristers. The *Tableaux* of the Order lists Jacques Godard, a future deputy to the Legislative Assembly, as having joined in 1783.

27. AN Z^{1A}593. These letters patent give extensive details on Le Roy's career. A second copy was preserved by the Order itself. See BCC 360, no. 22. As for Le Roy's possessions, see AN Y 14963. On the magistrates' fortunes, see Bluche, 106–11.

28. BN JF 312, fols. 9–29; Poirot, "Le milieu socio-professionel" (see Intro., n. 60), I:14.

29. Maurice Gresset noted that barristers caused him far more problems than magistrates and *procureurs*, being both "less homogeneous" and "less easily integrated into the strict hierarchy of the Old Regime." Gresset (see Intro., n. 16), 717. See also Berlanstein (see Preface, n. 8) and Poirot, passim.

30. Principally the Châtelet, the Grand conseil, the Cour des Aides, and the Chambre des Comptes. Barristers tended to plead more or less exclusively in a single court. See, for instance, the references to "avocats au Châtelet" and "avocats à la Cour des Aides" in BA 6192, fols. 16–45; also Edmond-Jean-François Barbier, *Journal historique et anecdotique du règne de Louis XV*, A. de la Villegille, ed., 4 vols. (Paris, 1847), IV:438–39 (I have cited this edition of Barbier because, while not the most accurate, it is the most accessible. The references have been checked against later editions); *MS* VI:9. However, there was no separate organization for the barristers in the "lower courts" and no opprobrium attached to pleading in them, as was the case in Toulouse (see Berlanstein, 17–18).

31. See discussion in Poirot, II:14–19. Throughout France, aspiring barristers had to be of the Catholic faith.

32. The most notable were the 1579 Edict of Blois reinforced and expanded by a royal edict of April 1679. See Denisart et al. *Collection de décisions* (see Intro., n. 66), II:708.

33. Poirot, II:18; Martine Acerra, "Les Avocats du Parlement de Paris (1661–1715)," *Histoire, Économie et Société*, I (1982), 215; Adeline Daumard and François Furet, *Structures et relations sociales à Paris au XVIIIe siècle* (Paris, 1961), e.g., 36 and 45.

34. As seen in Chapter 1, the *Tableau* was supposedly published every year, but in fact the frequent divisions in the Order often led to long gaps. The only sizeable collections of *Tableaux* are located in the BACA CBA and the BCC.

The annual list published in the *Almanach royal* often differed considerably from the *Tableau*. As part of his thesis, Albert Poirot compiled a biographical dictionary of every barrister who served between 1745 and 1790 (Poirot, I).

35. Denisart, II:708.

36. In practice, barristers referred to themselves by many titles, including *avocat en, avocat au, avocat à la cour,* and more than twenty other names (AN, computerized inventory of the Minutier Central des Notaires for 1751). Under Maupeou, the spectacle of three different categories of barristers gave rise to a much-quoted rhyme: "Amis d'*au*, d'*en* et *du* voici tout le mystère. / On découvre dans *au* la gloire et les talents; / Des *du* les griffes sont l'apanage ordinaire; / Le duc et le faquin compte *en* parmi ses gens." Quoted in Fournel, *Histoire des avocats* (see Intro., n. 61), 479.

37. On this subject, see especially Gresset, 135–74, and, more generally, Lucas, "Nobles, Bourgeois" (see Preface, n. 6). For the specific figures on Paris, see Acerra, 218; Poirot, II:120. The decrease from 66 to 54 percent probably occurred because as the profession increased in size, it recruited from more varied social backgrounds. See Richard L. Kagan, "Law Students and Legal Careers in Eighteenth-Century France," *Past and Present,* 68 (1975), 64.

38. Guillaume Blanchard compiled a manuscript (BCC 359) giving biographical details on hundreds of barristers from the fourteenth century onwards (including the Le Roys). For those practicing in 1725, he seems to have given details on all those he knew personally, identifying 58 out of 560 as sons of barristers. For Le Paige, see BSPR LP 460, no. 23.

39. BSPR LP 423, no. 60.

40. Guillaume Fericoq de la Dourie et al., *Mémoire pour plusieurs avocats du Parlement de Paris, opposants à l'arrêté et homologation du nouveau tableau mis au greffe de la cour* . . . (Paris, 1729), 4.

41. Poirot, II:131–34. Roughly half of the wealth consisted of *rentes,* drawn mostly on the state, and only one quarter consisted of land. Poirot, II:180. In Toulouse, on the other hand, barristers relied much more heavily on land, with two-thirds of their fortunes taking this form. See Berlanstein, 51–55.

42. While not calculating an average, Poirot reports that one ambitious young barrister was happy to receive the relatively small sum of 1,500 *livres* a year from his work, while a more established colleague could earn 15,000. See Poirot, II:177. For Gerbier, see Berryer, I:88.

43. Only twelve percent owned their apartments. By contrast, one-third owned a house of a sort in the country (sometimes this was only a cottage). Poirot, II:162–71. On *rentes,* see Poirot, II:181–82.

44. Law books made up 33 percent of all volumes. History came in a close second with 28 percent, followed by "belles-lettres" at 20 percent, theology at 14 percent, and natural science at only 5 percent. See Poirot, II:187–91.

45. For instance, Barbier, I:148; *MS* IV, 290–91; Ambroise Falconnet, *Le Barreau français: partie moderne,* 2 vols. (Paris, 1806-8), II:363.

46. Durey de Meinières to Le Paige, February 26, 1775. BSPR LP 574, no. 18.

47. On most occasions, after hearing initial oral arguments (and the press of business often led to these being dispensed with as well), the judges would "appoint" a case, with one of their number (the *rapporteur*) collecting additional material in written form and summarizing it. See P. Guilhermoz, "De la persistance du caractère orale dans la procédure civile française," *Nouvelle revue historique de droit français et étranger,* XIII (1889), 21–65.

48. Barristers could, however, file amicus briefs in criminal cases. In general on the barristers' practice, see the article "avocat" in Denisart; and Guyot (see Intro., n. 66).

49. Poirot, II:63–69, 88–93. For the classic exposition of the three categories as stages of a career, see Louis-Ferdinand Bonnet, *Discours prononcé à la bibliothèque des avocats, pour la rentrée de la S. Martin 1786* (Amsterdam, 1787).

50. Berlanstein, 9; Poirot, II:53–62 and 93–109.

51. On legal briefs, see the article "factum" in Denisart; Guyot; and *Encyclopédie méthodique, ou par ordre de matières; par une société de gens de lettres, de savans et d'artistes: Jurisprudence* (Paris, 1783–87). For the *factums* of the BN, the largest collection, see A. Corda and A. Trudon des Ormes, *Catalogue des factums*, 10 vols. (Paris, 1896–1936), which is widely available. Other important collections can be found in the BS and the BACA. On their political uses, see Maza, "Le tribunal de la nation" (see Intro., n. 11), esp. 75–78.

52. To be sure, one does not have to practice actively to remain a member of the bar in modern France, Britain, or America; however, the assumption is that people join the bar primarily to practice and not for honorific reasons.

53. Barbier, II:355; Eustache-Antoine Hua, *Mémoires d'un avocat au Parlement de Paris, Député à l'Assemblée législative*, E.-M.-François Saint-Maur, ed. (Poitiers, 1871), 12; Berryer, I:19.

54. AAE MDF 1297, fol. 72; *Tableau de 1731* (BACA), still in use four years later. In both Toulouse and Besançon, only 12–15 barristers out of more than 100 appeared regularly in court in any given year (Berlanstein, 14; Gresset, 96).

55. See Poirot, II:93–109, which shows that at least fifteen percent of barristers held such positions.

56. BCC 359, nineteenth-century copy, II:476 (for Meudon); *Grand dictionnaire historique de Moréri* (Paris, 1759), VIII:564 (for the *université* and Vincennes); AN Y 11935A (for the apartment); BN NA 2111 (for the registers).

57. BN JF 27, fol. 160.

58. [Pierre-Louis-Claude Gin], *Entretien d'un militaire et d'un avocat sur les affaires présentes* (n.p., 1771), 35. For the attribution to Gin, see the note by Le Paige on the copy of the pamphlet in BSPR LP 810, no. 3. The presence of barristers in the council of the house of Orléans, and in those of Louis XVI's brothers, can be traced in the pages of the *Almanach royal*.

59. According to the *Almanach royal* and the journal of Barbier, serving in the council of the house of Orléans were Louis Chevallier, Jacques-François Cellier, Claude-Pierre de la Monnoye, Georges Le Roy, Jacques-Charles Aubry, and Aubry's son-in-law Anselme-Joseph Doutremont. Serving in the council of Conti were Gerbier and his father, Pierre-Salomon Pothouin and his son Pierre-Charles, and Henry Duhamel. For the Jansenist sympathies of these barristers, see Ch. 3.

60. When d'Argenson was named lieutenant général de police, Barbier recalls that his father, who served twenty-five years as counsel to d'Argenson, took Edmond-Jean-François to pay hommage: "We went there . . . my father and I. He said to us: 'I know that you love me, and I ask your son to love me as well'." Barbier, I:13. On Barbier and his political views, see Michel Antoine, "Edmond-Jean-François Barbier (1689–1771), Avocat et chroniqueur," *Revue de la société internationale d'histoire de la profession d'avocat*, no. 3 (1991), pp. 23–34.

61. Guy-Jean-Baptiste Target, *Mémoire pour Me. Élie de Beaumont, Inten-*

dant des Finances de Monseigneur le Comte d'Artois, contre Monsieur le Procureur Général (Paris, 1780), 3–4.

62. BN JF 1247, fol. 272.

63. BN JF 2393, fols. 36–37.

64. For the most concise description of barristers' education, see Delbeke, *L'action politique et sociale* (see Preface, n. 7), 45–65. Also see most recently L. W. B. Brockliss, *French Higher Education in the Seventeenth and Eighteenth Centuries: A Cultural History* (Oxford, 1987).

65. Kagan (see Ch. 1, n. 37), esp. 40–41. See also Poirot, II:6–14.

66. Delbeke, 64.

67. Jacques-Pierre Brissot, *Un indépendant à l'ordre des avocats* (Berlin, 1781), 7. See also Delbeke, 63; Kagan, 41–42.

68. Jacques-Pierre Brissot, *Mémoires de Brissot (1754–1793)*, M. de Lescure, ed. (Paris, 1877), 170; cf. Delbeke, 63.

69. See the description of the *stage* in Louis-Anne Louvet, *Discours prononcé par M. Louvet, avocat au Parlement, le premier décembre, 1787, à l'ouverture des Conférences de l'Ordre des Avocats en l'Assemblée tenue à leur Bibliothèque* (Paris, 1787), 7. The pamphlet was reprinted in 1877.

70. Poirot, II:32.

71. Several folio *registres* contain the minutes of *conférences* held between 1710 and 1720. See BN Ms. 7565–67 and 10955–57, BN NAF 2476–77 and 2499, BN JF 2208 and BCC 364–67. The fact that they were aimed principally at *stagiaires* is clear from remarks in BCC 362, fol. 190. In 1718–20, during the general confusion of the *parlement*'s exile to Pontoise, various disputes led to their suspension. See the account in Louis Froland, *Mémoires concernans l'observation du Senatus-Consulte Velleien . . .* (Paris, 1722), ix–x. As for their later resumption, see BCC 360, no. 6; BCC 360, no. 8.

72. Berryer, I, 85–86; Hua, 19–20.

73. For details on the Basoche, see David A. Bell, "Lawyers and Politics in Eighteenth-Century Paris (1700–1790)," unpublished Ph.D. dissertation, Princeton University (1991), 61–78, 246–63, and 361–78.

74. The list is preserved in BN JF 2133, fols. 82–91. The calculations are as follows: roughly ten percent of the clerks listed later appeared on the *Tableaux des avocats*. Given a total of 1,300 clerks who each served for between ten and fifteen years—conservatively, 90–100 a year (see Bell, "Lawyers and Politics," 61–78)—it seems reasonable to conclude that a figure of ten percent means that 9–10 clerks per year became barristers. Total entries into the Order of Barristers averaged 27 per year between 1735 and 1750, yielding a figure of about one-third.

75. Berryer, I:81–85; Hua, 19–20; Brissot, *Mémoires de Brissot*, 39–40; Brissot, *Un indépendant*, 6; Louis Groustel, *Essai sur la profession de procureur* (Paris, 1749), 54.

76. William Farr Church, "The Decline of French Jurists as Political Theorists, 1660–1789," *French Historical Studies*, V, 1 (1967), 1–40; Delbeke, 62–65.

77. Osiel, "Lawyers as Monopolists, Aristocrats and Entrepreneurs."

78. Ibid., 2061–62.

79. Osiel himself points out that the substantial law-making powers of civil law courts before the French Revolution led to a greater reliance on common law-style "practical judgment." Ibid., 2062.

80. On the magistrates, see Bluche (see Ch. 1, n. 11), 205–31. For the Renaissance roots of this culture, see Fumaroli (see Intro., n. 19), 427–74.

81. The oath, as established by the *parlement*'s ordinance of March 11, 1345, was made in Latin, and is reprinted in Roland Delachenal, *Histoire des avocats au Parlement de Paris, 1300–1600* (Paris, 1885) 393–96. The early eighteenth-century text written down in BCC 362, fols. 1–3 is essentially similar.

82. Hua, 13–14.

83. For specific examples of these regulations being applied, see BN JF 312, fols. 2–43 and BN JF 186, fols. 291–304. The term *la mort civile* appears in BN JF 312, fol. 32; and letters to Claude-Joseph Prévost in BCC 361.

84. Montesquieu, *Lettres persanes* (Paris, 1964), 79.

85. Poirot, II:124. See also Anne Piriou, "Les avocats du Parlement de Paris de 1751 à 1799 d'après leurs inventaires après décès," unpublished *mémoire de maîtrise*, Université de Paris-IV (1986), 8. The same percentage also holds for Besançon (Gresset, 287). For the term a "noble profession," see Denisart et al. (see Intro. n. 66), II:739.

86. Denisart, II:739. For the texts of various *arrêts de parlement* confirming these privileges, see AN AD^{II}2.

87. François-Bernard Cocquart, *Lettres, ou dissertations, où l'on fait voir que la profession d'avocat est la plus belle des professions* (London, 1733), 24. In Grenoble, forty distinguished barristers of more than seven years standing made up a special "collège" of noble "*avocats consistoriaux*" (see Denisart, II:723). In 1789, some "orders of barristers" in France claimed the right to elect deputies to the *second* estate. See Ph. Torreilles, "Les élections de 1789 en Roussilon," *Société agricole, scientifique et littéraire des pyrénées-orientales*, XXXII (1891), 399.

88. AN Z^{1A}593.

89. BCC 360, no. 22.

90. Cocquart, 21–22; *De la nature de la Grace, Où l'on fait voir ce que c'est que la Grace de JESUS-CHRIST, considérée en général, & indépendamment du sujet: c'est-à-dire de l'être particulier où elle consiste, dédié à Messieurs les Avocats du Parlement de Paris* (n.p., 1739), 9; Chavray de Boissy (see Ch. 1, n. 7), 327.

91. See Roland Mousnier, most concisely in "Problèmes de méthode dans l'étude des structures sociales des XVIè, XVIIè et XVIIIè siècles," in *La plume, la faucille et le marteau* (Paris, 1970).

92. The chief works in a very limited bibliography are Bataillard and Nusse, *Histoire des procureurs* (see Intro., n. 61); Laure Koenig, *La Communauté des Procureurs au Parlement de Paris aux XVIIe et XVIIIe siècles* (Cahors, 1937); Gresset, esp. pp. 272–73, 283, 432. See also Bell, "Lawyers and Politics," 51–61, 121–29, 246–63, 361–79.

93. For details on the profession, see Guyot, s.v. *procureur*. Sons of *procureurs* were exempt from the apprenticeship. The best evidence that *procureurs* commonly possessed law degrees comes from the Maupeou crisis of 1771, when 87 of 130 *procureurs* who applied for the new position of *avocat du parlement* possessed law degrees. See *Tableau des Avocats en la cour du Parlement, créés par édit du mois de mai, 1771* (Paris, 1771), BN Recueil Z Le Senne 17(11).

94. Technically, this was the price of the *charge*, on which the *parlement* set a legal maximum of 15,000 *livres*, plus the price of the practice, which was determined by a special committee of senior *procureurs*. Figures are based on a sample of thirty-five contracts of sale representing all transmissions of offices from the

years 1724, 1744, and 1764 (contracts from earlier and later periods are missing from the archival records), AN X^{5B}6. See also Bataillard and Nusse, II:37–83. For the later price increase, see William Doyle, "The Price of Offices in Pre-Revolutionary France," *The Historical Journal*, 27 (1984), 850–51; Gresset, 62–63.

95. See Bien, "Offices" (see Ch. 1, n. 20); Koenig, 107–36; Bataillard and Nusse, II:37–83; and Bell, "Lawyers and Politics," 121–24.

96. Bien, passim. In the case of the *procureurs*, the organization was known as the *communaté des procureurs*, described in Koenig, 23–54.

97. The contracts are preserved in AN X^{5B}6. For the anecdotal evidence, see *Réflexions pour les Procureurs au Parlement de Paris* (Paris, 1790), 4; BSPR LP 569, no. 223: journal of Le Paige, 1771.

98. Mercier (see Ch. 1, n. 4), III:2–3.

99. Duvigneau, *Discours sur la profession de procureur* (Geneva, 1783), ix. See also Groustel; and Pierre Légier, *Traité historique et raisonné, d'après des loix, règlements et usages, sur les différentes procédures qui s'observent dans toutes les jurisdictions de l'Enclos du Palais* (Paris, 1780), xxviii.

100. Bell, "Lawyers and Politics," 121–29, 246–63, 361–79.

Chapter 2

1. See the useful discussion of these issues in Ramsey, *Professional and Popular Medicine* (see Intro., n. 56), 1–5.

2. See, for instance, Larson, *The Rise of Professionalism* (see Intro., n. 53); Gerald L. Geison, ed., *Professions and the French State, 1700–1900* (Philadelphia, 1984).

3. [Ambroise Falconnet], *Projets de création de charges d'avocats, ou plûtot de destruction de l'ordre inquisitorial et despotique des avocats au Parlement de Paris, par une société d'Avocats non-tablotants* (Berlin, 1789), 74.

4. See Eric Hobsbawm and Terence Ranger, eds., *The Invention of Tradition* (Cambridge, 1984).

5. Antoine-Gaspard Boucher d'Argis, *Histoire abrégée des avocats* (Paris, 1778); Fournel, *Histoire des avocats* (see Intro., n. 61); Gaudry, *Histoire du barreau* (see Intro., n. 3). For the background to these works, see, for the 1770's, Chapter 5, and Karpik, "Lawyers and Politics" (see Intro., n. 52).

6. Voltaire, *Histoire du Parlement de Paris* (Paris, 1835), 316.

7. [Ambroise Falconnet], *Mémoire sur les privilèges des avocats* (Paris, 1785), repr. in Falconnet, *Le barreau français* (see Ch. 1, n. 45); [Falconnet], *Projets de création*.

8. Delachenal, *Histoire des avocats* (see Ch. 1, n. 81) 23–34. He comments: "The authority that the *parlement* wielded over the barristers was absolute and uncontested" (p. 122). For the early seventeenth century, see Gaudry, II:1–44. The early expansion of the bar belies any notion that later changes were due to rising numbers.

9. Delachenal, 152–57, 189–226. To judge from Martin Husson's work, *De advocato libri quattor* (Paris, 1664), the disciplinary arrangements seem to have remained in force at least until the early 1660's.

10. Delachenal, 34–50. In theory, the confraternity and community remained separate during the period 1300–1600. In fact, Delachenal says, they were one and the same thing (p. 47).

11. In the eighteenth century, the title of *bâtonnier* generally passed uncontested in order of seniority, and was frequently declined (possibly because each *bâtonnier* was expected to give a gift of 1,000 *livres*). See Cresson, *Usages et règles de la profession d'avocat*, 2 vols. (Paris, 1888), II:209–11.

12. The phrase *ordre des avocats* was an old one, going back to the late Middle Ages. See Delachenal, 35. For a typical multicolumn definition of *ordre*, see, for instance, the *Dictionnaire de Furetière* (Paris, 1690).

13. Charles Loyseau, *Traité des ordres et simples dignitez*, in *Les oeuvres de maistre Charles Loyseau, avocat en parlement* (Paris, 1678), 1–6.

14. Antoine Loisel, *Pasquier, ou Dialogue des Advocats du Parlement de Paris* (*1602*), André Dupin, ed. (Paris, 1844), 5; Guy Du Faur de Pibrac, *Recueil des poincts principavx de la premiere et seconde remonstrance faicte en la Cour de parlement de Paris, à l'ouuerture des plaidoiries apres les festes de Pasques & la Sainct Martin* (Paris, 1573), fol. 12.

15. Loyseau, 1–4 and 48; F. A. Isambert et. al., *Receuil des anciennes lois françaises*, 29 vols. (Paris, 1821–33), XIV:107.

16. Loyseau, 5–6.

17. Loisel, 3; Du Faur, fol. 7; Loyseau, 50.

18. Miriam Yardeni, "L'ordre des avocats et la grève du barreau parisien en 1602," *Revue d'histoire économique et sociale*, XLIV (1966), 481–507.

19. The cost of the most common office in the Paris *Parlement* rose from around 12,000 *livres* around 1550 to 140,000 around 1720. See Marcel Marion, *Dictionnaire des Institutions de la France aux XVIIe et XVIIIe siècles* (Paris, 1923; repr. 1984), 431. During the same period, the *Parlement* of Paris turned highly restrictive in its recruitment. See Bluche, *Les magistrats* (see Ch. 1, n. 11) esp. 55–98. For recruitment between 1653 and 1673, see Albert M. Hamscher, *The Parlement of Paris after the Fronde, 1653–1673* (Pittsburgh, 1976), 45–46.

20. Loyseau, 50; Montesquieu, *Lettres persanes* (see Ch. 1, n. 84), 123.

21. See Ralph E. Giesey, "Rules of Inheritance and Strategies of Mobility in Prerevolutionary France," *American Historical Review*, 82 (1977), 271–89; Bluche, 19.

22. Fumaroli, *L'âge de l'éloquence* (see Intro., n. 19) 585–622.

23. Loisel; Du Faur; and Etienne Pasquier, *Lettre à Théodore Pasquier*, reprinted in Loisel, 204–11. See also the comments by Loyseau in *Traité des ordres*, 48–51. On all these men, see especially Kelley, *Foundations* (see Intro., n. 46), 241–300.

24. Du Faur, fol. 12; Loyseau, 50; Loisel, 60.

25. Pasquier, in Loisel, 205; Loisel, 14.

26. Pasquier, in Loisel, 208.

27. Loisel, 23; Du Faur, fol. 4.

28. Loisel, 22. The debate over the church courts focused on the so-called *appel comme d'abus*, which had greatly diminished the role of church courts by allowing litigants there to appeal to royal jurisdictions. See Moïse Cagnac, *De l'appel comme d'abus dans l'ancien droit français* (Paris, 1906), esp. 19–24.

29. Loyseau, 1–3. Cf. Seyssel, *Monarchy* (see Ch. 1, n. 19); Antoine, "La monarchie absolue" in *PCOR* 3–24.

30. Loisel, 125.

31. See, more generally, on the "anti-Ciceronianism" of the late sixteenth century, Fumaroli, 480–92.

32. See ibid., 475–94.

33. For information on the authorship of pamphlets, see Jacqueline Boucher, "Culture des notables et mentalité populaire dans la propagande qui entraîna la chute de Henri III," in Jean Nicolas, ed., *Mouvements populaires et conscience sociale: XVIe–XIXe siècles* (Paris, 1985), 339–49.

34. Robert Descimon, "La ligue à Paris (1588–1594): Une révision," *Annales: Économies, sociétés, civilisations*, XXXVII, 1 (1982), 72–101, esp. 85–91 and 97–99. These were hardly the only barristers of this period to indulge in pamphleteering. Antoine Arnauld, Pasquier, and Loisel all wrote pamphlets for Henri IV and against the Jesuits.

35. Ralph Giesey, "The King Imagined," *PCOR* 41–59; Hanley, *Lit de Justice* (see Ch. 1, n. 21).

36. Bossuet, *Politique tirée des propres paroles de l'écriture sainte*, in *Oeuvres de Bossuet*, 21 vols. (Paris, 1763), VIII:452 and passim.

37. For current views on "absolutism," see Beik, *Absolutism and Society* (see Intro., n. 38); Hamscher, 119–54.

38. François Bluche, "L'origine sociale des secrétaires d'état de Louis XIV (1661–1715)," *Bulletin de la société d'étude du XVIIe siècle*, nos. 42–43 (1959), 8–22; Beik, 303.

39. Yardeni, 507.

40. Neither Gaudry nor the current secondary sources have much to say on the possible role of barristers in the Fronde.

41. The original minutes of these meetings are in BCC 368. They were copied apparently in the early eighteenth century into BCC 362, to which this chapter will refer. Although the entries begin with the session of August 22, 1661, the entry for December 14, 1661 mentions meetings the previous year (fol. 34). On these documents, see Franck Bouscau, "Documents sur la discipline des avocats parisiens aux XVIIè et XVIIIè siècles," *Revue de la société internationale d'histoire de la profession d'avocat*, 1 (1989), 48–68; and Yves Ozanam, "Les sources de l'histoire de la profession d'avocat conservées par le barreau de Paris," *Revue de la société internationale d'histoire de la profession d'avocat*, 3 (1991), 75–88. For Montholon's noble status, see BCC 362, fol. 35.

42. BCC 362, fols. 33–34.

43. Ibid., fol. 34.

44. Henri-François d'Aguesseau, *Oeuvres complètes*, 13 vols. (Paris, 1759–89), X:407.

45. BN, JF 586, fols. 287–88. Durot wrote to the barristers of Besançon, who were in the process of reorganizing their troubled bar. Cf. Denisart (see Intro., n. 66) II:716; Boucher d'Argis, 21–22.

46. See, for instance, the 1778 oration by *bâtonnier* Jean-Prosper Duvert d'Émalleville, BCC 360, no. 8, fol. 1; the *conférence de discipline* of August 6, 1696, in BCC 362, fol. 104; Durot's report, BN JF 586, fols. 286–87.

47. In Brittany, the *premier président* simply inserted d'Aguesseau's 1750 observations, word for word, into a speech on the legal profession. See Gustave Saulnier de la Pinelais, *Le barreau du Parlement de Bretagne, 1553–1790: Les procureurs, les avocats* (Rennes, 1896), 170. For Rouen, see A. Sarrazin, *Le barreau de Rouen, hier et aujourd'hui* (Rouen, 1899), 16; and for Toulouse, Berlanstein (see Preface, n. 8), 135. The barristers of Besançon asked for a charter in 1707, but the experiment proved disastrous, and ended in 1770. See Gresset (see Intro., n. 16), 693–95.

48. BSPR LP 460, no. 23. The bound *registres* of the Order, which cover the years 1661 to 1731, are located in BCC 362–68.

49. Simon-Nicolas-Henri Linguet, *Appel à la posterité, ou receuil des mémoires et plaidoyers de M. Linguet, pour lui-même, contre la communauté des Avocats du Parlement de Paris* (Liège, 1779), 477.

50. *Exposition abrégé de la Constitution de l'Ordre des Avocats au Parlement de Paris* (Geneva, 1782), 12.

51. See, for instance, Anthony Black, *Guilds and Civil Society in European Political Thought from the Twelfth Century to the Present* (Ithaca, 1984).

52. See Jacques Revel, "Les corps et communautés," in *PCOR* 225–41, esp. 227.

53. The king was forced to register personally one of the relevant decrees concerning the *procureurs* in a *lit de justice*. See Bataillard and Nusse (see Intro., n. 61), I:153–64.

54. BCC 362, fol. 104; *Exposition abrégée*, 15.

55. It is true that one group of barristers, the *avocats aux conseils du roi*, were venal officers organized into a chartered corporation. However, the *avocats au parlement* had little respect for these colleagues, who combined the functions of both *avocat* and *procureur*. See Émile Bos, *Les avocats aux conseils du roi, Étude sur l'ancien régime judiciaire en France* (Paris, 1881).

56. BCC 362, fols. 27, 35, 42, 45.

57. The task proceeded slowly, as each bench had first to draw up its own list, and was not finished until May of 1663. BCC 362, fols. 27, 31, 58.

58. Ibid., fols. 27, 32–34, 63, 67, quotation from 34.

59. Norbert Elias, *The Court Society*, Edmund Jephcott, trans. (New York, 1983).

60. BCC 362, fol. 30. The registers do not comment on the *parlement*'s reaction.

61. Bluche, 37.

62. BCC 362, fol. 53.

63. BCC 362, fols. 53–63 passim. The dispute ended with an *arrêt de parlement* in the barristers' favor, which was duly copied into the registers of the *conférences de discipline*.

64. BCC 362, fol. 96. In May 1696, the *bâtonnier* decided to "renew the *conférences* held in 1661, 1662, 1663, 1664 and 1665."

65. Barthélémy Auzanet, "Lettre de Maître Barthélémy Auzanet, écrite à un de ses amis, Touchant les Propositions arrêtées chez Monsieur le premier Président" (unpaginated), in *Oeuvres de M. Barthélémy Auzanet, ancien avocat au Parlement* (Paris, 1708).

66. *Petit discours sur l'excellence de la profession des Advocats* (n.p., n.d.). The author was probably Jean Martinet or Pierre Chardon.

67. Isambert et al. (see Ch. 2, n. 15), XVIII:165.

68. "The public can only address itself, both for oral and written defense, to those it finds in the Tableau." François de Maraimberg, *Mémoire pour François de Maraimberg* (Paris, 1736) [in BSPR LP 449]. Further evidence for this point is found in AAE MDF 1271, fol. 281; BN JF 312, fol. 4; BN JF 586, fol. 289. When circumstances prevented the publication of the *Tableau*, young *stagiaires* had no choice but to wait patiently, as Le Paige describes in BSPR LP 460, no. 23.

69. The first edition (apparently) only appeared in 1680, and listed only

294 names. Over the next thirteen years, only two more *Tableaux* were published, listing 433, and 266 barristers. See BHVP C.P. 6482, and the collections in the BCC and the BACA.

70. *Arrêt de Parlement du 17 juillet, 1693*, reprinted in the *Tableau des Avocats* for 1781, 60.

71. See, for instance, Peter Burke, *The Fabrication of Louis XIV* (New Haven, 1992).

72. BCC 360, no. 5, fol. 7.

73. Riparfonds's will is reprinted in Alfred Franklin, *Les anciennes bibliothèques de Paris*, 3 vols. (Paris, 1873), III:177–80 (original is in BN ff. 22592, no. 17); Henri-François d'Aguesseau, "La décadence du barreau" (1698) in *Discours de Monsieur le Chancelier d'Aguesseau* (Paris, 1773), 92–121; quote from 99.

74. BCC 362, fols. 96–124.

75. Ibid., fols. 143–80.

76. Franklin, III:177–80; cf. BCC 362, fols. 164–66.

77. BCC 362, fols. 129–35; BN JF 2145, fol. 1.

78. BCC 362, fols. 178. See also the information in BCC 361, no. 63.

79. The victim, Jean Raoul, had offended against "the purity of the maxims of the bar" by performing dubious financial transactions for a noble client. See BN JF 575, fol. 85.

80. In 1774, Malesherbes wrote: "The barristers today claim that they are the masters of their *Tableau*, and that it is only out of politeness that they present it to the *avocats généraux*; the *avocats généraux* think the opposite . . . but carefully avoid compromising their authority or their claims." AN 263 AP 10, dossier 1, "Mémoire sur les Avocats," second draft, fol. 5. The two occasions were in 1727 and 1775. See Chs. 3 and 5, for details.

81. Joly de Fleury to Fleury, May 1739. BN JF 186, fol. 293.

82. Between 1710 and 1720, d'Aguesseau and the future *procureur général*, Guillaume-François Joly de Fleury, attended regularly. BCC 364, passim; Philippes Dumouchet Du Bac, *Traité des questions mixtes* (Paris, 1750), preface.

83. Charles de Ribbe, ed., *L'ancien barreau de Provence: extraits d'une correspondence inédite échangée pendant la peste de 1720* (Marseilles, 1861), 67 for legal seminars in the *Parlement* of Aix. In 1707, the barristers of Besançon formed their ill-fated *corps* (Gresset, 693–95). In Rouen, the *collège* approved articles of conduct for the profession in 1692, and established a series of *conférences* in a library in 1723 (Sarrazin, 16). In Rennes, an Order led by a *bâtonnier* had certainly come into existence by the 1730's (see Saulnier de la Pinelais, 169–71, 271).

84. The main sources for the life of Claude-Joseph Prévost are his professional papers, collected as BCC 360–61; his *inventaire après décès* and will, AN Minutier Central des Notaires, étude 116, no. 370; his *scellé*, AN Y 11935A; a *mémoire judiciaire* concerning a dispute over his estate, BN JF 1816, fols. 150 ff.; and the publisher's preface to his posthumous work, *Principes de jurisprudence sur les visites et rapports judiciaires de medecins . . .* (Paris, 1755).

85. BSPR LP 460, no. 23.

86. AN AB[XIX]3947, fol. 11c.

87. BCC 368, fol. 149. The drafts are still conserved in the *Bibliothèque des Avocats* in Paris, thankfully along with more legible copies. See BCC 360–61, passim. For the correspondence with Arrault, see BCC 361, no. 42.

88. BCC 361, no. 29.

89. Cocquart (see Ch. 1, n. 87), 44, 66; BCC 360, no. 86.

90. See BCC 360, no. 61; and Michel Duchemin, *Journal des principales audiences du Parlement*, 7 vols. (Paris, 1754), VII:484.

91. The simple reading of evidence, as opposed to the composition of an oral argument, did not require a university degree. A *procureur* could perform the task, and sometimes barristers actually brought forth *procureurs* as their "readers."

92. BCC 360, no. 61.

93. Mathieu Marais, *Journal et mémoires de Mathieu Marais, Avocat au Parlement de Paris, sur la Régence et le règne de Louis XV (1715–1737)*, M. de Lescure, ed., 4 vols. (Paris, 1863–68), II:189. Cf. Barbier (see Ch. 1, n. 30) I:103–4 and 253; BCC 360, no. 65.

94. See Ch. 3.

95. BN JF 2393, fols. 36–37; AAE MDF 1271, fol. 279.

96. Bataillard and Nusse, I:155–63; Koenig (see Ch. 1, n. 92), 13–17, 94–95.

97. Bien, "Offices, Corps and a System of State Credit," in *PCOR* 89–114, esp. 97–108.

98. See Koenig, 42, 111–12; Bataillard and Nusse, II:37–84.

99. The crown could also propose new privileges and higher *gages*—again in exchange for a hefty sum. See Koenig, 18.

100. *Réflexions sur le sort des procureurs au Parlement de Paris* (Paris, 1790), 8. See also Koenig, 117. Each payment was added to the nominal value of the office.

101. [Gin], *Entretien d'un militaire* (see Ch. 1, n. 58), 8.

102. Husson (see Ch. 2, n. 9); *Introduction au Barreau, ou Dissertations sur les choses principales qui concernent la profession de l'Avocat* (Paris, 1686); abbé de Bretteville, *L'éloquence de la Chaire et du Barreau* (Paris, 1698); Biaroy, *Règles* (see Intro., n. 59); François Fiot [or Fyot] de la Marche, *L'éloge et les devoirs de la profession d'Avocat* (Paris, 1713). Although such manuals were common in Renaissance Europe, in France, barristers included observations about "jurists" as part of general works. Relatively few works on the profession of barrister itself seem to have appeared before 1650.

103. The book was reprinted in 1740, 1742, and 1778, when it was heavily revised by Boucher d'Argis. For the physical advice, see the 1778 edition, 263, 359, 360, 371–72.

104. Ibid., 410–11 (1711 edition, 309–11).

105. Ibid., 272.

106. Ibid., 227–37.

107. Among many works on d'Aguesseau, see particularly Georges Frêche, *Daguesseau: Chancelier gallican* (Paris, 1969). For the citation from Fleury, see Peter Campbell, "The Conduct of Politics in France in the Time of the Cardinal Fleury, 1723–43," unpublished Ph.D. dissertation, University of London (1985), 245.

108. D'Aguesseau, "L'indépendance de l'avocat" in *Discours de … d'Aguesseau*, 122–43. In 1698, d'Aguesseau was not far removed from his own *stage* in the bar, and as *avocat général*, he continued to plead on a daily basis. Thus the oration represented not so much a lecture from on high, but rather the sentiments of a former colleague.

109. To take just three examples of citations: *Exposition abrégée* (see Ch. 2,

n. 50), 11; *Réflexions d'un militaire* (see Ch. 1, n. 7) 6; Louvet (see Ch. 1, n. 69), 27. On the *bâtonniers*, see: BSPR LP 460, no. 23 (Le Paige on Froland); BCC 360, no. 6 (de la Vigne); [Adrien Maillard], *Discours de M. le bâtonnier* (Paris, 1738); Barbier, I:410 (Le Roy de Vallières); BA 6192, fols. 254–63 (Merlet), quotation from fol. 261.

110. D'Aguesseau, "L'indépendance de l'avocat," 124.

111. Ibid., 126–27.

112. The barristers' virtue, d'Aguesseau wrote, "has never cost anything but the desire to obtain it." Ibid., 130.

113. Ibid., 128, 130, 138.

114. Karpik, "Le désintéressement" (see Intro., n. 52), 736, and "Lawyers and Politics" (see Intro., n. 52), 707–36.

115. See, for instance, AN U 859, which contains the *mercuriales* of Gilbert de Voisins (e.g., November 26, 1723, which mentions "le tribunal auguste du public," fol. 9; November 28, 1723—"Que le magistrat est tout au public"—and April 7, 1728).

116. For instance, d'Aguesseau, "L'indépendance de l'avocat," 136.

117. Ibid., 142–43. For a good treatment of republicanism in the French context, see Franco Venturi, "From Montesquieu to the Revolution," in *Utopia and Reform in the French Enlightenment* (Cambridge, 1971), 70–94.

118. On d'Aguesseau's republicanism, see also Nannerl O. Keohane, *Philosophy and the State in France: The Renaissance to the Enlightenment* (Princeton, 1980), 423–25.

Chapter 3

1. Bishop Joachim Colbert, quoted in René Taveneaux, *Jansénisme et politique* (Paris, 1965), 134.

2. Among the numerous works on eighteenth-century Jansenism, Edmond Préclin's *Les jansénistes du 18e siècle et la constitution civile du clergé* (Paris, 1929) remains fundamental. Among more recent works, see especially Dale Van Kley, *The Jansenists and the Expulsion of the Jesuits from France* (New Haven, 1975); and Catherine Maire, "L'église et la nation: du dépôt de la vérité au dépôt des lois, la trajéctoire janséniste au XVIIIe siècle," *Annales: économies, sociétés, civilisations*, XLVI, 5 (1991), 1177–1205; and Catherine Maire, "Port-Royal," in Pierre Nora, ed., *Les lieux de mémoire*, part III: *Les France*, 3 vols. (Paris, 1993), I:470–529.

3. For one of the clearest and most concise definitions of Jansenism, see Van Kley, *The Jansenists*, 6–36. On early Jansenism, see esp. Jean Orcibal, *Jean Duvergier de Hauranne, abbé de St. Cyran et son temps* (Louvain and Paris, 1947).

4. It was in response to these measures that Antoine Arnauld developed a distinction between matters of *droit* ("right"), on which the pope was infallible, and matters of *fait* ("fact"), on which he was not. This distinction became the justification for widespread refusal to sign the formulary.

5. Catherine-Laurence Maire, *Les Convulsionnaires de Saint-Médard: Miracles, convulsions et prophéties à Paris au XVIIIe siècle* (Paris, 1985), 55–57.

6. See Taveneaux, 138–40.

7. See Egret, *L'opposition parlementaire* (see Ch. 1, n. 3), 23–25; Taveneaux, 158–59.

8. Quesnel cited in Maire, *Les Convulsionnaires*, 33.

9. The historians include esp. Préclin and Van Kley. Richelieu is quoted in Solange Deyon, "Le jansénisme," in André Burguière and Jacques Revel, eds., *Histoire de France: Les conflits* (Paris, 1990), 185. On Quesnel's politics, see Taveneaux, 122–33.

10. For interesting reflections on the heavy legacy of the religious wars, see J.G.A. Pocock, "Conservative Enlightenment and Democratic Revolutions: The American and French Cases in British Perspective," *Government and Opposition*, XXIV, 1 (1989).

11. See Fumaroli, *L'âge de l'éloquence* (see Intro., n. 19), 623–32.

12. Lucien Goldmann, *Le dieu caché: Étude sur la vision tragique dans les Pensées de Pascal et dans le théâtre de Racine* (Paris, 1955).

13. Goldmann's work does not explain why Jansenism only appealed to a minority of *parlementaires*, nor why other members of the robe supported the Jesuits, nor why Jansenism had the most obvious sway over the magistrates in the mid-*eighteenth* century, long after their supposed "decline." See Van Kley, *The Jansenists*, 20–21.

14. See Fumaroli, 427–92 and 585–660.

15. Ibid., and particularly the study of Antoine Le Maître on 623–32.

16. Seyssel, *Monarchy* (see Ch. 1, n. 19), esp. 49–51; quote from 51.

17. Jean Soanen, *La vie et lettres de Messire Jean Soanen, Evêque de Senez*, abbé Gaultier, ed., 2 vols. (Cologne, 1750), I:217 (letter of January 5, 1728 to the Paris Order of Barristers). Dale Van Kley himself has speculated that Jansenism remained stronger in the *parlement* than in the Order until around 1741, because barristers only came to outnumber magistrates in Jansenist necrologies after that date. Yet many barristers who died between 1741 and 1760 would have been most active in the 1720's and 1730's. Consider also one additional perspective. Between 1715 and 1740, Jean Soanen wrote some 1,609 letters. Between 1715 and 1731, some 17 of these letters went to barristers, and 4 to magistrates. Between 1732 and 1740, however, only 8 went to barristers; 59 went to magistrates.

18. See the epigraph to Chapter III. For details on the "Parti Janséniste" in the *parlement* in the 1720's and 1730's, see Campbell, "The Conduct of Politics" (see Ch. 2, n. 107), 293–384. For the 1750's and 1760's, see Van Kley, *The Jansenists*, 37–61.

19. Barbier and d'Argenson, authors of two of the most important surviving journals, were hostile to Jansenism, and thus tended to find Jansenists everywhere. This fact has sometimes led to a skewed view of the eighteenth-century religious scene. See the quotations in Van Kley, *The Jansenists*, 27.

20. Ibid., 42–57. The *NE* is less useful for barristers, since they featured in its articles less often than magistrates.

21. The sources are: René Cerveau, *Nécrologe des plus célèbres défenseurs et confesseurs de la vérité du XVIIIe siècle*, 2 vols. (Paris, 1760) and 4 supplements, dated 1763–78; "Nécrologe de St. Médard," BN NAF 4264; the *NE* (see abbé Bonnemare, *Table raisonnée et alphabétique des Nouvelles ecclésiastiques, 1728–60*, 2 vols. [Paris, 1767]); and *Second recueil des miracles opérés par l'intercession de M. de Paris* (Paris, 1732). The sixteen are Jacques-Charles Aubry, Marc-Antoine Belichon, Louis Chevallier, Charles Comtesse, Henry Duhamel, Michel Duperray, Louis Fuet, Charles-Louis Guérin de Richeville, Philippes Guillet de Blaru, Jean Issali, Georges-Claude Le Roy, Louis Nivelle, Pierre-Salomon Pothouin,

Claude-Joseph Prévost, François-Denis Simon, and Pierre-François Soyer. Van Kley found sixteen barristers in Cerveau alone, but not all of them practiced in the *Parlement* of Paris. Catherine Maire, in "L'Église et la nation" (1185 and 1202), presents a different list of twenty-three barristers for the period 1727–31. She bases it on the "principal signatories of Jansenist *consultations*" and on BHVP CP 3481, fol. 3, "Liste d'ecclésiastiques et autres personnes de tout état attachés à l'oeuvre." The *consultations*, however, are not a reliable guide, as many non-Jansenists signed them out of Gallican sympathies. I could not consult the list at the BHVP, which appears to have been misplaced.

22. On Aubry, see the obituary in the *NE* for December 19, 1739. His son Guy-Charles was *bâtonnier* in 1782; his son-in-law, Anselme-Joseph d'Outremont, in 1779. On Chevallier, see *Grand dictionnaire* (see Ch. 1, n. 56), III: 604.

23. The *bâtonniers* from the Le Roy family were Georges himself and his brother, Pierre Le Roy de Vallières. Alexis Le Roy de la Tour also served in the Order. For the remark on the family, see Georges-Claude's obituary, which appeared in the same issue of the *NE* as Aubry's (see BSPR LP 414, no. 5). On Duhamel, see Le Paige's journal in BSPR LP 460, no. 23. For his link to d'Aguesseau, see Henry-François d'Aguesseau, *Lettres inédites du Chancelier d'Aguesseau*, D.-B. Rives, ed. (Paris, 1823), 460.

24. See Barbier (see Ch. 1, n. 30), I:411; II:100. For the library, see BN, Département des Imprimés, Q 8000.

25. Archives de la Famille Vinot Préfontaine: *Mémoires du conseiller Pierre-Augustin Robert de St. Vincent* (typescript copy), 10.

26. BN JF 1816, fol. 150; Duchemin, *Journal* (see Ch. 2, n. 90); Van Kley, *The Jansenists*, 58–59.

27. See Donald R. Kelley, *The Beginning of Ideology: Consciousness and Society in the French Reformation* (Cambridge, 1981), 169–211; cf. Fumaroli, 623–32; Dorothy Thickett, *Etienne Pasquier (1529–1615): The Versatile Barrister of 16th-century France* (London, 1979), 68–69, 95–121.

28. See Hubert Carrier, *La Presse de la Fronde (1648–1653): Les Mazarinades* (Geneva, 1991), II:23–27.

29. Fumaroli, 612–22; Carrier, II:23.

30. *Introduction au Barreau* (see Ch. 2, n. 102), 23–25; Biaroy, *Règles* (see Intro., n. 59), 9.

31. Fiot de la Marche (see Ch. 2, n. 102), 85, 100–36.

32. Ibid., 136, cf. 144.

33. Jean Barbier d'Aucour, *Onguent à la Brulure et plusieurs autres pièces* (n.d., 1670). On Barbier, see Antoine Joly de Blaisy, *Souvenirs d'un président au Grand Conseil sous Louis XIV*, Ernest Petit, ed. (Dijon, 1899), 15–18. Le Maître's pamphlet was called *Lettre d'un advocat au Parlement a un de ses Amis, Touchant l'Inquisition qu'on veut établir en France à l'occasion de la nouuelle Bulle du Pape Innocent VII* (n.p., [1657]).

34. See Lise Lavoir, "Factums et mémoires d'avocats au XVIIème et XVIIIème siècles," *Histoire, économie et société* 2 (1988), 221–42.

35. For background on the case, see Préclin, 54–61. On the connections between barristers and Jansenist clerics, see Maire, "L'Église et la nation," 1184–85.

36. The *mémoires* and *plaidoyers* are in BN JF 2298; and Département des Imprimés, *cote* Ld[4], nos. 773, 800, 801, 802, 812, 913, 933, 934, 935, and 936. For full titles, see the *Catalogue de l'Histoire de France*. See also the accompany-

ing material in BSPR LP 414. Prévost's declaration is in BN JF 2298, fol. 102, printed text, 2.

37. J. Cadry and J. Jouail, *Histoire du livre des Réflexions morales et de la Constitution Unigenitus*, 4 vols. (Amsterdam, 1723), I:685–92, quotation from 692.

38. The original draft of the speech is in BSPR LP 19, 11–36. A printed copy, without title, essentially identical to this draft, is in BN JF 2298, fol. 102. Compare with the reconstruction in BN Ld⁴802: *Plaidoyers de Mr. Joly, en faveur des trois chanoines, & des trois Curez de Reims, pour être déchargés de la Sentence d'excommunication prononcée contr'eux, le 17 juin 1715, au sujet de la Constitution Unigenitus* (n.p., [1716]), under title *Second Plaidoyer* with separate pagination.

39. BN JF 2298, fol. 48.

40. *Grand dictionnaire*, III:603–4; Chevallier, in *Plaidoyers de Mr. Joly*, first pagination, 19–20; Prévost, in BSPR LP 19, 1113, 1121.

41. Several briefs from the period paraphrased Quesnel closely. See, for instance, *Consultation de MM. les Avocats au Parlement de Paris, sur l'effet des Arrêts des Parlements, tant provisoires que définitifs, en matières d'appels comme d'abus des Censures ecclésiastiques* (Paris, 1718), 4–5. The authorship is uncertain.

42. *Plaidoyers de Mr. Joly*, first pagination, 4. For a quick summary of Quesnel's positions, see Taveneaux, 122–33.

43. Claude-Joseph Prévost, *Mémoire pour les trois docteurs et curez de Reims, au sujet des poursuites contre eux faites pour raison de la Constitution Unigenitus* (Paris, 1716), 7. On these theories of kingship, see above all Ralph E. Giesey, *The Royal Funeral Ceremony in Renaissance France* (Geneva, 1960); and Hanley, *Lit de Justice* (see Ch. 1, n. 21).

44. Prévost, 10.

45. See Van Kley, *Damiens* (see Intro., n. 63), 175 and 195; and Franklin Ford, *Robe and Sword: The Regrouping of the French Aristocracy after Louis XIV* (Cambridge, Mass., 1953), 92–95.

46. Van Kley, *Damiens*, 184–202. See, in comparison to Prévost's *mémoire judiciaire*, the 1731 remonstrance in Jules Flammermont, ed., *Remontrances du Parlement de Paris au XVIIIe siècle*, 3 vols. (Paris, 1888), I:232–40.

47. The *maître des requêtes* Richer d'Aube praised the regent for his prudence in BN NAF 9511, "Réflexions sur le gouvernement de France," 335.

48. Le Paige describes his friendship with Prévost in BSPR LP 460, no. 23, and later noted: "I was very linked with him during my first years at the bar" (BSPR LP 19, 141). In 1737, Prévost copied the *olim* registers for *Procureur général* Joly de Fleury (BN NAF 2111, quote from 11), and composed a series of observations on them (Bibliothèque du Sénat, Ms. 813). In his 1756 *Lettre sur les lits de justice* (n.p., n.d.), Le Paige seems to have drawn heavily on a 1730 study of the ceremony by Prévost, which is bound immediately after the pamphlet in the relevant volume of his library (BSPR LP 534, no. 18–19).

49. Maire, "L'église et la nation," 1187; BN JF 2298, fol. 102, printed text, *Consultation . . . sur l'effet des arrêts des Parlements*, 4.

50. Egret, 36; Barbier, I:15.

51. Egret, 37–38; Barbier, I:43.

52. BN JF 18, fols. 172–90.

53. Barbier, I:15. This *bon mot* enjoyed sufficient circulation to be repeated fifty-three years later, in a pamphlet in favor of Chancellor Maupeou, *Pensez-y bien* (n.p., [1771]), 3.

54. Barbier I:103. The six were motivated, so Barbier claimed, by undue sensitivity born of low birth; in fact, most were sons of *procureurs* or merchants and probably quite vulnerable to *parlementaire* scorn.

55. Barbier, I:69–70 and 13. On d'Argenson, see Egret, 36.

56. BSPR LP 460, no. 23.

57. BN JF 186, fol. 192 (a 1739 letter from Joly de Fleury to Fleury, which mentions the case); Barbier, I:43.

58. The Châtelet barristers briefly considered seceding from the Order. See Barbier, I:69–70, 81–82.

59. In 1727, *bâtonnier* Abraham Grosteste complained that the *parlement* was giving him no discretion to exclude candidates for admission, and was still accepting documents signed by disbarred barristers. BACA CBA, passim; *Arrest de la cour de Parlement*, July 23, 1727, cited in *Tableau* of 1781, BACA CBA.

60. See the description of events in Fericoq de la Dourie, *Mémoire* (see Ch. 1, n. 40), and the copy of the *Tableau de 1725* in the BACA. Prévost's papers make clear that he was undoubtedly the moving force behind the purge.

61. BACA, *Tableau de 1729*; *Troisième plaidoyer du mercredi 20 May 1716 . . .* (Paris, 1716).

62. BCC 361, 22–27; BACA, *Tableau de 1729*.

63. On the problem of unanimity in the Revolution, see Daniel Roche, "Sociabilité et politique de l'Ancien Régime à la Révolution," *French Politics and Society,* VII, 3 (1989), 7–13.

64. In general, on the history of Jansenism in this period, see Hardy, *Le Cardinal de Fleury* (see Intro., n. 2).

65. Maire, "L'Église et la nation," 1178–84. See also Françoise Bontoux, "Paris janséniste au 18e siècle: *Les nouvelles ecclésiastiques*," *Mémoires de la fédération des sociétés historiques et archéologiques de Paris et de l'Ile de France,* VII (1955), 205–20.

66. See Egret, 9, 23.

67. On the right to remonstrance, see Ford, *Robe and Sword,* 79–104, and esp. 99–101.

68. On Richerism, see Van Kley, *Damiens,* 173–84.

69. See particularly on this period, Hardy, 9–103; and Campbell, 192–210. Hardy calls Fleury "un véritable chef de parti" of theological anti-Jansenism (p. 17). Campbell, by contrast, sees the cardinal as mostly concerned with keeping the peace (p. 24). On the *parlement*, see Flammermont, ed., *Remontrances du Parlement de Paris au XVIIIᵉ siècle,* I:xiii–xiv.

70. See Maire, "L'Église et la nation," 1184–85.

71. *Consultation des Avocats du Parlement de Paris pour la cause de Monsieur l'Evêque de Senez* (Paris, 1727), 6. Aubry is credited with authorship in his obituary in the *NE* of December 19, 1739; however, Le Paige—usually a reliable source—gave the credit to Pothouin in BSPR LP 414, no. 2.

72. The Jansenists were Philippes Guillet de Blaru, Chevallier, Aubry, and Pothouin. The relatives were Guillaume Tartarin (brother or nephew of a woman listed in Cerveau), Jean-Louis Julien de Prunay (Tartarin's son-in-law), Cochin (related to Aubry), Georges Le Roy (father of Georges-Claude Le Roy), and Pierre Le Roy de Vallières (Georges-Claude's uncle). The nobles were Nicolas Guyot de Chesne, Tartarin, Nicolas de la Vigne, Cochin (all *secrétaires du roi*), Pothouin (a *capitoul* in Toulouse), Georges Le Roy (noble by letters patent), Guillet de Blaru, and Clément-François de la Verdy (of old noble

families). Le Roy, Aubry, Chevallier, de la Vigne, and Cochin had served in the council of Orléans. Cochin and Guyot de Chesne had served in the council of the Duc de Bourbon (house of Condé). Duhamel and Pothouin had served in the house of Conti. This information is taken from BCC 359; Barbier's journal; the *Almanach royal;* and BN JF 12, fol. 62. Tartarin was the *avocat général* to Marie Leszczinska.

73. *Consultation de MM. les Avocats du Parlement de Paris au sujet du jugement rendu à Ambrun contre M. l'Evêque de Senez* (Paris, [1728]). For the authorship, see *NE*, December 19, 1739. On the collaboration with Boursier, see Préclin, 119–20, 122.

74. *Consultation*, 12–13.

75. Barbier, I:271.

76. *NE*, 1727, 183–88. Cf. Barbier, I:269; Marais, *Journal* (see Ch. 2, n. 93), III:517.

77. Barbier, I:265–69; *NE*, 1728, 126.

78. Barbier, I:265, 270.

79. Marais, III:527, 540; Soanen, *Vie et lettres*, I:216–21; Barbier, I:268.

80. Barbier I:272; Émile Raunié, *Chansonnier historique du dix-huitième siècle*, 10 vols. (Paris, 1879–84), V:133–41, quote from 138; *Consultatie der advocaten van het Parlement van Paris over de sack van den hoogwaerde heer bisschop van Senez* (n.p., n.d.).

81. *NE* 1728, 201, 210.

82. AAE MDF 1268, fol. 63–64. According to Georges Hardy, Fleury "reserved all his resources" for the struggle against the barristers (p. 96).

83. Five of them appeared under the title *Lettre d'un avocat de province à M. Aubry* (and *Seconde lettre . . .*, etc.) (n.p., [1728]). See also [Poisson], *Avertissement donné aux vingt avocats sur leurs consultation du 1er juillet 1727 pour la cause de M. de Senez, ou Prelude de l'Avertissement qui sera donné aux cinquante avocats sur leur Consultation du 30 october 1727 au sujet du jugement rendu à Embrun contre M. de Senez* (Brussels, 1728), attribution to Poisson, a *cordelier* and client of Bissy's, in *NE* April 12, 1728, 11; Dominique Favier, *Lettre de M. Favier, ancien avocat au Parlement de Paris, à Monseigneur l'archevêque d'Embrun, ou il démontre principalement l'injustice du reproche de la Confidence* (n.p., [1728]); Jean Neutelet, *Réponse à la Question Nouvelle* (Paris, 1728).

84. For attacks by bishops of Embrun, Carcassonne, and Orléans, see Hardy, 95 and 151. For the attack by the bishop of La Rochelle, see *NE* March 22, 1729. For the papal brief, see Marais, IV:561. For the attempt to solicit a consultation, *NE*, Jan. 16, 1728, 197 and Jan. 28, 1728, 200.

85. Their finished work, published in late June, deemed many of Aubry's propositions "Richerist" and heretical. *NE* April 12, 1728, 10; and April 24, 13; *Lettre des Cardinaux, Archevêques et Evêques assemblez extraordinairement à Paris par les ordres du Roy pour donner à Sa Majesté leur Avis et Jugement sur un écrit imprimé qui a pour titre Consultation des cinquante Avocats . . .* (Paris, 1728). The work ran 63 pages. As for the royal condemnation, see BSPR LP 218, no. 17.

86. *Lettre d'un avocat au parlement de Bourgogne à un de ses amis, sur la Consultation des Avocats du Parlement de Paris contre M. l'Archevêque de Sens* (n.p., [1739]), 1; cf. Pierre-François Lafitau, *Histoire de la Constitution Unigenitus*, 2 vols. (Avignon, 1737–38), II:162.

87. For details on this group, see Bell, "Des stratégies d'opposition" (see

Intro., n. 3), 571, 585. Seven of the twenty-four were noble, five served as counselors to princely houses, and of fourteen whose parentage can be determined, thirteen were born into legal circles.

88. In general on 1730, see Hardy, 197–205; Egret, 26–27. Five of the briefs circulated only in manuscript, but were widely copied, and in one case, the barristers only refrained from publication as a favor to the Jansenist magistrate René Pucelle—yet more evidence that the barristers were taking a more radical stance than even Jansenist magistrates. See BCC 363, 620; Barbier, I:309. The works, signed by a total of 104 barristers, are: *Consultation de MM. les avocats du Parlement de Paris au sujet d'un bref de Rome contre le Mandement de M. l'évéque d'Auxerre sur la légende de Grégoire VII* (Paris, 1730); Philippes Guillet de Blaru, *Mémoire pour les docteurs de la Sorbonne*, in two separate parts, with a short "supplement," BN JF 129, fols. 1–24; BSPR LP 414, no. 10, written by Prévost; BA 10178, dated October 22, 1730; *NE* August 20, 1730, by Visinier; Maraimberg, *Mémoire pour les Sieurs Samson . . .* (see Intro., n. 1); BCC 363, 622–41; BN Manuscrits Clairambault 758, fols. 97–103, by Aubry (see Barbier, I:309).

89. Saint-Simon, in his *Mémoires*, accidentally wrote that Aubry represented Tencin's antagonist. His editor noticed the mistake. See *Mémories de Saint-Simon*, A. de Boislisle, ed. (Paris, 1925), XXXVII:12n.

90. See, for instance, *Lettre d'un avocat de province . . .* , 1; *Quatrième lettre d'un avocat de province . . .* , 7. Aubry's opponents also reprinted his original brief.

91. Aubry published this information in the *NE* May 14, 1728 and June 16, 1728, 67. The self-styled "provincial barrister" responded that the letters were forgeries. See *Cinquième lettre d'un avocat de province . . .* , 1.

92. *Deuxième lettre d'un avocat . . .* , 1.

93. Neutelet, 2; Raunié, esp. 138; *arrêt de conseil* of July 3, 3.

94. Poisson, *Avertissement*, 5.

95. Ibid., 8, 26, 35.

96. Ibid., 31, 29, 16.

97. Ibid., 28.

98. [Jérôme Besoigne], *Question nouvelle. A-t-on droit d'accuser Mrs. les Avocats du Parlement de Paris, d'avoir passé leur Pouvoir; & d'avoir traité des matières qui ne sont pas de leur Compétence, dans leur célébre Consultation sur le Jugement rendu à Ambrun, contre M. de Senez?* (n.p., [1728]). The attribution comes from Maire, "L'Église et la nation," 1203. Other defenses, which dwelt mostly on theology, were: *Defense de la Consultation de MM. les Avocats du Parlement de Paris en faveur de M. l'evêque de Senez* (n.p., 1729); Jacques Fouilloux, *Défense de la Consultation des 50 avocats* (Paris, 1728); *Apologie de la Consultation des avocats jansénistes* (n.p., [1728]).

99. Besoigne, 10.

100. Favier, *Lettre de M. Favier*, 14.

101. Besoigne, 9–10.

102. AAE MDF 1270, fols. 278–79 (for the list of fifty-three). See also AAE MDF 1271, fols. 223–24, 242–43, 273–74. Prévost is attacked by name in AAE MDF 1270, fol. 278 and AAE MDF 1271, fol. 273.

103. [Falconnet], *Projets de création* (see Ch. 2, n. 3), 46.

104. Fericoq, 19–23; AAE MDF 1271, fol. 223.

105. Barbier, I:313.

106. BCC 363, fols. 627–29.

107. [Maraimberg], *Mémoire pour les Sieurs Samson* . . . (see Intro., n. 1).

108. Ibid., 2.

109. Ibid., 1–3.

110. BCC 360, nos. 36, 38; Marais, IV:176.

111. Barbier, I:333.

112. For the full story of this bizarre incident, see Bell, "Des stratégies d'opposition," 572–73. The figure of two thousand comes from Lucien Febvre and Henri-Jean Martin, *The Coming of the Book: The Impact of Printing, 1450–1800* (London, 1976), 218–20.

113. BSPR LP 17, 794; BM 2357, 257; AAE CPR 715, fols. 406–7.

114. BN JF 97, fols. 281–82; AN U 375 (journal of magistrate Delisle). The *Nouvelles d'Amsterdam* of November 10, 1730 reproduced the ruling in its entirety. For the printing figures, see AN AB^{XIX}3947, fol. 8d.

115. See Bell, "Des stratégies d'opposition." Previous secondary treatments have failed to cover all the principal primary sources: BN JF 97–100; BN NAF 3333–35; AAE CPR 715–29; AAE MDF 1266–71; BCC 360–68; BSPR LP 414 and 449; AN U 375–77; and especially the incomplete *relation* by Jean-Louis Julien de Prunay, in AN AB^{XIX}3947 (my thanks to Michel Antoine for this reference).

116. See Christian Jouhaud, *Mazarinades: La fronde des mots* (Paris, 1985). Jeffrey Merrick starts from a similar standpoint in "'Disputes Over Words'" (see Intro, n. 44). Unfortunately, his account does not draw on Fleury's papers in the AAE or d'Aguesseau's notes in BSPR LP 17 and 449.

117. BSPR LP 449.

118. Bell, "Des stratégies d'opposition," 574–76. D'Aguesseau plotted out his strategy in notes conserved in BSPR LP 17, 801–14, and especially 806.

119. Bell, "Des stratégies d'opposition," 574–76. Evidence for the aborted strike is found in BCC 363, fol. 659; AN U 375; and BN JF 97, fol. 244 (d'Aguesseau to Joly de Fleury, November 6, 1730). The draft declaration was eventually published as *Requête de MM. les avocats au Parlement de Paris, au sujet de l'arrêt du Conseil d'Etat du Roi du 30 octobre, 1730* (Paris, 1730). On Prévost's responsibility for its clandestine distribution, see BN JF 97, fols. 255–56, and AN AB^{XIX}3947, fol. 11c.

120. On Le Normand, see the remarks by Barbier in II:457, and the pamphlet *Lettre de M. le Marquis de * * * Lt. Gén. des Armées du Roy, à M. Le Normant, Avocat en Parlement* (n.p., [1734]), esp. 3. On Julien de Prunay, see AN AB^{XIX}3947, passim and BCC 359.

121. AN AB^{XIX}3947, fols. 8b–8d.

122. See Bell, "Des stratégies d'opposition," 576–77. The final text was an *Arrest du Conseil d'Estat du Roi, Rendu au sujet d'une déclaration donnée, suivant l'Arrest du 30 octobre dernier, par 40 avocats au Parlement de Paris* . . . (BN JF 97, fols. 166–67). For the original text, with many last-minute corrections and the signatures of the barristers, see AN E 2105, fols. 293–98.

123. AN AB^{XIX}3947, fol. 7c.

124. *Arrest du Conseil d'Estat du Roi, Rendu au sujet d'une déclaration*, 1–2; AN AB^{XIX}3947 fols. 8b–8d; BCC 363, 676–85.

125. Marais, IV:185; AN AB^{XIX}3947 fols. 8c–8d. For the songs, see BSPR LP 449. One anonymous pamphlet, *Lettre de Mr *** (n.p., [1730]) tried to present the events as a defeat for the barristers.

126. The *Nouvelles d'Amsterdam* of December 7, 1730 reprinted the *arrêt*

in its entirety; AAE CPR 717, fol. 357; d'Argenson (see Intro, n. 7), I:71; BM 2357, 262. Other bishops officially condemned the original *mémoire*. See BSPR LP 449, passim, and the dispatches from Chauvelin to Ambassador Polignac in AAE CPR 729, fols. 2–19; 34–40; 79–88.

127. See Bell, "Des stratégies d'opposition," 577–79.

128. AN AB^{XIX}3947, fol. 10a; BN JF 100, fols. 39–43. The *maître des requêtes,* Richer d'Aube, was also taken in. See BN NAF 9511, 346.

129. AN AB^{XIX}3947, fols. 10a–10b.

130. Bell, "Des stratégies d'opposition," 579.

131. On the phenomenon, the principal works are Maire, *Les Convulsionnaires* (see Ch. 3, n. 5), and Robert Kreiser, *Miracles, Convulsions, and Ecclesiastical Politics in Early Eighteenth-Century Paris* (Princeton, 1978). For the correspondence between Fleury and Vintimille, see BM 2357, esp. fol. 399. On the connections between the barristers and Saint-Médard, see Maire, "L'Église et la nation," 1185.

132. For a detailed account of the affair, see Bell, "Des stratégies d'opposition," 579.

133. *NE* July 14, 1731, 140. For the exchange between Fleury and Vintimille, see AN AB^{XIX}3947, fol. 11d.

134. On Fleury's temporizing, see BM 2357, 492.

135. BCC 360, no. 46; AN AB^{XIX}3947, fol. 11d; "Procès verbal de ce qui s'est passé au Palais le 23 aoust et jours suivants," BN NAF 3334, fol. 364 ff; Le Normand to Chauvelin, AAE MDF 1270, fol. 124.

136. BSPR LP 449; AN AB^{XIX}3947, fol. 12c. Richer d'Aube described the chaos caused by the strike in BN NAF 9511, 340.

137. On the events of the summer of 1731 in general, see Hardy, 243–54 and Kreiser, 183–90.

138. Hardy, 240–41; BCC 360, no. 177, fol. 14; *NE* October 20, 1731, 187. The ten were Charles Comtesse, Louis Gin, Clément-François de Laverdy, Louis-Charles Lecomte, Le Roy de Vallières, René Pageau, Denis Paillet Des Brunières, Claude-Joseph Prévost, Jean-Baptiste Rousselet, and Pierre-François Soyer.

139. AAE MDF 1269, fols. 71–79; AAE MDF 1271, fols. 279–80.

140. AAE MDF 1271, fols. 273–95.

141. See BN JF 100, fols. 60–127; AN AB^{XIX}3947, fols. 13a–13c.; AN U 377.

142. *L'hérésie imaginaire des avocats, ou les jérémies de nos jours* (n.p., [1731]). The well-informed author knew, among other details, the barristers' allies in the ministry.

143. See Maire, *Les Convulsionnaires,* 55–57.

144. *L'hérésie imaginaire,* 22.

145. Ibid., 5.

146. Joly de Fleury threatened to resign in a letter to d'Aguesseau dated November 13, 1731 (BN JF 100, fol. 177). He first spoke only of "the proposition that was made to us." But the next day, he warned the chancellor that this "order of the king that one wishes to give to the barristers" would lead to the loss of many "great talents" (BN JF 100, fol. 178).

147. AAE MDF 1270, fol. 262 and *NE* December 19, 1739, 198 (for the collections); BA 3128, fol. 250 (for the song).

148. Le Normand to Joly de Fleury, November 8, 1731, BN JF 100, fol. 154.

149. AAE MDF 1271, fol. 209; BN JF 100, fols. 201–10.

150. AN AB[XIX]3947, fols. 13c–13d; *Arrest du Conseil d'État du Roy sur le mémoire des avocats au Parlement, 1er décembre, 1731* (Paris, 1731). The *mémoire* in question, hastily drafted by Le Normand, was not published, but a draft survives in BN JF 100, fol. 218.

151. See, for instance, Hardy, 252.

152. Barbier, I:380; BCC 359, iv. In 1735, Prévost lamented that the Order was not what it had been in 1731 (BSPR LP 460, no. 23). Le Paige would recall the declaration of November 25, 1730 as late as 1753. See BSPR LP 539, no. 93.

153. *JH* II, 280.

154. Voltaire, *Histoire du Parlement* (see Ch. 2, n. 6), 315.

Chapter 4

1. To take just the most obvious example, Alfred Cobban, *A History of Modern France*, I (London, 1963).

2. Baker, *Inventing* (See Preface, n. 4), 170.

3. Egret, *L'opposition parlementaire* (see Ch. 1, n. 3), 27–31.

4. Barristers and *procureurs* struck on three occasions: in May (see Barbier, *Journal* [see Ch. 1, n. 30], I:415); in June and July (ibid., 431); and in August through November (ibid., 449; and Egret, 30).

5. BN Ms. 10232, 66–67; cf. the "Réflexions" of Richer d'Aube, BN NAF 9512, 108–9. Both these sources are cited in Campbell, "Conduct of Politics" (see Ch. 2, n. 107), 338.

6. Egret, 30–31.

7. See Marais, *Mémoires* (see Ch. 2, n. 93), IV:496; and the Marquis d'Argenson in AAE MDF 1297, fol. 58.

8. AAE MDF 1297, fol. 73.

9. The ten were Aubry, Duhamel, Nicolas de la Vigne, Guillet de Blaru, Pierre Le Queulx, Georges Le Roy, Georges-Claude Le Roy, Pierre Le Roy de Vallières, Pierre-Salomon Pothouin, and Nicolas-Claude Visinier. All signed at least three of the following *mémoires* for convulsionaries: Jacques-Charles Aubry, *Acte d'appel au parlement interjeté par Anne Le Franc* (Paris, 1731); idem, *Requête présentée au Parlement pour Anne Le Franc, appellante comme d'abus* (Paris, 1731); idem, *Requête présentée au parlement par vingt-trois curés de la ville, faubourgs et banlieue de Paris* (Paris, 1735) (attributions in *NE* for December 19, 1739, 198); Georges-Claude Le Roy, *Consultation* [*pour Charlotte de la Porte*] (Paris, 1735) (in BSPR LP 414, no. 13); Pierre Le Queulx, *Requête présentée au Parlement par Charlotte de la Porte* (Paris, 1735), (attribution in *NE* of October 29, 1735, 169); *Requête présentée au Parlement pour Marguerite-Catherine Turpin dont les os se sont reformés...* (Paris, 1735); *Requête présentée au Parlement pour Denise Regné* (Paris, 1735). Police reports in BA 10196, dated July 27, 1731, speak of a group of eleven barristers who sent a deputy to St. Médard to investigate the case of a convulsionary nun—almost certainly the same group.

10. *Second recueil des miracles opérés par l'intercession de M. de Paris* (Paris, 1732). Charles-Louis Guerin de Richeville and Charles Comtesse appear on page

91 of this work. Prévost and Soyer accompanied Le Paige to hear the "prophet" Louis Sabinet. See BN NAF 4262, fol. 41. See also Ch. 3, n. 21. On Le Paige, see Maire, *Les Convulsionnaires* (see Ch. 3, n. 5), 26–27.

11. See Kreiser, *Miracles* (see Ch. 3, n. 131).

12. Ibid., 320–51.

13. AAE MDF 1297, fol. 58; AN U 375; Barbier, II:67; BSPR LP 460, no. 23.

14. *Lettre à Gilbert de Voisins Avocat-Général au Parlement de Paris* (n.p., [1731]); *Seconde lettre . . .* (n.p., [1731]); *Troisieme lettre . . .* (n.p., [1731]).

15. Guillaume-Hyacinthe Bougeant, *La femme docteur, ou la théologie tombée en quenouille* (Liège, 1731); *Critique de la femme docteur, ou de la théologie tombée en quenouille* (London, 1731); *Le saint déniché, ou la banqueroute des marchands de miracles* (The Hague, 1732). Quote from *Le saint déniché,* 18. Marais seems to refer to a performance in a letter of January 12, 1731 (Marais, IV:195). See also *Arlequin: Esprit Folet. Comédie* (n.p., 1732), which defends the barristers against Bougeant.

16. Cocquart, *Lettres* (see Ch. 1, n. 87). The anonymous *Examen de la lettre du fils à son père* (n.p., [1734]) alleged that the work was in fact a provocation written by an enemy of the barristers, but the identification is supported in Philippe Bourgeon, *Le barreau de Dijon au xvii᷍ et xviii᷍ siècles* (Dijon, 1885), 62.

17. Cocquart, 6, 21, 44–70.

18. [Demontcrif], *Réponse d'un fils à son père sur deux lettres ou dissertations qui parurent en 1733 au sujet de la profession d'Avocat* (n.p., 1734 or 1735), 6–7. A handwritten copy of this pamphlet, with the author identified as Demontcrif, *procureur au Châtelet,* survives in AN 4 AP 189.

19. The barristers voiced their suspicions, and protested their enormous respect for the *parlement,* in *Examen de la lettre du fils;* see also Barbier, II:66.

20. Barbier, II:32. See also Olivet, *Lettre de M. l'abbé Olivet de l'Académie Française à M. le Président Bouhier de la même académie* (n.p., 1733); *Lettre de M. le Marquis* (see Ch. 3, n. 120); *Lettre d'un académicien à M. le Marquis de *** pour servir de réponse à la lettre écrite à M. Le Normant* (n.p., 1734); *Lettre d'un jeune avocat pour servir de réplique à la réponse d'un académicien.*

21. AN U 384; *Mandement de Monseigneur l'Evêque de St. Papoul* (St. Papoul, 1735); BSPR LP 460, no. 23; *Lettre de MM. les Avocats au Parlement de Paris à M. l'Evêque de St. Papoul au sujet de son Mandement* (Paris, 1735).

22. D'Aguesseau to Joly de Fleury, April 2, 1735; BN JF 150, fol. 32; BSPR LP 460, no. 23.

23. BSPR LP 460, no. 23; Barbier, II:107–8. Georges-Claude Le Roy was the son of Georges.

24. AAE MDF 1297, fols. 58–59.

25. BSPR LP 460, no. 107 (a draft of a pamphlet by Le Paige on the strike, apparently never published); BSPR LP 460, no. 23.

26. BSPR LP 460, no. 23. For evidence that barristers could not practice until their names appeared on the *Tableau,* see AAE MDF 1271, fol. 281; BN JF 312, fol. 4; and BN JF 586, fol. 289. On Froland, see Barbier, II:68. On Maraimberg, see BN JF 2133, fol. 365. The *parlement* dismissed Maraimberg's demands for reinstatement.

27. AN U 384; BSPR LP 460, no. 23; Barbier, II:114.

28. BSPR LP 460, no. 23; cf. Barbier, II:119.

29. BSPR LP 460, no. 23; Barbier, II:120.

30. BSPR LP 460, no. 23; BACA CBA.

31. Portail to Chauvelin, undated. AAE MDF 1297, fol. 72. See also AN U 384; Barbier, II:119.

32. AN U 384 (July 22, 1735).

33. BSPR LP 460, no. 107; Barbier, II:122. The pamphlets were: *Remontrance que la raison fait aux advocats après leur rentrée générale au Palais du 23 Juillet 1735* (n.p., [1735]); *Amnistie en faveur des Avocats au Parlement de Paris* (n.p., [1735]); *Requête présentée aux avocats par les decrotteurs pour demander la réunion des deux ordres* (n.p., [1735]); *Arrest de la Basoche en faveur des Avocats du Parlement de Paris* (n.p., [1735]); *Brevet du Regiment de la Calotte en faveur des Avocats du Parlement de Paris* (n.p., [1735]). On their distribution, see BN JF 154, fol. 317.

34. *Brevet du Regiment de la Calotte*, 1–2; *Amnistie*, 2.

35. BN, Manuscrits Clairambault 526, 186; BSPR LP 460, no. 102.

36. BN NAF 10783, fol. 44; BSPR LP 19.

37. The total has been compiled from three sources: the *NE*, which discussed and sometimes even reprinted *mémoires* that do not appear to have survived elsewhere; BSPR LP 414; and the BN. For a complete list of texts, see Bell, "Lawyers and Politics" (see Ch. 1, n. 73), 427–29.

38. Fleury to Joly de Fleury, May 9, 1739, BN JF 186, fol. 289.

39. The group slowly changed as earlier members such as Aubry and Georges-Claude Le Roy died and were replaced by others, notably, Le Paige, Maultrot, Mey, Jacques-Joseph Texier, and Jean-Charlemagne Lalourcé. Le Paige himself took credit, in the copies in his library, for at least four *mémoires: mémoire* dated September 6, 1740 in *Recueil des Consultations de MM. les Avocats du Parlement de Paris au sujet de la procédure extraordinaire instruite à l'Officialité de Cambrai* (Paris, 1741, with Pierre Soyer); *Mémoire à consulter à MM. les Avocats de Paris, et la Response des avocats, pour refus de sacrements à Bayeux* (Paris, 1739); *Mémoire* in BSPR LP 510, no. 14; *Consultation de MM. les Avocats du Parlement au sujet du mandement de M. l'archevesque de Sens du 6 avril 1739* (Paris, 1739). The last was the second of two *mémoires* with identical titles, one dated August 2, the second September 1, 1739.

40. Prévost dictated a lengthy *procès-verbal* of one such meeting, concerning the case of a refusal of the sacraments in Bayeux in 1739, which took place at the home of Georges Le Roy (BSPR LP 414, no. 19, citation from section 6). See also Maultrot's letter to Le Paige in BSPR LP 515, no. 42.

41. *Recueil des Consultations de MM. les Avocats. . . .* This consists of nine separate consultations from 1739–40.

42. Le Paige family papers in BSPR; *Annales de la Religion, ou mémoire pour servir à l'Histoire des 18e et 19e siècles: par une Société d'Amis de la Religion et de la Patrie* (Paris, 1803), XVI:550.

43. See Maire, *Les Convulsionnaires*, 26–27. On Le Paige's moderation, see, for instance, his correspondence with the ministry in BSPR LP 580, nos. 61–68; and Egret, 174. On his collaboration with *bâtonniers*, see BSPR LP 539, no. 93.

44. *Annales de la religion*, XVI:546–47, 552. See also Yann Fauchois, "Jansénisme et politique au XVIIIe siècle: légitimation de l'État et délégitimation de la monarchie chez G.N. Maultrot," *Revue d'histoire moderne et contemporaine*, XXXIV (1987).

45. *Recueil des Consultations de MM. les Avocats.*

46. BSPR LP 533. Guy-Charles Aubry was the son of Jacques-Charles.

47. See Bontoux, "Paris janséniste" (see Ch. 3, n. 65).

48. Bishop of Auxerre to Soyer, 1741. Bound with BSPR LP 511, no. 5.

49. *NE* November 28, 1739, 186; January 10, 1740, 17; 1744, 173; September 18, 1749, 152; *De la nature de la Grace* (see Ch. 1, n. 90), 13.

50. On Languet's condemnation, see *NE* November 29, 1739, 186; *Réflexions sur la consultation des avocats contre le mandement de Msgr. l'Archevêque de Sens* (n.p., [1739]); BSPR LP 511, nos. 9, 11, 11 bis.

51. BSPR LP 511, no. 26; BSPR LP 515, no. 39.

52. *Consultation . . . au sujet du mandement de M. l'archevesque de Sens,* dated August 2, 1739, esp. 29.

53. Ibid., dated September 1, 1739, 2, 8.

54. *Mandement de Msgr. l'Archévêque-Duc de Cambray portant Condamnation d'un Ecrit qui a pour titre Recueil des Consultations de MM. les Avocats du Parlement de Paris* (BSPR LP 511, no. 11), 6.

55. The *vingtième,* an attempt to impose a permanent revenue tax in peacetime, met with fierce resistance from the *parlement* and the clergy. See Egret, 40–43. On the *rentrée en scène,* see Egret, 52.

56. In addition to the four *consultations* suppressed by the 1749 *arrêt de conseil,* see the *NE* October 30, 1750, 174, concerning a brief by Maultrot. On the crisis itself, see Egret, 56–67; and, most recently, Carroll Joynes, "Jansenists and Ideologues: Opposition Theory in the Parlement of Paris (1750–1775)," unpublished Ph.D. dissertation, University of Chicago (1981), 85–157.

57. Robert de Saint-Vincent (see Ch. 3, n. 25), 218. See also Van Kley, *The Jansenists* (see Ch. 3, n. 2), 99–100. The *Mémoire à consulter pour Jean Lioncy* alone, by Charlemagne Lalourcé, ran more than 500 pages. Other important mémoires included Mey's *Mémoire à consulter et consultation pour les quatres premiers Pères ou Abbés de l'Ordre de Cîteaux, contre l'Abbé de Cîteaux* (Paris, 1764).

58. Besides Van Kley's *The Jansenists,* see on this subject esp. Joynes; André Cocatre-Zilgien, "Les doctrines politiques des milieux parlementaires dans la seconde moitié du XVIIIe siècle," *Annales de la faculté de droit et des sciences économiques de Lille* (1963), 33–155; and J. M. J. Rogister, "The Crisis of 1753–4 in France and the Debate on the Nature of the Monarchy and of the Fundamental Laws," in Rudolf Vierhaus, ed., *Herrschaftsverträge, Wahlkapitulationen, Fundamentalgesetze* (Göttingen, 1977).

59. Louis-Adrien Le Paige, *Lettres historiques sur les fonctions essentielles du Parlement, sur le droit des pairs, et sur les Loix fondamentales du Royaume,* 2 vols. (Amsterdam, 1753–54). On the remonstrances, see Flammermont, *Remontrances* (see Ch. 3, n. 46), II:xv and passim.

60. Van Kley, *The Jansenists,* 60.

61. For the influence of the *Lettres historiques* on the remonstrances of 1755 and 1756, see Van Kley, *Damiens* (see Intro., n. 63), 190. On the role of Le Paige, Mey, and Maultrot in the composition of the "great remonstrances," see Van Kley, *The Jansenists,* 54–55.

62. Moreau, however, refused. Jacob-Nicolas Moreau, *Mes souvenirs,* 2 vols. (Paris, 1898–1901), I:49.

63. In his memorandum *Principes de conduite avec les parlements,* Bibliothèque

du Sénat 402, fols. 27–135. On this essay, see Baker, "Ideological Origins" (see Intro., n. 12), 215. On Moreau, see Dieter Gembicki, *Histoire et politique sous l'ancien régime: Jacob-Nicolas Moreau* (Geneva, 1976).

64. Moreau, *Mes souvenirs,* I:50; BSPR LP 535, no. 155.

65. On Bargeton, see Barbier, III:45 (I have not been able to identify the pamphlet listed); on Coquereau, see *Plaidoyer prononcé au Parlement, les Chambres assemblées, le 18 mars 1755, par M. Coquereau,* in BSPR LP 535, no. 136 (oddly, Coquereau is also generally identified as the author of the anti-Maupeou *Mémoires de l'abbé Terray*). On Darigrand, see *MS* VI:9.

66. Robert de Saint-Vincent, 148.

67. See particularly Joynes; Van Kley, *Damiens;* and Shanti Singham, "'A Conspiracy of Twenty Million Frenchmen': Public Opinion, Patriotism, and the Assault on Absolutism during the Maupeou Years, 1770–1775," unpublished Ph.D. dissertation, Princeton University (1991).

68. Van Kley, *Damiens,* 185.

69. Van Kley must write: "Even if, therefore, Le Paige himself did not explicitly enunciate the principle of national sovereignty in his *Lettres historiques,* it remains true to say that the book's premises 'invite' if not 'convoke' such a conclusion." Van Kley, *Damiens,* 188. Cf. Joynes, 186. In a later pamphlet, Le Paige went slightly farther and used the ambiguous phrase "the founders of the state." See [Louis-Adrien Le Paige], *Lettre sur les lits de justice* (n.p., n.d.), 9.

70. See Joynes, 187–88. For a view of Le Paige as essentially conservative, see Rogister, "The Crisis of 1753–54," 119–20.

71. Montesquieu, *De l'esprit des loix,* Jean Brethe de la Gressaye, ed., 4 vols. (Paris, 1950).

72. *Lettres historiques,* I:1–3.

73. Ibid., I:96. Likewise, in Le Paige's section on the Carolingians (I:155–202), his sole concern is to establish the unchanging nature of the institutions.

74. Maire, in "L'église et la nation" (see Ch. 3, n. 2) sees the concept as having solely Jansenist theological roots.

75. Van Kley, *The Jansenists,* esp. 57–61.

76. BSPR LP 531.

77. Lambert to Le Paige, November 3, 1753, BSPR LP 529, no. 110.

78. Robert de Saint-Vincent, 149; BN NAF 8496, 96, 102, 110. D'Erceville did not refer to Mey by name and disparaged the "condescension" with which he had supposedly treated his social superiors.

79. *Almanach royal,* passim, 1700–49. The barristers numbered among the twenty or so *administrateurs* who helped supervise the institution.

80. See the discussion in Chapter 1. Robert was the grandfather of the magistrate Robert de Saint-Vincent (Robert de Saint-Vincent, 18–19). On the Gerbiers and Conti, see BSPR LP 549.

81. On the *affaire de l'Hôpital général,* see Henry Légier Desgranges's *Madame de Moysan et l'extravagante affaire de l'hôpital général (1749–58)* (Paris, 1954), which is badly flawed by its ferocious hostility to the Jansenists.

82. BN JF 1247, fols. 1–36. Cf. Légier Desgranges, 116–20, 153–60.

83. BN JF 1230, fol. 171; *NE* September 4, 1749, 144. Cf. Légier Desgranges, 171–72, 205–6.

84. BSPR LP 516, no. 39.

85. In the end, the ministry managed to buy Arrault's cooperation, but other members of the Order continued the struggle. See Légier Desgranges, 324–30.

86. Van Kley, *Damiens*, 144; Jules Flammermont, *Le Chancelier Maupeou et les parlements* (Paris, 1883), xvi; Nina Rattner Gelbart, *Feminine and Opposition Journalism in Old Regime France: The Journal des Dames* (Berkeley, 1987), 95–132, quotation from 114; BN 22093, fol. 421 ff.

87. For Le Paige's letters to the prince, see, for instance, BSPR LP 547, no. 3; Robert de Saint-Vincent, 196.

88. BSPR LP 549, "Lettre du 12 février 1757"; Barbier, IV:195–96. On Le Gouvé, see also Van Kley, *Damiens*, 91.

89. [Edme-François Darigrand], *L'Antifinancier* (n.p., 1763), 6–7. His travails with the Order are recounted in *MS* V:90. Malesherbes refers to them in AN AP 263 9, dossier 4, ch. 6, fol. 42.

90. On Darigrand's imprisonment, see BA 12173, fols. 81–203.

91. On the judicial strikes, see Egret, 50–132 passim. On the *procureurs* during this period, see Bell, "Lawyers and Politics," 246–52.

92. [Gin], *Entretien* (see Ch. 1, n. 58), 8; *JH* II:281.

93. During the 1751 strike, rumors spread that a faction in the king's council had demanded the "decimation" of the Order to punish its resistance. See Barbier, III:317, 469; BSPR LP 516, no. 53.

94. Barbier, III:469–506; d'Argenson (see Intro., n. 7), VIII:294.

95. Barbier, IV:219; Moreau, I:47.

96. In the provinces, *querelles de préséance* took place throughout the century, notably, in Rouen (Lenard Berlanstein, "Lawyers in Pre-Revolutionary France," in Wilfrid Prest, ed., *Lawyers in Early Modern Europe and America* [London, 1981], 175); Grenoble (ibid.); Rennes (Delbeke, *L'action politique* [see Preface, n. 7], 93); Bordeaux (*JH* VII, 35); and Besançon (Gresset, *Gens de justice* [see Intro., n. 16], 721 and 734–41).

97. BA 6192, fols. 16–44. See also Barbier, IV:438–39. On Phelippes, see BN JF 2145, fol. 64. The only sign of rebellion from the leaders of the Order after 1735 came in 1741, when they published a brief for provincial colleagues on the same question of *préséance* that had led to the 1735 strike: *Consultation de MM. les Avocats du Parlement de Paris sur les questions suivantes . . .* (Paris, 1741), esp. 15.

98. BN JF 186, fol. 289.

99. Ibid., fols. 292–94. The barristers apparently agreed to reinstate the man in question, but he never again appeared on the *Tableau*.

100. *Consultation de Plusieurs Canonistes et Avocats de Paris, sur la compétence des Juges séculiers, par raport au refus des sacrements . . .* (n.p., [1753]); [Bertrand Capmartin de Chaupy], *Réflexions d'un avocat sur les affaires du temps* (London, 1756). See also *Lettre à M. *** Avocat au Parlement de Paris ou Défense de la Consultation de Plusieurs Canonistes et Avocats de Paris, sur la compétence des Juges séculiers, par raport au refus des sacrements, du 2 janvier 1753* (n.p., [1753]).

101. *NE* May 8, 1753, 75; *NE* October 22, 1756, 175.

102. BSPR LP 539, no. 93. As proof of the Order's devotion to royal authority, Le Paige cited eight lines of the barrister's declaration of November 25, 1730. On 1730, see BCC 363, 592. Cf. *NE* March 26, 1729, 1.

103. Barbier, II:203. Cf. Bos, *Les avocats aux conseils* (see Ch. 2, n. 55), 409–46.

104. See *Mémoire pour les Chancelier . . . de la Basoche du Palais . . . Contre le Sieur Jean-Baptiste-Thomas de Ruelle* (Paris, 1748); *Mémoire pour le Chancelier . . . de la Basoche . . . Contre Pierre Petitjean* (Paris, 1750).

105. Barbier, III:289.

106. BACA CBA. For an explicit link between overcrowding and the purges, see Barbier, III:289.

107. *Extrait des registres du Parlement. Du Mercredi 5 Mai 1751 du matin*, reprinted in the *Tableau* of 1781, 73–77, BACA CBA.

108. BACA CBA; BN JF 312, fols. 4–40.

109. BN JF 186, fol. 290.

110. BN JF 312, fols. 5, 9; BACA Collection Gaultier du Breuil, vol. 15, nos. 2, 5, 14; BACA CBA, handwritten note in 1761 *Tableau*; Barbier, II:341–43; Malesherbes in AN 263 AP 9, dossier 4, ch. 6, fol. 28 (Bidault in fact escaped *radiation*).

111. The Order did not, however, frown on what one *avocat général* had called "the noble vehemence and sacred boldness which forms part of the barristers' calling." Quoted in Charles de Fouchier, *Règles de la profession d'avocat à Rome et dans l'ancienne législation française, jusqu'à la loi des 2–11 septembre 1790* (Paris, 1895), 259.

112. BN JF 2133, fols. 347–53; Barbier, II:253; BN JF 312, fol. 30.

113. BN JF 2133, fol. 351.

114. BN JF 186, fols. 286, 302.

115. Le Paige wrote in a journal that if the two men accepted the offer, they would be disbarred. BSPR LP 516, no. 39. Cf. *NE* September 4, 1749, 144.

116. *Extrait des registres de Parlement* (Paris, 1751), 76; BN JF 312, fols. 5 and 12; BACA *Tableau* of 1763; Durot, "Mémoire sur les avocats" in BN JF 586, fol. 291.

117. BN JF 586, fols. 289–90. Malesherbes claimed that Darigrand, author of *L'antifinancier*, only escaped *radiation* in 1769–70 by appealing to the general assembly.

118. BACA CBA, passim.

119. For instance, Linguet, *Appel* (see Ch. 2, n. 49), 9; Jacques-Claude Martin de Mariveaux, *Récit pour Jacques-Claude Martin de Mariveaux, Avocat au Parlement* (Paris, 1776), 4.

120. François-Charles Huerne de la Mothe, *Liberté de la France contre le pouvoir arbitraire d'excommunication* (Paris, 1761), discussed in BN JF 575, fols. 64–94, quote from fol. 66. Huerne initially denied he had written the *mémoire* itself. Cf. John McManners, *Abbés and Actresses: The Church and the Theatrical Profession in Eighteenth-Century France* (Oxford, 1986).

121. Barbier, IV:391; BN JF 575, fols. 64–94, quote from fol. 79.

122. *MS* XIX:139–45.

123. Moreau, I:50; [Jacob-Nicolas Moreau], *Lettre du chevalier *** à Monsieur ***, Conseiller au Parlement; ou, Reflexions sur l'arrest du Parlement du 18 Mars 1755* (n.p., [1755]).

124. See BSPR LP 535, nos. 155–60. Cf. comments in *NE* June 26, 1755, 103.

125. BA 6192, fol. 45.

Chapter 5

1. See BSPR LP 580, nos. 61–68. On the expulsion of the Jesuits, see Van Kley, *The Jansenists* (see Ch. 3, n. 2).

2. For detail on the two judgments, see Van Kley, *The Jansenists*, esp. 108–36; and Edna Nixon, *Voltaire and the Calas Case* (New York, 1959), esp. 88–114.

3. [François Richer], *De l'autorité du clergé et du pouvoir politique sur l'exercice des fonctions du ministère ecclésiastique*, 2 vols. (Amsterdam, 1766). See on this issue Dale Van Kley, "Church, State and the Ideological Origins of the French Revolution: The Debate over the General Assembly of the Gallican Clergy in 1765," *Journal of Modern History*, LI (1979), 629–66.

4. For some of the continuing skirmishes, concerning, respectively, the Jansenist nuns of the Hôtel-Dieu and a French student in Rome, see BN JF 455, fols. 54–138; and *MS* IV:32–33. On the continuing *parlementaire* conflicts, see Egret, *l'opposition parlementaire* (see Ch. 1, n. 3), 158–81.

5. Voltaire, *Les oeuvres complètes de Voltaire*, Theodore Besterman, ed., 134 vols. (Oxford, 1970–76), CIX:203 (Voltaire to Feriol and Jeanne Du Bouchet, September 6, 1762).

6. On the development of the case, see Nixon, 153–69; Delbeke, *L'action politique* (see Preface, n. 7), 166–76.

7. Voltaire, CXII:479 (Voltaire to d'Alembert, March 25, 1765); CIX:352 (Voltaire to Élie de Beaumont, December 19, 1762); CX:22 (Voltaire to Damilaville, February 4, 1763). See also Voltaire's *Lettre de monsieur de Voltaire, à monsieur Élie de Beaumont* (n.p., [1767]).

8. On the careers of the three men, see Lenormand and Charrier, *Biographie des principaux magistrats, avocats et jurisconsultes français* (Paris, 1825); Paul Boullouche, ed., *Un avocat du XVIIIe siècle: Target* (Paris, 1893); Joseph Hudault, "Guy-Jean-Baptiste Target et la défense de statut personnel à la fin de l'ancien régime," unpublished *thèse de doctorat en droit* (Paris, 1970). On Gerbier's ennoblement, see Poirot, "Le milieu socio-professionnel" (see Intro., n. 60), I:93–94; and on Élie's, AN M 1039. Keith Baker has cogently analyzed the tension between the "public sphere" and the *parlements* as it appeared in the works of Malesherbes, a man closely linked to all three barristers. See Baker, *Inventing* (see Preface, n. 4), 120.

9. See Stéphane Rials, *La déclaration des droits de l'homme et du citoyen* (Paris, 1988), esp. 187–91; Hudault, 46–47; Van Kley, *The Jansenists*, 100–1.

10. Target, *Lettres d'un homme à un autre homme* (n.p., [1771]), 135, 180; *ML* II:7; *MS* XXVII:60 and V:82.

11. Hudault, 48. On the question of Protestant marriages, see Jean-Baptiste-Jacques Élie de Beaumont, *Question sur la légitimité des mariages protestants français célébrés hors du royaume* (Paris, 1764). On the château and the festival, see Alain de Mézerac, "Le château de Canon," in *Art de Basse-Normandie*, no. 37 (1965); and Sarah Maza, "The Rose-Girl of Salency: Representations of Virtue in Pre-Revolutionary France," *Eighteenth-Century Studies*, XXII, 3 (1989).

12. Jean-Baptiste-Jacques Élie de Beaumont, *Mémoire à consulter et consultation pour Pierre-Paul Sirven . . .* (Paris, 1767), 1–2.

13. Voltaire, CXII:479 (Voltaire to d'Alembert, March 25, 1765); CXIV:73 (Voltaire to Élie de Beaumont, Feb. 1, 1766).

14. Élie wrote a pamphlet for the *parlement* entitled *Lettres sur l'état actuel du crédit du Gouvernement en France* (n.p., [1772]); the plan for the plenary court is in the Élie de Beaumont papers, Château de Canon.

15. *GT* XXV:180. On the police suspicions, see BN Ms. 22101, fol. 97. On Gerbier *père*, see Cerveau, *Necrologie* (see Ch. 3, n. 21), II:425; For the invitations to Conti and Chartres and his appearance, *MS* IV:290–91; V:182; III:203–4. Gerbier received as much as 300,000 *livres* per case, but also accumulated debts on a noble scale, owing 15,000 *livres* annually in 1771. See Berryer, *Souvenirs* (see Ch. 1, n. 8), I:88, and BSPR LP 571, no. 9.

16. Robert de Saint-Vincent, *Mémoires* (see Ch. 3, n. 25) 235–36; Siméon-Prosper Hardy, *Mes loisirs, ou Journal d'événements tels qu'ils parviennent à ma conaissance*, Tourneux et Vitrac, eds. (Paris, 1912), 116–17.

17. *MS* II:175; VI:19.

18. BN NAF 10781–83. The figure of fourteen *avocats tablotants* comes directly from D'Hémery's lists. The other figures come from Robert Darnton, "A Police Inspector Sorts His Files: The Anatomy of the Republic of Letters," in *The Great Cat Massacre* (New York, 1984), 151. For the *Tableau* of 1770, see BACA CBA.

19. BACA CBA. On Loiseau, see Poirot, I:135. On Élie's unpopularity in the bar, see *MS*, XXXI:28, confirmed by Voltaire in CXIII:237 (Voltaire to Comte and Comtesse d'Argental, July 28, 1765). Other incidents involving Élie appear in the Élie de Beaumont papers, Château de Canon.

20. See Charles H. O'Brien, "The Jansenist Campaign for Toleration of Protestants in Eighteenth-Century France," *Journal of the History of Ideas*, XLVI (1985), 523–38.

21. Jean Cruppi, *Linguet: Un avocat-journaliste au XVIIIe siècle* (Paris, 1895), 54. In general on Linguet, see the meticulous biography by Darline Gay Levy, *The Ideas and Careers of Simon-Nicolas-Henri Linguet* (Urbana, 1980).

22. Quoted in Cruppi, 46.

23. [Linguet], *Nécessité d'une réforme* (see Ch. 1, n. 6), esp. 93–94.

24. Levy, 33–37.

25. Simon-Nicolas-Henri Linguet, *Aiguilloniana; ou, anecdotes utiles pour l'histoire de France au dix-huitième siècle, depuis l'année 1770* (London, 1777), 20–21.

26. He was the author of a play and a novel. Ferdinand Hoefer, *Nouvelle biographie universelle* (Paris, 1852–66), s.v. Falconnet; Quérard, *Les supercheries littéraires* (Paris, n.d.), I:711.

27. [Ambroise Falconnet], *Essai sur le barreau grec, romain et français, et sur les moyens de donner du lustre à ce dernier* (Paris, 1773), 175, 180. Falconnet's comments on the *parlement* and venality, making no mention of Maupeou's reforms, suggest an earlier date of composition.

28. Ibid., 196–203, 214, 210.

29. Poirot, I:95. Joël Félix, *Les magistrats du Parlement de Paris (1771–1790): Dictionnaire biographique et généalogique* (Paris, 1990), 103.

30. Pierre-Louis-Claude Gin, *De l'éloquence du barreau* (Paris, 1767). On his later translations, see *MS*, XXVIII:264.

31. Gin, 73, 285, 91–93.

32. See on this subject, Starobinski, "Éloquence antique, éloquence future," in *PCOR* 311–30.

33. Linguet, *Nécessité d'une réforme*, 93–94.

34. Linguet, *Aiguilloniana*, 34.

35. Linguet, *Aiguilloniana*; and BSPR LP 563, passim; Julian Swann, "'Fauteurs de toutes les maximes qui sont contraires à la monarchie': le gouvernement face aux magistrats jansénistes sous Louis XV," *Chroniques de Port-Royal*, no. 39 (1990), 165. Linguet lists barristers reputed to support the Jesuits in *Aiguilloniana*, 18.

36. Works on the "Maupeou Revolution" include Flammermont, *Le Chancelier Maupeou* (see Ch. 4, n. 86); Durand Echeverria, *The Maupeou Revolution: A Study in the History of Libertarianism* (Baton Rouge, 1985); Dale Van Kley, "The Religious Origins of the Patriot and Ministerial Parties in Pre-Revolutionary France," in Thomas Kselman, ed., *Belief in History: Innovative Approaches to European and American Religion* (Notre Dame, 1991), 173–236; William Doyle, "The Parlements of France and the Breakdown of the Old Regime," *French Historical Studies, VI* (1970), 415–57; Félix, *Les magistrats*; and the contributions by Shanti Singham and Sarah Maza to *Historical Reflections / Réflexions historiques*, XVIII, 2 (1992). See also the following dissertations: David C. Hudson, "Maupeou and the Parlements: A Study in Propaganda and Politics" (Columbia, 1967); Martin Mansergh, "The Revolution of 1771, or the Exile of the Parlement de Paris" (Oxford, 1971); and especially Singham, "A Conspiracy" (see Ch. 4, n. 67).

37. The crisis did, however, contribute to a burgeoning debate on legal reform. See John A. Carey, *Judicial Reform in France before the Revolution of 1789* (Cambridge, Mass., 1981).

38. *HE* I:65–75.

39. *JH* I:133–40.

40. BSPR LP 569, nos. 10, 39, 79; *JH* I:135–39; *HE* I:95.

41. *HE* I:65–70.

42. JH I:75–81; BSPR LP 569, no. 39.

43. BSPR LP 569, no. 39, 13; *HE* I:87.

44. AN AD[II]24; BSPR LP 569, no. 110 (Gillet to Le Paige, March 4, 1771); *HE* I:101.

45. BSPR LP 571, no. 9; *ML* III:209; *HE* I:194.

46. The complete list, compiled from Félix, and the *Tableau de 1770* (BACA CBA) was: Joseph Buynand, Gabriel-Marie-Joseph de Sacy de Belliveux, Antoine-Jean-Jacques Désirat, Nicolas-Eleonore Honoré de Corton, Pierre-Louis-Claude Gin, Claude Mangot de Dauzayée, Pierre-Jean Martin de Bussy, Pierre-François Muyard de Vouglans, and Jean-Pierre Reymond. Honoré and Mangot were sons of *conseillers* in the *Grand conseil*, performing their *stage* in the Order at the time of the reform. On Muyart, see Félix, 51–52.

47. See Félix, 26–37 and passim.

48. *HE* I:191–92; *ML* I:316; *JH* I:280–83; BSPR LP 569, no. 223.

49. AN AD[II]25; cf. BSPR LP 569, no. 261. The new venal offices were essentially the same as the old.

50. Le Paige noted that most members of the corps still had substantial debts to pay off for their now nonexistent positions. BSPR LP 569, no. 223.

51. *JH* I:360; II:46; BSPR LP 569, no. 261. A list of the new officers in BN Receuil Z Le Senne 17 (11), bearing the title *Tableau des Avocats en la cour du Parlement, créés par édit du mois de mai, 1771* (Paris, 1771), indicates that they had all in fact possessed law degrees for years.

52. *HE* I:194; AN AD[II]25; *JH* II:92.

53. AN 263 AP 10, dossier 1, text 2, fol. 16; BSPR LP 569, no. 173 (Darigrand to Le Paige, undated—the context suggests late spring, 1771).

54. See Van Kley, "Religious Origins," 203–10.

55. See Singham, 22.

56. For the figure of one hundred by August, see *JH* II:65. For the fullest information on the pamphlets of the Maupeou period, see Singham, esp. 162–214; and Van Kley, "Religious Origins", 189–203.

57. Echeverria, 40–41. For the figure of ninety, see *MS* VI:54. According to Le Paige in BSPR LP 810, no. 3, Gin composed *Entretien d'un militaire* (see Ch. 1, n. 58); Pierre Bouquet wrote *Lettres provinciales, ou Examen Impartial de l'Origine de la Constitution et des révolutions de la monarchie françoise* (n.p., 1772). Bouquet is not listed on the *Tableau* of 1770, but *Le palais moderne* (n.p. [1771]) implies that he was a *stagiaire* on the point of admission.

58. On eighteenth-century pamphleteering campaigns, see Jeremy Popkin, "Pamphlet Journalism at the End of the Old Regime," *Eighteenth-Century Studies*, XXII, 3 (1989).

59. *Annales de la Religion* (see Ch. 4, n. 42), XVI:551. Evidence of Le Paige's role appears in BSPR 569, 160 (collaboration with Armand-Gaston Camus on a pamphlet entitled "Observations sommaires sur les opérations du 10 avril 1771"); and BSPR LP 571, nos. 207 and 226 (evidence of pamphlets sent to exiled magistrates). Le Paige's 1788 comment comes in a note in BSPR LP 928, no. 6. On Blonde, see *La Bastille dévoilée, ou Recueil de pieces authentiques pour servir à son histoire* (Paris, 1789), IV:86.

60. The police's suspicions can be gauged by BA 12400, fol. 201 (interrogation of barrister Jean-François-Pierre Levasseur) and BA 12403, fol. 85 (testimony of Edme-Nicolas Moret). The "*lettres ostensibles*" are in LP 571, nos. 47–63. On Le Paige's flight, see *JH* III:276–78; *ML* II:93; BSPR LP 571, nos. 47–63.

61. *JH* II:351.

62. See Hudson, "Maupeou and the Parlements," 145–49. A letter to Le Paige by a close colleague (Pinault?) denies his authorship of the princes' manifesto. BSPR LP 571, no. 10.

63. J. M. Augeard, *Mémoires secrets de J.M. Augeard, Secrétaire des commandements de la Reine Maire-Antoinette*, E. Bavoux, ed. (Paris, 1866), 43–45; *ML* III:161.

64. For a close analysis of the "*parti patriotique*," see Singham, 162–214.

65. *Lettre de Monsieur ***, conseiller au parlement, à Monsieur le comte de *** (n.p., 1771); *Lettre d'un bourgeois de Paris à un provincial, à l'occasion de l'édit de décembre 1770* (n.p., [1771]). Attributed to Le Paige in Van Kley, "Religious Origins," 190. The use of the language of the king's two bodies comes especially in *L'avocat national, ou lettre d'un patriote au Sieur Bouquet* (Paris, 1774). See Hélène Dupuy, "Le roi dans la patrie," *Annales Historiques de la Révolution Française*, 284 (1991), esp. 146–47.

66. [Target], *Lettres d'un homme* (see Ch. 5, n. 10), 130, 180, 202–3. See also *Plan d'une conversation entre un avocat et M. le chancelier* (n.p., 1771).

67. Many of Target's positions would be echoed in [Gabriel-Nicolas Maultrot et al.], *Maximes du droit public françois* (Amsterdam, 1775; first published 1772).

68. They included: *Lettre d'un Avocat de Paris aux Magistrats de Rouen* (n.p., [1771]); *Lettre de M.D.L.V.* (n.p., [1771]); Gin, *Entretien d'un militaire*; *Le confiteor d'un ci-devant avocat qui n'étoit pas du commun* (n.p., [1771]);

L'ombre secourable, ou l'apparition salutaire a messieurs les avocats de Paris sur l'édit de création des cent avocats (n.p., [1771]); and *Pensez-y bien* (n.p., [1771]).

69. Gin, *Entretien d'un militaire,* 10–18, 33; cf. *Le mot d'un militaire* (n.p., [1771]), 12.

70. *Pensez-y bien,* 11–23; *L'ombre secourable,* passim. For particular venom, see *Le fin mot de l'affaire* (n.p., [1771]), 18.

71. *Nous y pensons* (n.p., [1771]), esp. 13; *Plan d'une conversation,* esp. 108, 119. According to *JH* II:262, both appeared *after* the *rentrée des avocats.*

72. The financial difficulties faced by various barristers are mentioned in BN Ms. 22101.

73. The account presented here draws primarily on the following sources: *HE* I:244–55; *JH* II:213–84; BSPR LP 571, nos. 7–10; ADCO E 642, anonymous barrister to Cortot, January 20, 1772; *ML* I:400–5; Pierre-Henri Caillau's recollections printed in Paul Templier, ed., *Documents relatifs à l'organisation de l'ancien barreau* (Paris, 1881); and *Le palais moderne.* On Rimbert, see Berryer, *Souvenirs* (see Ch. 1, n. 8), I:53; on Thevenot, see BSPR LP 582, no. 49 and *JH* II:213; on Bouquet, *JH* VI:320, and on Coqueley, Gelbart (see Ch. 4, n. 86), 233–4. The twenty-eight were: Pierre Ader, François-Simon Bailleux, Charles-Nicolas Bidault de Montréal, Pierre Bouquet, Abraham-Jacques Caillard, Jean-Baptiste-Charles Charon de Saint-Charles, Claude-Geneviève Coqueley de Chaussepierre, Jacques-Mathurin Colombeau, Nicolas Damien de Blancmur, Jean-Honoré de la Borde, Guillaume-François-Philippes de la Goutte, Louis-François Desbois, Jean Fursy Dournel, Pierre Gaborit, François-Brice Hennequin de Blissy, Louis-François Hochereau, Pierre Jabineau de la Voute, Pierre-Nolasque Le Blanc de Verneuil, Louis Le Roy, Louis-Claude Picart, Jean-Baptiste Pierret Desancières, Claude-Philbert Pion de la Roche, Silvain Prunget Des Boissieres, Louis-Claude Rimbert, Antoine Tessier du Breuil, Claude-François Thevenot d'Essaule, François-Marie Thorel, Pierre-Alexandre-Charles Timbergue.

74. *JH* II:213, 279.

75. BSPR LP 571, no. 7; ADCO E 642, letter of January 20, 1772; *HE* I:255. According to Le Paige, Thevenot asked for a monopoly on pleading for "*les vingt-huit.*"

76. *JH* II, 265; BSPR LP 571, no. 8, Gerbier to Le Paige, November 22, 1774.

77. BSPR LP 571, no. 8. Despite the claims of an anonymous correspondent (BSPR LP 571, no. 10), Maupeou honored the agreement.

78. *ML* II:7. See also *MS* XXVII:60.

79. *Le palais moderne,* passim. The figure of fifty percent does not include the 9 men who became magistrates. Of 540 barristers on the *Tableau* of 1770, 8 had since died, according to annotations in BACA CBA. On the reopening of *cabinets,* see *HE* I:280.

80. *Protestation de l'Ordre des Avocats*... reprinted in *Le Palais moderne,* 13–17.

81. See, for instance, *JH* II:262–63; BSPR LP 571, no. 7; and BN JF 588, fol. 88.

82. ADCO E 642, January 20, 1772; *HE* I:255; *JH* II:273; *ML* II:485.

83. *ML* II:40–41.

84. E.g., Gaudry, *Histoire du barreau* (see Intro., n. 3) II:269–70; Poirot,

II:225; Fitzsimmons, *The Parisian Order* (see Preface, n. 8), 25; Singham, 144.

85. The following discussion is based on the lists in *Le palais moderne*, and the *Tableau de 1770* (BACA CBA).

86. This may also explain why the percentage was lower for those who had joined between 1750 and 1765 (53%) than those who had joined between 1740 and 1750 (63%). The younger barristers would not have yet acquired clients, and so they too would have had less to lose.

87. Gresset, *Gens de justice* (see Intro., n. 16), 714–15. Barristers elsewhere followed varying patterns: compliance in Toulouse and Dijon, resistance in Rouen and Rennes.

88. See Linguet, *Aiguilloniana*, 17–18. The argument here parallels that advanced in Félix, 21–57.

89. BN JF 455, fols. 54–138. Supporting the nuns were: Guy-Charles Aubry, Armand-Gaston Camus, Henri Jabineau, Le Paige, Maultrot, Mey, Jean-Jacques Piales, Gabriel Piet Duplessis, Jacques Texier, André-Jacques Vancquetin, and Claude Viard. Appearing for Luker: Jean-Baptiste Boys de Maisonneuve, Boucher d'Argis, Raymond Donadieu de Noprats, Pierre Gillet, Paul-Augustin Guerin de la Cour, Louis-François Hochereau, Nicolas Mongeot de Conseveron, Muyard de Vouglans, Silvain Prunget des Boissieres, and Louis-François Rigault. Hochereau and Prunget belonged to the "twenty-eight." On Luker, see Félix, 51–52.

90. BSPR LP 563 and 564, passim. On d'Aiguillon's side were: Laurent-Jean Babille, Boucher d'Argis, Abraham-Jacques Caillard, Jacques-François Cellier, Gillet, Antoine-Lois de Laune, Marc-Antoine Laget-Bardelin, Linguet, Pierre Marguet, Muyard de Vouglans, Michel-Antoine Paporet, Rigault, Thevenot d'Essaule. On the other side: Lalourcé, Nicolas Lambon, Claude-Pierre de la Monnoye, Le Paige, Claude-Nicolas L'Herminier, Maultrot, Mey, Anselme-Joseph d'Outremont, and Viard.

91. Linguet, *Aiguilloniana*, 18.

92. For general information on Luneau and a complete list of the *mémoires*, see John Lough, "Luneau de Boisjermain v. the Publishers of the Encyclopédie," *Studies on Voltaire and the Eighteenth Century*, Theodore Besterman, ed. (Geneva, 1963), 115–77.

93. For instance, an unpublished lecture by Roger Chartier in his seminar at the École des Hautes Études en Sciences Sociales, Paris (1988–89).

94. See Linguet, *Mémoire signifié pour le Sieur Luneau de Boisjermain* (Paris, 1768); and *Derniere réponse signifiée et consultation pour le Sieur Luneau de Boisjermain contre les Syndic & Adjoints des Libraires de Paris* (Paris, 1769), particularly page 15 for Linguet's defense of the fundamental authority of the king over literary property.

95. Given the long time span of the case, I have not considered every barrister involved, but taken as exemplary the teams listed in *Derniere réponse signifiée et consultation pour le Sieur Luneau de Boisjermain . . .*; and *Mémoire à consulter et consultation pour les Libraires associés à l'Encyclopédie* (Paris, 1770). Luneau's barristers were Aubry, Henry-François Benoist, Pierre Firmin de la Croix, Jean-Baptiste Le Gouvé, Linguet, Paporet, Prunget Des Boissieres, Jean-Pierre Reymond, Rigault, Pierre-Alexandre-Charles Timbergue. Defending the *libraires* were: Armand-François Beviere, Geraud Boudet, Boys de Maisonneuve, Cellier, Jean Cochin, Gillet, de Lambon, and Jean-Louis Rousselet.

96. There was a considerable amount of overlap among the teams; however, only one barrister, Pierre Gillet, can be found on both a *parlementaire* and an anti-*parlementaire* team.

97. Linguet, *Aiguilloniana*, 59–60.

98. Among the radical royalist pamphlets were *Lettre de M.D.L.V.* and *Le fin mot de l'affaire*. Le Paige's sketch for "Molinisme d'état," which sets out the parallels between 1713 and 1771, is in BSPR 569, no. 173 bis.

99. BSPR LP 571, no. 26 (Le Paige to Murard, May 20, 1772). On the success of the reforms, see David Hudson, "In Defense of Reform: French Government Propaganda during the Maupeou Crisis," *French Historical Studies*, VIII, 1 (1973) 51–76.

100. BSPR LP 571, no. 26 (Le Paige to Murard, May 20, 1772); Van Kley, *Damiens*, 193; [Maultrot et al.], *Maximes*. For the influence of this work, see Dale Van Kley, "The Estates General as Ecumenical Council: The Constitutionalism of Corporate Consensus and the *Parlement*'s Ruling of September 25, 1788," *Journal of Modern History*, LXI (1989), 7–15.

101. Singham, 268.

102. [Jacques-Claude Martin de Mariveaux], *L'ami des loix* (n.p., 1775). On Saige, see Baker, *Inventing* (see Preface, n. 4), 109–52.

103. BSPR LP 571, no. 10.

104. See *Maupeouana* (n.p., n.d.), V:82 ("Supplément à la Gazette de France").

105. Only a *bâtonnier* could officially issue a new *Tableau*. Lambon, the official holder of the title, refused from 1771 to 1774, and the *rentrants* did not dare attempt to replace or bypass him. The *Almanach royal*, which usually republished the *Tableau*, simply reprinted the 1770 edition each year until 1775.

106. Poirot, I:81. Other barristers in this situation included Mille, struck from the *Tableau* in 1765, and La Morandiere, both mentioned in *HE* II:266; and Petit de Blacy, mentioned in *ML* II:237.

107. *HE* II:45–46; *JH* VII:83, II:280.

108. Gaudry (II:262–88) and Poirot (II:221–31) both devote chapters to the Maupeou *parlement*, but do not analyze the changed conditions of legal practice.

109. *MS* VI:105, 299.

110. Cited in John Renwick, *Voltaire et Morangiès 1772–1773, ou les lumières l'ont échappé belle* (Oxford, 1982), 11.

111. Fournel, *Histoire des avocats* (see Intro., n. 61), II:482.

112. *HE* I, passim.

113. Lough; *MS* VI, passim; *MS* IX, 282. In general on these *causes célèbres*, see Sarah Maza's forthcoming book, tentatively titled *Private Lives and Public Affairs: The Causes Célèbres of Prerevolutionary France* (Berkeley, 1993).

114. *Mémoires de Beaumarchais dans l'affaire Goezman*, Valentin Lipatti, ed. (Paris, 1974). Louis de Loménie, *Beaumarchais and His Times: Sketches of French Society in the Eighteenth Century, From Unpublished Documents*, Henry S. Edwards, trans., 4 vols. (London, 1856).

115. Cruppi, *Linguet* (see Ch. 5, n. 21), 327, 287.

116. *JH* IV:271.

117. *HE* II:211–12.

118. Louis Groustel, *Mémoire relatif à l'affaire du comte de Morangiès* (Paris, 1773), 3.

119. Groustel left his *procureur*'s office in 1762, and so it would not have been confiscated during the chancellor's reforms as Regnaud's had been. See Ibid., 1–2.

120. *ML* II:172; *HE* II:135, 266–67.

121. *MS* VI:196; *HE* I:342. See also Cruppi, 298–302; Levy, *Ideas and Careers* (see Ch. 5, n. 21), 149–50.

122. The fracas began when thirty of Linguet's enemies, led by Gerbier, secretly met and decided not to take part in any cases he was involved in. Linguet published a vitriolic pamphlet in response, and the *parlement* used its appearance as the occasion to bar him from the court. See *ML* II:285–89.

123. *HE* II:136. In doing this, Maupeou indicated that despite the Order's travails, barristers still possessed sufficient *esprit de corps* to defend themselves against the crown.

124. *Déclaration du Roi portant Réglement concernant les Mémoires à consulter. Donnée à Versailles le 18 Mars 1774* (Versailles, 1774). BN JF 535, fol. 346 ff.

125. Cruppi, 336.

126. BSPR LP 573, no. 90, entry dated February 3, 1775. Le Paige's journal echoes Regnaud closely enough to make one suspect that he had read the *procureur*'s work.

127. *HE* II:213.

128. *MS* VII:133–34. For the most detailed description of the two men's rivalry, see *JH* V:170-75.

129. One has only to skim newsletters such as the *Mémoires secrets* to gauge the increasing attention given to barristers during the Maupeou years. In some months, accounts of sensational trials took up more than half the coverage. For indications that *mémoires* were sold for profit, see Maza, "Le tribunal de la nation" (see Intro., n. 11), 77–78.

130. On these cases, see Maza, *Private Lives*, chs. 1 and 3. I depart here from Maza's argument that the Véron and Beaumarchais cases became a means of continuing the battle between *parlements* and crown.

131. *HE* II: 212–13. On Falconnet's admittance to the Order, see Poirot, I:81.

132. See esp. Chartier, *Cultural Origins* (see Intro., n. 22), 38–66; Daniel Carroll Joynes, "The *Gazette de Leyde*: The Opposition Press and French Politics, 1750–1757," in Censer and Popkin, eds., *Press and Politics*, 133–69.

133. AN AP 263 10, dossier 1, no. 2, fol. 28; Simon-Nicolas-Henri Linguet, *Réflexions pour Me. Linguet, avocat de la comtesse de Béthune*, in *Appel à la posterité* (see Ch. 2, n. 49), 178. Cf. Levy, 145.

134. On this subject, see Doyle, "The Parlements of France" (see Ch. 5, n. 36).

135. A copy of the edict is in BN JF 589, fol. 168.

136. Élie de Beaumont, untitled printed text in BSPR LP 573, no. 95; Pierre-Paul-Nicolas Henrion de Pansey, *Éloge de Mathieu Molé . . . Discours prononcé à la rentrée de la conférence publique de messieurs les Avocats au Parlement de Paris* (Lausanne, 1775), 4–5.

137. On Malesherbes, see Pierre Grosclaude, *Malesherbes Témoin et Interprète de son temps* (Paris, 1961). On the two essays on the bar, see 291–303.

138. The two reports are preserved in the archives du Château de Rosanbo, fonds Lamoignon-Malesherbes, in AN 263 AP 9, dossier 4, ch. 6; and AN 263 AP 10, dossier 1 (there are three drafts in this second dossier; all citations are

taken from no. 2, which is 61 folios in length). For the remonstrances, see Elisabeth Badinter, ed., *Les "Remontrances" de Malesherbes, 1771–1775* (Paris, 1978), 167–284. Certain sections, esp. 269–70, are taken almost word for word from the *Mémoire sur les avocats*.

139. AN 263 AP 9, dossier 4, ch. 6, fols. 1, 36; AN 263 AP 10, dossier 1, no. 2, fol. 20.

140. AN 263 AP 9, dossier 4, ch. 6, fols. 39, 42–44, 59.

141. AN 263 AP 10, dossier 1, no. 2, fol. 28; AN 263 AP 9, dossier 4, ch. 6, fol. 21.

142. AN 263 AP 10, dossier 1, no. 2, fols. 1, 18, quote from 59.

143. Ibid., fols. 23, 6–7, 11, quote from 1.

144. The speakers before the *parlement* included Target (Guy-Jean-Baptiste Target, *Discours prononcés en la Grand'Chambre par M. Target, Avocat, le 28 novembre 1774, à la Rentrée du Parlement* [Paris, 1775]); Élie de Beaumont (printed text in BSPR LP 573, no. 95); Jean Blondel (*Discours prononcé par Me. Blondel, Avocat, à l'ouverture des Audiences de la Tournelle, le Samedi 3 Décembre 1774* [Paris, 1775]); and Claude-Ponce Sarot (reported in *MS* VIII:17–18). Jean-Baptiste Darigrand, brother of the now deceased Edme-François, spoke in the *Cour des aides* (*Discours prononcé à la Cour des Aydes le 13 Décembre 1774, par Me. Darigrand, Avocat* [Paris, 1775], BSPR LP 573, no. 135), as did Jacques Carlier (reported in *JH* VII:65). Jacques-Claude Martin de Mariveaux spoke in the Châtelet (*Discours prononcé au Châtelet par M. Martin de Mariveaux, avocat* [Paris, 1775] and *Suplément* [sic] *au discours de rentrée du Châtelet* [Paris, 1775]).

145. Jean Darigrand, *Discours*, 3–4; Target, *Discours*, 2, 4.

146. *JH* VII:61.

147. Pidansat (in *JH* VII, 61) charged that he had spoken too zealously, given that he himself had allegedly practiced under Maupeou. See also *ML* III:3.

148. Martin de Mariveaux, *Suplément [sic] au discours de rentrée du Châtelet*, 1–2.

149. Malesherbes's exhortations to mercy are quoted in Pierre-Jean-Baptiste Gerbier, *Mémoire pour Me. Gerbier, ancien avocat au Parlement* (Paris, 1775), 41–42. See also, *HE* III:326.

150. Templier, *Documents* (see Ch. 5, n. 73), 21–28. The twenty-eight were now, due to death and resignation, twenty-four.

151. Ibid.

152. On Linguet's disbarment, see the accounts in Levy, 155–65; Cruppi, 326–91; and Henri Carré, *Le barreau de Paris et la radiation de Linguet* (Poitiers, 1892).

153. Linguet, *Appel à la posterité*, 202–214, 112, quote from 259. For the images of light and darkness, see, for example, 9, 232.

154. For instance, on January 29, the Order once again convened to expel him. On February 1, his pamphlet *Supplément aux réflexions de Me. Linguet, avocat de la comtesse de Béthune*, was already being distributed. See *JH* VII:69–77.

155. BSPR LP 573, no. 90. Le Paige's account of the assembly (not seen by Cruppi, Carré, and Levy) is, ironically, the one fairest to Linguet. See *JH* VII:78–97 for Pidansat's ferociously anti-Linguet account.

156. For details, see Carré, *Le barreau de Paris*.

157. BSPR LP 574, no. 22.

158. BSPR LP 573, no. 90, entry dated March 5, 1775.

159. Guy-Jean-Baptiste Target, *La censure, lettre à* *** (n.p., [1775]), quote from 5.

160. Ibid., passim.

161. Ibid., 3.

162. For its reception in Besançon, see Gresset, 735. "Censorship" was picked up as the key argument in a *Consultation sur la discipline des avocats* (Paris, 1775), written by fifteen Parisian barristers for the bar of Poitiers. Embarrassingly for the Order, their clients lost the case.

163. According to Jacob-Nicolas Moreau, Linguet had declared à propos of his estranged former client the Duc d'Aiguillon, "he must fear me, but I fear him not." Moreau claimed that this statement excited the magistrates' class prejudices, despite their hatred of the duke, and led them to change their minds. See Moreau, *Mes Souvenirs* (see Ch. 4, n. 62), II:132.

164. See BSPR LP 574, no. 27.

165. The *JH* (VII) devoted more than fifty pages to the events of February and March alone.

166. E.g., Linguet, *Appel à la posterité*, 164, 168.

167. Levy, 172–224.

168. Habermas, *Structural Transformation* (see Intro., n. 25), esp. 31–43.

Chapter 6

1. As Burke observed soon afterwards. See Edmund Burke, *Reflections on the Revolution in France*, J.G.A. Pocock, ed. (Indiannapolis, 1987), 72.

2. The five were: Etienne Mallet, Jean-Pierre-Victor Féral, Claude-André Dassy, Jean-Baptise Borde de Charmois, and Martin de Mariveaux (compiled from BN JF; *MS*; and BACA CBA). Despite claims in the *MS*, Alexandre-Balthazar Laurent Grimod de la Reynerie was not disbarred. See Gustav Le Brisoys Desnoireterres, *Grimod de la Reynerie et son cercle* (Paris, 1877), 141. For reprimands and suspensions, see the cases of Ader (*MS* XXXII:38–39); and Legrand de Laleu (*MS* XXXV:326–27).

3. *MS* XV:245–46 (case of Manoury); *MS* XXVII:79, 105–12 (case of Polverel).

4. Gabriel-Nicolas Maultrot, *Lettres de M. Maultrot, avocat au Parlement, à M. Le Camus d'Houlouve, bâtonnier des avocats* (Paris, 1783), 7. See also Maultrot, *Première lettre écrite le 5 juillet 1783 à M. Le Camus d'Houlouve, bâtonnier des avocats* (Paris, 1783). In a quarrel between Maultrot and Claude-Christophe Courtin, Maultrot was humiliatingly summoned to appear before the *députation*. See *ML* V:336–39; also *MS* XXI:8–13; XXIII:46–49, 60, 89, 94.

5. BCC 360, no. 8, 1–2. Duvert also drew on Target's notion of "censorship" and attacked Linguet.

6. Chavray de Boissy, *L'avocat* (see Ch. 1, n. 7), 243–44.

7. *GT* VII:327. From the 1780's, see, for instance, *Exposition abrégée* (see Ch. 2, n. 50), 10, 12; Maultrot, *Lettres*, 2.

8. *GT* XIX:188–90.

9. *MS* XI:199; XXXII:268.

10. *MS* X:260. For the projected regulations of 1780, see BN JF 535, fols. 325–46; for 1787, *MS* XXXV:227.

11. Quoted in Maza, *Private Lives* (see Chapter 5, n. 113), ch. 5.

12. The *MS* (VIII:127–28 and 150) get the details slightly wrong. For a

more accurate record, see BN JF 464, fols. 199–202; and BN JF 587, fols. 118–22. Further details on Martin's career and eventual expulsion are found in *ML* V:482; *MS* XXVI:99; and Martin de Mariveaux, *Récit présenté à Monseigneur de Calonne* (see Ch. 4, n. 119).

13. *MS* XV:272. On Treilhard, see Jean Treilhard, "Jean-Baptiste Treilhard, Ministre Plénipotentiel de la République au Congrès de Rastadt," unpublished law thesis, Paris (1939).

14. *GT* I:1–4.

15. Maza, *Private Lives*, chs. 4, 6.

16. Simon Schama, *Citizens: A Chronicle of the French Revolution* (New York, 1989), 378.

17. *GT* XIX:157–60 and 188–90.

18. Target was hailed as follows: "Toi qui, sur les bords de la Seine,/ Du barreau de Rome et d'Athène / Rappelle l'antique splendeur . . ." *GT* XV:141. Gerbier, "the oracle of France," received similar treatment (e.g., *GT* IV:141). For the award by New Haven, CT, see *MS* XXIX: 135.

19. Poirot, "Le milieu socio-professionel" (see Intro., n. 60), I: passim.

20. Godard to Cortot, June 19, 1783, ADCO E 642.

21. In Toulouse, membership jumped from 119 in 1750 to 215 in 1789 (Berlanstein, *The Barristers of Toulouse* [see Preface, n. 8], 12). In Paris, the pamphlet *Réflexions d'un militaire* (see Ch. 1, n. 7), spoke of "mobs" of prospective barristers flooding the Order (p. 1).

22. Chavray de Boissy, 241–47; *Réflexions d'un militaire*, 19–20; *Exposition abrégée* . . . , 6. The size of the Order rose dramatically in 1775 and 1776 to accomodate the graduates of the Maupeou period, but soon fell back sharply.

23. *Thémis dévoilée, dédiée aux Etats-Généraux* (Paris, 1788), 29; Brissot, *Un indépendant* (see Ch. 1, n. 67), 35; [Falconnet], *Mémoire sur les privilèges des avocats* (see Ch. 2, n. 7), II:486.

24. On the split with the *procureurs*, see Formé, *Mémoire pour la Communauté des Procureurs . . . Contre Me. Antoine-Elisabeth-Evrard Mollien* (Paris, 1782); *MS* XX:294–95; BN JF 642, fols. 26–34. Godard to Cortot, October 28, 1788 (ADCO E 642) confirms the rule about the library, but said that the requirement for 1,500 *livres* of *rentes* had been rejected. See also *Lettre de MM. les Avocats du Parlement de Rouen, à. MM. les Avocats du Parlement de Paris, 6 Septembre 1777* (Rouen, 1777).

25. *MS*, IX:131; cf. [Falconnet], *Essai sur le barreau* (See Ch. 5, n. 27), handwritten note in copy in the BN. See also Poirot, II:238–40, which treats the pamphlets on both sides somewhat uncritically, and in general exaggerates the strength of the Order during this period.

26. *Lettre de M. *** Avocat au Parlement de Paris à M. *** son Confrere, Ce 27 avril 1782* (n.p, [1782]), 2.; *Exposition abrégée*, 36.

27. For examples, *Lettre de M. ***;* and *Exposition abrégée*, 35–36.

28. Poirot (II:240–46) dismisses this debate as the criticism of a handful of *exclus* against a content majority. Yet in doing so, he does not give sufficient weight to the obvious popularity of Linguet, Falconnet, and Gin's views in the Order. Furthermore, if the critics' ideas were rejected by most barristers, why did the *status quo ante* of the 1760's not return?

29. Boucher d'Argis, *Histoire abrégée* (see Ch. 2, n. 5). Boucher's updated version of *Règles pour former un avocat* succeeded the original as the principal manual of the profession.

30. [Falconnet], *Mémoire sur les privilèges des avocats*. Morizot was an *avocat en parlement* who had taken the oath but did not belong to the Order.

31. MS XXX:97; *Thémis dévoilée*, 23–37; [Falconnet], *Projets de création* (see Ch. 2, n. 3). In his collection *Le barreau français*, which reprints the original *mémoire*, Falconnet does not mention the later pamphlet, but it is hard to believe he had no hand in its composition. More likely, when he had become a crusty pillar of the French legal establishment (and a ferocious legitimist), he declined to identify himself with this radical document of 1789.

32. [Falconnet], *Projets de création*, 24–25.

33. Camus, *Lettres sur la profession d'avocat* (Paris, 1772). As late as 1787, Louis-Anne Louvet still argued for the traditional course of study in *Discours* (see Ch. 1, n. 69), 8–17.

34. Lacretelle, "Fragments sur l'éloquence," *GT* III:156–57, later revised and published in Pierre-Louis Lacretelle, *Mélanges de jurisprudence* (Paris, 1778).

35. Brissot, *Un indépendant*, 11–12.

36. Ambroise Falconnet, "Essai sur les mémoires" repr. in *Le barreau français*, I:ix–xxxii; Jacques-Vincent Delacroix, *Réflexions sur les mémoires* (Paris, 1775).

37. Falconnet, "Essai sur les mémoires," xxi.

38. Delacroix, 13–14, 8.

39. Brissot, *Un indépendant*, 22.

40. Chavray de Boissy, 59.

41. *Le triomphe de Thémis, pour servir de réponse au Parallèle entre le Capucin et l'avocat, quant à l'utilité publique* (Paris, 1783), 5.

42. Ibid., 48; Chavray de Boissy, 278.

43. Brissot, *Un indépendant*, 43; Falconnet, "Essai sur le mémoires," I:xxxi.

44. Brissot, *Un indépendant*, 46; [Falconnet], *Projets de création*, 77; *Thémis dévoilée*, 34.

45. François Furet has pointed to similarities between "absolutist" representations of sovereignty in traditional monarchical theory and in Rousseau's *Social Contract*. The stance adopted by these barristers supports the point. See Furet, *Penser* (see Intro., n. 25), 60–61.

46. Koenig, *La Communauté des Procureurs* (see Ch. 1, n. 92), 133; BN JF 542, fols. 41–42.

47. BN JF 542, fols. 41–42.

48. AN AD^{II}25, *Délibération de la Cour du 5 Septembre 1783;* AN AD^{II}25, passim; *Mémoire pour Me. Guillaume Cotton . . . contre Me. Claude Leseneschal, aussi Procureur de Communauté, Défendeur* (Paris, 1782); and *Mémoire justificatif pour Me. Seneschal. . . contre Me. Cotton* (Paris, 1782).

49. Bien, "Offices" (see Ch. 1, n. 20), 111.

50. The *Exposition abrégée* in response to Brissot, and *Le Triomphe de Thémis* in response to the *Parallèle entre le capucin et l'avocat*.

51. BN Ms. 10364, II, fols. 303–5.

52. Godard to Cortot, October 28, 1788, ADCO E 642.

53. *MS* XX:150–54; Mercier, *Le tableau de Paris* (see Ch. 1, n. 4), II:40–43; VI:281.

54. On this journal, see Jeremy Popkin, "The Pre-Revolutionary Origins of Political Journalism," in *PCOR*, esp. 216–20.

55. Beaumarchais, *Avertissement de M. de Beaumarchais* (Paris, 1787), 1. On Bergasse, see Louis Bergasse, *Un défenseur des principes traditionnels sous la Révolution: Nicolas Bergasse: Avocat au Parlement de Paris, député du tiers état*

de la sénéchaussée de Lyon aux États-Généraux (*1750–1832*) (Paris, 1910). Despite the title of this book, Bergasse was not a *avocat au parlement*. He never appeared on any *Tableau*, and wrote in 1788 that he "never had any intention of joining the bar": Nicolas Bergasse, *Mémoire pour le Sr. Bergasse dans la cause du Sr. Kornmann* (Paris, 1788), 139.

56. For an overview of these pamphlets, see Fitzsimmons, *The Parisian Order of Barristers* (see Preface, n. 8), 33–37.

57. *Réplique d'un citoyen à la réponse d'un avocat* (Paris, 1789), 6–7.

58. Pierre Firmin de Lacroix, *Mémoire pour le sieur Pierre-Paul Sirven . . . Contre les Consuls & Communauté de Mazamet, Seigneurs-Justiciers de Mazamet, Hautpoul & Hautpouloi* (n.p., 1771), 127–28. See Voltaire's comments in *Les oeuvres complètes* (see Ch. 5, n. 5) CXX:68 (Voltaire to Élie de Beaumont, March 3, 1770).

59. Pierre-Louis Lacretelle, *Réponse particulière du défenseur du comte de Sanois . . .* (Paris, 1787), reprinted in Lacretelle, *Oeuvres* (see Intro., n. 13), II:281–82.

60. Maza, *Private Lives*, ch. 5.

61. Guy-Jean-Baptiste Target, *Les États-Généraux convoqués par Louis XVI* (Paris, 1789), 67–68.

62. See, most recently, Dale Van Kley, "New Wine in Old Wineskins: Continuity and Rupture in the Pamphlet Debate of the French Prerevolution, 1787–1789," *French Historical Studies*, XVII, 2 (1991), 447–65. See esp. 460.

63. Munro Price, "The Comte de Vergennes and the Baron de Breteuil: French Politics and Reform in the Reign of Louis XVI," unpublished Ph.D., Cambridge (1989); and idem, "The 'Ministry of the Hundred Hours': A Reappraisal," *French History*, IV, 3 (1990), 317–39, esp. 318–19. Cf. Baker, *Inventing* (see Preface, n. 4), esp. 120–23.

64. Bailey Stone, *The Parlement of Paris, 1774–1789* (Chapel Hill, 1981), 121–53. On the Parlement and the Estates General, see 156–60.

65. Charles-Marguerite Dupaty, *Mémoire justificative pour trois hommes condamnés à la roue* (Paris, 1786), 240.

66. BN JF 607, fol. 55v.

67. *ML* VII:371. For Séguier's speech, see Maza, *Private Lives*, ch. 5.

68. Lacretelle, *Oeuvres*, II, 112. On the case, see Maza, "Domestic Melodrama" (see Intro., n. 31).

69. Lacretelle, *Oeuvres*, II, 451; Guillaume-Alexandre Tronson du Coudray, *Mémoire pour la Comtesse de Sanois . . . Contre le Comte de Sanois, Défendeur* (Paris, 1786), 6.

70. Munro Price's study focuses mainly on the court, and Bailey Stone's on the magistrates. Jean Egret's indispensable *The French Pre-Revolution*, Wesley D. Camp, trans. (Philadelphia, 1976) is limited to the years 1787–88.

71. See Lacretelle's notes on his cases in *Oeuvres*, II:442–45, and compare to Cardinal Fleury's campaign against the barrister Aubry.

72. [Charles-Alexandre de Calonne], *Lettre d'un avocat à M. de la Cretelle concernant l'opinion émise par ce dernier sur les lettres de cachet* (n.p., [1786]), attribution in Antoine-Alexandre Barbier, *Dictionnaire des ouvrages anonymes* (repr., Hildesheim, 1963). Lacretelle, after the Revolution, may have confused this piece and Calonne's supposed *mémoire* in the Compagnie des Indes case (which I have failed to locate). Alternately, Barbier may have attributed the *Lettre* to Calonne, when he really meant the elusive piece in the other affair.

73. David Yale Jacobson, "The Politics of Criminal Law Reform in Pre-Revolutionary France," unpublished Ph.D. dissertation, Brown University (1976) 401–2; *MS* XXXII:210.

74. Armand Lods, "L'avocat Target défenseur des Protestants," *Bulletin de la société de l'histoire du protestantisme français*, XLIII (1883), 606. This article uses the full text of Target's journal, which was lost in World War II.

75. Élie de Beaumont, the original barrister in the case, died before it was resolved. See the Élie de Beaumont papers, Château de Canon.

76. Quoted in Lods, 607.

77. *MS* XXXV:314.

78. Guy-Jean-Baptiste Target, *Consultation sur l'affaire de la dame marquise d'Anglure, contre les sieurs Petit, au conseil des Dépêches, Dans laquelle l'on traite du mariage & de l'état des Protestans* (Paris, 1787), 76, 103. On the case, see Geoffrey Adams, *The Huguenots and French Opinion, 1685–1787: The Enlightenment Debate on Toleration* (Waterloo, 1991), pp. 285–93.

79. Target, *Consultation*, 162–63.

80. Ibid., 162.

81. Jacobson, esp. 200–84; Cesare Beccaria, *On Crimes and Punishments*, Henry Paolucci, trans. (Indianapolis, 1963), esp. 14–17. Jacobson suggests that despite Michael Fitzsimmons's claim to the contrary, Parisian barristers did contribute heavily to the movement for legal reform (Fitzsimmons, 30).

82. Michel de Servan, "Discours sur l'administration de la justice criminelle" (1766), reprinted in *Oeuvres édites et inédites de Servan*, Xavier de Portrets, ed., 5 vols. (Paris, 1825), II:75.

83. See Jacobson, 394–429.

84. Robert de Saint-Vincent, *Mémoires* (see Ch. 3, n. 35), 7–8.

85. Jean Le Maître, *Les adieux du bonhomme Le Maître, à Messieurs les Avocats de Paris, députés à l'Assemblée, dite nationale* (Paris, 1790); idem, *Discours de M. Lemaître, doyen des avocats et procureurs au Parlement de Paris, et doyen de tous les officiers en charge du Royaume* (Paris, 1790); idem, *Reveil du bonhomme Le Maître, à Messieurs les Avocats du Parlement de Paris députés à l'Assemblée Nationale* (Paris, 1790). See particularly *Discours*, 6, 9–10; and *Les adieux*, 2–3. Michael Fitzsimmons, following Seligman, says these pamphlets were pseudonymous and "almost certainly emanated from the Order" (p. 62). But Le Maître's title, *doyen des avocats et procureurs au Parlement*, suggests a reference to the *Communauté des avocats et procureurs au Parlement*, the name of the *procureurs'* corporate body until 1781. The *Listes des procureurs* confirm that in 1789, the senior *procureur* (i.e., the *doyen*) was none other than a certain Jean Le Maître! (BN JF 2133), so in fact the texts are *not* pseudonymous. Incidentally, they also praise *procureurs* effusively.

86. Jean Egret writes about 1788 in *The French Pre-Revolution* that most lawyers who supported the *parlements* did so out of fear of "revenants" rather than ideological conviction (p. 165).

87. Fournel, *Histoire des avocats* (see Intro., n. 61) II:510.

88. The efforts of Target's coterie are chronicled in the Godard–Cortot correspondence, ADCO E 642. For Le Paige's comment, see BSPR LP 928, no. 6.

89. See, for instance, *Mémoire à consulter et consultation pour Madame la Vicomtesse du Chaylat, niece de feu M. de Caylus, Evêque d'Auxerre* (Paris, 1784), signed by all the familiar Jansenist barristers. In 1789, the Jansenists drafted sev-

eral Richerist *mémoires* to support the lower clergy's claims to greater representation at the Estates General.

90. For attribution of remonstrances to Jabineau in 1784, see BN Ms. 10364, II:73 (journal of Lefebvre). On the 1778 incident, in which the *garde des sceaux* accused Jabineau of devising a "plan of attack" for the *Parlement* of Normandy, see *La Bastille dévoilée* (see Ch. 5, n. 59), II:96–98; and *ML* IV:50.

91. [Pierre-Jean Agier], *Le jurisconsulte national, ou principes sur la nécessité du consentement de la nation pour établir et proroger les impôts* (n.p., 1788), three parts paginated separately; Charles-Alexandre de Calonne, *Lettre adressée au Roi, par M. de Calonne, le 9 Février 1789* (London, 1789), 7.

92. See Simon-Nicolas-Henri Linguet, *Réflexions pour Me. Linguet, avocat de la comtesse de Béthune* (Paris, 1774); idem, *Observations sur un imprimé ayant pour titre, Mémoire pour Me. Gerbier, ancien avocat* (Paris, 1775). In 1777, Élie de Beaumont protested the Order's failure to disbar Gerbier. See the Élie de Beaumont papers, Château de Canon.

93. *MS* XXXV:45; cf. Egret, *The French Pre-Revolution*, 22.

94. BN Ms. 10364, II:303.

95. Moreau, *Mes Souvenirs* (see Ch. 4, n. 62), II:365.

96. *Observations d'un avocat sur l'arrêté du Parlement de Paris du 13 août, 1787* (n.p., [1787]). The attribution to Blondel is not entirely certain. The *MS* (XXXVI:37, 112) and *Réponse d'un françois aux observations d'un avocat* (n.p., [1787]), 6, attributed it to Moreau. Le Paige tentatively called Morellet the author (AN AB^{XIX}4149). The Catalogue of the BN opts for the abbé Maury. Hardy, however, gave the credit "assuredly" to Blondel on August 28 (*ML* VII:199), and Lefebvre tentatively concurred (BN Ms. 10364, II:304). Both these sources are generally more credible than the *MS*, and given Blondel's employment at the ministry, and the repeated calls for his disbarment, he seems the most likely author.

97. *Observations d'un avocat*, 19.

98. The responses include: *Réponse d'un françois; Dénonciation de l'écrit intitulé observations d'un avocat . . .* (n.p., [1787]); *Courte réponse à l'auteur des Observations d'un avocat sur l'arrêté du Parlement* (n.p., 1788); *Avis au peuple françois par un avocat* (n.p., [1787]); and a printed *arrêt* of the *Parlement* de Rennes (BSPR LP 915, no. 13). See Godard to Cortot, October 28, 1788, ADCO E 642, for rumors about disbarment and the remark about partisans.

99. Some of this correspondence, located in ADCO E 642–43, has been reprinted as A. Huguenin, ed., "Correspondance inédite de l'avocat [Jacques] Godard de Paris à l'avocat [Jean] Cortot de Dijon, 1786 à 1789," *Mémoires de l'académie des sciences, arts et belles-lettres de Dijon*, 4th ser., X (1905). See also Henri Carré, "La tactique et les idées de l'opposition parlementaire d'après la correspondance inédite de Cortot et de Godard (1788–89)," *La Révolution française*, XXIX (1895).

100. See particularly Godard to Cortot, June 10 and July 2, 1788, ADCO E 642.

101. Ibid., July 4 and August 17, 1788.

102. Ibid., July 4, 1788.

103. Ibid., May 29, 1788.

104. Ibid., June 5, 1788.

105. Ibid., December 8, 1788.

106. Ibid., January 30, 1789.

107. Ibid., February 3, 1789.

108. See Van Kley, "The Estates General" (see Ch. 5, n. 100), 42–43, 47.

109. This is a point Henri Carré discusses in "La tactique et les idées."

110. For Bordeaux, see BSPR LP 922, no. 26. For the others, see Egret, *The Pre-Revolution*, 155. For Le Paige's possible authorship of one Rennes declaration (there were at least three), see annotations in BSPR LP 929, no. 3.

111. On the events in Rennes, see Saulnier de la Pinelais, *Le barreau* (see Ch. 2, n. 47) 281–320. On the Paris elections, see Fitzsimmons, 34–35.

112. BSPR LP 924, no. 32: *Précis historique de ce qui s'est passé à Rennes, Depuis l'arrivée de M. le Comte de Thiard, Commandant en Bretagne* (Rennes, 1788), 36.

113. See, for instance, [Pierre Firmin Delacroix], *Mémoire sur la prochaine tenue des états généraux* (Paris, 1788); *Second mémoire de M. Delacroix, avocat au parlement, sur la tenue des états généraux, en réponse à M. le Comte de Lauraguais* (Paris, 1788); *Mémoire à consulter et consultation sur la question suivante: Quels sont les moyens que doivent employer les habitants de Paris pour obtenir de nommer eux-mêmes leurs Représentans aux prochains États-Généraux?* (Paris, 1788).

114. Fitzsimmons, in *The Parisian Order of Barristers and the French Revolution*, has wisely focused on the organization of the profession, rather than trying to track several hundred disparate individuals through every twist of their revolutionary careers.

115. Target, *Les Etats-généraux*, 1, 7, 11, 14.

116. For a full discussion of the elections, see Fitzsimmons, 34–39.

117. Bailly, *Mémoires* (see Intro., n. 13), I:53; Fitzsimmons, 39.

118. Jules Mavidal and Émile Laurent, eds., *Archives parlementaires de 1787 à 1860*, 1st ser., 82 vols. (Paris, 1862–1913), V:286.

119. Ibid., 282–88, quote from 288.

120. Edmond Seligman, *La justice en France pendant la Révolution (1789–1792)*, 2 vols. (Paris, 1901), I:134. See, for instance, *Reproches au Tiers-Etat de Paris et avis aux Electeurs pour l'exclusion des gens de Robe à la Députation des Etats-Généraux* (Paris, 1789), 6; *Les idées d'un citoyen de Paris sur le danger qu'il y aurait que la noblesse choisît des députés dans le Tiers Etat et sur le choix qui a été fait des Electeurs* (Paris, 1789), esp. 5–6.

121. The only such example I have found is in *Réponse d'un avocat*, 4.

122. These figures are taken from a comparison of the lists in the following sources: the *Tableaux des Avocats* of 1770 and 1789, in BACA CBA; *Le Palais moderne* (see Ch. 5, n. 57); Charles-Louis Chassin, *Les élections et les cahiers de Paris en 1789*, 4 vols. (Paris, 1888–89), I:402; Sigismond Lacroix, ed., *Actes de la commune de Paris pendant la Révolution*, 1st ser., 7 vols. (Paris, 1894–98), I:2–8.

123. This connection has recently been advanced most forcefully by Dale Van Kley, particularly in *Damiens* (see Intro., n. 63), 223–25.

124. A committee chaired by Bergasse in the summer of 1789 called institutions such as the *parlements* unnecessary and even dangerous. See Nicolas Bergasse, *Rapport du comité de constitution, sur l'organisation du pouvoir judiciaire, présenté à l'Assemblée Nationale par M. Bergasse* (Paris, 1789).

125. Larson, *The Rise of Professionalism* (see Intro., n. 53), 119; Osiel, "Lawyers" (see Ch. 1, n. 25), 2026.

126. On the abolition, see Fitzsimmons, 33–64, and André Damien, "La suppression de l'ordre des avocats par l'Assemblée Constituante," *Revue de la société internationale d'histoire de la profession d'avocat,* 1 (1989), 81–86.

127. Isser Woloch, "The Fall and Resurrection of the Civil Bar, 1789–1820's," *French Historical Studies,* XV, 2, (1987), 241–62; *La désolation des procureurs et autres personnes du Palais, ou le petit mystère* (Paris, 1789), 2.

128. Woloch, 245.

129. The National Assembly calculated the value of *procureurs'* offices—and thus of their reimbursements—using extremely low evaluations. See esp. *Observations sur le classement des procureurs au Parlement de Paris* (Paris, 1790).

130. *Archives parlementaires,* XVIII:493.

131. Seligman, 280–328.

132. *Archives parlementaires,* VIII:395; Bergasse, *Rapport du comité de constitution,* 46–67.

133. See Fitzsimmons, 42–62. Fitzsimmons comments on the Order's "almost complete failure to react to the proposal to abolish it" (p. 60).

134. Simon-Nicolas-Henri Linguet, *Annales politiques, civiles et littéraires du dix-huitième siècle,* 19 vols. (London, Brussels and Paris, 1777–92), XVII:38–39 (1790).

135. For the evidence concerning Jean Le Maître, see Ch. 6, n. 85.

136. Fitzsimmons, 58–59.

137. Cited in Damien, "Suppression," 83.

138. Fitzsimmons, 54–55. See also Fournel, II:541–42.

139. Fitzsimmons, 94; See also Berlanstein, *The Barristers of Toulouse* (see Preface, n. 8), 182.

140. See Fournel; Hua, *Mémoires d'un avocat* (see Ch. 1, n. 53); and Berryer, *Souvenirs* (see Ch. 1, n. 8).

Conclusion

1. Target, *Discours prononcés en la Grand'Chambre* (see Ch. 5, n. 144), 5.

2. BACA CBA.

3. Poirot, "Le milieu socio-professionel" (see Intro., n. 60), passim; BACA CBA, *Tableau* of 1727.

4. As Dale Van Kley astutely pointed out in *Damiens* (see Intro., n. 63).

5. *Recueil des Consultations de MM. les Avocats du Parlement de Paris* (see Ch. 4, n. 39).

6. AAE MDF 1297, fol. 73.

7. Dale Van Kley, "The Jansenist Constitutional Legacy in the French Prerevolution," in *PCOR* 169–201.

8. BSPR 414, no. 19.

9. *L'hérésie imaginaire des avocats* (see Ch. 3, n. 142).

10. See Bernard Bailyn, *The Ideological Origins of the American Revolution* (Cambridge, Mass., 1967), esp. 144–59.

11. On the use of biblical exegesis, see again Maire, "L'église et la nation" (see Ch. 3, n. 2).

12. On these changes, and the monarchy's attempts to increase its authority, see again Michel Antoine, "La monarchie absolue," (see Intro., n. 39) and, more broadly, Michel Antoine, *Le conseil du Roi sous le règne de Louis XV* (Geneva, 1970).

13. See on this subject, Doyle, "The *parlements* of France" (see Ch. 5, n. 36).

14. AAE CPR 715, fols. 406–7; BN JF 186, fol. 290.

15. See Sarah Maza's forthcoming *Private Lives* (see Ch. 5, n. 113). Also on these themes, see Chartier, *Cultural Origins* (see Intro., n. 22), esp. 195–96.

16. See particularly Lynn Hunt, *Politics, Culture and Class in the French Revolution* (Berkeley, 1984), 19–51.

17. Burke, *Reflections* (see Ch. 6, n. 1), 37.

18. For d'Argenson's prognostications, his *Journal et mémoires* (see Intro., n. 8), VII:295. On Mably, see Baker, *Inventing* (see Preface, n. 4), 86–106.

19. Montesquieu, *The Spirit of the Laws*, Anne M. Cohler et al., trans. and ed. (Cambridge, 1985), 56.

20. For an illuminating discussion of the United States as a countermodel to Revolutionary France on these issues, see Marcel Gauchet, *La Révolution des droits de l'homme* (Paris, 1989), 36–38.

21. See Gauchet, passim; Philippe Raynaud, "La déclaration des droits de l'homme" in Colin Lucas, ed., *The French Revolution and the Creation of Modern Political Culture*, 3 vols. (Oxford, 1987–89), II:139–49; Dale Van Kley, ed., *The French Idea of Freedom: The Declaration of the Rights of Man*, forthcoming.

22. Lambert to Le Paige, November 3, 1753, BSPR LP 529, no. 110.

23. See Bien, "Offices" (see Ch. 1, n. 20); Roche, "Sociabilités" (see Ch. 3, n. 63). See John Keane, "Introduction," in John Keane, ed., *Civil Society and the State: New European Perspectives* (London, 1988), pp. 1–31, esp. p. 19; and Victor Pérez-Diaz, "Civil Society and the State: Rise and Fall of the State as the Bearer of a Moral Project," *The Tocqueville Review / La revue Tocqueville*, vol. XIII, no. 2 (1992), pp. 5–30, esp. p. 7. Obviously, these works are just the tip of the iceberg of a vast literature on the concept of civil society.

24. D'Aguesseau, *Discours* (see Ch. 2, n. 73), 127.

25. Habermas, *Structural Transformation* (see Intro, n. 25).

26. See Darnton, *Literary Underground* (see Intro., n. 20), 1–40. Even if one doesn't accept Darnton's argument that these critics came from the depths of Grub Street one must still recognize the sincere loathing that ran through their condemnation of the literary "aristocrats" of the salons and the academies.

27. Baker, *Inventing*, 167–99.

28. On the "anticorporate" spirit pervading so much revolutionary legislation, see William H. Sewell, Jr., *Work and Revolution in France: The Language of Labor from the Old Regime to 1848* (Cambridge, 1980), 86–91.

29. Mercier, *Tableau de Paris* (see Ch. 1, n. 4), II:42.

30. Raynaud, 140.

31. Fitzsimmons, *The Parisian Order of Barristers* (see Preface, n. 8), 122–24.

32. Ibid., 111–92.

33. Ibid., 178, 181–82.

34. Karpik, "Lawyers and Politics" (see Intro., n. 52), 716–17.

Bibliographical Note

The material available in Parisian archives and libraries on Old Regime barristers is immense, and considerations of space do not permit the publication of a complete bibliography here. An attempt at such a bibiography can be found in David A. Bell, "Les avocats parisiens d'ancien régime: Guide de recherches," *Revue de la société internationale d'histoire de la profession d'avocat*, no. 5 (1993). An earlier version is available in David A. Bell, "Lawyers and Politics in Eighteenth-Century Paris, 1700–1790," Ph.D. dissertation, Princeton University (1991), 407–44 (available from University Microfilms International, Ann Arbor, Michigan).

The archives consulted for this work are listed at the beginning of the notes. Among the books and pamphlets consulted, the majority are located at the Bibliothèque Nationale, and are listed in the *Catalogue de l'Histoire de France*, particularly under the headings Lb^{37}, Lb^{38}, Lb^{39}, and Ld^4. The other important collections used were those of the Bibliothèque de la Société de Port-Royal, the Bibliothèque Historique de la Ville de Paris, the Bibliothèque de l'Arsenal, and the Bibliothèque des Avocats à la Cour d'Appel de Paris. As for the printed legal briefs called *factums* or *mémoires judiciaires*, the majority of those consulted are also located at the Bibliothèque Nationale, and are listed in A. Corda and A. Trudon des Ormes, *Catalogue des factums*, 10 vols. (Paris, 1890–1936). Among other collections consulted, the most important were those of the Bibliothèque de la Société de Port-Royal (especially Collection Le Paige, vol. 414), the Bibliothèque des Avocats à la Cour d'Appel de Paris (Collections Chanlaire et Gaultier du Breuil), and the Bibliothèque du Sénat.

Index